VOCABULARY POWER MADE EASY

Advocate Siddhartha K Garg practices in the Supreme Court of India. He has worked with Shri Prashant Bhushan and was a law clerk-cum-research assistant to the former Chief Justice of India, Hon'ble P. Sathasivam. He has previously taught in Rahul's IAS and is on the mock interview panel of Ambition Law Institute. He was a former research scholar in the law and economics department at the University of California, Berkeley, and has also studied corporate law at the London School of Economics.

Ms Vinamrata Chawla is a former judge from Haryana. She was posted as civil judge-cum-judicial magistrate in the Haryana judiciary. Before that, she was a law clerk-cum-research assistant to the Hon'ble Justice Dalveer Bhandari in the Supreme Court of India, who is currently posted as a judge in the International Court of Justice at The Hague. Gold medallist and university topper in her academic journey, her expertise lies in preparing students for competitive exams. Ms Chawla has previously taught in Rahul's IAS and various other exam-preparation institutes in India.

'I highly recommend this book. It is a must read for all competitive exams.'

—**Justice Jasti Chelameswar**
Former judge of the Supreme Court of India

'I highly recommend this for all judiciary exams.'

—**Rahul Yadav**
Proprietor and director of Rahul's IAS

'This is an excellent book.'

—**Dr Faizan Mustafa**
Former vice-chancellor of NALSAR University of Law

VOCABULARY POWER MADE EASY

MASTER WORD LIST FOR UPSC, JUDICIARY, SSC, PSC, CUET, CAT, CLAT, SAT, GRE, GMAT, TOEFL, IELTS, GATE

SIDDHARTHA K GARG *and*
VINAMRATA CHAWLA

RUPA

Published by
Rupa Publications India Pvt. Ltd 2024
7/16, Ansari Road, Daryaganj
New Delhi 110002

Sales centres:
Bengaluru Chennai
Hyderabad Jaipur Kathmandu
Kolkata Mumbai Prayagraj

P-ISBN: 978-93-6156-572-4
E-ISBN: 978-93-6156-243-3

First impression 2024

10 9 8 7 6 5 4 3 2 1

Printed in India

CONTENTS

FOREWORD

Judiciary exams are a class apart and becoming a judge not only brings prestige but also the chance to work for an egalitarian society. However, becoming a judge and clearing these exams is not an easy task. It requires immense dedication and focus on each underlying element. One such essential element, that can make or break this exam, is language and general knowledge. Without concentrating and preparing these two subjects, it is impossible to fulfil the dream of becoming a judge. Command over language is essential not only to clear the P.T.(Physical Training) and Mains Judicial Services Exam but also to elevate the overall personality in order to befit the character of a judge.

This is where this book comes in. It fills the vacuum of quality material for this subject in the market. Proficiency in English is the key to clearing judiciary exams of many states, especially Delhi Judicial Services Exam. The method of 'batching technique' that this book utilizes is not only effective and efficient but also infuses a degree of ease and fun in the studying process. I am happy to learn that this book has been produced after extensive analysis of past year papers and utilizes innovative techniques to make education both easy and fun. I highly recommend this book to anyone preparing for judicial services exam.

I have known the author and founder of ASAP Edu for a long time. She has been my student and protégé, and brought me immense happiness and pride when she cleared her judicial services exam in the first attempt and became a judge. I have full faith in her abilities and highly recommend this book to all those preparing for judiciary exams.

Rahul Yadav
Proprietor and Director, Rahul's IAS

PREFACE

Firstly, thank you for purchasing this book and reposing your faith in us. We promise that the money you spend to buy this book and also the time you spend studying it will not go to waste. This book will help you sail through the **GRE** (Graduate Record Examinations) and also the SAT (Scholastic Aptitude Test), GMAT (Graduate Management Admission Test), TOEFL (Test of English as a Foreign Language), IELTS (International English Language Testing System), UPSC (Union Public Service Commission), CUET (Common University Entrance Test), etc.

Why This Book Works Better than Any Other—Because of the Rigorous Process We Followed in the Production of This Book:

1. Past year papers of all major competitive exams analysed to get the important words.
2. Then the words were **'batched' or grouped theme-wise and subject-wise**—for example, all the words related to shiny (like resplendent, refulgent, effulgent) are in one batch. Similarly, all the words related to wealth (like opulence, affluence) are in another batch.
3. Then, for each word, the **synonyms, antonyms, homonyms, etc., were added**—this way, by learning the meaning of one word, you learn many more in one go.
4. Then we **added sentences** to explain the word better.
5. Next we added the **variants of the words** like noun form, adjective form, verb form, adverb form and even verb tenses.
6. And finally, we added the **etymology** of the word covering its origins and **Latin or Greek word roots**.

And ta-da! You get the most exhaustive, well-researched, exam-focussed book there is in the world for vocabulary building!
Basically, we converted a large, unorganized mass of words into an organized word list, where for every word you learn, you actually gain five, all in one shot.

An Illustration of Our Methodology:

Take the batch below as an example:

Fume: to be visibly very angry
He was fuming when his driver banged up his new car.
*Synonyms: **seethe** (He was seething with anger), **incense** (He was incensed at everyone being late), **infuriate** (The false charges infuriated him)
*Adjective form: fuming, **irate** (The irate customer demanded a full refund), **livid** (He was livid at not being invited), furious, infuriated, incensed, **enraged**, seething, **apoplectic** (*pronounced as ap-uh-plek-tik. The CEO would become apoplectic at the mere mention of the rival company's name)
*Etymology: relating to apoplexy [a stroke], from the Greek *'apoplektikos'*, meaning to be disabled by a stroke
Wrath: fierce and extreme anger

He feared his father's wrath because he wrecked the family car.

*Pronounced as rath

Rage: violent and uncontrollable anger

There has been a rise in road rage incidents.

*Adjective form: enraged

*Synonym: fury (The Gods unleashed their fury on the evil mortals; *adjective forms of fury: furious, infuriated)

Dudgeon: a feeling of anger for being offended

They left in high dudgeon because of the mistreatment by the host of the party.

*Pronounced as duj-un

Glare: to stare angrily

The wife glared at the husband for being late for their anniversary dinner.

Scowl: an angry expression

He walked out of the useless meeting with a scowl on his face.

*Synonyms: **glower** (The angry manager glowered at his team for missing the deadline), **frown** (The teacher frowned because all his students had failed)

A Brief Explanation of How We Batched up the Words:

- This batch contains all the words that are related to being very angry. The first entry is fume, a verb meaning 'to be visibly very angry'.
- For this word, we added its synonyms like seethe, incense and infuriate.
- Then, for every synonym, we added a small sentence to show how this particular synonym can be used in a sentence.
- Then we added the adjective form of fume (the adjective form of the verb fume is fuming, and fuming means 'to be very angry'). The words added as the adjective form—all of which means 'to be very angry' —are irate, livid, furious, infuriated, incensed, enraged, seething and apoplectic.
- To further explain things and make your knowledge even more complete, we added the pronunciation and etymology of the word apoplectic.
- Then, we added other such words related to fume like wrath, rage, dudgeon, glare, scowl, glower and frown. These words do not exactly mean 'to be angry' and hence were put as a separate entry in this batch, where all the words are related to the general theme of anger. Then the synonyms, adjective form, adverb form, verb tenses, pronunciation, antonyms and etymology were also added whenever needed for all these related words.

How to Study This Book:

- We recommend **just doing one page per day and spending five minutes per page**—this way, you will have a super strong vocabulary in less than a year, and there will not be a single word in the exam hall that you do not know the meaning of! And the reason we recommend that initially you do one quick reading of the book and not spend more than five minutes per page is because, in a Multiple Choice Question (MCQ) exam, you do not need to know the exact meaning of every word. As long as you have a general idea, you can see the choices and answer the question correctly.
- For example, one batch in the book is about boats and the words in that batch are skiff, yacht, barge, frigate, flotilla, armada, gondola, galley. Now all these are different types of boats or ships but for many exams you don't tend to remember the exact differences and definitions. **So, in such situations, just remember that all these are types of boats and that should be enough.** Similarly, there is a batch for various kinds of axes and the words in that batch are hatchet, tomahawk, machete. Again, for most exams, just remember that these are types of axes. That's it. No need to remember the details.

Clarifications:

- Most important words are bolded.
- In the synonyms of some verbs we add 'to' before a word. For example, consider the word 'grouse', where we have put 'to grumble, to gripe, to whine, to bleat, to quibble, to crib, to carp' as synonyms. Technically, the 'to' before every synonym is not required but we have put it for the purpose of clarity on how the synonyms are to be used in a sentence. In an exam you can just write the synonyms without the 'to' before it.
- For many explanation sentences we use just 'he'. There is no particular reason for this except for keeping uniformity throughout the book rather than putting in names of a person and possibly offending a person of that name.
- Many times we use phrases instead of full sentences to explain the usage of a word. This is done for brevity, to get the main point across as crisply as we can.
- Many places or characters that come from popular movies or TV shows are used in the explanation sentences. We want to clarify that all such characters and names are intellectual property of their respective studios, etc., and we are only doing fair use.
- We tried our best to make sure that there is no error in the book, but if you do find one then we apologize in advance and we request you to please email us about the error so that we can fix it in the next edition. Thank you.

We wish you the best in your journey. We are certain that with your hard work you will definitely hit your target. Best of luck!

WORD MEANINGS

Democracy: a government run by the people by electing representatives through voting
Oligarchy: a government run by a few powerful and dominant people
Autocracy: a government run by one person with unlimited powers
Monocracy: a government run by one person only
Plutocracy: a government run by the wealthy
Aristocracy: a government run by the nobility
Stratocracy: a government run by the military
Kakistocracy: a government run by the least competent people
Kleptocracy: a government run by thieves
Theocracy: a government run in the name of God, with God being seen as the supreme leader and laws derived from religious scriptures
Hagiocracy: a government run by a body of persons who are regarded to be holy or saintly
Episcopacy: a government run by the Church through its bishops
*Etymology: from Latin *'episcopus'* meaning bishop
Ergatocracy: government run by the workers.

■

Antebellum: before war
Antenatal: before birth
Antenuptial: before marriage
Antediluvian: before the flood; outdated; obsolete
*Antonym: **postdiluvian**

■

Anthropology: the study of mankind (its origins, physical evolution, cultural development, etc)
Anthropocentric: considering humankind as being the central and most important of the universe
Anthropocene: the current geological age, Industrial Revolution onwards, during which the earth's environment has been massively influenced by human beings

Anthropomorphic: having the appearance or characteristics of a human being
For example, Rocket Raccoon is an anthropomorphic raccoon in the Marvel movies.
*Noun form: anthropomorphism
Anthropoid: resembling a human being in form
For example, gorillas and chimpanzees are anthropoid apes.
Anthropoglot: an animal having a tongue similar to human beings, which allows for human-like speech. For example, a parrot is an anthropoglot.
Misanthrope: a hater of humankind
Philanthrope: a lover of humankind

■

Misogyny: hatred of women
Misandry: hatred of men
Misogamy: hatred or aversion to marriage
Misology: hatred of knowledge
Bigamy: the practice of having two marriages
Polygamy: the practice of having multiple marriages
Polygyny: the practice of having multiple wives
Polyandry: the practice of having multiple husbands

■

Parricide: the killing of one's parents
Patricide: the killing of one's father
Matricide: the killing of one's mother
Fratricide: the killing of one's brother
Sororicide: the killing of one's sister
Filicide: the killing of one's son or daughter
Uxoricide: the killing of one's wife
Avunculicide: the killing of one's uncle
Nepoticide: the killing of one's nephew
Regicide: the killing of a king
Tyrannicide: the killing of a tyrant
Feticide: the destroying of a foetus; an abortion
*It is also written as foeticide. Both are pronounced as fee-ti-side.

Carnivore: an animal that feeds on other animals
Herbivore: an animal that feeds on plants
Frugivore: an animal that feeds on fruits
Nectarivore: an animal that feeds on the nectar of flowering plants
Graminivore: an animal that feeds on grass
Granivore: an animal that feeds on seeds
Omnivore: an animal that feeds on both plant and animal
Pantophagist: an animal that eats all kinds of food
Lacto-ovo-vegetarian: a vegetarian who eats eggs and dairy products
Vegan: a person who doesn't eat or use any animal products and even milk

■

Philopatridomania: a compulsive desire to return to one's home or native land; homesickness
Mythomania: a compulsive desire to exaggerate or tell lies
Oniomania: a compulsive desire to buy; compulsive buying disorder
Oenomania: a compulsive desire to drink wine
Dipsomania: a compulsive desire to drink alcohol
Phagomania: a compulsive desire to eat
Gamomania: a compulsive desire to get married
Gynecomania: a compulsive desire for female sex partners
Andromania: a compulsive desire for male sex partners
Nymphomania: a compulsive sexual desire in a woman
Satyriasis: a compulsive sexual desire in a man
Plutomania: a compulsive desire to gain wealth
Megalomania: a compulsive desire to acquire power

■

Xenophobia: fear of foreigners
Paedophobia: fear of children
Gerontophobia: fear of old people
Thermophobia: fear of heat
Acrophobia: fear of height
Agoraphobia: fear of the outside
Ochlophobia: fear of crowds
Nyctophobia: fear of the dark
Photophobia: fear of light
Heliophobia: fear of sunlight
Chronophobia: fear of the time
Ergophobia: fear of work

Bibliomancy: the practice of predicting the future by interpreting a randomly chosen passage from a book, typically the Bible
Anthropomancy: the practice of predicting the future by the inspection of human entrails (entrails mean intestines), especially by sacrificing girls
Cubomancy: the practice of predicting the future by interpreting the numbers which appear after the throwing of a dice
Osteomancy: the practice of predicting the future by the examination of bones
Chiromancy: the practice of predicting the future by interpreting the lines on the palms of people's hands; palmistry
*Pronounced as kiro-man-cee
Graphomancy: the practice of predicting the future by handwriting analysis
Tasseomancy: the practice of predicting the future by interpreting the pattern formed by the tea leaves in a cup
Necromancy: the practice of predicting the future by talking to the dead

■

Hypothermic: below the normal temperature
Hypodermic: below the skin
Hypogastric: below the stomach
Hyperaesthesia: excessive sensory feeling
Hyperbaric: excessive pressure

■

Bibliopole: a person who buys and sells books, especially rare ones
Bibliophile: a lover of books; a book collector
Biblioklept: a person who steals books

■

Endogenous: having an internal origin or cause
The economic crash was caused by factors endogenous to the United States (US) like corporate corruption and not caused by exogenous factors like increase in oil prices from the Middle East.
Exogenous: having an external origin or cause
Entomology: the study of insects

■

Theology: the study of God and religion

Theomachy: a war against God or among the gods

■

Synonym: a word having the same meaning as another word

Antonym: a word having the opposite meaning to another word

Homonym: a word having the same pronunciation as another word

Eponym: a name derived from the name of a person

For example, *Gandhi* (the title of the movie) is an eponym derived from the name of the central character

*Etymology: from Greek '*epi*' (upon) + '*onoma*' (name)

Toponym: a name derived from the name of a place.

For example, badminton (the sport) is a toponym as it is named after the town of Badminton in Gloucestershire, England, where it was invented.

*Etymology: from Greek '*topos*' meaning place

Pseudonym: a pen name; a stage name

Eric Arthur Blair is better known by his pseudonym George Orwell and under this pseudonym, Blair wrote many famous books like *Animal Farm* and *1984*.

*Etymology: from Greek 'pseudo' (false, lying) + '*onoma*' (name)

■

Unanimous: in complete agreement

The board of directors unanimously decided to remove the badly performing CEO of the company.

Eponymous: giving one's name to something

Gandhi ji was portrayed on screen in the eponymous titled movie *Gandhi*, which was released in 1982.

Anonymous: of unknown name

The activist received an anonymous threat-letter.

■

Etymology: the origin of a word; the study of the origin of words

*Etymology: from Greek '*etumos*' meaning true

Onomatopoeia: the formation of a word by using the sound associated with that word, e.g. cuckoo, meow or boom

*Pronounced as ono-mato-pia

*Etymology: from Greek '*onoma*' (word) + '*poiein*' (to make)

Palindrome: a word that reads the same backwards as forwards, e.g. madam *Etymology: Greek '*palin*' (again) + '*drom*' (to run)

Teknonymy/paedonymic: the practice of referring to parents by the names of their children

*Etymology: Greek '*tékn*' (child) + 'ónym' (name)

■

Appellation: a name or title

New York City has the appellation of being the 'capital of the world'.

*Synonyms: **nickname, moniker**

Sobriquet: a person's nickname

His rude and domineering nature earned him the sobriquet 'dictator'.

*Pronounced as soh-bruh-kay

*Synonym: **cognomen** (cognomen also means a surname)

Alias: a false identity

The spy operated under the alias Mr Smith.

Titular: relating to the title

The movie *Gandhi* was released in 1982 with Ben Kingsley portraying the titular role.

Titular also means existing in title only and not having any real powers. For example, Queen Elizabeth II is the United Kingdom's titular Head of State.

*Synonym: **nominal** (a nominal head).

Hypocorism: a pet name; a nickname that displays love and affection

For example, 'Joey' is a hypocorism for 'Joseph'.

Honorific: giving honour

Heads of state are commonly referred to by using the honorific title 'Excellency'.

Misnomer: an incorrect name, term, designation, etc.

Morning sickness is a misnomer as the uneasiness can occur at any time of the day.

Neologism: a newly coined word or expression

For example, 'webinar' is a neologism and it means a seminar on the web.

Nomenclature: the system of naming in a particular field.

Taxonomy: the branch of science dealing with classification and organization into categories.

■

Genesis: the origin of something

There is a lot of research going on into the genesis of life on earth.

*Pronounced as jen-uh-sis

Conception: the process of forming the concept of something
The CEO wanted to reduce the time between the conception and market delivery.
Inception: the establishment of something
Since its very inception Harvard has aimed to be the top university in the world.
Commencement: the start of something
The Dean gave the commencement address at the start of the academic year.
Stem from: to start as a result of something
All major fights stem from minor misunderstandings.

■

Denouement: the ending; climax
During production, the denouement of *Avengers: Infinity War* was a closely guarded secret.
*Pronounced as dey-noo-mahn
*Synonym: **culmination**
Upshot: the end result
The upshot of the entire litigation was that no party gained anything major and it was only the lawyers who profited.
Brunt: the chief impact of an unpleasant action
The call centre executive bore the brunt of the customer's anger.
Climactic: relating to the climax
The audience was stunned in the movie's climactic scene.
*Pronounced as clime-actic
Anticlimax: an ending that disappoints after the initial hype
The travel blogger felt that coming back home after a long trip was an anticlimax.
Closure: the act of closing; also means the sense of resolution and completion at the conclusion of something
The parents finally achieved closure when the killer of their child was hanged.
*Pronounced as klo-zhur
Finale: the last part of a musical piece or a show; the last episode in a TV show's series
*Pronounced as fi-naal-ay
*Plural: finales
Fruition: fulfilment; attainment of the desired result
The education policy reached fruition as the literacy rates increased.
*Synonym: actualization

■

Fallout: the adverse result of an action
The emotional fallout from the divorce was tough for him to handle.
*Etymology: fallout means the falling on the ground of the radioactive particles that were ejected into the atmosphere because of a nuclear explosion.
Repercussion: an unintended consequence, especially a negative one
The repercussions of the 9/11 attacks are still felt today in world politics.
*Synonym: **reverberation** (The move had far and wide reverberations)
Ramification: the possible result of an action, especially when such result is complex and negative in nature
Any change in the free speech laws is bound to have tremendous legal ramifications.
*Etymology: in botany, a ramification is a branch or a structure formed of branches.
Aftermath: the consequences of a major disastrous event
Thousands died in the aftermath of the nuclear explosion.
*Synonym: after-effects.
By-product: an unintended and unforeseen result of some action
Jealousy in others is a by-product of one's success.
*Etymology: by-product is a secondary or incidental product that is produced in the manufacturing of something else. For example, selenium is a by-product of copper refining.
*Synonym: **backwash** (The economic backwash of the war was huge)
*etymology: backwash is the water which is thrown backward by the motion of propellers, paddle wheels, etc., when an object moves through water.
Blowback: unintended negative reactions such as criticism, protest or anger to political actions
Fearing blowback, the government decided to withdraw the proposed tax hike.
*Etymology: blowback is the process in which gas expands and then travels in the opposite direction in an internal-combustion engine or other such mechanical device.
Backlash: a strong negative reaction by a large number of people to some major social or political change
The government ordered an inquiry after the strong public backlash.
*Etymology: in mechanics, backlash is the recoil that arises between different parts of a machine.
In the wake of: following something as a consequence

The inquiry committee was set up in the wake of massive protests.
*Etymology: wake is the trail of disturbed water left after the passage of a ship.

■

Scotch: to conclusively put an end to something
The party spokesperson scotched the rumours of the president resigning.
Quell: to conclusively put an end to something by using force
The dictator quelled the rebellion by firing at the protestors in the town square.
Snuff: to extinguish a candle or flame
The air coming from the ceiling fan snuffed out the candles on the birthday cake.
*Synonym: to stub out

■

Matriculation: the process of enrolment at a university
Convocation: the formal ceremony at the end of an academic year where the university degrees are handed out
Alumnus: a male graduate
*Plural: **alumni**
Alumna: a female graduate
*Plural: **alumnae**
Alma mater: the university, school or college that one has graduated from
*Etymology: Latin for 'generous mother'
Varsity: the principal team that represents a school or college in athletic or other types of competitions; varsity also means a university

■

Belie: to contradict
His shaking hands belied his calm voice.
Belabour: to over-elaborate
The students were bored because the lecturer kept belabouring on basic topics.
*Homonym: **labour under** (labour under means to be misled; for example, he laboured under a misapprehension)
Betray: to reveal
The loud growling of his stomach betrayed his hunger.
Begrudge: to resent someone for their good fortune

He begrudged Jack the promotion. She begrudged Jennifer her wealth.
Befall: to fall upon someone
Tragedy befell his aunt.
Bear upon: to have an influence on something
The lawyer argued that the earlier judgment bore upon his case as the facts were identical.
Bring to bear: to apply
A lot of pressure was brought to bear on the witness to withdraw his testimony.

■

Empathy: the ability to feel someone else's pain and suffering
Animal rights activists have a heightened sense of empathy.
Apathy: lack of interest; complete and utter indifference towards something
The court expressed shock over the government apathy towards the poor.
*Synonym: indifference, impassivity
*Antonyms: interest, passion
Sympathy: feelings of sorry and pity for someone for their misfortune

■

Grouse: to complain about small and trivial things, usually persistently and irritatingly
The lead actress would grouse about everything on the movie set.
*Synonyms: to **grumble,** to **gripe,** to **whine,** to **bleat,** to **quibble,** to **crib,** to **carp** (No one enjoyed his perpetually carping company), to **cavil** (They cavilled at the cost of the fries at the burger joint)
*Verb tenses: cavil, cavils, cavilled, cavilling), to **harp** (The headmaster would always harp on about having good attendance)
Querulous: a person who complains a lot about small and trivial things
The diva was very querulous.
*Synonyms: **captious, carping**
Fastidious: fussy about details
The bride was fastidious about every detail.
*Synonyms: **pernickety/persnickety** (The pernickety accountant wanted receipts for every expense), **pettifogging** (The pettifogging lawyers made it difficult to conclude the deal), **finicky, finical, dainty, hair-splitting**

Censorious: severely critical of others; fault finding
The group tried to posture as the censorious champions of sexual chastity.
*Synonyms: hypercritical, condemnatory, **castigatory,** denunciatory, **deprecatory, reproachful,** reproving, **censuring**
*Antonyms: complimentary, approving

∎

Petulant: moody; irritable; bad-tempered
The parents were tired of tantrums of the spoiled petulant teen.
*Synonyms: **peevish, irascible** (His boss was an irascible old man and very difficult person to work with; *pronounced as ee-ras-uh-bul), crabbed, crabby, grumpy, grouchy, **crotchety,** testy, **surly, dyspeptic, splenetic, snitty**
Cantankerous: argumentative and uncooperative
The children called the school headmaster a cantankerous old fossil.
*Synonyms: **curmudgeon** (The children did not like their curmudgeon uncle; *pronounced as kur-muj-uhn), **choleric** (The choleric old man irritated everyone)
Belligerent: hostile and aggressive; quarrelsome; confrontational; combative
Everyone came into the meeting extremely belligerent and just looking to start a fight.
*Synonyms: **bellicose** (The dictator made many bellicose statements about his country's nuclear strength; *pronounced as belly-kohs), **fractious** (The young candidate quit because he got fed up with the fractious nature of politics; *pronounced as frack-shus), **pugnacious** (Everyone in the office avoided the pugnacious manager), **truculent** (He had a truculent temperament), **disputatious**
*Noun form: belligerence, pugnacity, bellicosity, truculence
*Antonyms: friendly, peaceable

∎

Fume: to be visibly very angry
He was fuming when his driver banged up his new car.
*Synonyms: **seethe** (He was seething with anger), **incense** (He was incensed at everyone for being late), **infuriate** (The false charges infuriated him); *Adjective form: fuming, **irate** (The irate customer demanded a full refund), **livid** (He was livid at not being invited), furious, infuriated, incensed, **enraged,** seething, **apoplectic**

Wrath: extreme and fierce anger
He feared his father's wrath because he wrecked the family car.
*Pronounced as rath.
Rage: violent and uncontrollable anger
There has been a rise in the incidents of road rage.
*Adjective form: enraged
*Synonym: fury (The Gods unleashed their fury on the evil mortals; *adjective forms of fury: furious, infuriated)
Dudgeon: a feeling of anger because of being offended
They left in high dudgeon because of the mistreatment at the party.
*Pronounced as duj-un
Glare: to stare angrily
The wife glared at the husband for being late.
Scowl: an angry expression
He walked out of the useless meeting with scowl on his face
*Synonyms: **glower** (The angry manager had a glower on his face), **frown** (The teacher had a frown on his face)

∎

Gesticulate: to make dramatic gestures while speaking
The debater gesticulated excessively rather than focusing on speaking clearly.
Pout: to push out one's lips forward as a sign of irritation or to make one look sexually attractive
The spoilt child pouts whenever he hears a no.
Purse one's lips: to contract one's lips, usually as a sign of anger
He pursed his lips when he heard about his son's low college attendance.

∎

Moan: to make noises in pleasure
He moaned while eating the burger.
Groan: to make noises in pain
The wrestler groaned when the physiotherapist examined his injury.
*Synonyms: whimper, sniffle, mewl
Howl: to cry out or scream in pain
The child howled in pain.
*Synonyms: **wail,** bawl, yawl, **yelp, shriek, squeal, squall,** squawk, screech
Keen: to wail in grief for the dead
He fainted while keening for his mother.
Weep: to cry
Everyone wept at his funeral

*Synonym: **sob**
Snivel: to cry lightly, usually in a fake manner
His friends snivelled when they heard about his fever and were happy that he would miss his exam.

■

Slipshod: careless
He was fired because of his slipshod work.
*Synonyms: **shoddy, slapdash, haphazard, lax, slack**
Remiss: negligent
The cook was remiss for not washing his hands.
*Adverb form: remissly (negligently)
*Noun form: remissness (negligence)
Feckless: irresponsible and good-for-nothing
She was tired of babysitting her feckless younger brother all day.
Delinquent: a young person who has committed a minor crime
*Noun form: delinquency
*Synonyms: **wayward, shirker, deviant**
Truant: a student who misses school without permission
Derelict: a negligent person
*Noun form: dereliction (He was punished as he committed grave dereliction of duty)
Malingerer: someone who pretends to be ill to avoid work

■

Malfeasance: a crime, especially by a public official
The financial advisor was convicted for corporate malfeasance.
*Pronounced as mal-fee-zuns
Misdemeanour: a minor crime
*Synonyms: a **venial offence** (for example, shoplifting), **peccadillo** (The candidate dismissed the shoplifting incident in his youth as a mere peccadillo)
High-crime: a major crime that is tried before the highest courts of the land because of its severity and which may incur the gravest punishments
Treason is considered a high-crime in the US.
Jaywalk: to unlawfully walk on the road; for example, not using the zebra crossing or not following the walk or not walk sign
Pilfer: to commit petty theft
He was caught pilfering from the company storehouse.
*Noun form: pilferage
Purloin: to steal; to thieve

The lawyer argued that purloined memos were inadmissible in court.
*Synonyms: to filch, to snitch
Larceny: theft of personal property
Heist: a robbery
*Pronounced as hahyst.
Embezzlement: misappropriation of funds
*Verb form: to embezzle
Siphon: to draw out, often illegally
The CEO was caught siphoning from the company.
*Etymology: from Greek 'siphon' meaning pipe
Felony: a major crime usually involving a long prison sentence
Impropriety: improper behaviour
The CEO warned that even a hint of impropriety could be dangerous as the investors would definitely flee.
Lapse: a brief failure of memory or judgement (He apologized for his lapse in judgement); the passage of time (The limited window of applying lapsed)
Default: the failure to pay a loan on time (He routinely defaulted); a preselected option (Chrome is the default browser in Android phones)

■

Scrupulous: ethical; principled; honest
He was always liked because of his scrupulous dealings with clients.
*Synonym: **dinkum** (He was known in the office as a dinkum guy)
*Noun form: scruples (meaning principles)
Compunction: a feeling of unease before doing something wrong
He had no compunction in stealing from his office.
*Synonym: **qualm** (The hitman has no qualms about killing someone)
Misgiving: apprehension; doubt
The board expressed serious misgivings about the awful running of the company.
*Synonym: **reservation**
Probity: honesty and decency
The company always maintained the highest standards of financial probity in all its dealings.
Propriety: rightness or justness
Politicians have lost the spirit of propriety.
Rectitude: morally correct behaviour
The pastor was a model of rectitude.
*Synonyms: **righteousness**, saintliness

■

Irreproachable: faultless and beyond any criticism
The committee found his behaviour irreproachable.
*Synonyms: **irreprovable, unexceptionable**
Impeccable: perfect
He scored full marks because of his impeccable answers in the exam.
*Synonym: exemplary
Immaculate: spotlessly clean, perfectly neat and tidy
He wore an immaculate white suit to the award ceremony.
Inimitable: incapable of being imitated or copied; of matchless quality
The inimitable style of actress made her a favourite with the fashion magazines.
Infallible: incapable of making a mistake or being wrong
The dictator considered himself as infallible.
*Synonym: **unerring**

■

Copacetic: in excellent order; fine; completely satisfactory
Everything was copacetic between the young couple.
*Pronounced as coh-puh-setic
Pristine: pure; in perfect condition
The pristine mountain air did wonders for his health
*Synonyms: untarnished, unblemished, unsullied, undefiled
Intact: unbroken; undamaged
The car was intact even after hitting the tree.
*Synonyms: unscathed, **unmarred**
*Antonym: marred
Fray: to become undone; to separate or disentangle the threads of a woven fabric
The cheap shawl frayed at the edges.
*Synonym: to **unravel**
Threadbare: to become thin and tattered with age and use
The room had a threadbare carpet.
*Synonyms: worn out, **moth-eaten, mangy**, ragged
Bare bones: the most essential parts which cannot be further removed
A bare bones account of the case.
*Synonym: the **irreducible minimum**
Shopworn: to become dirty and damaged because of constant display and handling at a shop
There was a discount on the shopworn fridge.

■

Protégé: a pupil; student; trainee
*Pronounced as pro-tuh-zhay
*Synonym: **apprentice**
Prodigy: a genius
*Synonym: **savant**
Precocious: unusually advanced in mental development
Mozart was a precocious child.
*Pronounced as pre-ko-shus
Maven: an expert on a subject
Virtuoso: a highly skilled musician
*Pronounced as vir-chu-oso
Past-master: a very skilled person
Phenom: an outstandingly talented person; a star
Laureate: a person who has received a major award for intellectual achievement
*Pronounced as law-ree-yet
Luminary: a very eminent person in a particular field (for example: a luminary in the field of global warming)
*Synonym: a **leading light**
*Antonym: nobody
Veteran: a very experienced person; an ex-member of the armed forces
Doyen: an authority of a field
Journeyman: a very skilled worker but one who is not yet a master
Jurist: an authority in law
Polymath: a person who knows a lot about many fields
Protean: able to do many different things; protean also means ever-changing
He is a protean performer who can brilliantly act, sing and dance.
*Synonym: **versatile**
*Etymology: protean comes from Proteus, the Greek Sea God, known for his ability to assume different forms.
Aficionado: an enthusiast; a fan; a very passionate and knowledgeable hobbyist
He is a flag aficionado.
*Pronounced as uh-fish-yuh-nado
Cognoscenti: an expert in arts and literature
Wiseacre: a very knowledgeable person who is mocked by others as a know-it-all
*Etymology: from Old Dutch *'wijssegger'* meaning wise man
Erudite: intellectual
The erudite professor had won many academic awards.
*Synonyms: **sagacious** (meaning sage-like), **profound**

■

Obscurant: a person who makes intense efforts to prevent the increase and spread of knowledge; also written as obscurantist.

Amateur: a person who engages in a pursuit (for example, a sport) for fun rather than to earn money
*Antonym: a professional player; amateur also means an incompetent person
*Pronounced as am-uh-chur or am-uh-tur

Layperson: a non-ordained member of a Church; a person who attends a church to pray but is not a priest or a nun; layperson also means a person without specialized knowledge on a particular subject
*Antonyms: clergyman, expert

■

Omniscient: all-knowing
*Pronounced as omni-see-unt
*Noun form: omniscience (*pronounced as omni-see-uns)
Omnificent: having unlimited powers of creation
*Pronounced as omni-fi-sunt
*Noun form: omnificence (pronounced as omni-fi-suns)
Omnipotent: all-powerful
God is described in theology as an omnipotent being.
*Pronounced as omni-puh-tunt
*Noun form: omnipotence

■

Flagship: the most important product made by an organization
*Etymology: flagship carries the commander of the fleet and displays his flag
Figurehead: a head of an organization who has no real powers
The Queen is the figurehead of Britain.
*Synonyms: titular head, nominal leader
Frontman: the lead singer of a music group; a person who is the nominal head of an organization and the organization's public face

■

Grandiose: grand; epic; magnificent
The tourists marvelled at the grandiosity of the Empire State Building in New York City.
*Synonyms: **stupendous, sublime,** awe-inspiring, monumental
Superlative: of world class quality
Leonardo DiCaprio gave a superlative performance in

the movie *Revenant*.
*Synonyms: **prodigious, virtuoso, pre-eminent, marquee** (Cristiano Ronaldo is a marquee footballer; *pronounced as mar-kee)
*Antonyms: **abysmal, crummy,** substandard
Excelsior: ever upward; of top quality
Excelsior is the motto of the State of New York
*Etymology: from Latin ex (beyond) + celsus (lofty)
Exquisite: having a quality of rare excellence in art or workmanship
Michelangelo's exquisite painting of the Sistine Chapel Ceiling
August: distinguished and impressive
The august gathering of scholars from all over the world
*Synonyms: respected, eminent, exalted, esteemed
Nonpareil: having no match or equal
J.K. Rowling is a nonpareil storyteller
*Pronounced as non-pur-el
*Synonyms: unrivalled, unparalleled, **peerless**
Adroit: very proficient
Cristiano Ronaldo is an adroit footballer
*Synonyms: **adept, dextrous,** expert, masterful
*Antonym: maladroit
Meritorious: someone has a lot of merit; for example, the meritorious student.
Nimble: quick-moving and loose-jointed
The Leopard is famous for its nimble manoeuvring when catching prey
*Synonyms: flexible, fit, agile, **limber, lithe, lissom, supple, spry, sprightly**
*Antonyms: stiff, unfit
Prowess: mastery; expertise; competence; proficiency
Sir Elton John is famous for his prowess on the piano
*Synonyms: skilfulness, **adroitness, adeptness, aptitude, dexterity**, finesse, deftness, know-how
Ingenious: clever; original; inventive
He came up with an ingenious way to produce electricity.
*Synonyms: innovative, resourceful
*Noun form: **ingenuity**
*Homonym: **ingenuous** (unsuspecting and easily trusting)

■

Maladroit: clumsy; incompetent; unskilful
The captain was upset by the maladroit performance of his team
*Synonyms: **inept**, bungling, bumbling, ungainly, unhandy, uncoordinated, cloddish, clodhopping

Gauche: socially awkward
The gauche teenager was mocked by his peers
*Pronounced as goh-sh
*Synonyms: **tactless, gawky**
*Noun form: gaucherie (pronounced as go-sherry)
*Antonyms: elegant, sophisticated
Lummox: a clumsy and stupid person
Slob: a lazy and messy person
Sluggard: a lazy and sluggish person
*Synonym: **gold brick**
Laggard: a person who lags behind others in terms of progress
The laggard students were told to attend extra classes after school.
Haggard: looking exhausted and unwell, typically due to fatigue, worry or anxiety
He looked pale and haggard after the 80-hour work week.
Busywork: work done just to show others (like one's boss) that one is busy and productive but in reality the work being done is of little real value; for example, making official calls that are not necessary or required.

∎

Meticulous: paying great attention to detail; careful
Michelangelo meticulously painted the ceiling of the Sistine Chapel in the Vatican City.
*Synonyms: **rigorous, conscientious, painstaking**
Diligent: hard-working; industrious
The diligent worker was always praised by his boss.
*Synonyms: **assiduous** (The teachers liked the assiduous student), **sedulous** (The sedulous student came first in his class)
Formidable: inspiring fear or respect or awe
Cristiano Ronaldo is a formidable footballer.
*Synonyms: intimidating, **redoubtable, daunting**
Staunch: very committed
He was a staunch supporter of the LGBTQIA+ rights.
*Synonyms: devoted, dedicated
Stalwart: a very loyal and dependable supporter of an organization
A function was organized to honour the stalwarts of the political party.

∎

Indomitable: unconquerable
Wonder Woman has an indomitable spirit.

*Synonyms: invincible, unconquerable, unbeatable, unassailable, invulnerable, unshakeable
*Antonyms: weak, vulnerable
Insuperable: impossible to overcome
He had insuperable financial difficulties because of years of gambling.
*Synonyms: **insurmountable** (*etymology: surmount means to mount on top of something; for example, he surmounted Mount Everest), unconquerable
*Antonyms: superable, surmountable
Indefatigable: untiring
Erin Brockovich is an indefatigable environmental rights activist.
*Synonyms: **unwearying, unflagging, unjaded**
Inexorable: unceasingly intense and severe
Due to the inexorable march of technology, no field is immune from automation.
*Synonyms: **relentless**, **unremitting**, unrelenting, unbending, unyielding

∎

Resolute: determined; unwavering; unyielding; unshakeable; resolved
He won because of his resolute nature.
*Synonyms: **adamant, doughty, headstrong, unfaltering, steadfast** (steadfast loyalty to his boss)
Resilient: the quality to be able to withstand a lot of difficult situations and then recover from them
The soldier had a resilient nature.
*Synonyms: strong, tough, **hardy**
*Noun form: resilience, hardihood
Persevere: to persist despite difficulties
He persevered in his crusade to fight organized crime.
*Synonyms: plod on, plough on, grind away
*Antonyms: to give up, to quit
*Adjective forms: persevering, persistent, **pertinacious** (a pertinacious salesman), **tenacious, dogged, mettlesome, gritty**
*Noun form: perseverance, persistence, tenacity, mettle, grit
Leapfrog: to surpass or overtake
With five straight wins, the team leapfrogged from fifth place to first place in the points table.

∎

Reliable: dependable
*Synonym: **tried and tested**

*Antonyms: unreliable, **dodgy**
Foolproof: unfailing
The house was protected by a state of the art foolproof security system.
Erroneous: containing an error; wrong; incorrect
The judgment was erroneous.
*Synonym: **fallacious** (*pronounced as fal-ay-sheus; for example: the judge rejected the lawyer's argument as it was based on fallacious reasoning)
Untenable: indefensible; undefendable; especially an argument or point of view
The minister's position that the economy is doing well is untenable in face of the falling Gross Domestic Product (GDP).
*Antonyms: tenable, defensible, defendable

■

Intrepid: fearless; brave; courageous
The intrepid soldier.
*Synonyms: **dauntless, valorous, valiant, gallant, fortitudinous**
*Noun forms: bravery, valour, dauntlessness, gallantry, fortitude
*Antonym: coward
Feisty: brave and courageous in a spirited and lively way
The champion was faced with a feisty challenger.
*Synonyms: **spunky, plucky** (She fought pluckily), **gamely** (He fought gamely)
*Antonyms: timid, meek
Audacious: daring; willing to take bold risks; recklessly brave
Opening his own store in the middle of the recession was an audacious move.
*Synonyms: **temerarious, gumptious** (*Pronounced as gump-shus), **venturesome** (the venturesome explorer)
*Noun forms: audacity, temerity, gumption, venturesomeness, **chutzpah** (The young army officer's chutzpah impressed the generals; *pronounced as hoot-spah)
Bravado: bold behaviour with the aim to impress or intimidate
James Bond has a lot of bravado.
*Synonym: **swagger**
Swashbuckling: boldly engaging in daring and romantic adventures
He played the role of the swashbuckling Robin Hood in his last movie.

■

Recreant: a coward; traitor
Pusillanimous: cowardly; fearful
The mayor had a pusillanimous approach towards organized crime.
*Synonyms: **craven** (a craven apology), **trepid, timid, timorous, tremulous**
Milquetoast: a timid and weak person who is easily bullied and intimidated *Pronounced as milk-toast
*Etymology: from a cartoon of the same name

■

Coy: a woman who uses her shyness to flirt
She gave him a coy smile when he walked into the bar.
Coquette: a flirtatious woman
*Pronounced as koh-ket.
Demure: a shy woman
*Pronounced as dim-your
Demur: to object
The lawyer demurred.

■

Docile: tame; ready to accept directions, compliant, weakly submissive
The management wanted a docile workforce who would not question anything. *Pronounced as doh-sile
*Noun form: docility
*Synonyms: **biddable, lamblike, meek, nebbish, acquiescent** (*pronounced as ak-wee-es-unt; *etymology: acquiesce means to agree to somebody without any protest)
Diffident: shy or timid due to a lack of self-confidence
He disliked networking because of his diffident nature.
*Synonym: bashful
Deferential: showing deference; polite and respectful
He was very deferential to his seniors in the profession.
*Etymology: deference means polite and respectful submission
Pliable: easily flexible; easily influenced
The pliable minds of children must be kept away from the gory violence on TV.
*Synonyms: **pliant, prone, impressionable, susceptible,** suggestible, maniable, manipulable

■

Laborious: requiring a lot of time and effort to accomplish; difficult; tough

The job required years of laborious training.
*Synonyms: **Herculean, arduous, strenuous, onerous, gruelling, exacting**
*Antonym: easy
Unwieldy: difficult to move because of its size or weight
The large gun was unwieldy for the young soldier.
*Synonyms: unmanageable, unmanoeuvrable
*Antonyms: manageable, manoeuvrable, **dainty**
Cumbersome: burdensome because of being complicated
The reimbursement procedure was cumbersome to dissuade any applications.
Cinch: an extremely easy task
The new phone was a cinch to use.
*Pronounced as sinch

■

Calisthenics: gymnastic exercises done for physical health and well-being, usually done without any equipment
*Pronounced as kal-us-thenics
Decathlon: an athletic event that consists of 10 different events such as long jump, shot-put, high jump, pole vault, etc.
Triathlon: an athletic event that consists of three different events, which usually are swimming, cycling and long-distance running
Marathon: a long-distance running race
*Antonym: **sprint** (a short distance running race usually less than 400 metres)

■

Abash: to make someone feel embarrassed
The rude manager abashed the new hire by yelling at her in front of the entire office.
*Adjective forms: abashed, **mortified, red-faced**, to have a sheepish look.
Daunt: to intimidate someone
The elderly can sometimes be daunted by the infusion of technology into every aspect of daily life.
Discomfit: to make someone uneasy; to agitate someone; to upset and disturb someone
The new hire was discomfited by the manager's inappropriate questions.
*Synonyms: to discompose, to discomfort, to **disconcert**, to **discombobulate** (pronounced as discum-bob-you-late; the stand-up comic was discombobulated by the

heckler's jeering), to **perturb,** to **unnerve**, to ruffle, to fluster
*Noun forms: discomfiture (pronounced as dis-cum-fi-cher), discombobulation, perturbation, disquietude, restlessness, fretfulness, malaise, angst
*Adjective forms: discomfited, disquieted, discombobulated, disconcerted, discomposed, discomforted, uneasy, tense, **antsy, restive** (The passengers in the plan became restive after the take-off was delayed by two hours), **overwrought, highly strung, keyed up, on edge,** edgy, **jangled** (The footballer's nerves were jangling before the crucial match), **jittery,** nervous, **fidgety**, perturbed, unnerved, fretful, ruffled, flustered, fazed
*Antonyms: **mellow**, calm, relaxed, serene, unfazed
Skittish: easily scared, typically used to refer to a nervous horse
His horse is very skittish, so he keeps him away from traffic.
Frantic: panic-stricken
The student was frantic due to the last minute exam announcement.
*Synonym: **frenetic**
Tempestuous: having strong and conflicting emotions
They had a tempestuous love affair that culminated in a beautiful marriage.
*Synonyms: stormy, **turbulent, tumultuous**
*Antonyms: **placid**, calm, peaceful
Consternation: fear or anxiety that comes when things don't go as plan
Much to his consternation, the electricity generator wouldn't start.

■

Flabbergasted: shocked; stunned; astounded; astonished
He was flabbergasted when he failed his exams.
*Synonyms: **startled, stupefied, stumped, dazed, gobsmacked, nonplussed, benumbed, baffled, bewildered, woolly-headed, transfixed, taken aback** (The parents were taken aback by the rude reply of their teenage son)
Confounded: to be surprised and confused when something goes not as per expectations
The doctors were confounded when the test results of the food poisoning patient came back negative for a stomach infection.
*Synonyms: **dumbfounded, bamboozled**
Befuddled: confused

The students were left befuddled after the math teacher did a horrible job in explaining basic algebra.
*Synonyms: **flummoxed, perplexed, muddled, addled, bemused**

■

Neurotic: mentally unstable
His neurotic behaviour worried everyone.
Sadism: a mental condition in psychiatry in which the person derives sexual pleasure from the pain or humiliation of others
Masochism: a mental condition in psychiatry in which the person derives sexual pleasure from the pain or humiliation of oneself and not others
Demented: crazy; mad; insane
Everyone suspected that the dictator was demented.
*Synonyms: **lunatic, deranged, unhinged**
Delirious: in a mental state characterized by restlessness, illusions and the inability to speak intelligibly
He was delirious after consuming the drugs.
*Synonyms: **raving, hysterical, frenzied**
*Noun forms: delirium, hysteria
Maniac: a person exhibiting wild or violent behaviour
Berserk: wild; out of control
He was berserk with anger after his team lost.
Amok: out of control
The children ran amok in the classroom because there was no teacher present.
Rampage: wild, violent and destructive movement
The escaped rhinos rampaged through the city.

■

Psychokinesis: the supposed ability to move objects by just thinking
*Synonym: **telekinesis**
Kinetic: relating to motion or movement
*Etymology: from Greek *'kinein'* meaning to move.

■

Dizzy: feeling as if one is spinning around, losing balance and about to faint
He got dizzy whenever he looked down from the roof of the building.
*Synonyms: unsteady, shaky, **giddy, wobbly, woozy, light-headed, weak at the knees**
*Noun form: dizziness, giddiness, **vertigo**
Groggy: unable to think clearly, usually after lack of

sleep or after being hit on the head
*Synonyms: **dazed, befogged, muzzy, punch-drunk**
Stupor: a state of near-unconsciousness
He got fired because he reached work in a drunken stupor.
*Synonyms: **daze, dwam, trance, narcosis**
Reverie: a daydream
He was lost in a reverie in the middle of the meeting.

■

Chagrin: irritation
Much to her chagrin, the irritating questions wouldn't stop.
*Synonyms: annoyance, **vexation, pique** (pronounced as peak)
Vex: to irritate someone
The elder sister loved to vex her little brother by asking him about his girlfriend from school.
*Synonyms: to **irk**, to **nettle**, to **niggle**, to **gnaw**, to **rankle**, to **rile**, to **disgruntle,** to needle
Antagonize: to make someone hostile by irritating them
The government antagonized the banking industry by rolling out harsh regulations.
Alienate: to make someone become indifferent and lose affection
He alienated his brother by never replying to his call.
*Synonym: to **estrange** (After years of living apart, his estranged wife finally filed for a divorce)
Affront: an insult
He took the jokes about his haircut as a personal affront.
*Synonyms: **slur, aspersion**
Indignation: a feeling of annoyance at unfair treatment
His indignation at not being invited to the party was warranted.
Umbrage: to take offence
He took umbrage at the jokes about his new clothes.
*Synonym: to be affronted

■

Piqué: to arouse; piqué also means irritation (She finally left in a fit of piqué)
His curiosity was piquéd by the amazing presentation.
*Verb tenses: piqué, piqués, piquéd, piquing
*Pronounced as peak
*Synonyms: to stimulate, to **whet** (The burger's aroma whetted his appetite), to **kindle**, to **stir**, to **spur**
*Adjective form: piquant (pronounced as pee-kunt)

Hone: to sharpen (He honed his knife on a whetstone); to refine and make perfect over time (He honed his skill by working with expert coaches)

■

Acicular: needle-shaped
*Etymology: from Latin *'acicula'* meaning small needle
*Synonym: **acerose**
Acuminate: tapering to a sharp point; for example, acuminate skyscrapers
*Etymology: from Latin *'acuminatus'* meaning pointed
Mucronate: having an abrupt, pointed and sharp end; for example, a mucronate leaf
*Etymology: from Latin *'mucron'* meaning point

■

Embroiled: deeply involved in a controversy or problem
He was embroiled in a match fixing controversy.
*Synonyms: **entangled, enmeshed, mired**
Extricate: to free from a constraint or difficulty
He went to the bathroom to extricate himself from the awkward situation.
*Synonym: to **disentangle**
Beset: to be troubled
The poor guy was beset with all sorts of issues.
Bedevil: to cause someone great trouble
The company was bedevilled by a shortage of cash.
*Synonyms: to **afflict**, to **torment**
Besiege: to surround a place with armed forces
The fort was besieged by enemy forces.
*Synonyms: to **beleaguer**, to **encircle**, **to hem in**, to **engulf**
Browbeat: to bully someone
The goons tried to browbeat the business owner into signing away his property.
*Synonyms: to **hector** (The seniors tried to hector the fresher), to **cow** (The young intern was cowed into silence)
Harass: to pressurize and bother someone
There strict rules against sexual harassment at workplace.
*Synonyms: to **pester**, to **badger**, to **bate**, to **hound**, to **harrow**, to **harry** (The senior tried to harry the junior)
Heckle: to harass a public speaker with loud and abusive language
Ambush: to wait for someone in a concealed position and then suddenly and unexpectedly attack them, thereby taking them by surprise

The military convoy was ambushed by the rebels
*Synonyms: to **bushwhack**, to **waylay** (waylay also means to hide and wait for someone and then unexpectedly stop them to talk; for example: the superstar was waylaid by his fans)
Accost: to approach someone and then speak to them aggressively
The tourists were accosted by the taxi drivers at the arrival terminal.
Cosset: to pamper
The child was always cosseted by her family.
*Synonyms: **mollycoddle, coddle**, spoil, overindulge.
Countervail: to counter by providing an equal but opposite force
A strong judiciary is required to countervail the dominance of the government.

■

Bombard: to attack continuously with bombs
The enemy forces bombarded the town with missiles from fighter planes.
*Synonyms: to shell, to torpedo, to pound, to **blitz**, to **strafe** (The soldiers were strafed by machine-gun fire from the enemy), to pepper, to strike, to batter, to **broadside** (The minister was broadsided by the media for his insensitive remarks)
*Etymology: historically, broadside meant a firing of all the guns from one side of a warship, to **buffet** (The hut was buffeted by the strong winds), to **volley** (They volleyed abuses at us)
*Noun forms: **barrage** (The enemy faced a barrage of cannon fire), **hail** (They went down in a hail of gunfire), **salvo** (salvo means gun fire; for example, the first salvo was fired by the enemy camp), **cannonade** (The German attack on Poland began with a cannonade; *pronounced as canon-aid), **fusillade** (The politician faced a fusillade of questions from the media; *pronounced as few-suh-laid)
Onslaught: a violent, fierce and destructive attack
The enemy could not withstand the army's onslaught.
*Plural: onslaughts
Dogfight: an aerial battle between fighter planes at close range
Predation: preying; attacking; for example, the predation of deer by the tiger in the jungle.
*Related word: predator, which means attacker
Clobber: to hit someone very hard
*Synonyms: to **batter**, to **drub**, to **thrash**, to **thwack**,

to **pummel** (*Etymology: pummel is derived from **pommel** which is the rounded knob on the end of the handle of a sword), to **wallop**, to **smite** (May God smite our enemies. Also, smite means to be strongly attracted: he was smitten with the new girl in the class)
Combat: battle; fight
Many soldiers died in the fierce combat.
Assail: to attack
The activists assailed the regressive judgment.
Slay: to kill someone violently
*Adjective form: slain, which means killed.
Swat: to smack; to hit
He swatted the mosquito with a rolled-up magazine.

■

Embargo: an official ban on trade with a particular country
During the Cold War, the US imposed an embargo on Cuba.
Stockade: a barrier formed by using upright wooden posts
The fort was protected by a stockade on all sides.
*Synonym: **palisade**
Barricade: a barrier to stop the movement on a road
The police installed barricades on the road.
*Synonyms: barrier, obstacle, roadblock
Blockade: a barrier erected to completely seal off entry or exit
The government's blockade of the town square was lifted after massive anger.
Bulwark: a defensive wall
*Pronounced as bull-work
Rampart: a defensive wall of a castle
*Synonym: fortification
Parapet: a low protective wall on the edge of a balcony
*Synonyms: **balustrade** (*pronounced as bahl-uh-strade), railing

■

Garrison: a military fort or camp
*Synonym: **cantonment**
Citadel: a fort
Barracks: a large building to house soldiers or a group of such buildings
*Pronounced as bar-uks
Billet: a non-military place, especially the house of a civilian, where soldiers are temporarily lodged

*Pronounced as bil-it
Bastion: a stronghold; a place that strongly maintains an ideology
Harvard university is said to be a bastion of liberal values.
Lair: a secret hiding place; a resting place of a wild animal
The meetings took place at his secret lair.
*Pronounced as layer
Acropolis: the fortified part of an ancient Greek city, usually built on a hill and containing important buildings like temples to Greek Gods.

■

Gargoyle: a horrifying carved human or animal face on a building, which is projecting from the gutter of a building for spouting away rain water
Weathervane: a revolving pointer mounted on top of a building to indicate the direction of the wind

■

Buttress: a brick structure built against a wall to support it
Undergird: to secure by passing ropes under and around it
Underpin: to support a building by laying a solid underground foundation

■

Posterior: situated at the backside
Anterior: situated at the front side
Lateral: situated at the sides
Dorsal: relating to the upper side or backside of an organism's body
Ventral: relating to the underside of an organism's body; abdominal

■

Abscess: a boil on the skin
*Pronounced as ab-ses
*Plural: abscesses
Blister: a small bubble on the skin filled with serum
Blisters are usually caused by friction or burning.
*Homonym: **bluster** (bluster means the loud roar of the wind or the loud talk by a person with the aim to bully someone)

*Adjective form for bluster: blustery, gusty, windy, squally

Cyst: a small sac that grows under the skin and contains liquid or semi-liquid matter *Pronounced as sist
*Plural: cysts

Wart: a small and hard growth on the skin

Nodule: a small and abnormal swelling

He went to the dermatologist to have the nodule on his ear checked out.

Excrescence: an abnormal and usually harmless growth on a plant or animal
*Etymology: from Latin *'ex'* (out) + *'crescere'* (grow)

Lesion: a wound; a region of damaged tissue caused due to injury etc.

Contusion: a bruise; a region of damaged tissue where blood capillaries have burst due to an injury and caused a swelling underneath the skin

Concussion: a brain injury caused by a severe blow to the head; symptoms include headaches and loss of memory

Whiplash: a neck injury caused by the forceful and quick back-and-forth movement of the neck; whiplash usually occurs in car accidents

Pang: a sudden and sharp pain

He started experiencing hunger pangs after he missed his breakfast.
*Synonyms: spasm, ache, cramp, twinge

Throes: intense pain, usually associated with massive change or struggle

The economy was in the throes of recession.
*Pronounced as throws

Haemorrhage: heavy bleeding
*Pronounced as hem-er-age

■

Auscultation: the act of listening to the sounds of bodily organs like heart, lungs, etc., typically with a medical instrument like a stethoscope, for the purposes of a medical diagnosis.

Bloodletting: a bitter quarrel inside an organization

The disappointing quarterly sales report led to a lot of bloodletting inside the boardroom.

Anaphylaxis: a severe allergic reaction of the body to a foreign substance *Pronounced as anuh-fuh-lak-sis
*Adjective form: anaphylactic

Prophylaxis: treatment given to prevent the occurrence of a disease
*Pronounced as pro-fuh-lak-sis

*Adjective form: prophylactic (He took a prophylactic rabies injection before going on the African safari; *pronounced as pro-fuh-lactic;
*Synonyms: preventive, preventative, precautionary, pre-emptive, preclusive, anticipatory)

Hypochondriac: a person who is excessively preoccupied and anxious about his/her health
*Synonyms: **valetudinarian, valetudinary, neurotic**

Psychosomatic: a disease that is caused by mental factors such as stress

He suffered from psychosomatic acidity before the debate.

Paraplegic: a person whose both legs and lower body are paralysed due to spinal disease or injury

Spastic: having muscular weakness because of brain damage

Bubonic: related to bubo (Bubo is an inflammatory swelling of a lymphatic gland in the groin or armpit region)
*Pronounced as byu-bo
*Plural: buboes

Catatonic: immobile or unresponsive

The patient lay on the floor catatonic.

Rigor mortis: the stiffening of the joints and muscles of a body a few hours after death, caused by chemical changes in the muscles post mortem

Euthanasia: the painless putting to death of a patient who is incurably ill with a painful disease
*Synonym: mercy killing.

■

Soporific: sleep-inducing

The warm milk had a soporific effect.
*Synonyms: **sedative, dormitive, tranquillizing, hypnagogic**

Sedate: to make someone fall asleep typically by using medical drugs
*Synonyms: **tranquillize**, give a sedative to, put under sedation

Anaesthetize: to make someone lose feeling in a body part or the full body, typically by using medical drugs, for a surgical operation

Palliative: pain-killing

At later stages of cancer only palliative medication works as there is no cure.
*Synonyms: **analgesic, calmative**

Anodyne: a pain-killing drug
*Synonyms: **opiate** (a drug derived from opium used to

reduce pain; *adjective form: opioid)

Laxative: a drug that facilitates bowel movement and helps one excrete more frequently
*Synonyms: **purgative, lenitive, aperient, evacuant**
Diuretic: something that causes the increased passing of urine
*Etymology: Greek for *'dia'* (through) and *'ouron'* (urine)
Antipyretic: a drug used to reduce fever
Antihistamine: an anti-allergic drug; a drug taken to reduce or eliminate the body's allergic reaction to foreign substances
Narcotic: an addictive drug, usually illegal, which affects the behaviour
Carcinogen: a substance capable of causing cancer
*Adjective form: carcinogenic

■

Casualty: a person who is injured or killed in a war or accident
Fatality: a person who is killed due to a disease, accident, war, etc.
Mortality: death, especially caused on a large scale due to war, famine, etc.

■

Regimen: a prescribed course of medical treatment
The doctor prescribed a strict regimen of antibiotics twice a day for two weeks.
Inoculate: to vaccinate
*Synonym: **immunize**
Cauterize: to burn the skin of a wound with a heated instrument or a caustic substance in order to prevent infection or stop bleeding
Catheter: a flexible tube which is inserted into a bodily cavity through a narrow opening, usually to drain a liquid for medical purposes
Gauze: thin, loosely woven cloth used for medical dressings
Swab: an absorbent piece of material used in surgery for cleaning wounds, applying medication, etc.
*Homonym: **swap** (swap means to exchange).
Panacea: a remedy for all diseases; a solution for all problems
The one-child policy is no panacea for population control.
*Synonym: **cure-all**

Nostrum: a medicine prepared by an unqualified person, which results in no cure
*Synonym: **quack remedy**
Tincture: a medicine made by dissolving a drug in alcohol
Elixir: a magical option
Emollient: a balm; a preparation that soothes the skin
*Synonyms: ointment, moisturizer, **salve** (*pronounced as salv), **unguent, unction**
Embrocation: a rubbing liquid used relieve body pain
*Synonym: **liniment**
Poultice: a soft and moist mass of material (like flour, herbs, etc) applied to the body to relieve soreness and inflammation
*Pronounced as pole-tis
Triage: the process in medicine of determining which patients should be treated first as per the severity of their condition

■

Podiatrist: a foot doctor
Paediatrician: a child doctor
Obstetrician: a baby delivery doctor
Orthopedician: a bone doctor
Orthodontician: a teeth doctor
Paramedic: a person who is not a qualified medical doctor but is trained to give emergency medical assistance to an injured person
Midwife: a person, usually a female, who is not a qualified medical doctor but is trained to assist women in childbirth

■

Regurgitate: to vomit; to repeat information without analysing it
*Pronounced as re-gur-ji-tate
*Synonym: **disgorge**
Retch: to almost vomit; to make the sound and movement of vomiting
*Synonym: **dry-heave**
*Homonym: **wretch** (a dishonest person)
Belch: to repeatedly and loudly burp
Nausea: a sickness of the stomach which causes an impulse to vomit
The car ride made him feel nauseous
*Adjective form: nauseous, **queasy**
Flatulence: intestinal gas; farting

*Pronounced as fla-chu-lence
*Adjective form: flatulent (gassy)

■

Gasp: to catch one's breath with an open mouth because one is shocked
Wheeze: to breathe with a whistling sound as a result of obstruction in the air passages
Pant: to breathe with short, quick breaths because of exertion
Hyperventilate: to breathe very rapidly when over excited or nervous

■

Denude: to strip
Illegal mining has denuded the forests of its trees.
Dishabille: the state of being semi-clothed or very scantily clothed
Many portraits showed the Greek goddess in a state of dishabille.
Foliage: the leaves of a plant referred to collectively
Defoliate: to strip a tree or an area of land off all its leaves
Exfoliate: to shed off or peel off in scales or layers

■

Chafe: to rub up against something and make it sore (The tight collar chafed his neck); to irritate someone (The manager chafed the employees)
Abrade: to slowly erode away
The seawater abraded the coastline.
Scuff: to make a mark by brushing up against the surface of something
She accidentally scuffed her new shoes against the sides of the brick wall.
Scour: to remove dirt, grease, etc., by hard-rubbing the surface with an abrasive material
The hotel cleaner scoured the dirty pots and pans.
Scrape: to drag a sharp object across something's surface
The chef told the assistant to scrape the dirt off the radish with a knife.
Rake: to sweep a surface while looking for something
The divers raked the sea floor looking for pearl oysters.
Dredge: to clear a river bed by scooping and dragging out mud, rubbish, etc.
He did not like it when his wife would dredge up old issues.

Grate: to shred something
He grated the vegetables for the noodles.
Graze: to superficially touch or rub lightly in passing
The bullet only grazed the police officer's arm.
*Graze also means to eat grass in a field.
Gnash: to grind one's teeth in anger or irritation
He would gnash his teeth every time his staff made a mistake.
*Pronounced as nash
Pulverize: to reduce something to fine particles
The cement blocks were pulverized to make building material.
*Synonyms: **granulate**, **grind**, crush
Mince: to chop up something into small pieces
He minced the meat.
Knead: to work moistened flour, etc., into dough by pressing and folding with one's hands
*Pronounced as need

■

Ding: to dent something
The speeding driver dinged the side of his car.
Vandalize: to damage public property
The mob vandalized the bus.
Warp: to bend or twist out of shape
The heat from the lamp warped the plastic toy lying next to it.
*Synonyms: **distort, deform, misshape, malform, gnarl** (*pronounced as nahrl).
Wring: to squeeze and twist something
He wrung the dish washing sponge over the sink to drain the liquid from it.
Buckle: to bend under pressure
The government buckled and decided to withdraw the controversial bill.
*Buckle also means to fasten with a buckle.

■

Macerate: to make something soft by soaking it in liquid
The beans were macerated in water all night before cooking.
*Pronounced as mas-uh-rate
Maculate: to put spots on something
He maculated his white office shirt by dropping tomato sauce on it.
Mutilate: to inflict a disfiguring injury
The detectives uncovered mutilated bodies from the

psychopath's backyard.
*Synonyms: **mangle, maim, maul**
Lacerate: to make deep cuts into something
The attacker lacerated his neck with a knife.
*Noun form: **laceration, gash**
Desiccate: to dehydrate something, usually in order to preserve it
She loved to eat the desiccated apricots.
Decapitate: to cut off someone's head
The psychopath would brutally decapitate his victims.
*Synonyms: to **guillotine**, to **decollate**
Dismember: to cut off someone's limbs, arms and legs
Disembowel: to cut open a dead body and remove the internal organs
*Synonyms: **eviscerate, to gut, remove the innards from**
Deracinate: to uproot
The child was deracinated from her home.
Amputate: to surgically cut off a limb to prevent the spread of infection

∎

Bobbitize: to cut off someone's penis
*Etymology: in US 1994, a lady by the name of Lorena Bobbit cut off her husband's penis
Emasculate: to make somebody/something less powerful or effective; to deprive a man of his manliness
*Synonyms: **castrate, neuter, geld, sterilize**, unman
Emaciated: extremely weak because of illness or a lack of food
*Pronounced as ih-may-shee-ey-tid
Enfeeble: to make extremely weak and powerless
The new court ruling in favour of the corporates, further enfeebled the consumers.
*Synonyms: **debilitate, enervate, devitalize, incapacitate**
Effeminate: unmanly
He was mocked by his friends for his effeminate handshake.
*Synonym: **effete** (*pronounced as eh-feet)
Languish: to grow weak by being forced to stay in unwanted place
They languished in jail.
*Synonym: deteriorate
*Antonyms: thrive, flourish

∎

Feeble: weak; lacking physical strength
*Synonyms: **frail, infirm**, impotent
*Noun form: weakness, frailty, infirmity, feebleness, enfeeblement, **debility** *Antonym: potent
Tenuous: very thin; weak; insubstantial
Any claim made without evidence is tenuous.
*Synonym: **flimsy**
*Antonyms: convincing, substantial, strong
Fragile: something which can be easily broken or damaged
Trust is a fragile commodity.
*Synonyms: delicate, **brittle, frangible**

∎

Robust: strong
*Synonyms: sturdy, rugged, durable, built to last
Ironclad: impossible to change, weaken or break
The law firm was famous for drafting ironclad contracts.

∎

Defunct: no longer existing or functioning
Many consider the Non-Aligned Movement (NAM) a defunct organization.
*Synonyms: inoperative, unused
Decrepit: worn out due to long use or neglect; broken-down
He bought the decrepit house to renovate it and then sell it off for a quick profit.
*Synonyms: **dilapidated, ramshackle, rundown, tumbledown**
Desuetude: a state of disuse
The marine docks fell into desuetude after fishing was banned in the area
Rickety: likely to collapse; shaky
The rickety old chair was not meant for sitting but to be only used for decorative purposes.

∎

Taut: tight
The Bungee jumping instructors were taught to always check that the ropes were taut to avoid any accidents.
Snug: tight-fitting
He bought snug jeans so that people could see the shape of his strong legs.

∎

Slack: loose
He slackened the tie after the meeting got over.
Limp: not stiff nor firm; lacking internal strength
*Synonym: **flaccid** (*pronounced as flas-id)
*Antonyms: rigid, firm, stiff, taut, energetic
Wilt: to limp and droop because of excessive heat, lack of water, etc.
He began to wilt because of the enormous office stress.
Wither: to become dry and shrivelled
The grass in the park began to wither due to the oppressive summer heat.
Tender: soft; gentle and kind
He bit into the tender steak.

■

Ossify: to turn into bone
Without regular reforms, traditions can ossify and turn regressive
*Adjective form: osseous (Latin for bony).
Petrify: to turn into rock
She was petrified at the sight of the tiger near her house
*Etymology: from Latin *'petra'* meaning rock
Thaw: to defrost
The Arctic thaw is a great cause of concern.
*Adjective form: freeze

■

Lithic: relating to stone
Lapidary: a person who cuts, polishes or engraves ornamental gems

■

Physique: the shape and size of a person's body; bodily structure
He had a muscular physique.
*Pronounced as fi-zeek
*Synonym: **anatomy**
Musculature: the muscular system or the arrangement of muscles on the body of an organism
The wrestler had a strong and sturdy musculature.
Rotund: round in shape; plump; fat;
*Synonyms: **corpulent** (*etymology: from Latin *'corpus'* meaning body), tubby, roly-poly, portly, dumpy, chunky, **Falstaffian**
*Noun form: rotundity
*Antonyms: thin, slim, slender, skinny
Cherubic: having a plump and pretty appearance

The child had a cherubic face.
*Pronounced as shay-rub-ik
*Synonym: angelic
Girth: the circumference; especially of a person's waist
Stout: fat and bulky
The stout middle-aged man was unattractive.
Thickset: muscular; having a thick, heavy or solid built; for example, the thickset bodyguard
*Synonyms: stocky, bull-necked, chunky, beefy, meaty, **hefty** (the hefty book; *etymology: heft means weight), **husky, burly, brawny, sinewy** (*pronounced as sin-yoo-ee; *etymology: like a sinew, which is a piece of tough fibrous tissue connecting the muscle to bone)
Clunky: awkwardly solid and heavy
The old clunky cassette players.
Lanky: thin and tall
The lanky teenager.
*Synonyms: **gangly**, wiry (like a wire), stringy (like a string), spindly (like a spindle)
Gaunt: unattractively skinny
*Synonyms: **scrawny**, scraggy
Buxom: having big breasts
The buxom blonde worked as a model.
*Synonyms: bosomy, large-bosomed
*Pronounced as buk-sum
Voluptuous: having a curvy and sexually attractive body
*Pronounced as vo-lup-chu-us
*Synonyms: **curvaceous, Rubenesque**
Petite: having an attractively small and trim figure, usually refers to a woman
The petite woman was having a hard time carrying the heavy boxes.
*Etymology: from French *'petit'* meaning small

■

Wispy: feathery
He had wispy tufts of hair above his ears.
Frizzy: curly; formed into a mass of tight and small curls
He has frizzy hair.
Flocculent: woolly; resembling wool; soft and fluffy
A flocculent mass of fresh snow covered his lawn.
*Pronounced as flock-yoo-lent
Hirsute: hairy
The hero liked to show his hirsute chest.

■

Malleable: capable of being hammered or pressed into

the shape of a sheet without breaking or cracking
Ductile: capable of being drawn out into a thin wire
Tractile: capable of being drawn or stretched out in length
Tensile: capable of being pulled apart without breaking or cracking and thus able to resist such tension
Sectile: capable of being cut smoothly with a knife
Friable: capable of being easily crumbled or reduced to powder
Brittle: hard but easily breakable into pieces
Glass is a brittle material.
Prehensile: capable of grasping
Some monkeys have prehensile tails.

■

Traction: the extent to which an idea or a product gains popularity or acceptance among people
The notion of free medical care for all is gaining a lot of traction.
*Synonym: **purchase**
Adhesion: the sticking onto a surface
The glue was used for adhesion of the photos onto the scrapbook.
*Adjective form: adhesive, sticky, gluey, gummy, **mucilaginous**
*Verb form: adhere
*Noun form: adherence
Cohesion: the sticking together as a united whole and not breaking up into smaller units
A common goal helps in the cohesion of a group.
*Adjective form: cohesive
*Verb form: cohere
*Noun form: coherence

■

Supernumerary: additional; extra
Some of the guests were supernumerary and were removed from the guests list.
Centenary: the hundredth anniversary
*Pronounced as sen-tenary
*Adjective form: centennial (*pronounced as sen-tenial)
Sesquicentenary: the one-hundred-and-fiftieth anniversary
*Pronounced as ses-kwis-sen-tenary
*Adjective form: sesquicentennial
Millennium: a period of a thousand years
Quintuplet: one of the five children born of one pregnancy

Penultimate: second last
The penultimate episode of the show.

■

Fortnight: a period of two weeks
Eve: the day immediately before an event
They met on Christmas eve.

■

Triad: a group of three (be it people, things etc)
*Adjective form: triadic.
Troika: a group of three people, especially a group of three government officials
He was removed from the minister's troika of close advisers.
Triumvirate: a group of three very powerful people
*Etymology: from Latin 'trium virorum' which means 'of three men'

■

Denarian: someone whose age is 10 to 19 years
Vicenarian: someone in their twenties
Tricenarian: someone in their thirties
Quadragenarian: someone in their forties
Quinquagenarian: someone in their fifties
*Pronounced as kwin-kwuh-juhn-air-ean
Sexagenarian: someone in their sixties
Septuagenarian: someone in their seventies
Octogenarian: someone in their eighties
Nonagenarian: someone in their nineties
Centenarian: someone whose age is 100 years or more
Supercentenarian: someone whose age is 110 years or more with no upper limit

■

Ramify: to branch out
The government built a complex system of waterways and canals, ramifying throughout the territory.
Bifurcate: to divide into two branches
The city developed at the point where the river bifurcates.
Trifurcate: to divide into three branches
Divaricate: to diverge widely; to spread apart
The river divaricated near the edge of the plateau.

■

Escalate: to increase rapidly
The prices escalated because of the scarcity caused by the drought.
*Antonym: **plunge** (to decrease rapidly)
Proliferate: to increase rapidly in number
Many countries decided to sign the Nuclear Non-Proliferation Treaty.
*Synonyms: to **mushroom**, to **snowball**, to **burgeon** (for example, the burgeoning population; *pronounced as bur-juhn)
*Antonyms: to **dwindle**, to **shrink**
Ramp: to sharply increase something
The firm ramped up production.
Ratchet: to gradually increase or decrease, usually in an irreversible manner
The tension between the nations ratcheted up after the attack.
Amplify: to louden
*Synonym: to **boost**
Distend: to swell
His leg distended because of the bone fracture.
*Synonym: to **tumefy** (His hand tumefied after the fracture)
*Noun form: **distention,** bulge, bloat
*Adjective form: distended, swollen, enlarged, **tumescent, tumefied, tumid, turgid, engorged, bloated, bulging, bulbous, protuberant**
*Antonym: to **contract**
Dilate: to become wider
The doctor dilated his eyes to do a thorough check-up.
Constrict: to become narrower
The cholesterol in his blood caused a constriction of the arteries.

■

Truncate: to shorten something by cutting off the top or the end
The judge told the lawyer to truncate his arguments and be brief.
*Synonym: to **dock**
Curtail: to reduce in size or degree; to impose a restriction on something
People's civil rights were curtailed.
*Synonyms: **diminish,** shrink
Pare: to trim something by cutting away its outer coating or layer, especially when done to a fruit or vegetable
*Synonym: to **peel** off
Prune: to trim a tree, shrub, etc., by cutting away dead or

overgrown branches with the aim of encouraging growth
*Synonym: to **pollard**
Lop: to cut off a branch from the main body of a tree
The gardener lopped off the branch that obstructed the view from the window.
Whittle: to carve an object from a block of wood
The initial list of candidates was whittled down to the final two.

■

Subside: to become less intense
The fever subsided after the medication.
*Synonyms: **tail off, peter out**, to **abate** (abate also means to stop entirely; for example, the suit abated after the party died).
Taper: to become thinner towards the end
The patient's amputated leg tapered off just above the knee.
Retard: to delay or hold back; slow down; hold up
The progress of the startup was retarded due to the founder's mismanagement.
*Synonym: **decelerate**
*Antonyms: accelerate, **expedite**, speed up
Recede: to move back
The enemy receded.
*Noun form: recession
Dwindle: to decrease in size or strength
The membership numbers dwindled after the party president was caught rebuking a lady volunteer.
Dissipate: to disappear: All the anger dissipated after he apologized

■

Exacerbate: to worsen
The conditions were exacerbated by the water shortage.
*Pronounced as ek-zas-er-bate
*Synonym: to **aggravate**
Mitigate: to improve (The conditions after the economic crash were mitigated by the fall in oil prices); to lessen the severity (His lack of education was treated as a mitigating circumstance by the judge and hence he was awarded a lesser sentence)
*Synonym: **extenuate** (to make an offence less serious; for example, the judge refused to listen to any extenuating circumstances like poverty and awarded him the maximum sentence)
Modulate: to soften; to tone down

He modulated his voice to appear calm and gentle.

*Synonyms: to moderate, to **temper**

Attenuate: to make thin

He attenuated to half his size due to illness.

Alleviate: to lessen suffering

The government did not do enough to alleviate the wide-spread poverty and hunger.

Ameliorate: to make bad conditions better

The NGO tried to ameliorate the living standards of the local community by providing free clean water.

Accentuate: to highlight

The dark jacket accentuated his fair complexion.

Underscore: to emphasize something

The security advisor underscored the dangers of war.

*Etymology: underscore means to underline a text

■

Appease: to give into unjustified demands at the expense of justice and morality

The government should not appease anyone.

Assuage: to calm down intense feelings

The manager tried to assuage the angry customers.

*Synonym: to **allay** (allay the fears)

Propitiate: to win someone's favour by doing something that pleases them

The tribe propitiated the Gods by making sacrifices during the full moon.

Placate: to calm a person down; to stop someone from being angry or discontented The principal tried to placate the angry students.

*Synonyms: to **mollify** (The government tried to mollify the farmers), to **pacify**, to **conciliate** (He conciliated his girlfriend)

*Noun forms: placation, pacification, mollification, conciliation

*Antonyms: to provoke, to enrage, to agitate

Reconcile: to restore friendly relations between two fighting parties

The couple reconciled over a relaxed getaway in the hills.

Lull: to send a person to sleep by making soothing sounds

The mother lulled the baby to sleep.

*Noun form: **lullaby**

Buffer: something that acts like a cushion between two incompatible things

Family and friends are a buffer against stress.

Pander: to fulfil someone's immoral desire

The producer pandered to the crowd by putting multiple sex scenes in his movie.

Gratify: to satisfy someone's desire

He gratified the audience by performing an extra 30 minutes.

*Antonyms: to frustrate, to displease

Satiate: to satisfy completely; to sate

He satiated his craving by eating the entire box of ice cream.

*Pronounced as say-shee-ate

*Noun form: satiety, satisfaction

*Antonyms: to starve, deprive

Quench: to satisfy one's thirst by drinking

He quenched his thirst by downing a chilled beer.

*Synonym: to slake

Delectation: enjoyment; pleasure; delight

He had made homemade pasta for the guest's delectation.

■

Rapacious: extremely greedy

The rapacious landlord doubled the rent.

*Synonyms: grasping, **avaricious**, acquisitive

Voracious: someone who can't be satisfied

He is a voracious eater who eats a large pizza for breakfast.

*Synonyms: insatiable, unquenchable

Covet: to crave, usually something that belongs to another person

He coveted his friend's new jacket.

*Antonyms: benevolent, generous, giving

■

Touchy: oversensitive

She is touchy about her age.

*Synonym: **thin-skinned**

*Antonyms: **thick-skinned, with a hide like an elephant**

Touchy-feely: a derogatory term referring to anyone who becomes too uncomfortably physically close

Her male co-star got very touchy-feely.

■

Sensory: relating to the senses

Ocular: relating to the sense of sight

Aural: relating to the sense of hearing

*Synonyms: auditory, **acoustic**

Olfactory: relating to the sense of smell

Tactile: relating to the sense of touch
*Synonyms: **tactual, haptic**
Gustatory: relating to the sense of taste
*Pronounced as gus-ta-tuhree

■

Anaptic: unable to feel touch
Anosmic: unable to smell
Ageusic: unable to taste
*Pronounced as uh-gyu-zik
Insentient: unable to feel emotions
Inanimate: lifeless; showing no sign of life
Insensate: unconscious; knocked out

■

Converge: to come together from different directions and meet
The pilgrims from all over the world converged on to the holy site.
*Noun form: **convergence, juncture, intersection, node**
Congeal: to become hardened or thickened especially because of evaporation or cooling
The cheese from the pizza congealed onto the tray.
*Pronounced as cun-jeel
*Synonym: **inspissate**
Coalesce: to come together to form single mass
All the ideas of the scientist coalesced into one grand theory.
*Pronounced as koh-uh-less
Coagulate: to change from liquid state to a solid or semi-solid state
The blood of the victim coagulated on the floor.
*Pronounced as koh-ag-you-late
Corrugate: to fold or contract into wrinkles
His eyebrows corrugated when he concentrated.
*Etymology: from Latin 'corrugat' meaning wrinkled
Confabulate: to make up a false memory about an event which never happened, with the intention to deceive
The defence lawyer argued that the witness was not credible because he had a history of confabulating.
Confluence: a junction or joining of different things
A confluence of factors, like high food prices and corruption, which led to the Arab Spring.
Amalgamate: to combine or join together
The two companies amalgamated to form one giant corporation company.
*Synonym: **splice**

Weld: to join together two metal parts by heating the surfaces to the point that they melt and fuse together
Solder: to join two metals together using an alloy of lead and tin
Curdle: to separate into lumps like lumps of curds; to shock or horror (The movie made his blood curdle); to sour or turn bad (Their relationship soon curdled)
*Synonym: **clabber**
Palpitate: to expand and contract rapidly
His heart began to palpitate with fear before the exam.
*Synonyms: to **throb**, to **pulsate**
Precipitate: to trigger an event; to spark off
The High Court ruling precipitated a constitutional crisis.
*Synonym: to **prompt**
Effectuate: to bring into effect
The Minister was hailed in the press for the reforms he effectuated.
*Pronounced as ih-fek-choo-ate
Juxtapose: to place side by side
The annual economic report juxtaposed the GDP figures from the past few years.
*Pronounced as jux-tuh-pohz
Disseminate: to spread something, especially information
The NGO's aim is to disseminate information about the prevention of water borne diseases.
Serrated: having a jagged edge; saw-edged; having a row of sharp points along the edge
A serrated edge knife is used to slice up bread.

■

Proprietary: relating to ownership
The company gave out licenses to use its proprietary software.
*Noun form: proprietor (owner)
Expropriate: to take over a property from someone so that this property can be used for public benefit, usually done so by the government
Appropriate: to take something for one's own use without the permission or consent of the owner
The crooked manager appropriated the funds.
Arrogate: to claim something for oneself without any legal right to do so
The courts cannot arrogate to themselves the power to legislate.
Requisition: an authoritative and formal demand for something to be supplied, usually for military purposes or public needs

Commandeer: to officially seize private property for military purposes
Some houses were commandeered by the army to store guns.
Co-opt: to adopt an idea for one's own use
After initially denouncing it, political parties eventually co-opted the Black Lives Matter movement.
Confiscate: to seize someone's property with due authority
His car was confiscated by the customs officials.
*Synonyms: **impound, sequestrate**
Conscript: to compulsorily enlist someone in the army
*Synonym: to **draft** (also written as draught)
Consign: to formally deliver
The case files were consigned from the lower court to the high court for the appeal hearings.
*Pronounced as cun-sign
Coup: a sudden and usually violent seizure of power by the military from a democratically elected government
*Synonyms: regime change, takeover
*Verb form: to **overthrow**, to **oust**, to **depose**, to **dislodge**, to **topple**
Usurp: to illegally take power by the use of force
Game of Thrones is all about one usurper fighting another.
*Synonym: to **accroach**
Usury: lending money at very high rates
The students were crushed by the usurious study loans.
Pawn: to deposit something which is valuable and movable, with a pawnbroker as a security for a loan taken from this pawnbroker
He raised money for the surgery by pawning his Rolex watch.
Loan shark: a money lender who charges extremely high and excessive interest rates
*Synonym: usurer (For example, the character of Shylock from the play *Merchant of Venice* is a usurer)

■

Despot: a dictator
Kim Jong-un is the despot currently ruling over North Korea.
*Synonyms: **tyrant, autocrat**, oppressor
Potentate: an autocratic ruler.
Puissant: powerful
The puissant dictator was much feared.
*Pronounced as pyoo-sunt
*Etymology: in Latin *'posse'* means to have power

Monarch: a sovereign head of state, especially a king or a queen
Navarch: an admiral; the leader of a ship
Honcho: the leader of an organization; the person in charge
Tycoon: a very powerful businessman; industry leader
*Synonyms: **magnate, mogul, baron**
Satrap: a local leader
*Etymology: a satrap was a governor in Persia
Shogun: the real ruler of feudal Japan as he held all the military power and the Emperor of Japan (The Mikado) was only the titular ruler
Mandarin: a powerful official or senior bureaucrat
*Etymology: a mandarin was a top official in the imperial Chinese civil service
Incumbent: currently holding office; in power; reigning
Due to the ailing economy, the incumbent president faces a tough re-election.
Alpha male: the most dominant male in a group
Beta male: a male who is lower in rank than the alpha male in the group

■

Subjugate: to bring under control, especially by conquest
Genghis Khan subjugated most of the population of Central Asia in the thirteenth century.
Annex: to add territory to one's own territory, usually by the use of force
Germany annexed a portion of Czechoslovakia in 1939.
Tyranny: a cruel, oppressive and arbitrary rule, usually by an autocratic ruler
The tyranny of Nazism ended in World War II.
*Synonyms: **yoke** (the yoke of colonialism), **despotism, autocracy, totalitarianism, fascism**
Draconian: excessively harsh and severe
Stalin's USSR was infamous for the clampdown on freedom of expression.
*Synonyms: **ruthless, tyrannical, repressive, iron-fisted**, brutal, oppressive
Hegemony: the dominant control by one nation over others
The freedom war ended the British hegemony over America.
*Synonym: **ascendancy**
Suzerainty: a relationship where a dominant nation controls the foreign policy of a smaller nation but allows autonomy in internal affairs
Paramountcy: the quality of being paramount; the domination of a large state over a smaller one

The British had paramountcy over its colonies.

Preponderance: predominance; the superiority in power, numbers, etc.

The preponderance of votes was against the tax hike proposal.

Emancipate: to liberate; to release from slavery or servitude

Abraham Lincoln emancipated the slaves.

*Synonym: **manumit**

■

Allocate: to distribute

The Finance Minister allocated a large amount for education in this year's budget.

*Synonyms: **allot**, assign

Apportion: to divide and share

The profits were apportioned as per the partnership agreement

Earmark: to set aside funds for a particular purpose

The government earmarked a hundred million dollars for infrastructure development.

Expend: to spend

The ministry was criticized for expending precious taxpayers money in wasteful publicity events.

Disburse: to pay out money

The corrupt government disbursed huge loans to undeserving crony capitalists.

Reimburse: to repay someone for expenses incurred on one's behalf

He was reimbursed by the company for the flight ticket.

Recoup: to regain something

The Company was keen to recoup their losses after a bad last quarter.

Mete out: to distribute or dispense something

In the past, schoolteachers meted out physical punishment to their students. *Pronounced as meet out

Dole out: to distribute something in small portions

The campaign manager got volunteers to dole out pamphlets to the audience before the rally began.

Defray: to pay the cost or bear the expenses

The grant from the university helped defray the expenses of the student's research trip to Antarctica.

Bankroll: to financial support; to fund

The vaccination project in the town was bankrolled by the local wealthy industrialist.

Payroll: a list of the employees of a company and the amount of money they are to be paid as remuneration for services rendered

■

Compensation: money paid in recognition of loss incurred or injury suffered by the other person, typically in order to make amends

*Verb form: compensate

*Synonym: **recompense**

Indemnification: monetary protection given to someone to secure against a future loss

The insurance company indemnified the house owner.

Reparation: the compensation paid by the defeated country to the other country for the damage caused and losses suffered because of the war

Restitution: the restoration of something, which was lost or stolen, back to its original and proper owner

The tribes demanded the restitution of land.

Remuneration: payment made for work or services rendered

Google offers handsome remuneration to its engineers.

*Verb form: remunerate

Redressal: a remedy or payment made to correct a wrong

Affirmative action is a method to redress the historical wrongs suffered by minorities.

■

Croupier: the person in charge of a carb game table

Purser: the officer on a ship who handles all the financial accounts

Bursar: a person who manages the financial affairs of college

Bursary: the office of a bursar

Bullion: gold bars

Bourse: the stock exchange of a European and non-English speaking country like France

Treasury: a place where the funds of an organization are deposited, kept and disbursed

Tranche: an instalment of money

The first tranche of the home loan was released by the bank.

*Pronounced as tranch

■

Gratuity: a tip given to a waiter, attendant, taxi driver, etc.

Annuity: a fixed sum of money paid out annually to a person

Alimony: the maintenance given by a spouse after a divorce

Allowance: a sum of money paid regularly to a person to meet their general living expenses
*Synonym: pocket money

Pension: a regular payment made by the government to the old or disabled

Perquisite: a perk; an additional benefit or privilege above one's regular salary
The perquisite of job was the free use of the company car.
*Homonym: **prerequisite** (a precondition)

Stipend: a periodic payment made to a student or intern

Subvention: a government grant
*Plural: subventions

Fellowship: a university grant given to a scholar to conduct research

■

Haggle: to bargain a lot over the price of something
Shopkeepers did not like him as he would haggle over everything and wasted their time.

Concession: a preferential lower rate
The middle class wanted tax concessions in the new budget.

Rebate: a partial refund
As per company policy, the customer was entitled to a 30 per cent rebate off the MRP by mailing the invoice of the product.

■

Freebie: something that is provided free of charge, usually done to promote a business
The company gave out caps, pens and other such freebies.

Gratis: free
The shoe company provided an extra set of shoe laces gratis.

Gratuitous: uncalled for
The debate was filled with gratuitous insults and personal comments.
*Synonyms: unwarranted, unprovoked

Gratitude: gratefulness; thankfulness
He sent his neighbours some to express his gratitude for the dinner invitation.
*Antonym: ingratitude

Ingrate: an ungrateful person
He loathed his friends as he considered them a bunch of ingrates and freeloaders.
*Antonym: grateful (thankful)

■

Fiduciary: based on utmost trust
The company has a fiduciary relationship to its shareholders.

Profiteer: to make excessive and unfair amounts of profit
The greedy company profiteered from the war by selling bandages at a 200 per cent margin.

Lucre: money, especially black money
The corrupt official accepted the filthy lucre to award the contract.
*Pronounced as loo-kur
*Synonym: **pelf**

Blood money: money obtained through the death or suffering of others; for example, the money earned by contract killers for killing someone

■

Bottom line: it is the line on the accounts graph that shows the profit

Top line: it is the line on the accounts graph that shows the revenue

Line-item: an item on a financial statement that is mentioned on a separate line, which signifies a separate category; for example, 'Rent & Utilities'

■

Retrenchment: the reduction of expenses, typically done by dismissing people to reduce salary expenditure
*Synonym: **cutbacks**

Downsize: to make an organization smaller by dismissing some of the staff

Layoff: the dismissal of workers
*Antonyms: **recruitment**, hiring

■

Itinerary: a detailed plan for a journey
*Pronounced as i-tin-uh-ruree

Repertoire: the stock of skills and techniques of a person in a particular field; the entire list of songs and dances that a performer can perform

Roster: a list of persons or items; a list of people's names along with their duties
*Synonym: **rota** (the duty rota of a hotel)

Agenda: a list of items to be discussed or voted on at a formal meeting; agenda also means the underlying intentions or motives of someone

Inventory: the stock of a merchant's goods which are currently in hand or the complete list of all items in such a stock

■

Anomalous: inconsistent; unusual; exceptional; peculiar; out of the ordinary; queer; freakish
Global warming is a major cause for the anomalous weather conditions.
*Synonyms: **aberrant, abnormal, atypical, incongruous, inconsonant, dissonant, discordant, deviant, divergent, discrepant, variant**
*Noun form: anomaly (anomaly means something that deviates from what is standard or normal), **outlier**, aberration, abnormality, incongruity, dissonance, discordance, discrepancy, divergence, variance
*Antonyms: normal, usual, typical

Disparity: a great difference
Many economists are worried about the growing disparity between rich and poor.
*Synonyms: imbalance, inequality, unevenness, disproportion
*Antonyms: **parity** (The firefighters of the city took to the streets demanding pay parity with police), uniformity, equality, **equivalence**, sameness, consistency, levelness, evenness

Deficit: shortfall; the amount by which a sum is not enough
The country's trade deficit increased last month.
*Antonym: **surplus**

Differential: the difference between amounts of things
The differential between gold and silver prices is not vast.
*Synonym: **delta**

Commensurate: corresponding in size or degree
The punishment must be commensurate with the seriousness of the crime. *Pronounced as cum-en-ser-it
*Synonym: proportionate
*Antonym: disproportionate

Tantamount: equivalent
His refusal to answer the police's questions was seen as being tantamount to an admission of guilt.

Virtually: nearly
The fire destroyed virtually all the houses in the area.

■

Prodigal: wastefully and recklessly spending money
The prodigal son wasted all of his father's fortune.
*Synonyms: **improvident, profligate** (Shopping malls are profligate consumers of energy), **thriftless**

Parsimonious: stingy; miserly
The parsimonious shop owner paid his employees very less.
*Synonyms: **skinflint, tightwad, niggardly, close-fisted, penny-pinching, cheese-paring**

Penury: poverty; strained financial circumstances
Facing penury he got job so that he could pay his bills.
*Synonyms: **impecuniousness, impoverishment, indigence, destitution, privation, deprivation**, pennilessness, beggary
*Adjective form: penurious, penniless, impoverished, **impecunious, destitute, indigent**

Frugal: very careful with spending
A frugal person lives well within his means.
*Synonyms: **thrifty**, sparing, economical, saving

Scrimp: to severely limit the use; to economize; to save on money by cutting necessary expenditures
One should not scrimp on adequate travel insurance when going abroad.
*Synonyms: to **skimp**, to **stint**

Squander: to waste away something
He squandered all his wealth on fancy cars.
*Synonym: to **fritter** away
*Noun form: squanderer, **spendthrift, wanton, wastrel**

Scrounge: to borrow money or food with no intention of repaying or returning it
He never buys cigarettes and instead scrounges off his friends.

Cadge: to try to get something from someone without paying for it
The unethical lawyer had a reputation for cadging free meals off his clients.

Insolvent: unable to pay one's debts
*Synonyms: **bankrupt, defaulting, liquidated, wiped out**
*Antonym: solvent, creditworthy

Mendicant: a beggar

Affluent: extremely rich
*Synonyms: well off, **with deep pockets**

Opulent: luxurious
The King lived in an opulent palace.
*Synonyms: **sumptuous, palatial, lavish, luxuriant, decadent** (a decadent lifestyle)

Austere: characterized by living life in a very simple and plain manner without any luxuries

Mahatma Gandhi lived a very austere life.
*Synonyms: sober, **Spartan**, moderate, temperate, self-restrained, non-indulgent
Ascetic: characterized by living life in severe self-denial and not indulging in basic comforts, usually done for religious reasons
The nuns lived an ascetic lifestyle.
*Pronounced as uh-set-ik
*Synonyms: monastic, monkish
Hermit: a person living all alone and away from society
*Synonyms: **ascetic, troglodyte**
Recluse: a person who lives a solitary life, usually for religious reasons
After the fight with his friends, he became a recluse.
Creature-comforts: material comforts like good food and comfortable accommodation that contribute to one's physical ease like a TV

■

Luxuriate: to enjoy luxury
He luxuriated by taking a long warm bath.
*Synonym: to **indulge oneself**
Wallow: to lie in mud or water to keep cool or avoid biting insects
The buffalo keeps cool by wallowing in mud.
*Pronounced as wo-low
Bask: to lie in the sunlight for warmth and relaxation
The cat climbed on top of the wall to bask in the winter sun.
Relish: to enjoy greatly
He relished his mother's home cooked food.
*Synonyms: to **savour**, to **lap up**, to **drool over**
Sprawl: to lie with one's arms and legs stretched out
He sprawled on the beach everyday on his vacation.
Loll: to sit, lie or stand in a very lazy and relaxed manner
The tourists lolled in the hotel lounge chairs.

■

Magnanimous: generous in forgiving an insult or injury
The team's captain was very magnanimous in victory and praised the losing team.
Munificent: very generous
The alumni association donated a munificent sum of money to the university.
*Pronounced as myoo-ni-fis-unt

Philanthropic: charitable
He gave scholarships to poor students through his philanthropic organization.
*Noun form: philanthropy (meaning charity)
Altruistic: unselfishly concerned about the welfare of others
A true altruistic act is never publicized.
*Antonym: **egoistic**
Humane: compassionate; showing concern for others pain
It is more humane to kill an incurably ill animal rather than to let it suffer for a long time.
Lenient: merciful
The judge took a lenient view and only imposed a fine and no jail term.
*Synonym: **clement**
*Antonyms: merciless, severe, strict
*Noun forms: **leniency, clemency**

■

Aegis: support; protection; sponsorship; backing
The free vaccination camp was set up under the aegis of the Department of Health.
*Synonym: **auspices** (The country got aid under the auspices of the UNO)
Benevolent: desiring to help others; having a positive effect
He had a benevolent nature.
*Synonym: benignant
*Antonym: malignant, malevolent
Beneficent: conferring benefits; helping people
He had a beneficent uncle who would regularly send him pocket money.
*Pronounced as beni-fis-unt
Beneficiary: a person who receives some benefit
Benefactor: a donor
Benefaction: a donation or a gift
Patron: a person who gives financial or other support
The industrialist was a patron to many NGOs.
*Patron also means a regular customer or client.
Patronage: the support given by a patron
Patronize: to give financial support to an organization, cause, etc.

■

Legacy: the money or property left in a will
*Synonyms: **bequest, inheritance, heritage**

Legatee: a person who receives some property left in a will
*Synonyms: **heir, inheritor**
Legator: a person who leaves some property in a will
Bequeath: to leave someone property in a will
He bequeathed all his money to his wife and children.
*Pronounced as bih-kweeth
*Noun form: **bequeathal** (the process of bequeathing)
Heirloom: a valuable object that has belonged to a family for generations
The antique piano was a precious family heirloom and thus not for sale.
Patrimony: property inherited from one's father

■

Mortal: a human being subject to death and with a definite life span
*Antonym: **immortal**
Morale: the feeling of confidence and enthusiasm
The morale of the army was up after victory in the battle.
Moral: a principle of right and wrong
Morality: the system consisting of the various morals that distinguish between right and wrong
Amoral: lacking morals but not immoral
A machine is amoral.
Immoral: wanting to violate moral principles
A villain is immoral.

■

Bestow: to grant
The Queen bestowed upon him the title of Knight.
*Synonyms: to **confer**, to **accord** (The constitution accords wide powers)
Vouchsafe: to grant but as if doing a favour to the receiver
The teacher requested the student to vouchsafe a reply to the teacher's question.

■

Manna: something very beneficial that appears unexpectedly
A cold drink on a summer day is like manna from heaven.
*Synonym: **godsend** (The food packets were a godsend)
*Antonyms: **scourge, curse**
Windfall: an unexpected gain or profit, especially a large one
*Synonyms: **jackpot, pennies from heaven**

Bonanza: a situation in which suddenly large profits are made
The rise in real estate prices meant a bonanza for the house sellers.
Boon: a blessing; something that is greatly beneficial
The sudden rains were a boon to the farmers who were facing a water crisis.
Largesse: a large and generous gift
The corporates got largesse from the government in the form of a giant tax cut.
*Synonym: **bounty**
Endowment: money that is gifted to a college, hospital, etc.
Handout: food or clothing given to a needy person
Sop: something given to quiet down or temporarily please someone
The farmers got sops like free hand pumps just before the elections.
Pittance: a very small amount of money
The factory owner paid his workers a pittance.
Alms: money or food given to poor people

■

Hedonist: someone who believes that the sole purpose of life is to seek pleasure and live in luxury
*Synonyms: **sybarite, sensualist, voluptuary** (*pronounced as voh-lup-chu-ary), **bon vivant**
Gourmand: a person who excessively eats and drinks
*Synonyms: **glutton, gorger**
Gourmet: an expert judge in taste of food and drinks
*Synonyms: **gastronome, epicure, connoisseur** (*pronounced as con-uh-soor)
Subsistence: the act of maintaining oneself at a very minimal level
He practised subsistence farming where he consumed whatever he produced.
Sustenance: food and drink; nourishment
The family derived sustenance from the income they received by selling their cow's milk.

■

Pantry: a small room where food is stored
Larder: a large room where food is stored
Grocery: food and other commodities like tea, sugar, spice, etc.
Confectionery: sweets and chocolates
Condiment: a substance such as salt or pepper or ketchup that is used to add flavour to food

Dollop: a chunk of food
He put dollops of ketchup on his burger.
Fillet: a boneless piece of meat
*Pronounced as fi-ley
Venison: deer meat
Veal: meat from a young calf
Leaven: a substance (like yeast) that is used to make dough or batter rise
Fermentation: the chemical process where sugar changes into alcohol; for example, wine is made by fermenting grape juice.
Crockery: plates, dishes, cups, etc.
Cutlery: knives, forks, spoons, etc.
Utensil: a tool used in the kitchen for cooking food
Goblet: a drinking glass with a foot and a stem
*Synonyms: **chalice** (pronounced as chal-is), **grail**
Flute: a tall, narrow wine glass
Colander: a metal bowl with tiny holes used to strain off liquid from food
Sieve: a utensil consisting of a wire mesh on a circular frame used to strain off liquid from food while cooking
*Synonyms: **strainer, sifter**
Spatula: a kitchen utensil comprising of a blunt metal blade on a wooden handle used to mix things on a pan
Shears: large scissors
Rolling pin: a metal or wooden cylinder used to flatten dough into shape
Ladle: a long spoon used for serving soup
Skillet: a frying pan
Mitten: a kind of a glove used mostly in baking
Mallet: a hammer
Gavel: the small hammer used by a judge or an auctioneer
Kiln: a special kind of an oven or furnace used for firing pottery or baking
Whetstone: a fine-grained stone used for sharpening knives, swords, etc.
Chopping block: a block of wood on which food is kept to be chopped
Cookie cutter: a device with sharp edges used to shape cookies and it also means anything formulaic and mass-produced
Brim: the upper rim of a cup or bowl
Cauldron: a large metal pot used to cook food in
Cistern: the water tank in a toilet
Cesspool: an underground container for collecting and storing human waste and household sewage
Ullage: the free space left in a water tank to accommodate the expansion of the liquid
*Pronounced as uh-lij

Hose: a water pipe

■

Quill: a pen made from a tail feather of a bird
Blubber: the fat of sea mammals like whales, used as food or fuel
Tallow: a hard fatty substance made from animal fat, used in making candles and soap
Talon: a bird's claw
The mouse was caught in the eagle's talons
Wick: a piece of string placed in the centre of a candle

■

Appetite: hunger
*Related word: **ravenousness** (extreme hunger)
Aperitif: an alcoholic drink taken before a meal to stimulate the appetite
Appetizer: a light snack served before a meal to stimulate one's appetite
Repast: a meal
They had stew for the afternoon repast.
Supper: an evening meal; dinner
Sundae: an ice cream topped with syrup, whipped cream, fruit, etc.
Cuisine: a style of cooking, usually characteristic of a particular country or region; for example, Italian cuisine
*Pronounced as kwi-zeen
Marinade: a mixture of oil, spices, etc. in which meat is soaked
Stew: a dish which is slowly cooked in a liquid in a closed pan
Casserole: a dish which is slow cooked in an oven
Braise: to cook meat by first frying it and then slowly cooking it in a liquid
Fricassée: a dish of fried meat pieces served in white sauce
Sauté: to pan-fry with a little amount of butter, oil, etc.

■

Delectable: delicious
The guests were offered some delectable handmade pastries.
*Synonym: **toothsome**
Luscious: extremely tasty, usually referred for sweet food items
Everyone was blown away by the luscious red apples.
*Pronounced as lush-us

Succulent: tender, juicy and tasty

The succulent kebabs at the party made his mouth water.

*Pronounced as suk-you-lent

Savoury: salty or spicy in taste

Everyone liked the savoury dish.

Tangy: sour in taste; having a strong smell or sharp acidic flavour

Everyone liked the tangy salad.

*Synonyms: zesty, tart, piquant

Appetizing: appealing; tempting; stimulating one's appetite

The breakfast buffet looked very appetizing.

*Antonyms: off-putting, unappealing

Palatable: pleasant-tasting

The food was palatable but not awesome.

Edible: fit to be eaten; eatable

Kerosene is not an edible oil.

*Synonym: **esculent** (*pronounced as es-kyu-lent)

*Antonym: inedible

■

Reagent: a substance that is used in a chemical analysis

Antigen: a toxin or a foreign substance that causes the body's immune system to produce antibodies

Analyte: a substance or its chemical constituent which is being analysed

Histamine: a compound released by the body's cell as a response to an allergic reaction, which causes physiological effects, muscle stiffness, etc.

■

Solvent: the liquid in which a substance (solute) is dissolved to form a solution

In a sugar water solution, water is the solvent and sugar is the solute.

Solute: the substance which is dissolved in a liquid to make a solution

Miscible: capable of being mixed

Alcohol and water are miscible.

*Antonyms: **immiscible** (Oil is immiscible with water)

Viscid: thick and sticky

Molasses is a viscid product made by refining sugarcane.

*Pronounced as vis-id

*Synonyms: **viscous, glutinous**

■

Potable: drinkable

Brine: seawater or any water with a high salt concentration which is typically used to preserve food

*Adjective forms: briny, salty

Brackish: slightly salty

*Synonym: **salin**

Beverage: any drinkable liquid other than water; for example, tea, coffee

Brew: a kind of beer

*Synonym: **ale**

Liquor: a distilled alcoholic beverage like brandy or whiskey; such a distilled alcoholic beverage is different from fermented alcoholic beverages like wine or beer

Liqueur: a sweet tasting alcoholic drink, usually drunk after a meal

*Pronounced as lik-your

Hooch: illegally sold liquor that is very cheap because of its low quality but it is sometimes unsafe to drink and thus causes death

Tipsy: slightly drunk

*Adjective form: **mellow**

Inebriated: drunk

The inebriated driver was arrested.

*Synonyms: sloshed, **besotted** (Romeo was besotted with her)

*Antonym: **sober**

Toper: a drunkard

*Pronounced as toh-per

Dipsomaniac: an alcohol addict

Adipsia: loss of thirst

Polydipsia: excessive thirst

Proof: the measure of the content of ethanol (alcohol) in an alcoholic beverage *Etymology: earlier on, soldiers would pour some rum on their gunpowder. If this wet gunpowder burnt on being lit then it was a 'proof' that the alcohol content was high enough

Tavern: a bar

*Synonym: **saloon**

Coaster: a small piece of wood or plastic that is used to put a glass or cup on, in order to protect the surface of the table from heat or liquid

Aphrodisiac: a food or drink that arouses sexual desire

*Etymology: from Greek *'aphrodisiakos'* meaning relating to love or desire

Ambrosia: the food of the Gods as per Greek and Roman mythology

*Etymology: from Greek *'ambrosios'* meaning 'of the immortals'

Philter: a love potion

Libation: a liquid (for example wine) that is poured out in honour or as an offering to a deity

Nectar: the sugary fluid that is secreted by plants in order to attract birds and insects for pollination

■

Abattoir: a slaughterhouse
*Pronounced as ab-uh-twaahr
Broiler: a kitchen equipment used to grill meat by direct exposure to heat
Brewery: a beer making factory
Vintner: a wine merchant; a winegrower
*Pronounced as vint-ner
Bistro: a small restaurant
Bodega: a small corner store that sells groceries and wine, usually in a Spanish-speaking neighbourhood of a metropolitan city
Patisserie: a French pastry shop
*Pronounced as puh-tee-suh-ree
Roaster: a business that processes coffee beans from raw form to edible form
*Homonym: **roster** (a list or schedule)

■

Barista: a person who serves coffee in a café
Busboy: a young person who works in a restaurant removing the dirty dishes from the table of the customers and bringing clean ones
Bellboy: an attendant in a hotel employed to perform services such as carrying guest's luggage, running errands, etc.
*Synonym: **bellhop**
Sommelier: a waiter in a restaurant who is in charge of the wines
*Pronounced as saw-muh-lee-yay
Concierge: a hotel employee who assists the guests in various things like making dinner reservations, booking tickets, etc.
*Pronounced as con-see-airzh
Maître d'hôtel: the manager of a hotel
*Pronounced as may-truh-dho-tel
Motel: a roadside hotel, primarily catering to motorists, which provides lodging and free parking
Executive Chef: the head chef of a restaurant, who is responsible for everything in the kitchen
Sous-chef: the person ranking next after the executive chef
*Pronounced as soo-shef

*Etymology: sous-chef is French for under-chef

■

Peckish: hungry: He was peckish after the long metro journey
Famished: extremely hungry
He was famished after a full day of fasting
*Synonyms: **ravenous**, starving
Ingest: to consume
In the era of the Internet, we unknowingly ingest a lot of information.
*Antonym: **egest** (egest means to excrete)
Partake: to eat or drink something; usually refers to consuming alcohol
The monk refused to partake in the drunken festivities.
Nibble: to eat in small bites
He nibbled on some cookies before dinner.
Gnaw: to persistently bite or chew on something
The dog gnawed on the bone for hours.
*Pronounced as naw
Masticate: to chew food
He had digestive problems as he never masticated his meals properly.
Devour: to quickly and hungrily eat
The hungry soldiers devoured the meal.
*Synonyms: to **gorge**, to **snarf** up (He snarfed up the pudding)
Chomp: to chew noisily
The hungry kid chomped down his burger.
Carouse: to engage in drunken revelry and merry-making
He had a reputation for carousing.
*Synonyms: to **binge-drink**, to go on a **pub crawl**
Quaff: to drink very heartily
He quaffed a whole gallon of beer at the bar.
*Synonyms: **chug** (he chugged a glass of Pepsi), to **guzzle** down, to **gulp** down, **swill** (they loved swilling glasses of wine at the bar), **swig** (he swigged the entire glass of Coke in two gulps), **slug**
Slurp: to eat or drink with loud sucking noises
He liked to slurp warm tea.
Lap: to drink with quick movements of the tongue
He lapped up the soup.
Abstinence: the practice of restraint in one's consumption of something, usually alcohol or sex
After a decade of abstinence, he started drinking again.
*Synonyms: **teetotalism, temperance, sobriety, abstemiousness, forbearance**
*Verb forms: to abstain, to refrain, to forbear, to desist,

to hold back
*Adjective forms: **abstinent, abstemious, sober**
*Antonyms: intemperance, overindulgence, immoderation
Abstention: the act of abstaining or the act of practicing abstinence, especially when someone declines to vote
The vote on the Impeachment Motion had 10 abstentions.
Simple example: an abstinent person likes to abstain as he/she is practicing abstinence and every act of abstaining is called an abstention.
Wean: to accustom an infant to eat food other than its mother's milk

■

Lurid: shocking, sensational; trashy; cheap; tasteless
The tabloid published lurid details of the heroine's affair.
Lewd: sexually offensive
The drunk audience passed lewd comments.
Lecherous: expressing sexual desire to someone who is not interested
He lecherously looked at the female passengers in the bus.
*Noun form: **lechery** (the quality of being a lecher), a **lecher** (a lecherous person); *Homonym: **leech** (a bloodsucking worm), **leach** (to drain away)
Lustful: expressing or filled with sexual desire; for example, the lover's lustful gaze
*Synonym: **concupiscent** (*pronounced as con-kyu-pi-sunt)
Libidinous: having great desire for sex
The libidinous old man would chase young girls.
*Noun form: libido (great desire for sex)
Licentious: having many sexual partners
*Pronounced as lie-sen-shus
*Synonyms: **promiscuous, bacchanalian, dissolute**
*Antonym: **chaste**
Libertine: a licentious person
*Synonyms: **wanton, debauchee** (*pronounced as deb-aw-shee), **philanderer**
Prurient: sexual
Playboy magazine publishes nude pictures to satisfy the prurient interests of its reader
*Synonyms: **lascivious** (*pronounced as luh-siv-ee-us), **carnal** (carnal desires), **amatory** (He boasted about his amatory exploits), **amorous** (She rebuffed his amorous advances), **amative**
Salacious: obscene; vulgar
The trashy magazine published salacious stories about the celebrity couple.
*Synonyms: **lubricious, smutty, sleazy**
Ribald: referring to sex but in a joking manner
He shared ribald jokes at the party.
*Pronounced as rib-uld
*Synonyms: **earthy** (earthy comments), **bawdy** (bawdy stories), **Rabelaisian** (Rabelaisian humour; *etymology: François Rabelais, a French satirist who wrote bawdy jokes)
Risqué: sexually suggestive and slightly indecent
Her risqué dress turned heads.
*Pronounced as ris-kay
*Synonyms: **racy, saucy, sultry**
Pornography: sexually explicit material like videos, photos, writing, etc.
Erotic: sexually arousing
The government banned erotic literature.
Erogenous: sensitive to sexual stimulation.
Fornicate: to have sexual intercourse with someone out of wedlock
Copulate: to mate; to reproduce
*Synonym: **procreate**
Coitus: sexual intercourse
Orgasm: the climax of a sexual activity
*Adjective form: orgasmic
Orgy: a sex party
*Synonyms: **bacchanalia, debauchery** (*pronounced as deb-aw-shu-ree)
Sodomy: anal intercourse
Fellatio: oral stimulation of a man's penis
*Pronounced as fell-ashio
Cunnilingus: oral stimulation of a woman's genitals
Virile: manly; capable of procreating; having a strong sex drive
Nubile: a sexually attractive young woman; a marriageable young woman
Lolita: a young girl who behaves in a very sexual way and dresses up very seductively or provocatively; a sexually precocious girl
Nymphomaniac: a woman with an uncontrollable sexual desire
Satyromaniac: a man with an uncontrollable sexual desire
Continence: self-restraint or abstinence, especially with regard to sex
Complete continence is a pre-condition to be a priest.
*Continence also means the ability to control urinary discharge or faecal discharge.
Contraception: the deliberate prevention of pregnancy

after sexual intercourse by methods such as condoms or birth control pills

Celibate: a person who abstains from marriage and sex, especially for religious reasons
*Pronounced as sel-uh-bit
*Noun form: celibacy

■

Genitals: a person's external organs of reproduction
*Synonym: **genitalia**
Groin: the region of the genitals
*Synonym: **crotch**
Phallus: an erect penis or the image of an erect penis used as a religious symbol to signify reproductive potency
*Plural: phalli or phalluses
*Adjective form: phallic (The rowing boat was phallic shaped)
Loins: the region of the body that is between the lower ribs and the hips and regarded as the seat of sexual power
Perineum: the area between the anus and the scrotum or vulva
Udder: the mammary gland of female cattle.
Bosom: a woman's breasts
Noggin: a person's head
Gut: stomach
Innards: internal organs
Entrails: intestines
Viscera: the internal organs which lie inside the main cavities of the body, especially those in the abdomen; for example, the stomach and intestines
Offal: the animal parts that are discarded as waste after the butchering process because they are unfit for human consumption
Underbelly: the soft underside or lower abdomen of an animal; underbelly also means a vulnerable area or weak point and it also means the dark, hidden and usually crime-ridden part of society
Paunch: a large or protruding belly
*Synonyms: pot-belly, beer-belly
Haunch: the buttock and thigh considered together
Derrière: the buttocks
*Pronounced as dare-ee-air
*Synonym: rump
Snout: the projecting nose and mouth of an animal like a dog or horse
Tusk: a long pointed and protruding tooth as commonly seen in the elephant, walrus and wild boar

Fang: a large sharp tooth of an animal like a dog, wolf, snake, etc
Flank: the side of a person's body
Flank also means to be on each or on one side of; for example, The president was flanked by senior advisors.
Midriff: the region of the front of the body between the chest and the waist
Diaphragm: the dome-shaped muscular partition that separates the thoracic (chest) cavity from the abdominal cavity in mammals
Solar plexus: a network of nerves situated at the upper abdomen.
Sternum: the breastbone
Torso: the trunk of the human body
*Plural: torsi or torsos.
Thorax: the chest area; the part of the body between the neck and the abdomen
*Adjective form: thoracic (*pronounced as tho-rasic)
Jugular: relating to the throat or neck
Cuticle: the dead skin at the base of a toenail or fingernail
Epidermis: the outermost layer of the skin
Subcutaneous: under the skin: The layer of subcutaneous fat
Shin: the front of the leg below the knee
Tendon: a strong fibrous tissue that attaches a muscle to a bone
*Synonym: **sinew**
Ligament: a strong fibrous tissue that connects two bones at a joint
Cartilage: a strong connective tissue found in joints
Cartilage is sometimes replaced by bones during growth
*Pronounced as car-til-ij
Limb: the arm or leg of a person or the wing of a bird, that is a part of the body of an animal that is distinct from the head or the trunk
*Plural: limbs
Digit: a finger, thumb or toe
*Plural: digits
Tentacle: one of the long, thin and flexible parts of animals, which look like arms and used for feeling, catching and holding things and moving

■

Pulmonary: relating to the lungs
*Synonym: **pneumonic**
Alimentary: relating to the alimentary canal, i.e., the digestive system
Venereal: related to sexual transmission

HIV is a venereal disease.
Vascular: relating to the circulatory system

■

Beget: to cause; to generate
Violence begets only more violence.
*Synonyms: **engender, sire** (He sired two children out of wedlock)
Synthesize: to make something by combining various elements, especially when done chemically
Nylon is a synthetic fibre.
*Noun form: synthesis
Spawn: to release or directly deposit eggs into the water, like fishes and frogs
The first *Fast and Furious* movie spawned a generation of sequels.

■

Imbue: to fill something with a quality
The judgment imbued animals with personhood.
Imbibe: to absorb
The devotees imbibed lessons in morality.
Intersperse: to scatter something among other things; to intermix
His serious speech was interspersed with some funny jokes.
Instil: to gradually establish an idea or a belief in a person's mind
He instilled a sense of duty in the mind of his son.
*Synonym: **ingrain**
Inculcate: to instil something by consistent instruction
The teacher tried to inculcate a sense of patriotism in his students.
Saturate: to fill with; to soak something with a liquid
The air was saturated with a foul smell.
*Synonym: to **steep** (The military is steeped in honour)
Permeate: to spread
The smell of the freshly baked cake permeated through the air.
*Synonyms: **pervade** (Modern technology has pervaded all facets of society), **infuse, diffuse, suffuse, perfuse, metastasize** (The cancer metastasized to other parts of the body)
Penetrate: to go into or pierce something, especially with force
The bullet from the gun penetrated his skull.
Porous: allowing liquid to pass through

The porous borders posed a national security risk.
*Synonyms: **permeable, pervious, penetrable**

■

Infiltrate: to secretly and illegally enter into an organization or place
The government was infiltrated by spies from the rival country.
Impregnable: something that cannot be broken into
The impregnable fortress of the rebels.
*Synonyms: **impenetrable**, well-fortified
Inviolable: something that can never be violated or infringed
The inviolable oath of marriage.
Inalienable: something that can never be taken away
The inalienable right to live with dignity.
Impervious: not allowing liquid to pass through
The box was sealed with an impervious layer of rubber.
*Synonyms: **impermeable, impenetrable**
Impetus: something which helps a process move more quickly
The investment provided an impetus to the company.
*Synonyms: **fillip** (the tax cut gave the necessary fillip to the economy), **stimulant, catalyst**
Incentive: a benefit offered to someone to do an act
The buyers were offered 20 per cent cashback as an incentive to shop more.

■

Dribble: to trickle
Rain dribbled down the window.
Percolate: to trickle down
The chemicals trickled down to the water table.
Leach: to drain away
The minerals in the soil were leached away by rain.
Ooze: to discharge a liquid
Pus was oozing out of his wound.
Disgorge: to discharge or eject forcefully
The new printing press disgorged a heavy stream of newspapers.
*Disgorge also means to vomit.
Seep: to leak in
After the rains, water seeped into the house.
Gush: to flow out rapidly
Water gushed out of the hole in the dam wall.
*Synonym: **outpour, cascade** (Water cascaded down from the mountain top), **spurt** (Blood spurted out of his

wound), **spout** (The geyser spouted hot water), **spew** (The factory spewed pollution)

Gout: a drop or spot of something, especially a liquid
Gouts of blood erupted from the stab wound on the neck of the poor victim.

Squirt: to eject a liquid from a small opening
He squirted some lemon juice on to the salad.

Surge: a quick and strong rush
He felt a surge of anger.
*Synonym: **groundswell** (a groundswell of opposition to fascism)

Upsurge: an upward surge; a dramatic increase
There was an upsurge in crime during the economic downturn.

Uptick: a small increase
There was an uptick in tourism after the introduction of visas on arrival.

Ripple: a small wave
*Synonym: **wavelet**

Sodden: completely soaking wet
His clothes were sodden after he got caught in the rain.
*Synonyms: drenched, soused.

Souse: to soak or immerse in a liquid
The pickle was well soused in oil.

Douse: to pour liquid over; to extinguish
The brave firefighters doused the fire in the house.
*Synonym: to **drench**
*Homonym: **delouse** (to free of lice and other parasitic insects)

Decant: to pour a liquid from one container to another
He decanted the red wine into some fancy glasses for the guests to enjoy.

■

Evacuate: to remove people from a dangerous place
The building was evacuated after the earthquake.

Emanate: to flow from
The entire fight emanated from a small disagreement.

Emulate: to copy someone as a model; to model oneself on; to mirror; to echo
Ronaldo emulated the legendary player Pele when growing up.

Exude: to radiate
The student exuded tremendous confidence.

Extrude: to expel
On eruption the volcano extruded lava and gas
*Synonyms: to **shunt** out, to **oust**, to **eject**

■

Protrude: to stick out
He was smacked in the head by the protruding steel beam.
*Noun form: protrusion (something that is sticking out), protuberance

Obtrude: to force something on someone
He always obtruded his thoughts on others.

Intrude: to forcefully enter
The robbers intruded into the house by breaking down the door.

■

Cadaver: a dead body
*Synonym: a **corpse**

Carrion: the decaying flesh of dead animals

Stillborn: born dead, failed to develop
The tax plan was stillborn when it was shelved indefinitely by the government.

Coroner: an official whose job is to investigate the deaths of people who
*Pronounced as kaur-on-er

Mortuary: a room in which dead bodies are stored for medical examination or identification
*Synonym: **morgue** (*pronounced as mawrg)

Funeral home: a place where the dead bodies are prepared for viewing before a cremation or a funeral

■

Septic: to be infected with bacteria
The wound became septic as it was not cleaned properly by the doctor.

Aseptic: free from any bacteria, virus, etc
*Synonym: **sterile**

Sanitary: hygienic; clean; germ-free
The restaurant was shut down by the health officer as it did not have a sanitary cooking environment.

Pathogen: a microorganism that can cause disease; for example, virus etc.

Fester: to develop pus as a result of bacterial action
The wound went untreated and was allowed to fester.
*Synonym: **suppurate**

■

Salutary: beneficial; promoting good health
The clean mountain air had a salutary effect on his lungs.

*Synonym: **salubrious** (The vacation had a salubrious effect on his mental health)

Sanguine: optimistic and positive when facing a tough situation

He remained sanguine about the prospects of his company despite the recession.

Exsanguination: extreme loss of blood

The patient died due to exsanguination caused by an untreated knife wound to the stomach.

■

Putrid: rotting and emitting a foul smell

The putrid body of the dead zebra.

*Synonyms: putrefying, putrescent

*Noun form: putrefaction

Rancid: to go stale and emit a foul smell

The pickle became rancid.

Malodorous: foul-smelling; smelly, stinking

The malodorous toilets in the government offices.

*Synonyms: **noisome, reeking, fetid**

*Antonyms: **fragrant, aromatic**, **redolent** (the redolent mountain air), sweet-scented, perfumed

*Noun form: malodour, **miasma**, foul smell, stink, **stench**, reek

Pungent: sharp smelling

The pungent smell of onions.

*Antonym: mild

Odour: a distinctive smell, especially foul smelling

His foul body odour.

Aroma: a distinctive smell, especially pleasant smelling

The aroma of freshly brewed coffee.

*Synonym: fragrance

Whiff: a brief and faint of smell

He caught a whiff of the stew cooking in the kitchen.

*Pronounced as wif

*Synonym: **trace**

Waft: to gently move through the air

The smell of freshly baked cookies wafted from the kitchen.

■

Candid: frank; open; truthful

The interview panel was surprised by the candid answers given the student.

*Synonyms: blunt, straightforward, unvarnished

*Noun forms: candour, frankness, candidness, forthrightness

Callous: insensitive and heartless

The psychopath killer made callous remarks about his victims.

*Synonyms: unfeeling, cold-hearted

■

Rookie: a new recruit in the army or the police force; an athlete in a professional sports team who is playing his or her first season

Freshman: a first-year student at a university; a student in ninth grade (ninth grade is considered as the first year of high school)

Sophomore: a second-year student at a university; a student in tenth grade (tenth grade is the second year of high school)

*Pronounced as sof-more

Novice: an inexperienced newcomer; a beginner; an immature person

The book was full of advice on the stock market for the novice investor.

*Synonyms: **neophyte, tyro, fledgling** (*etymology: a fledgling is a young bird that has just fledged, that is developed wing feathers that are large enough for flight), **callow** (The new law firm team consisted of callow young lawyers), **greenhorn** (*etymology: the horns of young animals are not fully hardened and are usually green in colour)

*Antonyms: expert, veteran

Neonate: a newborn child; an infant less than four weeks old

Nescient: lacking knowledge; ignorant

Many young voters are nescient regarding politics.

*Pronounced as nes-see-unt

*Noun form: nescience

*Synonym: **unversed** (He was unversed in the ways of the city)

Nascent: being in the earliest stage of development

The nascent electric car industry was supported by grants.

*Noun form: nascency

*Synonyms: **embryonic, incipient** (He developed an incipient potbelly), infant, **germinal** (His germinal idea about joining the club flopped as the club disbanded)

Rudimentary: very basic; not advanced

He had a rudimentary knowledge about the matter.

*Synonyms: elementary, immature, undeveloped

■

Adolescent: a teenager
Adolescence: teenage years
Juvenile: relating to young people, especially teenagers
Puberty: the period or age at which a person becomes capable for the first time of sexual reproduction; usually 13 years for males and 12 for females
Pubescent: arriving or arrived at puberty
*Pronounced as pyoo-bes-ent
Pubescence: the time when puberty begins; the state of being pubescent *Pronounced as pyoo-bes-ens

■

Homeostasis: the tendency of a system to maintain equilibrium
Tranquil: peaceful; quiet; calm; for example, the tranquil mountain town
*Noun form: tranquillity
*Synonym: **placid** (the placid lake; *pronounced as plas-id)
Equanimous: calm and composed; not easily upset or worried especially in a crisis
The teacher remained equanimous even in the face of rowdy students.
*Synonyms: **equable** (He had an equable temperament), **imperturbable** (He had a remarkable imperturbable composure), **unflappable** (He remained unflappable even in the most tumultuous situations), **unruffled**
*Noun form: equanimity, equability
Stolid: showing little emotion; blank; impassive
The boy stood stolidly while his mean elder brother destroyed his tree house.
*Synonyms: **phlegmatic** (He had a phlegmatic disposition; *pronounced as fleg-matik; *etymology: phlegm is mucus or nasal discharge), **petrous, deadpan** (She was famous for her deadpan performance), glazed, poker-faced, straight-faced
Staid: having a very settled character; serious; boring and old-fashioned
He got a job in a staid old law firm.
*Antonyms: capricious, whimsical
Stoic: someone who can endure pain without showing their feelings
He exhibited a stoic resignation when he heard about his bad medical reports.
Stern: strict and severe
The students got a stern warning.
*Synonym: **dour** (the manager's dour criticism)
*Antonym: lenient

Stringent: strict and precise
The government came out with stringent guidelines on car emissions to battle air pollution.
Drastic: extremely severe
To solve global warming we need a drastic reduction in the burning of fossil fuel.
*Antonyms: mild, moderate
Dire: extremely serious or urgent; terrible
The planet is in dire circumstances.
*Synonym: **dreadful**

■

Nonchalant: appearing unconcerned or indifferent or unexcited
Her reaction to the bad news was nonchalant.
*Pronounced as non-shuh-lahnt
Insouciant: carefree
The irresponsible child responded an insouciant shrug.
*Pronounced as in-soo-see-unt
*Noun form: insouciance
Cavalier: showing a lack of due concern
The student's cavalier attitude about his grades infuriated the class teacher.
*Noun form: cavalierness
Flippant: showing a lack of respect and seriousness
The candidate's flippant remarks shocked everyone.
*Noun form: flippancy
Facetious: treating serious issue with inappropriate humour
Everyone was shocked by his facetious answers.
*Pronounced as fuh-see-shus
Blithe: cheerful and carefree
He had a blithe disregard for the traffic rules.
Blasé: unimpressed or indifferent
He travels to Paris so often that he has become blasé about it.
*Pronounced as blah-zey
Levity: the treatment of a serious matter with humour and without due care or the seriousness that the matter deserves
The host's attempt to introduce a brief moment of levity in the solemn proceedings was a major flop.
Jocular: joking and playful
His jocular remarks about her weight angered everyone.
*Synonyms: **jesting, jocose, waggish, droll** (droll remarks)

■

Mantle: responsibility
The mantle of leadership is tough.
*Synonym: onus
Helm: a position of leadership
With Steve Jobs at the helm, Apple was certain of success.
*Etymology: helm is the steering wheel of a ship
Vantage: a position that gives a clear and good view
From the vantage point on the top of the tower, we can see the full city.
*Pronounced as van-tij

■

Gravity: seriousness
Everyone understood the gravity of the situation when the police came.
*Adjective forms: grave, serious, solemn
*Synonym: **momentousness**
*Antonym: triviality
Gravitas: dignity and seriousness in conduct or speech
The old chairman of the company was a man of gravitas.
*Antonym: frivolity
Solemn: formal and dignified
The solemn occasion of a funeral.
*Pronounced as sawl-um
*Synonym: **sober**
*Noun form: solemnity
Magnitude: enormousness
The students felt daunted by the magnitude of the syllabus.
*Synonym: immenseness
*Antonym: smallness

■

Adage: a wise saying or proverb
The old adage 'Look before you leap'.
*Synonyms: **aphorism**, **apothegm** (*pronounced as ap-uh-them), **maxim**
Axiom: an accepted truth
It is an axiom in medicine that the first duty of doctors is to do no harm.
*Synonym: **truism**
Tenet: a fundamental belief
The central tenet of feminism is that men and women must be treated equally.
*Synonyms: doctrine, **precept, article of faith, dogma, canon**

Credo: the guiding philosophy
Gandhi's credo was the use of non-violence to achieve political change.
*Synonym: **ethos**
Dictum: a formal order: The government is bound to follow the Supreme Court's dictum
*Synonyms: **mandate, decree, fiat, edict, ukase** (*pronounced as u-kayz), ordinance
Behest: an order or command
The noblemen assembled at the behest of the King.
*Synonym: bidding (He came running at wife's bidding)
Commandment: a divine command, especially one of the Ten Commandments.
Ultimatum: the final offer, the rejection of which will result in breakdown in relations He gave his wife an ultimatum to stop overspending or else.

■

Pronouncement: a formal or authoritative declaration
The people distrusted the government's pronouncements about the economy.
Proclamation: the public or official announcement about an important matter
To save water, the government restricted its use by proclamation.
Promulgation: an official proclamation that puts a law into effect
The law promulgated in 1900.
*Verb form: promulgate

■

Desideratum: something that is needed or wanted
Honesty is a desideratum in the modern business world.
*Plural: desiderata
Prerequisite: something that is required as a prior condition for something else to happen
A law degree is a prerequisite before enrolling as an advocate.
*Pronounced as pre-rek-wuh-zit
*Homonym: **perquisite** (an additional benefit above one's regular salary)
Mandatory: compulsory
It is mandatory to wear a helmet when riding two-wheelers.
*Synonyms: obligatory, binding
*Antonym: optional

Illicit: illegal
He started his criminal career by selling illicit liquor.
Elicit: to evoke or draw out a reaction
The stand-up comedian was not able to elicit any laughter from the audience.
Proscribe: to forbid by law
The sale of cigarettes near schools has been proscribed by the government.
*Synonym: **interdict**
*Noun forms: proscription, prohibition, interdiction
*Homonym: **prescribe** (to advise: the doctor prescribed antibiotics; *noun form of prescribe: prescription)
Injunction: a formal command to not do something
Writ: a formal command by a legal authority
Impinge: to enter into an area belonging to someone else
The new law impinged on the citizen's rights.
*Synonym: **encroach** on
Infringe: to break the terms of a contract or break the law
He infringed the terms of the contract.
*Synonym: **contravene**
*Antonym: to comply with
Transgress: to go beyond the limits
He transgressed the boundary set by his parents.
*Noun form: transgression
Perpetrate: to commit, especially a crime
The attack was perpetrated by the local gang.
*Noun form: perpetrator (the person who commits the crime)
Probe: an investigation into a crime
Forensics: the scientific methods and techniques used in the investigation of a crime to find the culprit; for example, DNA analysis.
Rogatory: relating to asking or requesting information
Inquisition: long and intensive questioning
Inquisition also means an official investigation or a judicial inquiry.
Inquest: a judicial inquiry to ascertain the facts regarding an incident
Impugn: to question
The new law was impugned in the Supreme Court.
Indictment: a formal charge or accusation in a court of law
He was indicted by the prosecutor for selling drugs.
*Pronounced as in-dite-ment
Arraign: to be called before a court of law to answer to an indictment
The accused pleaded not guilty in his arraignment.

*Pronounced as uh-rain
Prosecute: to conduct legal proceedings against a person for a crime they allegedly committed
Persecute: to subject someone to ill-treatment because of their identity
Jews were persecuted in World War II.
Prosecutrix: the female victim of a crime on whose behalf the state prosecutes the accused.
Amicus curiae: an impartial adviser appointed by a court to assist it in a case
*Etymology: Latin for 'friend of the court'
*Pronounced as amicus-cure-ay
*Plural: amici curiae (*pronounced as um-ichi-cure-ay)
Inculpate: to incriminate a person in a crime; to accuse or blame
The recovered gun was used as inculpatory evidence in the murder trial.
Exculpate: to clear a person of a crime
The rock solid alibi with the CCTV footage was used as exculpatory evidence by the defence lawyer.
Exonerate: to declare innocent of a crime
*Synonyms: **absolve, acquit**
*Noun form: exoneration, absolution, acquittal
Erring: having done wrong, having committed an error
The erring husband begged his wife to take him back.
*Synonym: **errant**
Comeuppance: well-deserved punishment
The villain finally got his comeuppance in the end of the movie.
*Synonym: **just deserts**
Culpable: guilty
He was held culpable of bribing government officials
*Synonyms: errant, erring
*Antonym: innocent
Culprit: a person guilty of breaking the law
Complicit: involved with others in an illegal or wrong activity
He was complicit in the murder of his boss's wife.
Accomplice: a person who helps another commit a crime
He was an accomplice of the robbers as he drove the car.
*Synonym: accessory
Abscond: to secretly and hurriedly leave, usually to avoid arrest
The cashier of the bank absconded with the money.
*Synonym: to decamp
Detenu: a detainee; a person who has been detained by the authorities; detenu is also written as detenue
*Pronounced as de-ten-you
*plural: detenus

Miscreant: a criminal; a villain

Inmate: a person who is confined in a prison or in a hospital as an inpatient

Incarcerate: to imprison

*Noun form: incarceration

Immure: to confine someone against their will
The kidnappers immured the boy in a farm shed.
*Pronounced as im-your
*Noun form: immurement

Internment: the imprisonment of someone in a camp for military reasons; for example, the Japanese Americans were put in internment camps in US in the 1940s during the World War II
*Plural: internments

Penitentiary: a jail
*Pronounced as peni-ten-shu-ree

Probation: the release of a convicted person rather than sending him/her to jail, subject to good behaviour and under supervision; probation is also the trial period in a newly started job.

Parole: the permanent release of a convict before the expiry of a sentence, subject to good behaviour and under supervision

Patrol: to keep a watch over an area by regularly walking in it or passing through it The police patrolled the area in groups of three

Superintendence: supervision
*Related word: superintendent (supervisor)

Surveillance: the close observation of a person by the government

Vigil: a period of staying awake at night to keep a watch; also means staying up at night and praying on the eve of a Church festival; also means a stationary and peaceful protest
*Pronounced as vij-ul

■

Impunity: exemption from punishment
He walked around with a sense of impunity because his father was the principal.
*Synonym: **immunity**

Scot-free: to be let off without any punishment
The corrupt politician went scot-free.
*Etymology: Scot was a kind of a royal tax in Old England.

Sunset clause: a clause in a contract or statute that provides that a particular provision will cease to exist after the passage of a certain amount of time
The sunset clause in the new tax plan said that the tax

cuts for the middle class will expire in 2025.

Grandfather: apart from the obvious, father of one's father, to grandfather means to exempt
When he increased his fees every year, he grandfathered his most loyal clients.
*Etymology: in the nineteenth century, some Southern states in the US, created restrictions on voting rights on the basis of literacy and property holdings but exempted those people whose grandfathers had the right to vote before the Civil War. The aim was to disenfranchise black people (as they were usually illiterate and landless) but not deprive the poor and illiterate whites of the right to vote.

■

Vigilante: someone who takes the law into their own hands and punishes alleged criminals

Lynch: to hang someone for an alleged crime and without a proper legal trial
*Etymology: this comes from Lynch's law, which was named after Captain William Lynch, who headed a self-constituted judicial tribunal in Virginia, US, around 1780 where he would hang black people for alleged crimes without a proper trial.

Kangaroo court: a mob-operated court, without any legal backing, that disregards the law and punishes alleged criminals
*Etymology: this expression refers to how these courts are quickly convened without the proper legal procedure and thus these courts seem as if they have 'jumped up' out of nowhere like a kangaroo. Furthermore, these courts jump to conclusions without any logical basis.

■

Barrister: a lawyer qualified to appear before a court and argue

Solicitor: a lawyer not qualified to appear and argue before a court but qualified to do documentation and instruct a barrister on behalf of a client

Paralegal: a person who has some legal training and assists a lawyer, but is not qualified to practice law by themselves

■

Rejoinder: a reply, especially a sharp and witty one; a response to a reply
The debaters gave quick rejoinders.

*Synonym: **retort**
Riposte: a quick and sharp reply to an insult
She gave a clever riposte.
*Etymology: a riposte is a quick return thrust in fencing (sword fighting).
Rebuttal: a counter-argument; a counterclaim
Surrejoinder: the reply to a rejoinder
Surrebuttal: the reply to a rebuttal

■

Wordplay: the witty use of words to make jokes
Pun: a humorous use of words where they sound alike but have different meanings, for example 'Carazy Drivers' is a pun which refers to car drivers who drive like crazy people.
Portmanteau: a word formed by mixing two words, for example brunch (a mix of breakfast and lunch)
*Pronounced as port-man-toh
Repartee: a conversation consisting playful and friendly exchange of teasing remarks *Synonyms: **banter, badinage, raillery, crosstalk, persiflage** (*pronounced as persi-flazh)
Epigram: a witty and joking remark
His epigrams on every movie scene were more entertaining than the movie.
*Synonyms: a **quip**, a **jest**, a **jape**, a **wisecrack**, a **witticism**

■

Satire: the use of humour to poke fun at others, especially in politics
He is famous for his political satire in US.
*Adjective form: satirical
*Synonym: **lampoon** (The president was lampooned by the satirist)
Caricature: a picture that makes a person look cartoonish for the purposes of satire The president was caricatured as having a giant head.
Mimic: to make fun of someone by doing their imitation The audience loudly laughed at the comedian's mimicry.
*Noun form: mimicry
Pastiche: an artistic work that imitates the style of other artists
*Pronounced as pah-steesh
Spoof: a light-hearted and humorous imitation of something or someone for the purpose of satire
*Synonym: **parody**

Pasquinade: a satire which is delivered in a public place
*Synonym: **pasquil** (*pronounced as pass-kwil)
Squib: a short piece of satirical writing; squib also means a type of a small firework; squib also means a short news story used as filler in a newspaper

■

Mime: the theatrical technique of expressing without using any voice or sound but using only gesture, expression and movement
Pantomime: the theatrical technique used mainly for children's entertainment, involving music, jokes and slapstick comedy
Vaudeville: the theatre style consisting of light comedy and songs, popular in the US in the early twentieth century
*Pronounced as vaw-duh-vil
Revue: a play which consists of songs, dances and satire
Slapstick: a style of comedy, popular in the nineteenth century, involving exaggerated physical activity like cartoonish chase sequences
Burlesque: a humorous stage show with slapstick comedy and striptease
Kabuki: a form of traditional Japanese theatre consisting of highly stylized songs, dances and drama
Karaoke: a form of entertainment in which people take turns to sing songs into a microphone over pre-recorded music
Serenade: a piece of music sung at night in open air, typically sung by a lover under the window of his beloved, complimenting her beauty

■

Limerick: a short humorous poem
Haiku: a short Japanese poem
Ballad: a song or poem that tells a story
Sonnet: an English poem with exactly 14 lines
Bard: a poet
*Synonyms: versifier, verse-maker, rhymer, sonneteer
Ode: a poem that is meant to be sung
*Plural: odes
Epode: a poem in which a long verse is followed by a short one
Jingle: a short catchy slogan or tune, typically used in advertising

■

Mock: to ridicule; to make fun of someone or something
The opposition mocked the government's decision.
*Synonym: **deride**
*Adjective form: derisive
*Noun form: derision
Contempt: the feeling that someone or something is worthless and hence unworthy of one's consideration or respect
The mean school girls stared at her with contempt.
*Adjective form: contemptuous
*Synonyms: **disdain** (He disdained new age rock music), **scorn** (He has nothing but scorn for her)
*Antonym: admiration
Catcall: a shrill, loud whistle or shout made at a public performance to express disapproval or dissatisfaction; also means a loud sexual comment
Wolf whistle: a whistle made by a man to express sexual attraction to a woman
He got punched in the face when he made a wolf whistle at her.
Jibe/gibe: to taunt; to make insulting or mocking or sarcastic remarks
The media constantly jibed at his methods.
*Synonym: to **jape**
Jeer: to shout rude and mocking remarks
The rowdy young men jeered at female dancers on stage.
*Antonym: cheer
Smirk: to smile in an irritatingly smug way; to smile in a way that shows ones superiority to others
The rude child smirked at everything.
Snigger: to laugh in a half-suppressed and disrespectful way
The teacher told the students to stop sniggering.
*Synonym: **snicker**
Sneer: to smile by raising a corner of one's upper lip to show contempt or to mock someone
The rude young girl sneered at new dress of her classmate.
*Synonym: **to curl one's lip**
Snarky: critical and mocking in an indirect way
He passed snide remarks about her new haircut.
*Synonym: **snide**
Snipe: to criticize someone with petty and unpleasant words and in an indirect way
The frustrated Governor started to snipe at his colleagues.
Scoff: to laugh at something in a mocking way so as to completely disregard it
People scoffed at his ideas.
Sarcastic: to mock or criticize someone by using remarks that say something but mean the opposite

*Noun form: sarcasm
Sardonic: mocking with the aim to make the other person or thing seem worthless
The cruel manager passed sardonic comments.
Wry: using mocking humour
The comedy movie was full of wry one-liners.

■

Pillory: to criticize someone severely in public
The minister was pilloried for making the offensive remarks against the sexual assault victim.
*Etymology: pillory was a form of punishment in which the offenders were bound in a wooden framework and then exposed to abuse by public such as throwing of rotten tomatoes.
*Synonyms: **censure** (The student was censured by his parents after failing in the exams), **lambaste** (Cristiano Ronaldo was lambasted by the media after the defeat), to **crucify** (Crucify literally means to put someone to death by nailing them to a cross like was done to Jesus Christ), to **lash or flog** someone (Lash or flog literally means to whip or beat with a stick), to **flay** someone (Flay literally means to strip the skin off someone), to **flagellate** someone (Flagellate literally means to whip or beat with a stick for religious reasons or sexual pleasure; *pronounced as flaj-uh-late), to receive **flak**, **rail** against, **rant** against, **revile** (He was reviled by the media), **fulminate** against (The public fulminated against the petrol price hike), **excoriate** (The civil society excoriated the government over corruption; *etymology: in medicine, excoriate means to the damage or strip the skin; from Latin 'excoriare' = 'ex' [out] + 'corium' [skin]), **inveigh** (The media inveighed against the move; *pronounced as in-vey), to **throw brickbats**, to **animadvert** (The opposition animadverted upon the government policy), to **pan** (The movie was initially panned by the critics)
Chastise: to severely scold
The teacher chastised the student for bunking his classes.
*Synonyms: **chasten** (Chasten also means to restrain or to subdue; for example, age and complacency has chastened his ambition), **castigate, chide, reprimand, rebuke, reprove, reproach, admonish, upbraid, berate**, take to task, pull up
*Noun form: admonishment, stricture (a critical remark), reproof (an expression of disapproval or scolding)
Disparage: to belittle; to represent something as being

of little value

The company disparaged the product of its competitor.

*Synonyms: **denigrate** (the local politician denigrated the efforts of the aid workers), **derogate** (derogatory comments), **pejorate** (pejorative remarks), **abase** (Steve Jobs would routinely abase his employees in front of the entire office)

Besmirch: to defame someone; to befoul someone's reputation

The actor was besmirched by everyone when his adultery scandal hit the press.

*Synonyms: **malign, calumniate** (He calumniated the Church with baseless accusation; *pronounced as kuh-lum-niate; *noun form: calumniation, calumny), to **cast aspersions** on (Aspersions means defamatory statement; for example, the campaign director told him to stop casting aspersions on the rival candidate), **sully, smear, traduce** (The family name was traduced by the media), **vilify** (He was vilified in the press), to **slander** (Slander means a spoken defamatory statement), to **libel** (Libel means a written defamatory statement; *pronounced as lie-buhl; *adjective form: libellous)

Scurrilous: abusive, baseless and defamatory

He made a scurrilous attack on his integrity.

Tirade: a harshly criticizing speech; sharp and bitter outburst; an abusive attack; insulting condemnation

The CEO received a lot of tirade because he increased the price of the asthma drug.

*Synonyms: **diatribe, harangue** (*pronounced as huh-rang; *verb form: harangue, harangues, harangued, haranguing), **animadversion, castigation, fulmination, invective** (A steady stream of invective from the press continues to attack the president), **vituperation** (The debate was full of vituperation; *adjective form: vituperative), **obloquy** (The honest president endured years of obloquy from the biased media; *pronounced as ob-luh-kwee. Obloquy also means the disgrace resulting from public criticism), **contumely** (The office of the president should not be exposed to contumely; *plural: contumelies), **philippic** (His lecture was a sharp philippic against the culture of consumerism; *etymology: from Greek *'philippikos'* which was the name given to the speeches delivered by the Greek orator Demosthenes against Philip, King of Macedon, in fourth century BC).

Polemic: a piece of writing or a speech strongly attacking or sharply criticizing something

The peace activist published a series of polemical anti-war essays.

*Pronounced as poh-lem-ik

Profanity: abusive or obscene language

The movie contained a lot of profanity and violence.

Expletive: a swear word

The dictator was greeted by a stream of expletives from the protestors.

*Adjective form: expletory

Epithet: a word or phrase that is used to describe someone, usually negatively

The politician's corrupt ways earned him the epithet 'Mr Dirty'.

Trenchant: sharply critical; cutting; biting; stinging

The CEO got trenchant criticism for the mismanagement.

*Pronounced as tren-chunt

*Etymology: from Old French 'trenchant' meaning 'cutting'

*Synonym: **mordant** (He received mordant criticism; *etymology: from French 'mordre' meaning to bite)

*Noun form: trenchancy, mordancy

*Antonym: mild

Caustic: corrosive; burning

He regularly passed caustic comments.

*Synonym: **blistering**

Acerbic: sour or bitter

He has an acerbic wit.

*Etymology: from Latin *'acerbus'* meaning sour-tasting

*Synonyms: **acidulous** (acidulous criticism), **acrid** (acrid remarks)

Acetic: acidic

He passed acetic comments.

*Pronounced as uh-set-ik

*Etymology: from Latin *'acetum'* meaning vinegar, which is acetic acid

*Synonyms: **astringent** (astringent humour), **tart** (a tart reply)

Acerbate: to make sour or bitter

Acidulate: to make slightly acidic

■

Vitriolic: malicious; spiteful; hostile; venomous; vicious

Her Twitter handle was flooded with vitriolic tweets by trolls.

*Etymology: Vitriol is another name for sulfuric acid.

*Synonyms: **bilious** (A bilious attack by the biased media; *etymology: bilious means relating to bile. Bile is the fluid produced by the liver that helps in digestion), **virulent** (a virulent attack on his reputation; virulent also means highly harmful: the virulent strain of influenza caused the food poisoning; virulent also means highly infectious and its antonym is non-contagious; *etymology: from Latin 'virus' meaning poison)

Invidious: discriminatory and unjust

The media house was invidious as it did not equally cover the blatant lies of all politicians.

*Synonyms: prejudicial, discriminatory, **iniquitous**, **lop-sided**

Vengeance: the punishment inflicted by an injured person on the person who has caused this injury

Tony Stark told Loki that even if Loki succeeds, the Avengers will seek vengeance.

*Synonyms: **revenge, retribution, retaliation, requital, reprisal**

Vendetta: a blood feud in which the family of a murdered person seeks to avenge the murder by killing the murderer or the murderer's family

Vindictive: a person who strongly wants to take revenge; grudge-bearing

In *Game of Thrones*, Cersei Lannister was a very vindictive person.

*Synonyms: vengeful, revengeful, avenging

Vindicate: to be proven to be correct

He felt vindicated after the police removed him from the list of suspects.

■

Disapprobation: strong disapproval

He braved his father's disapprobation and slipped out to go party.

*Synonym: condemnation

Deplore: to publicly condemn

The father deplored the actions of his errant son.

*Synonyms: **denounce, decry, execrate** (He execrated the actions of his son), **deprecate** (The teacher deprecated coming late to class)

Disavow: to deny any responsibility or support for something

The spy's home country disavowed him immediately on his arrest.

*Synonyms: disown, disclaim, wash one's hands of

Repudiate: to reject and renounce something

The young voters repudiated the politics of hate.

*Synonyms: **abjure** (Politicians must abjure corruption), **eschew** (We must eschew violence), shun

Forswear: to give up something

The prime minister declared that his nation would forswear the use of harmful chemical fertilizers.

Forsake: to abandon

The bride's heart was broken as she was forsaken by the groom at the altar.

*Synonyms: to **desert**, leave high and dry

Forgo: to waive something; to go without something, usually something desirable

He decided to forgo the drinks so that he could drive back home safely.

*Synonyms: **abstain** from, refrain from, to **forbear**

Abdicate: to renounce one's throne

The King had to abdicate after the people's revolution swept the country.

*Synonym: **abnegate**

*Abdicate and abnegate also mean to fail in one's responsibility; for example, the governor abdicated his responsibility of upholding the Constitution.

Capitulate: to surrender

In World War II, Japan capitulated after the US dropped nuclear bombs on Hiroshima and Nagasaki in 1945.

*Synonyms: **yield** (He was unyielding in the face of adversity), **succumb** (He succumbed to the pressure), **cede** (Cede means to surrender, especially territory; for example, the president said that the country wouldn't cede one inch of land to the enemy; *noun form: cession; *pronounced as session), **concede** (Concede also means to admit to something being true after denying it initially; for example, he finally conceded that he made a mistake; *noun form: concession), **relinquish** (Relinquish also means to give up a claim)

Maroon: to abandon someone all alone on an island

The passengers were marooned on the tropical island when their plane crashed.

Strand: to leave a ship, fish, etc., on the shore in a helpless situation where it can't do anything

He was left stranded by the dishonest tourist guide.

■

Vanquish: to defeat thoroughly

He vanquished his rivals.

*Synonyms: **conquer, trounce** (US trounced Australia in the semi-finals), **rout** (He routed his rival in the finals), **drubbing** (Our team received a drubbing at the hands of the visitors), **checkmate** (Napoleon was checkmated at Waterloo)

Clinch: to win

The team played really well and clinched the title.

*Homonym: clinch (an extremely easy task)

*Clinch also means to settle a matter decisively; for example, the investigator's findings clinched the matter

in his favour.

Trifecta: a run of three consecutive wins

Thwart: to prevent someone from accomplishing something

The Avenger's thwarted Thanos' plan to destroy the world.

*Synonym: **foil** (Batman foiled Joker's evil plans)

Repulse: to drive back an attacker using force

The Justice League was able to repulse the invasion of Earth by Steppenwolf.

*Synonym: **repel** (The military repelled the rebels)

■

Scuttle: to sink one's own ship by making holes in it

Upend: to turn something upside down

The financial crash upended the world economy.

*Synonyms: to overturn, to **invert**

Dismantle: to disassemble; to pull down or take apart a machine or structure

The repairman dismantled the engine to figure out the fault.

Disband: to break up or dissolve an organization

The special task force was disbanded due to budget cuts.

*Antonyms: **assemble**, convene

Dismount: to get off a horse, cycle, etc.

The biker first slowed his bike and then dismounted.

*Synonym: to alight

*Antonym: mount

■

Malfunction: a failure of a machine

The printing press malfunctioned right at the time of peak demand.

*Synonym: **glitch**

Dysfunction: an abnormal behaviour

Cancer is a dysfunction of the body where it produces excessive cells.

Entropy: disorder

There is complete entropy in the fish market in the busy hours of the evening.

Awry: away from the expected course

He knew that something was awry because of the worried look on his son's face.

*Pronounced as uh-ry

*Synonyms: **astray**, **amiss**

Haywire: out of control; in disorder

The city's transportation system went haywire because

of the simultaneous bus and taxi strike.

Ruffle: to disorder or disarrange, especially someone's hair with your hands

■

Impede: to obstruct; to hinder; to hamper; to inhibit; to constrain

The wedding procession impeded the flow of traffic during rush hour.

*Synonyms: to put a brake on, to check, to **curb**, to cramp, to **stymie** (The heavy regulations stymied any innovation)

Stultify: to cause to lose enthusiasm and creativity because of a boring and monotonous routine

His mind was stultified by his boring job as a typist.

Stunt: to hinder the full and proper growth or development

Childhood abuse stunted his personality.

*Antonym: **foster** (to foster new ideas)

Stint: to severely limit the use of something; to restrict the supply of something; stint also means a period of time spent doing something

Hamstring: to cripple

The company was hamstrung when the government decided to cancel its license.

Intercept: to obstruct by stopping something in its path and thus cutting it off from its intended destination

The police intercepted a large shipment of weapons.

*Intercept also means to overhear messages, transmissions, etc.; for example, the intelligence agencies intercepted the enemy's secret radio messages.

Occlude: to block by clogging up the passage or opening

She got pimples because the thick make-up occluded her facial pores.

Caulk: to fill up and thus seal the cracks and gaps in a building in order to make it watertight and airtight

*Pronounced as kawk

Derail: to obstruct the progress by diverting something from its intended course

The false harassment accusations derailed his career for two years.

Encumbrance: an impediment; obstruction

*Synonyms: **hindrance, hurdle, hitch, obstacle, snag**, restraint, constraint, handicap

Bottleneck: a narrow section of a road that obstructs the flow of car movement and thus causes a traffic jam

Ligature: something, like a band or a cord, which is used to bind or tie up another object; for example, a cord used in surgery to tie up an artery

Circumscribe: to draw a line around; to encircle; to restrict; to limit; to confine
His powers were circumscribed.
*Synonyms: to **curb**, to **delimit**

Pinion: to cut off or bind the flight feathers of a bird to prevent the bird from flying The crooks pinioned the police man to the ground.
*Homonym: **pillion** (The seat for a passenger behind a motorcyclist)

Manacle: handcuff-type restraints to fasten the hands or ankles
The prisoners were kept in manacles in the jail.
*Synonyms: **shackle, fetter**

Trammel: a three-layered fishing net; trammel also means a restriction or an impediment or a hindrance
The many trammels of custom.

Straitjacket: a garment with long sleeves which can be tied together, used to control mental patients

Tether: to tie an animal with a rope to restrict movement

Unbridled: free to move and without any restraints
*Synonyms: unencumbered, unmanacled, unshackled, unfettered, untrammelled, untethered, unimpeded, unintercepted, unhindered, uninhibited, unconstrained, unchecked, unobstructed, unsaddled, rampant

■

Recant: to withdraw a statement
The witness recanted his testimony.
*Synonym: **retract**

Renege: to go back on one's word
The buyer reneged on his promise.
*Pronounced as re-neg

Resile: to abandon a position earlier taken
He shamelessly resiled from the agreement.

Rescind: to cancel one's offer
The store rescinded their offer of buy one get one free.

Revoke: to officially cancel something and declare it invalid
The department's notification was revoked by the governor.
*Synonyms: **repeal, abrogate, quash** (Quash also means to reject as invalid, especially through a court judgment; for example, The Supreme Court quashed his conviction on appeal), **countermand** (The senior officer countermanded the orders of the junior), **annul** (The marriage was annulled on the grounds of fraud), nullify, declare null and void, overrule, override

Refute: to deny
The young politician refuted all allegations of corruption by the opposition.
*Synonym: **controvert** (The accused tried to controvert the evidence)

Rebut: to disprove
The defendant tried to rebut the prosecution's accusations.
*Synonym: **confute** (The debater tried to confute to the rival's argument)

Rebuff: to reject someone or something in an abrupt and blunt manner
She rebuffed him when he asked her out on a date.
*Synonyms: to **snub**, to **spurn** (She spurned his advances)

Debunk: to expose the falseness of something
The media debunked his conspiracy theory.

Gainsay: to deny or contradict
The impact of social media on modern politics cannot be gainsaid.
*Verb tenses: gainsay, gainsays, gainsaying, gainsaid
*Antonym: **confirm**

Corroborate: to confirm
His claims were corroborated by the eye-witness.

Conflate: to confuse two different things together
He confuted causation with correlation.

Obfuscate: to make matters unclear
The accused tried to obfuscate the issue by questioning the motive and the timing of the charges against him.
*Synonyms: to **obscure**, to **bedim**

Negate: to deny the existence of something
The sham investigation tried to negate the influence of money on politics.
*Negate also means to nullify or cause to be ineffective; for example, the antidote negates the effects of the poison.

Nix: to cancel something
Netflix nixed the fourth season of Daredevil.

■

Ward off: to keep something away and thus prevent it from causing harm to oneself She used her umbrella to ward off the UV rays from the sun.

Fend off: to send away an attacker
She fended off the purse snatcher.

Stave off: to temporarily avoid an unwanted situation or person
The CEO tried to stave off the uncomfortable firing decisions until Christmas.

■

Impute: to assign a quality or blame on someone
The investigation committee imputed that the NASA scientists were to blame for the rocket crash.
*Synonyms: to **attribute** (He attributed loyalty to his team mates. Attribute also means to regard something as being caused by something; for example, he attributed his bad mood to lack of sleep), to **ascribe** (Everyone ascribed the failure of the team to the bad leadership of the captain), to **accredit**
*Noun forms: imputation, attribution, assignment, ascription, accreditation
Allude: to imply or hint at something
The judge alluded to passing a favourable order.
*Noun form: **allusion**
Elude: to avoid getting caught
The dacoits eluded the police search party.
*Synonyms: to **evade** (The defendant evaded the service of summons *adjective form: evasive), to **dodge**
Flee: to escape from
The thief fled from custody.
Forestall: to prevent something from happening
The family forestalled any attempts of theft by installing CCTV cameras in their house.
*Synonyms: **pre-empt** (The government pre-empted a coup attempt by locking up all the military generals), **preclude** (His stressful job precluded him from leading a balanced life), **obviate** (The use of seatbelts can obviate disaster. Obviate also means to remove a need; for example, a peaceful settlement would obviate the need for a military strike)
Sidestep: to avoid trouble
The soldiers sidestepped the mines.
Circumvent: to go around; to bypass
They circumvented the legal restriction by finding a rarely used exception in the law.
Parry: to deflect
Jon Snow parried the attack from the White Walker.
Avert: to turn away
He averted his eyes when he was shown the obscene picture.
*Avert also means to prevent; for example, by planning they averted a crisis.
Shirk: to avoid responsibility
He shirked his duty of cleaning the dishes.
*Synonyms: **shuffle off, shrink from duty, play truant**
Equivocate: to avoid answering a question by giving vague, evasive and ambiguous (roundabout) answers

The politician equivocated when asked about the corruption allegations.
*Synonyms: to **prevaricate**, to **pussyfoot**, **be non-committal**, to beat about the bush, to **tergiversate**

■

Procrastinate: to delay; to put off doing something, especially something which requires immediate attention
Students must never procrastinate.
Putter: to cut time in a relaxed way doing odd jobs that are not very important
He puttered around the house on the weekend.
Defer: to postpone
The confirmation of Judge Brett Kavanaugh was deferred till the completion of the FBI investigation.
*Synonym: **adjourn**
*Noun forms: deferment, postponement, adjournment, **continuance**
*Defer also means to respectfully yield to someone's judgment or opinion; for example, everyone deferred to him in critical matters because of his vast experience.
Dawdle: to be very slow in doing something because of lack of interest
The manager scolded the cleaning staff for dawdling.
Dilly-dally: to waste time by aimlessly wandering
The coach scolded the team for dilly-dallying and not practicing.
Dilatory: deliberately causing delay
The general employed dilatory tactics during the war so that the enemy would run out of food.
Temporize: to delay taking a decision so as to gain time or some advantage
He temporized the signing of the contract hoping to get a better rate.
Shelve: to indefinitely stop moving ahead with a project
The project was shelved after the budget committee pointed out the cost overruns.
Stall: to delay especially by the use of evasion or deception
The accomplice stalled the police so that the robber could get away.
Stonewall: to delay a process by not answering questions
The politician stonewalled the enquiry by not answering any questions.
Filibuster: to give a long speech in a legislative house so that the time runs out and the vote is delayed and consequently the bill lapses.
Circumlocution: the use of excessive words or

roundabout expression while answering so as to be evasive

The court got angry at the circumlocution in the government affidavit.

*Synonym: **periphrasis**

Hold-out: the act of refusing to accept an offer in order to get a better deal later

The land owner planned to hold out for a better contract.

Linger: to wait around a place because of reluctance to leave

The principal told the students not to linger near the gate and go home.

*Synonym: to **tarry** (He tarried near her house gate)

Loiter: to aimlessly stand or wait around a place

The teacher got angry at the students for loitering near the toilet.

■

Indolent: lazy

The child's indolent attitude worried the parents

*Synonyms: **work-shy, slothful, languid** (The languid worker got fired), **languorous**

*Noun form: indolence, languidness, languor, slothfulness

Lassitude: lack of energy; weakness; weariness

Overcome by lassitude by the end of the day, he quickly took a bath and went straight to bed.

*Synonyms: **listlessness, lethargy, sluggishness, torpor** (Torpor is also written as torpidity; *adjective form: torpid; *related word: torporific, which means causing torpor: the passenger became torpid because he took torporific sleeping pills and these pills caused him to enter into a state of a state of torpor)

*Antonyms: vigour, energy

Jaded: tired, exhausted

He was jaded after the exam

*Synonyms: **weary, fatigued, sapped, frazzled**

*Antonyms: fresh, energized

Sluggish: slow-moving; inactive; lacking energy

After the global financial meltdown, the world economy became sluggish.

*Synonyms: **lethargic, stagnant, static, dormant, torpid, inert, glacial**

Sclerotic: rigid and unresponsive

The sclerotic legal system is costing the economy billions.

*Etymology: sclerosis is hardening of bodily tissue

Ennui: extreme boredom

The boring history lecture produced an inescapable ennui.

*Pronounced as en-wee

Tardy: late

The manager scolded the intern for always being tardy

Tentative: provisional; not fixed

The book launch was tentatively set for next week, depending on the hall availability.

■

Slumber: sleep

He took some sleeping pills and fell into a gentle slumber.

Bleary: looking tired and sleepy

The bleary eyed truck driver took a nap.

Repose: to lay to rest

She reposed her faith in her best friend.

Comatose: in a coma

He has been comatose for six months.

Aphasia: the inability to speak as a result of brain damage

*Synonym: **aphonia**

Somnolent: sleepy

He was somnolent after working all night.

*Synonyms: drowsy, heavy-eyed

*Etymology: from Latin *'somnus'* meaning sleep

Somnambulism: sleepwalking

*Related word: somnambulist (a sleepwalker)

Somniloquism: sleep talking

*Pronounced as som-nilo-quism

*Related word: somniloquist (a sleeptalker), somniloquy (meaning sleep-talk)

Jetlag: extreme tiredness caused by the disruption of a person's normal biological rhythm due to flight travel across different time zones

Circadian: relating to a person's normal biological rhythmic cycle which recurs every 24 hours even in the absence of sunlight variations

■

Alacrity: cheerful readiness and willingness

The alacrity of the employee to take on new tasks really impressed the CEO.

Celerity: swiftness; quickness

They joked that his celerity on the field was matched only by the tortoise.

■

Abscise: to cut off

The gardener abscised the protruding branches of the bushes.

*Pronounced as ab-size

*Noun form: abscission

Ablation: the surgical removal of bodily tissue; for example, the removal of abnormal growth tissue like a tumour

*Synonym: resection

Ablution: an act of washing oneself

He always did worship after finishing his daily ablutions.

Excise: to cut out surgically

The surgeons excised the tumour.

*Noun form: **excision**

*Synonym: to **exscind**

Exorcise: to drive out an evil spirit from a person by using religious prayers and ceremonies

The priest exorcized demons from the possessed child.

*Pronounced as eck-sawr-size

*Noun form: **exorcism**

Expunge: to erase

The judge ordered that his past minor crimes be expunged from his record.

*Synonym: **efface** (Time effaced the bitter memories of his childhood)

Expurgate: to censor; to remove objectionable or offensive material from a text

The Censor Board expurgated the script to make to children friendly.

*Synonym: to **bowdlerize** (*pronounced as bohd-luh-rize)

Purge: to cleanse (especially to remove unwanted people from an organization)

The dictator purged the government of all naysayers.

Redact: to censor parts of a text for legal and security purposes

The committee redacted all the sensitive information from the report.

■

Glib: fluent but insincere

The politician has a reputation of being a glib talker.

*Synonyms: slick, smooth-talking, fast-talking, **honey-tongued, silver-tongued, oily tongued, soft soap** (The director tried to soft-soap the junior actress)

*Antonyms: sincere, **earnest**, solemn

Sycophant: a person who praises people in power or tries to please them and acts like their slave in order to gain favour

The minister was surrounded by sycophants.

*Pronounced as sik-oh-fant

*Adjective form: sycophantic (The boss loved his sycophantic assistant)

*Synonyms: **toady, brown-noser, apple polisher, lickspittle**

Ingratiate: to gain favour with someone by excessively praising him/her or trying to please them

He made many attempts to ingratiate himself with his boss.

*Etymology: from Latin *'in gratiam'* meaning 'into favour'

Unctuous: excessively flattering but in order to gain favour

To get his promotion the young associate was unctuous towards the senior partners at the office party.

*Pronounced as uhnk-choo-uss

*Synonyms: smarmy, greasy, soapy, oily, sycophantic, ingratiating, fawning

Obsequious: obedient and attentive but to an excessive degree, which makes one look like a slave

The guests at the party were served by obsequious waiters.

*Pronounced as ub-see-kwee-us

*Etymology: from Latin *'obsequi'* meaning to follow or comply with

Servile: excessive eager and willing to serve or please others

The King had many servile flatterers.

*Etymology: from Latin *'servilis'* meaning like a slave

*Synonym: slavish

Subservient: excessively and unquestioningly submissive

He was subservient to his wife.

Complaisant: excessively and unquestioningly compliant

The complaisant employee always followed the orders. of the manager, even when they were wrong.

*Etymology: from Latin *'complacere'* meaning to please

*Homonym: **complacent** (Complacent means to become falsely confident about oneself; for example, students should not become complacent)

Simper: to smile in an ingratiating manner

All that the courtiers needed to do to please the King was to simper and bow.

Fawn: to gain favour with someone by acting their slave

The courtiers fawned over the king.

*Etymology: from Old English *'fagnian'* meaning to make glad

*Adjective form: fawning
Fulsome: excessively flattering
The ministers heaped fulsome praise on the dictator.
Flummery: insincere flattery
The Dictator enjoyed the flummery at events.
Minion: a slavish follower of a powerful person
*Synonym: **hanger-on**
Yes-man: a person who always agrees with their superior
The CEO never got any real feedback because he was surrounded by yes-men.
Henchman: a follower who would even commit crime for their master
The don had his henchmen spread all over the city.
*Synonym: myrmidon (*etymology: Myrmidons were the soldiers who went with Achilles to Troy)

■

Obeisance: a movement of the body (like a bow or kneel) expressing deep respect to a superior
The supplicant paid obeisance to the prince before placing the request.
*Pronounced as oh-bey-suns
Kowtow: to kneel and touch the ground with the forehead in worship or submission as part of Chinese custom
He kowtowed to his boss.
Genuflect: to lower one's body briefly by bending one knee to the ground as a sign of respect or worship
*Etymology: from Latin *'genuflectere'* = genu (knee) + *flectere* (bend)
*Synonyms: **to bend the knee** (to touch one knee to the ground as a sign of submission)
Grovel: to lie on the ground with one's face touching the ground to ask or beg for favour or mercy
*Synonyms: to **truckle** (*etymology: truckle refers to sleeping in a truckle bed, which was is a low bed on wheels which goes underneath a large bed), to **prostrate** (He prostrated before his wife to beg for her forgiveness; *etymology: from Latin *'prosternere'* = *'pro'* (before) + *'sternere'* (lay flat);*homonym of prostrate is prostate, which is a gland near the urinary bladder of male mammals)
Kneel: to get down on one's knees as sign of respect or worship
He kneeled before the Queen.
Bow and scrape: to make a deep bow with the right leg drawn back (thus scraping the floor), left hand pressed across the abdomen and right arm held aside; this is done as a sign of respect or worship

The knight was seen bowing and scraping to the new king.
Hunch: to lean forward and bend with one's shoulders raised, so that one's upper body goes into a rounded shape
They always found the professor hunched over some book in the library.
*Hunch also means an intuition.
Stoop: to bend the top half of one's body forward and downward
Stoop also means to lower one's own standards to do something which one would otherwise never do. For example: he would never stoop to lying to his own mother.
Droop: to bend or hang down in a limp manner, usually because of defeat
The players walked back from field with drooped shoulders.
*Synonyms: to sag, to slouch, to slump
Deign: to do something which one considers to be beneath his/her dignity
The autocrat did not deign to answer any questions.
*Pronounced as dayn

■

Effusive: expressing pleasure or approval in an unrestrained and heartfelt manner They effusively praised their child.
*Synonym: gushing
Euphoric: feeling intense excitement and happiness
He was euphoric when he won the Oscar.
Exuberant: full of energy, excitement and enthusiasm; in high spirits
The exuberant crowds led the protests during the Arab Spring revolution.
*Synonyms: **ecstatic, ebullient** (He was in an ebullient mood)
Enthuse: to cause to become enthusiastic
His parents were enthused over his new book.
Elated: extremely happy
He was elated after reuniting with his family.
*Synonyms: **exhilarated, blissful** (The couple spent a blissful month together in Paris; *etymology: in theology, bliss means the joy of heaven)
Beatific: appearing very calm and happy, especially in a holy way
In the paintings, the angels have beatific smiles.
*Pronounced as bee-uh-tif-ik
Buoyant: cheerful; joyful

He was in a buoyant mood at the holiday party.
*Pronounced as boy-unt
*Etymology: from Spanish *'boyante'* meaning 'to float'
*Synonyms: **jolly, jaunty** (He had a jaunty smile on his face), **jocund** (He enjoyed himself at the jocund birthday party)
*Buoyant also means able to float in a liquid; for example, cork is a buoyant object.

Jubilant: feeling great happiness and delight on a triumph
The protestors were jubilant after the dictator resigned.
*Synonyms: **rejoicing, exultant** (The new president waved to the exultant crowds), **gleeful** (He had a gleeful smile on his face), **chuffed** (The child was chuffed with his present), **cock-a-hoop** (The team was cock-a-hoop after winning the trophy)

Jollity: cheerful and lively celebrations or festivities
He had a great time being a part of the jollity at the New Year party.
*Synonyms: gaiety, **mirth** (Mirth also means amusement expressed in laughter; for example, his weird habits were a source of considerable mirth), merriment, frolics

Revelry: lively and noisy festivities, especially involving a lot of drinking and dancing The sounds of revelry kept the neighbours awake all night.
*Plural: revelries
*Verb form: to revel (He revelled with his guests)

Felicity: extreme happiness or joy
The couple enjoyed years of marital felicity.
*Synonyms: bliss, elation, exultation, glee (The child opened his presents with glee), **gaiety** (He loved the gaiety of the festive season; *pronounced as gay-uh-tee; *plural: gaieties)

Ridibund: easily brought to laughter
The ridibund child would laugh at all the silly jokes.

Risible: evoking laughter because of its absurd nature
The movie had many risible scenes which the audience loved.

■

Fervent: intensely passionate
Dr Martin Luther King Jr was a fervent supporter for equal rights.
*Etymology: from Latin *'fervent'* meaning boiling
*Synonyms: **vehement** (There was vehement opposition to the new policy), **ardent** (He is an ardent supporter of Manchester United), **fervid** (He is a fervid debater), **perfervid** (He is a perfervid nationalist), zealous

*Noun forms: fervour, vehemence, ardour, zeal

Gusto: hearty enjoyment and enthusiasm in doing something
He danced with a lot of gusto.

Zest: great excitement, eagerness and enthusiasm in doing something
The politician campaigned with zest.
*Adjective form: zesty

Zeal: intense passion for a cause or objective
The CEO had a zeal for maximizing the profits.
*Adjective form: zealous
*Noun form: zealot

■

Vivacious: attractively lively and animated, especially used to refer to a woman or girl
The vivacious actress caught the director's eye at the audition.
*Pronounced as vi-way-shus
*Etymology: from Latin *'vivac'* meaning lively
*Synonyms: **effervescent** (She had an effervescent personality; effervescent also means bubbly or fizzy), **sprightly** (the sprightly young gymnast)
*Noun forms: vivacity, vivaciousness, verve, sparkle, éclat (brilliant display or effect; for example, he finished her speech with great éclat; *pronounced as ey-klah), **brio** (He performed on stage with a lot of brio; *pronounced as bree-oh), **oomph** (The casting director said that the newcomer had a certain oomph. Oomph also means sex appeal), **pizzazz** (Her dance performance was full of pizzazz; pizzazz also means glamour)

Vigour: energy or strength or power, be it physical or mental
Due to his regular yoga practice, he is full of vigour, even in his eighties.
*Synonyms: **vitality, verve** (He delivered his speech with a lot of verve)
*Adjective form: vigorous (He was tired after the vigorous exercise)
*Adverb form: vigorously (They vigorously debated on the news show)
*Etymology: from Latin *'vigere'* meaning lively
*Related word: invigorate (to give strength or energy to someone; to give vigour to someone; for example, the hot water shower invigorated him after the tiring day at the office)

Vivify: to make lively; to enliven
Visits to museums vivify the education for young students.

Rev: to make more active or energetic
The bank robber revved up the car engine and then drove away with the loot.

■

Cavort: to jump and dance around with excitement
He cavorted around the room after he got his admission letter.
Caper: to play around
The children capered about the room.
*Synonyms: to **gambol** (The kids gambolled in the park), to **romp**, to **frolic**, to **skylark**
Horseplay: rough and rowdy play
The students engaged in horseplay.
Escapade: a stunt; a reckless act involving adventure and excitement
The child's latest escapade was to go swimming in the sea.
Antics: silly and playful behaviour
His antics entertained everyone.
Shenanigans: mischief; children's playful misbehaviour
The nanny had a hard time putting up with the children's shenanigans.

■

Giggle: a light, silly laugh
The children giggled.
*Synonym: **titter**
Chuckle: a small, suppressed laugh
His friends chuckled when he said that he was royalty.
Chortle: a loud laugh caused by amusement and sounds like a mix of snorting and laughing
His friends chortled when he slipped on the wet floor.
Guffaw: a very loud, hearty laugh
He guffawed when he heard the joke.
*Synonym: **belly laugh**
Grin: a broad smile (like from ear to ear)
He grinned when he saw his gift.
Gloat: to feel great pleasure over one's own success or someone else's misfortune or failure
The cruel king gloated over the sudden death of his enemy.
*Synonym: to **crow over**
Snarl: to growl and bare fangs (show teeth)
The guard dog snarled at him.
Hilarious: very funny; evoking boisterous laughter
The hilarious comedy made everyone laugh their stomachs out.
*Noun form: hilarity, funniness

■

Luncheon: a formal lunch
*Pronounced as lunch-un.
Banquet: a large and lavish feast
*Pronounced as ban-kwit
Soirée: an evening party with music and dance
*Pronounced as swah-rey
Shindig: a large and lively dance party
Fiesta: a festival
*Etymology: Spanish for a feast
Carnival: a public celebration with lots of entertainment and processions
Gala: a social occasion with special entertainment and performances
Jamboree: a large lavish party
Jubilee: a special anniversary, typically celebrating 25 or 50 years

■

Bereft: deprived of or lacking something
His article is bereft of any logic.
Bereavement: the deprivation of a loved one due to death
There was a prayer meeting held to mark one year since the bereavement in the family.

■

Scarcity: shortness of supply
There was a scarcity of water because of the monsoon failure.
*Synonyms: **dearth, paucity, meagreness, sparseness, scantiness, deficiency**; *Adjective forms: scarce, meagre, paltry, sparse, scant, skimpy, **exiguous** (He had hard time surviving on his exiguous income)
*Antonyms: abundance, surplus, surfeit
Snippet: a small piece which has been snipped off something or a small piece of information, often interesting
Modicum: an extremely small amount
He did not show even a modicum of remorse when convicted of the crime. *Synonyms: **iota, scintilla** (*pronounced as sin-till-aa), **smidgen**, speck, fleck, mite, mote, morsel, scrap
Minuscule: extremely small; tiny
The farmers were only able to sell a minuscule amount of grain in the market. *Synonyms: **puny** (Puny also means small and weak; for example, he was easily

beaten up because of his puny frame), **diminutive** (He was picked on because of his diminutive size), **miniature** (He made miniature sized dolls for children), **Lilliputian** (His reputation was Lilliputian compared to his mentor), **infinitesimal** (Even infinitesimal amounts of radioactivity can kill a person; *pronounced as in-fini-tesi-mul), **minute** (The minute pollution particles in the air get lodged in our lungs; *pronounced as mine-yoot)
*Antonyms: vast, huge
Midget: a dwarf; a person who did not fully physically grow due to some medical condition
Pygmy: a member of the pygmy tribe from Africa who do not grow more than 5 feet in height
Puisne: inferior in rank; junior
*Pronounced as pyoo-nee
*Etymology: French for '*puis*' (afterwards) and '*ne*' (born)
Microcosm: a community or a place that encapsulates the characteristic of something much larger; a little world; for example, Little China in San Francisco is a microcosm that represents modern China
*Antonym: macrocosm (The large entire world or the total complex structure of something)
Granular: resembles granules (grains)
The fabric had a granular texture.
*Synonym: **grainy** (resembling grains)
*Granular also means highly detailed; for example, the boss wanted the data analysis on a granular level.
Nurdle: a small plastic pellet that is used as a raw material in manufacturing
Smithereens: small pieces
The city was bombed to smithereens.

■

Maximal: relating to maximum
The reduction of the income tax rate had a maximal effect on the economy.
*Antonym: minimal
Gargantuan: huge; enormous
The wrestler had a gargantuan size.
*Pronounced as gar-gan-choo-un
*Synonyms: **colossal, gigantic, humongous, elephantine, mammoth, Brobdingnagian** (*pronounced as brob-ding-nag-eun; *etymology: Brobdingnag was the land where everything was huge in the book *Gulliver's Travels* by Jonathan Swift)
Monolith: a large tall block of stone, usually carved to serve as a pillar or a monument; a large uncaring

organization that is slow to change
Monotheistic: relating to only one God
Christianity, Islam and Judaism are monotheistic religions.
*Antonym: polytheistic
Behemoth: a huge or monstrous creature; a large and extremely powerful organization
Samsung is a behemoth company.
*Synonym: **leviathan** (*Etymology: a leviathan is a giant sea monster as mentioned in the Bible)
Juggernaut: a very large and heavy truck; juggernaut also means a huge, overpowering force
Apple is a juggernaut in consumer electronics.
Boulder: a large rock, usually rounded in shape, worn smooth by erosion

■

Replete: filled with something
The politician's speech was replete with false claims and lies.
*Synonym: **fraught** (The move is fraught with risk)
Rife: widespread
Before Batman, Gotham City was rife with crime.
Awash: flooded with something
The movie set was awash with fans.
Ubiquitous: present everywhere
Pollution is ubiquitous in the city.
*Pronounced you-bik-wit-us
*Synonym: **omnipresent**
*Antonym: rare
Endemic: commonly found but among only a certain group of people or a certain geographical area
Kangaroos are endemic to Australia.
Pandemic: widespread; universal
There is a pandemic fear of nuclear war.
*Synonym: **pervasive** (a pervasive smell of cigarettes in his room)
Epidemic: a widespread occurrence of an infectious disease
There was a malaria dengue epidemic in the village after the heavy rains.
Outbreak: a sudden occurrence of something bad like war or disease
There was a cholera outbreak.
*Synonyms: **eruption, flare-up, breakout**
Contagion: the spread of a disease
The hospital room was sanitized every day to prevent contagion.
*Pronounced as cun-tey-jun

Rampant: spreading unchecked
There was rampant crime in the city.

■

Manifold: large in number and of various types
He has manifold duties as the chief hotel manager.
*Synonym: **multifarious** (The finance reporter wrote about the fraudster's multifarious business activities)
Multitudinous: numerous; consisting of many parts or elements
The dancers showcased their multitudinous talents.
Multifaceted: have many sides
He has a multifaceted personality.
Myriad: extremely large in number, innumerable
They tried to count the myriad stars in the clear summer sky.
*Pronounced as mir-ee-uhd
*Synonym: **umpteen** (umpteen number of excuses)
*Antonym: few
Galore: in abundance
The party had food and drinks galore.
Profuse: given in large quantity; abundant
After accepting the blame, he offered profuse apologies.
*Synonyms: **copious** (He took copious notes during the lecture), **bountiful**, **ample** (There was ample time for discussion)
Prolific: producing in large quantities; a prolific writer
He is a prolific writer with a hundred novels published in various languages.
Plethora: a large amount of something; oversupply; overabundance; an excess of something
There is a plethora of books on how to develop one's personality.
*Synonyms: **profusion** (He had never witnessed such a rich profusion of flowers), **surfeit** (The poor country had a surfeit of cheap labour; *pronounced as sur-fit), **superfluity** (There were layoffs because of the superfluity of staff in the company), **glut** (There is a glut of smartphone on the market), **plenitude** (The company has a plenitude of vacancies for data scientists), **slew** (The politician was asked a slew of questions)
Cornucopia: an abundant supply of good things
The feast offered a cornucopia of all kinds of food and drinks.
Ream: large quantity of paper
The daily reams of useless press releases.
Heap: a pile; a stack; a large and untidy collection of objects.

Capacious: spacious; roomy
The waiting lounge at the airport was capacious.
*Synonyms: **commodious** (The couple moved into their new commodious apartment), sizeable
*Antonyms: cramped, small
Exorbitant: unreasonably high
The hotel charged exorbitant rates.
*Synonym: **extortionate**
Inordinate: disproportionately large; excessive; not within reasonable limits
The court case had taken up an inordinate amount of time of the company.

■

Superfluous: extra and unnecessary
The brochure provided superfluous details of the property.
*Synonyms: **redundant** (for example, the use of 'single' in 'single unmarried women' is redundant), **tautological** (for example, 'woman' in 'widow woman'; *related word: tautology, which means needless repetition).
Otiose: useless; serving no purpose
Artificial intelligence will make much of the labour force otiose.
*Pronounced as oh-she-os
Overkill: excessive use or action
The two hour speech was considered as overkill by everyone.

■

Imperative: absolutely necessary
It was imperative for the doctor to operate.
*Synonyms: vital, crucial, critical
*Antonym: optional
Staple: a principal or main part of something
Rubber and rice are the staples of the Vietnamese economy
Utility: usefulness; utility also refers to essential public services like gas, electricity, water, etc.
The students questioned the utility of morning school assemblies.
*Adjective form: utilitarian (Utilitarian means useful rather than attractive; for example, the factory had a utilitarian building design)
*Antonyms: **futility** (uselessness: the public has realized the futility of war)

■

Concomitant: naturally accompanying; related
Car brings with itself concomitant heavy maintenance costs.
*Synonyms: attendant, associated
Collateral: secondary; additional but subordinate
The media praise was collateral to his primary goal of earning a lot of money.
Ancillary: providing necessary support to the primary work; supplementary
The law firm hired ancillary workers like typists to assist its lawyers.
*Synonym: auxiliary (The hospital hired auxiliary staff like cleaners)
Tertiary: third in order or level
The doctor informed the patient that the tertiary stage of the disease has the most painful symptoms.
Consummate: to complete a process or transaction
The lawyers consummated the deal well before the deadline.
*Consummate also means to make a marriage complete by having sexual intercourse.
Arrant: utter
The movie was arrant nonsense and waste of time and money.
*Synonyms: **unalloyed, sheer**, downright, outright, undiluted

■

Ludicrous: laughably absurd; nonsensical; ridiculous; preposterous
The underprepared students gave ludicrous answers to the questions asked by the teacher.
*Synonym: **cockamamie** (He had many cockamamie ideas)
Farce: an absurd or disorganized event; a ridiculous sham
The debate quickly turned into a drunken farce.
*Adjective form: farcical
Puerile: childishly silly
The editor scolded the young reporter for the puerile piece of writing.
*Etymology: from Latin 'puer' meaning boy
*Pronounced as pure-ile
*Synonyms: **infantile** (like an infant), **juvenile**
Inane: stupid
The students bothered the teacher with inane questions.

*Synonyms: **asinine**, **daft**, **fatuous** (He made a fatuous comment; *pronounced as fatch-oo-us), **vacuous** (mindless: his vacuous remarks irritated everyone), **imbecilic** (like an imbecile), **witless**
Ignoramus: a stupid person; an idiot
*Synonyms: moron, halfwit, **imbecile** (*pronounced as im-buh-sil), cretin, clod, dolt, dunce, dullard, nincompoop
Obtuse: slow to understand; slow-witted; dull; blunt
The student was deliberately obtuse to irritate the teacher.
Folly: foolishness
He had no excuse for his folly.
*Synonyms: stupidity, idiocy, imbecility, silliness, inanity
Foolhardy: reckless; rash; hasty; incautious; careless
He made a foolhardy attempt to climb the electricity pole to recover his kite.
*Synonyms: **heedless** (Heedless of the risks involved, he went swimming in the open ocean), **unheeding, impulsive, impetuous** (He immediately regretted his impetuous decision), devil-may-care (The young man has a devil-may-care attitude), **headlong** (He rushed into the fight headlong)
Tomfoolery: foolish behaviour
He was scolded for his tomfoolery.
*Synonym: buffoonery

■

Recumbent: lying down
He was recumbent on the hospital bed.
Erect: standing up straight
Despite his age, he had an erect posture.
Prone: lying down face downwards
The drunkard was seen lying prone on the road.
*Prone also means susceptible; for example, children are prone to diseases.
Supine: lying down face upwards
The supine bodies soaking up the sun.

■

Cringe: to experience a shudder (a quick trembling movement) due to embarrassment or disgust
He cringed at the awful acting.
Wince: a brief facial expression or a shrinking body movement, caused by pain or embarrassment
The mere idea of eye surgery makes him wince.
Grimace: an ugly or contorted facial expression, that

indicates disgust or pain
She grimaced at the cheesy pickup lines.

Moue: a pouting facial expression used to convey disgust or distaste
The irritated lady had a moue on her face.
*Pronounced as moo
*Plural: moues

Twitch: a quick, sudden and jerking movement, usually involuntary
He got a twitch in the corner of his eye whenever he got angry.

Flinch: to suddenly draw back as an instinctive reaction to surprise or horror
The kid flinched at the sight of incoming football.
*Synonym: **recoil** (The child recoiled at the sight of blood; recoil also means to rebound)

Crouch: to adopt a bodily position in which the knees are bent and the upper body is lowered to avoid detection
The thief crouched in the bushes to avoid the guards.
*Synonyms: to squat, to duck, to hunker

Cower: to crouch down in fear
The children cowered under the tables when the intruders barged into the house.

Convulse: to suffer muscle spasms and body contortions due to a disease
He convulsed due to his epilepsy.
*Noun form: convulsion

Contort: to twist or bend out of shape
The circus had many body contortionists to amaze the audience.
*Noun form: contortion.

Crass: lacking sensitivity
His crass comments on the sexual assault shocked everyone.

Quake: to shiver or tremble in fear
The student was quaking in his boots.
*Synonym: **quiver** (His bottom lip started to quiver in fear), **quaver** (His voice quavered with fear), **quail** (He quailed at the sound of his wife's angry voice), **waver** (His voice wavered when the creditor called)

■

Exigency: urgency; emergency
The government had to act due to the economic exigency.
*Adjective form: exigent (exigent circumstances)

Extirpate: to exterminate; to root out
The new president vowed to extirpate corruption from the government.

Decimate: to kill or destroy a large proportion of
The inhabitants were decimated by the plague.
*Etymology: it means to kill off one in ten

Wreak: to cause harm or inflict punishment
Godzilla wreaked havoc on the town.
*Pronounced as reek
*Homonym: **reek** (reek means to a strong and unpleasant smell; for example, his breath reeked of garlic and onions), **wreck** (wreck means to completely damage or destroy; for example, he wrecked his car), **wrack** (wrack means wreckage; for example, the wrack and ruin that follows war)

Turmoil: a state of great disturbance, utter confusion and immense uncertainty
The country was in turmoil after the military coup.
*Synonyms: **upheaval, turbulence, tumult** (The stock markets were in tumult)

Annihilation: complete destruction
Thanos annihilated many planets.

Obliteration: erasure of existence
*Synonym: **eradication**

Damnation: condemnation to hell for eternal punishment

Perdition: complete and utter ruin
*Synonyms: **doom, ruination**

Carnage: the killing of a large number of people
The bomb explosion caused a lot of carnage.
*Pronounced as car-nij
*Synonyms: slaughter, **massacre** (*pronounced as mas-uh-kur)**, bloodbath**

Cataclysm: a large-scale and violent event
WWII was the biggest cataclysm of our time.

Catastrophe: a disaster
*Synonyms: **calamity, tragedy**

Havoc: widespread destruction
The hurricane caused havoc in the city.

Internecine: destructive to both sides
Both clans suffered heavily due to the internecine feud.
*Pronounced as inter-neeh-sine

Genocide: large scale, organized and targeted killing of a particular community
The World War II genocide of the Jews still shocks the conscience.
*Synonym: **pogrom** (The Nazis started a pogrom against the perpetrated by the German Nazi regime)

Armageddon: a catastrophic event that can destroy the human race
*Etymology: it is the final battle between good and evil in the Bible

■

Conflagration: a massive fire
Nero fiddled while Rome was destroyed by a conflagration
*Synonyms: **blaze, inferno, firestorm**
Incendiary: something that starts a fire; fire-producing; for example, incendiary agents like petrol and kerosene on it
The politician made incendiary speeches to spark a riot.
*Pronounced as insen-dee-uhree
*Synonyms: **combustible, flammable, inflammable**
Arson: the criminal act of setting a property on fire
*Synonym: **incendiarism**
*Related word: arsonist (a person who commits arson)
Pyromania: the compulsion to set things on fire
Immolate: to kill by burning, especially as a sacrifice
The cruel King would immolate convicts.
*Pronounced as im-uh-late
*Noun form: immolation
Detonate: cause to explode
The anarchists detonated two bombs.
Stoke: to add coal or other such solid fuel to a fire, furnace, etc.
The politician was accused of stoking up religious hatred in the province.

■

Inundate: to flood
The island was inundated by the Tsunami.
Deluge: a severe flood
The village was submerged by the deluge.
Torrent: a strong rushing stream of water
He endured a torrent of abuse.
Spate: a sudden flood in a river; outpouring
There was a spate of attacks.
Cascade: a small waterfall
Cataract: a large waterfall
Avalanche: a large mass of snow falling down rapidly from a mountain
Blizzard: a snowstorm
*Synonyms: **snow squall**, white-out
Tempest: a windstorm, typically bringing rain and hail
Whirlwind: a tornado
*Synonyms: **gale storm, typhoon, cyclone**
Whirlpool: a typhoon on the sea with rotating mass of water caused when conflicting currents meet
*Synonyms: **vortex, maelstrom**

Eddy: the circular movement of water during a whirlpool
Flurry: a quick shower of snow
There was a flurry of activity in the office.
Floe: a sheet of floating ice on the surface of the sea
*Pronounced as floh
Draught: a current of cold air blowing through a room, usually causing discomfort
*Pronounced as draft
*Homonym: drought (water shortage)
Drizzle: light rain
Hail: pellets of frozen rain
Sleet: a mixture of rain and snow
Slush: partially melted snow or ice
The streets were covered with slush.
Slurry: a semi-liquid mixture of substances like cement or clay in water
Zephyr: a mild gentle breeze
*Pronounced as zef-ur

■

Epoch: an era
Currently we are living in the Anthropocene epoch
Eon/Aeon: a very long time
He ran his last marathon eon ago.
Yore: of long time ago
The days of yore when there was no internet.
Vintage: the year of the production of something, usually referring to the year of the production of a high quality wine

■

Superficial: not thorough, not deep, existing only at the surface (He did not go to the hospital as the wound was superficial); ignoring the complexities of something (The research paper was rejected because its analysis was very superficial)
*Synonyms: **facile** (The facile explanation did not satisfy the professor; facile also means easily achieved: the college football team won a facile victory over the local high school team), **cosmetic** (The changes in the company were only cosmetic), **cursory** (He gave the articles a cursory glance)
*Antonyms: thorough, detailed
Perfunctory: done hastily, without interest or effort; done superficially
The intern was fired because of his perfunctory research.
*Synonym: **peripherally** (Peripherally means to not go

deep into a matter and stick to its periphery: he was only peripherally involved with the project)

Desultory: aimless; lacking a plan or purpose; lacking enthusiasm

The bored students danced in a desultory fashion in the boring dance class.

*Desultory also means haphazard or random; for example, the students interrupted the professor's flow with a desultory remark.

Lackadaisical: half-hearted and lazy

The café's service was lackadaisical.

Shrift: to give very little attention

The manager gave short shrift to the customer's complaint.

*Etymology: shrift is the brief confession to a priest or the quick absolution given to a condemned prisoner before the execution

Extempore: done without prior thought or planning or preparation or rehearsal

At the debating club audition, the orators were asked to speak extempore. *Synonyms: **offhand** (Offhand means without prior thought or preparation: he got caught because he couldn't think of a believable excuse offhand); **impromptu** (The CEO suddenly announced his resignation in an impromptu press conference), **on the spur of the moment** (On the spur of the moment, he decided to quit his job), **off-the-cuff** (He did not get time to prepare his speech so he just spoke off the cuff; *etymology: this refers to the notes that some speakers used to make on their shirt cuffs to serve as a movement aid)

*Adjective form: extemporaneous (meaning unplanned and unpremeditated) *Antonym: premeditated (the murder was premeditated and not spontaneous)

Spontaneous: occurring as a result of a sudden natural impulse and without any premeditation or external cause

The audience broke into spontaneous applause before he started performing.

Adlib: to speak or perform in public without prior practice or previous preparation of one's words

The street play actor had to adlib because he had forgotten the dialogues.

■

Specious: misleading; superficially believable but deceptive

The judge reprimanded the lawyer for deploying specious arguments.

Sophistry: use of clever arguments with the intention to deceive

The fake sage used sophistry to deceive the followers

*Adjective form: sophistic

*Synonym: **casuistry** (*pronounced as cazh-oo-uh-stree).

Chicanery: trickery; the use of deception to achieve one's goals

The insurance salesperson resorted to chicanery to meet his sales target.

*Synonyms: **guile** (The politician used all his political guile to stay in power), **skulduggery** (He was hired to investigate the firm's skulduggery)

Hoodwink: to cheat or trick or deceive someone

The Enron corporation executives hoodwinked investors of millions of dollars. *Synonyms: **dupe** (He was duped into investing in the company), **swindle** (He was convicted of swindling investors), **cozen** (The financial advisor cozened his clients of millions), **gull** (The insurance agent gulled him into believing that the insurance documents were genuine), **finagle** (The CEO finagled the investors out of a fortune), **fleece** (He was fleecing investors by showing fake profits), **bilk** (The trickster bilked the investors of millions), **deceive** (Deceive means to trick or mislead someone by making a false statement: he deceived the investor by posing as a rich industrialist; *noun form: **deception** [the action of deceiving someone: he obtained the painting through deception], **deceit** [the practice of deceiving someone: the newspaper exposed his deceit])

Allure: to attract or fascinate or charm someone

The firm allured graduates by promising high salaries.

*Synonym: **lure** (The shop lured the customers with heavy discounts)

Beguile: to trick someone by charming them

He was beguiled by her looks.

Connive: to conspire; to plot a crime

Sam connived with Pam

*Synonym: **collude** (He was caught colluding)

*Noun forms: connivance, collusion

Coerce: to convince someone by using force or the threat of force

He was coerced into making a confession.

*Synonym: **dragoon** (The mobster dragooned him into signing the contract)

Entrap: to trap someone; to trick someone into committing a crime, usually this trickery is carried out by the police to secure someone's prosecution

The defendant claimed before the judge that he was entrapped by the police.

*Synonym: **ensnare** (The spider ensnared the fly in its web)

Entice: to convince someone by promising great rewards or pleasure
Advertisements entice customers into buying stuff they don't need.
Seduce: to persuade or induce someone into sexual activity
He was seduced by his secretary.
Inveigle: to trick someone using flattery
He was inveigled into signing the contract.
*Pronounced as invey-guhl
*Synonym: **wheedle** (He wheedled a new laptop out of his father)
Volition: the power to make one's own decision based on free choice
He left the job as per his volition and not out of coercion.
Veritable: something which can be verified, often used to add emphasis to something
The movie was a veritable blockbuster.
*Noun form: **veracity** (truthfulness: everyone doubted the veracity of his statement)
*Antonym: false (*noun form of false: **falsity**, falseness)
Certitude: certainty
The question as to who killed JFK may never be answered with certitude.

■

Contrive: to scheme; to devise; to plot
The candidate contrived a clever plot to get all the votes.
*Noun form: contrivance
Pretence/Pretense: a false display of feelings or intentions
The journalist kept up a pretence of neutrality.
*Pretence also means fake or affected or flaunting behaviour: Mahatma Gandhi spoke without any pretence of being morally superior to others.
Dissemble: conceal one's true feelings or emotions
The spy dissembled his true feelings towards the smugglers so that he could enter their gang.
*Synonym: to **dissimulate** (He did not try to dissimulate his irritation)
Simulate: to pretend to have a particular feeling or emotion
He simulated pleasure at seeing his rival.
*Noun form: simulation
Masquerade: to pretend to be someone else
He was caught masquerading as a rich industrialist.
*Pronounced as mas-kuh-raid
Stilted: writing or talking in an unnatural and awkward manner as if standing on stilts

The rivals made stilted conversation.
*Synonyms: strained, stiff, self-conscious, wooden, unrelaxed
*Antonyms: natural, effortless
Semblance: a false display, an outward appearance which hides the reality
He put on a semblance of guilt when confronted with the crime.
*Synonyms: **guise** (He visited the company in the guise of a police officer), **facade** (Behind his façade of friendliness was a cruel competitor; *etymology: façade is the front of a building that faces on to a street), **veneer** (He hid his corruption under a veneer of respectability), **patina** (He carries the patina of civility to fool everyone), **charade** (The bankrupt family kept up their charades of wealth in front of their rich friends; *pronounced as shu-raid)

■

Knave: a dishonest person
*Pronounced as nayv
*Synonyms: scoundrel, rascal, rogue, **reprobate**, hoodlum, thug, goon, wretch
Charlatan: a fraud person who claims to be possessing some special knowledge or skill
There are many charlatans posing as spiritual gurus.
*Synonyms: cheater, swindler, fraudster, trickster, **quack** (a fraud doctor), **shyster** (a fraud lawyer), **mountebank** (*pronounced as moun-tey-bank), **hoodwinker, hoaxer, dissembler, racketeer, con-man, con-artist, grifter, goldbricker** (*etymology: tricksters would sell fake gold bricks)
Impostor: a person who pretends to be someone else in order to deceive others
*Synonyms: **impersonator, masquerader**
Ignoble: dishonourable
His ignoble actions brought shame on us all.
Mendacious: dishonest; lying; insincere
The mendacious politicians used fake news to garner votes.
*Synonyms: **disingenuous, dissembling**
Machiavellian: cunning, scheming, manipulative, especially in politics
The entire political party was wary of his Machiavellian ways.
*Pronounced as mac-ee-uh-vel-ee-uhn
*Etymology: from the name of the Italian statesman and political strategist Niccolò Machiavelli (1469-1527)

*Synonyms: **crafty, wily, artful, guileful, devious, sly**
Nefarious: evil; wicked
In *Game of Thrones*, Cersei Lannister always had some nefarious plans up her sleeve.
*Synonyms: **insidious, sinister, dastardly, diabolical** (*etymology: in Italian *'diabolo'* means the devil).
Depravity: wickedness
His depravity knew no bounds.
*Synonyms: **turpitude, degeneracy, perverseness, corruption, vice, villainy, immorality, unscrupulousness, underhandedness**
*Adjective forms: depraved, pervert, **degenerate**, corrupt, unscrupulous, underhanded
*Antonyms: **moral, virtuous, righteous, scrupulous, irreproachable,** upright, upstanding, principled, honourable, honest, noble, law-abiding
Duplicity: double-dealing; speaking to two different people in two different ways regarding the same matter
*Etymology: from Latin *'duplicitas'* meaning twofold
*Adjective form: duplicitous
*Synonym **Janus-faced** (*etymology: Janus was the Roman God of beginnings and endings and had two faces as he looked both ways)
Perfidy: disloyalty
King Julius Caesar fell prey to the perfidious plans of Brutus
*Synonyms: **treason, treachery, deceit, unfaithfulness**
*Adjective forms: perfidious, treacherous, treasonous, traitorous, deceitful, disloyal, unfaithful
*Antonyms: loyalty, allegiance, fealty
Pernicious: harmful; the pernicious effect of fire-crackers on lungs
*Synonyms: ruinous, detrimental, **deleterious, inimical, malevolent, malignant, minatory, menacing, baleful**, baneful, antagonistic
Perversion: a shocking distortion from what was originally intended
The perversion of justice was shocking.
*Synonym: **travesty** (travesty of justice)

■

Venal: corrupt; open to bribery
Venal politicians are ruining the world.
Venial: pardonable
Using a swear word when very angry is a venial sin.
Vice: a bad habit; immoral behaviour
The city was a den of vice and crime.

■

Hired gun: a person hired to kill to someone; a professional killer
*Synonyms: **assassin, mercenary, hatchet man** (Hatchet man also means a person who is hired to write defamatory attacks on political opponents)
Bagman: a person who collects the bribe on behalf of another person
Fence: a person who deals in stolen goods
Shill: an accomplice of a trickster, who poses as a genuine customer to entice others to also trust the trickster
*Plural: shills
Patsy: someone on who doesn't commit the crime but is blamed for the crime due to the trickery of the actual criminals
*Synonyms: **scapegoat** (*etymology: this refers to the Biblical practice where a goat is let loose in the wilderness after a Jewish priest symbolically lays the sins of the people on its head), **fall guy, Aunt Sally** (*etymology: Aunt Sally is a game played in Britain where players throw balls at a wooden dummy), **whipping boy**

■

Subterfuge: a trick
*Synonyms: **hoax, artifice, humbug, feint, ruse**
Stratagem: a strategic plan
*Synonyms: **manoeuvre**, tactic, ploy
Smokescreen: a cloud of smoke created to conceal military operation
Camouflage: to hide using your surroundings like a sniper camouflaged among the bushes and the trees
Incognito: disguised
The princess always travelled incognito for safety reasons.
*Synonym: undercover
Decoy: a fake animal used by hunters to attract other animals
Bait: the food (like a worm) which is placed on a fishing hook to lure the fishes
*Homonym: **bate** (to restrain: the audience was unable to bate its enthusiasm and cheered for the concert to begin early)
Snare: a trap used to catch birds and animals, consisting of a wire noose
Flimflam: insincere talk
Critic's and their pseudo-intellectual flimflam.
Muleta: the red cloth used in a bullfight by a matador to attract the bull.

Machination: an evil scheme
*Pronounced as maki-nation
*Synonym: **intrigue**
Gimmick: a trick intended to attract publicity like a marketing ploy
Gambit: it is an opening move in chess where the player sacrifices a pawn to gain an advantage

■

Opprobrium: public shame
He could not handle the opprobrium of being in a family accused of honour killing.
*Synonyms: **ignominy** (the ignominy of being locked up in jail), **humiliation**, disgrace, dishonour, loss of face
*Adjective forms: shameful, opprobrious, ignominious, humiliating
Stigma: a mark of disgrace
The stigma of jail-time still haunts him wherever he goes for a job interview.
Notoriety: the state of being famous of negative things
The movie has gained notoriety because of its songs celebrating underage drinking.
*Synonym: **infamy**
*Adjective form: notorious, infamous
Disrepute: the state of having a low reputation in public
The company's name was in disrepute as it was not paying its workers their monthly wages.

■

Ingenuous: unsuspecting and easily trusting; someone who is easily fooled
It was very ingenuous of him to request a stranger to guard his luggage, while he went to the bathroom.
*Synonyms: **gullible** (The gullible old retired school teacher was duped of his retirement pension by fraudsters), **credulous, artless, dupable, naive** (*pronounced as naa-eve), **naïf** (*pronounced as naa-eef)
*Noun form: ingenuousness, gullibility, credulousness, naivety (*pronounced as naa-eve-uh-tee), naiveté (*pronounced as naa-eve-uh-tay)
*Related word: **ingénue** (a gullible young woman, especially in a film or a play; *pronounced as on-jhuh-noo).
Sceptical: cautious; suspicious; careful; alert
Thor was always chary of Loki's intentions.
*Synonyms: **chary, wary, leery, prudent, heedful, circumspect, vigilant, incredulous**

*Adjective forms: gingerly, warily, charily, discreetly, guardedly, prudently, watchfully, observantly
Balk: to hesitate and be unwilling to accept a proposal
The CEO balked at idea of giving everyone an extra day off.
*Pronounced as bawk
Cynical: believing that people are motivated by self-interest and not to do good for others
*Synonyms: having reservations, taking something with a pinch of salt, doubtful, questioning
*Noun form: cynic (a cynical person)

■

Optimist: someone who always looks at the positive side
Pessimist: someone who always looks at the negative side
Realist: a person who accepts the situation as they are
Idealist: a person who is guided more by ideals rather than real world practical considerations
Pragmatist: a person who is guided more by real world practical considerations rather than by ideals
Naysayer: a person who is always pessimistic, objects to ideas and says that failure is certain
He ignored all the naysayers and critics around him.

■

Condone: to approve or sanction something, usually a morally wrong act
The politician was accused of condoning violence against women.
Countenance: someone's face; to approve
The court made it clear that it would not countenance any contempt of its orders.
*Homonym: **continence** (self-restraint or abstinence)
Visage: a person's facial expression, a person's facial features
There was anger behind his cheerful visage.
*Pronounced as viz-ij
Credence: belief in something as true
The idea of nuclear fusion as a feasible form of clean energy is now gaining credence.
Cogent: convincing
The prosecution provided cogent evidence.
Plausible: superficially believable
It is plausible that a foreign government had a role in the assassination of John F. Kennedy.
Feasible: workable; doable

With the advancement in technology it will soon become feasible to clone human beings.

Incontrovertible: something that cannot be controverted (denied)

There was incontrovertible proof to prove the corruption charges.

*Synonyms: indisputable, incontestable, undeniable, **irrefutable, unassailable, indubitable**, undebatable, unanswerable

■

Berth: a space in a dock for the ship to anchor

*Synonyms: docking site, **anchorage**

*Berth also means a bed in a ship or train.

Moor: to dock a ship to the shore using ropes and anchor

Moorings: the ropes, chains, or anchors used to dock a ship in a moor

Promontory: a rocky cliff jutting into a body of water

Precipice: a very steep cliff

The car fell of the precipice after the driver lost control.

*Synonyms: **escarpment, scarp**

Atoll: a ring-shaped island formed by coral

Archipelago: a group of islands

Moat: a ditch filled with water surrounding a castle and used as a defence against an attack

Culvert: a tunnel carrying a stream of water

*Synonyms: **conduit** (He acted as a conduit carrying the messages from the underground resistance), **arroyo, duct, channel, aqueduct**

Pier: a platform on pillars projecting into the sea from the shore, typically used as a market place and entertainment gallery

Quay: a dockyard for ships; a port

*Synonyms: **wharf, marina, jetty**

Dyke: an embankment (stone wall) built to prevent flooding

*Synonym: **levee** (*pronounced as lev-eee)

■

Skiff: a small boat

*Synonyms: **raft, dinghy**

Yacht: a mid-sized boat used for fun sailing

*Pronounced as yaht

Barge: a large boat

*Synonyms: **vessel, trawler**

Frigate: a warship

*Pronounced as frig-it

*Synonym: **galleon**

Flotilla: a small fleet of ships

Armada: a fleet of warships

Dromond: a large medieval ship used for battle or trade

Pontoon: a flat-bottomed hollow metal cylinder boat used with other such boats to support a temporary bridge made over it

Gondola: the light boat used in the canals of Venice, Italy

Galley: a kitchen in a ship or plane; a printed manuscript

Scull: each of a pair of small oars used by a single rower to propel a boat

■

Capsize: when a boat turns upside down

The boat capsized and many drowned.

*Synonyms: **topple over, flip over, keel over, turn turtle**

Jettison: to throw something overboard from a ship into the sea

Jetsam: items that have been jettisoned from a ship and then washed ashore as debris

Flotsam: the debris found floating on the sea

■

Skipper: the captain of a ship

Yeoman: a petty officer in the navy

*Related word: yeoman service (an excellent and loyal service)

Stevedore: a person who works at the docks, loading and unloading ships

*Pronounced as stee-vi-dor

Coxswain: a person who steers a ship

*Pronounced as cock-sun

■

Mast: a tall pole on a ship on which the sails or flag is attached

Masthead: the highest part of a ship's mast; also means the title of a newspaper which is placed at the head of the first page

Hull: the main body of a ship comprising of the bottom, sides and deck but not the masts

Bilge: the lowest internal part of a ship's hull

*Pronounced as bilj

■

Debris: scattered pieces of rubbish
*Synonyms: **detritus, dross**, litter, scrap, chaff, rubble, wreckage
Dregs: the leftovers of a liquid that are sedimented at the bottom of a glass
Bauble: small worthless thing used for temporary amusement
*Synonyms: **trinket, trifle**, knick-knack, boondoggle, bagatelle, plaything
Odds and ends: miscellaneous items
*Synonyms: **paraphernalia, miscellanea**, bric-a-brac, sundries, bits and bobs
Nugatory: worthless, having no value or importance
His entire contribution to the meetings was one nugatory comment.
*Synonyms: **trifling, trivial**
*Etymology: related to the nougat (candy)
Minutia: minor or trivial details about something
Look at the big picture and ignore the minutiae of the problem.
*Pronounced as minoo-she-aa; also written as minutiae (*pronounced as minoo-she-ay)

■

Stub: the small sized remainder of a pencil, candle, etc.; the returned portion of a ticket; to extinguish a candle, etc.; to accidentally strike something
Stump: the bottom part of a tree which remains projecting from the ground after the main part of the tree (trunk and branches) has been cut
Stalk: the main stem of a plant; also means to stealthily pursue someone
The cat stalked the pigeon and then finally pounced on it.
Stubble: the stalk of the crops that is left projecting out of the ground after the grain from the crops has been harvested
Remnant: the remains of something
The statues are remnants of an era bygone.
*Synonyms: **vestige**, leftovers, residue, residuum

■

Relic: an object surviving from an earlier time
Fax machines are a relic from the pre-Internet era.
Artefact: a handmade object like a clay pot, especially the one's found at an archaeological excavation
Antique: a collector's item
Antiquity: the ancient times

Antiquities: an object from the ancient past
The antiquities museum in Egypt contained the actual tomb of the famous Pharaoh Tutankhamun
Antiquary/Antiquarian: a person who studies or collects antiquities

■

Appurtenance: an item accessory to the main activity
*Synonyms: **appendage, adjunct, incidental**
Accoutrement: equipment
The necessary accoutrements for hiking include first aid box, torchlight, etc.
*Pronounced as uh-koo-ter-ment
*Verb form: to accoutre
*Synonyms: **apparatus, appliance, rig**
Trappings: the outward signs associated with a particular situation
He revelled in the trappings of power such as an armed bodyguard and a driver.
Souvenir: something kept as a reminder of a place, event, etc.
*Pronounced as soo-vuh-neer
*Synonyms: **token memento, keepsake, remembrance**
Plaque: an ornamental tablet or plate made of metal or wood, used as a commemoration of a person or event
*Pronounced as plack
*Plural: plaques
*Synonym: **plaquette** (*pronounced as pluh-ket)
Cartouche: a carved tablet resembling a scroll; also means a cartridge

■

Indurate: to harden
Constant betrayals indurated his heart.
Inure: accustomed
The editors were inured to abuses by online trolls.
Inveterate: ingrained
He is an inveterate drunk who drinks like a fish.
*Synonyms: **incorrigible, entrenched, deep-rooted, dyed-in-the-wool**
Pathological: compulsive and obsessive
He is a pathological liar.

■

Congenital: hereditary, but used negatively
He is a congenital liar.
Innate: inborn; for example, Mozart's innate talents

*Synonyms: **inherent, immanent**
Intrinsic: from within
The intrinsic motivation to do good.
Extrinsic: from outside
Some students require extrinsic motivation to study like extra pocket money.

■

Chronic: long-standing and recurring; for example, a chronic back injury.
Acute: sharp but of short duration
The acute injury healed quickly.
Perennial: annual
The Masters is a perennial golf event held in the US.
Sempiternal: eternal; for example, the sempiternal agony of losing a loved one.
Protract: to prolong
The protracted war started to take its toll.
Perpetuate: to make something go on forever
Increasing the supply of deadly weapons will only perpetuate the war, not stop it.
Incessant: continuing without interruption; non-stop; unending
He was disturbed by the incessant noise from the construction site.
*Synonyms: **ceaseless, unabating, interminable, everlasting,** perpetual, enduring, lasting, persisting, permanent
*Noun form: incessancy, incessantness
Sporadic: off and on; not regular
Regular steps yield bigger results than sporadic Herculean steps.
*Synonyms: **intermittent**, occasional, inconstant, fitful, **spasmodic** (*etymology: in the nature of a spasm), **episodic** (*etymology: in the nature of an episode)
Temporal: relating to time; also means short-lived; also means worldly, as opposed to spiritual
He renounced all his temporal joys to become a monk.
Intertemporal: describing any relationship between past, present and future
It is an intertemporal choice we save today for a rainy day tomorrow.

■

Conceptual: relating to mental concepts
He failed the exam because his conceptual understanding was very weak.

Theoretical: relating to theory
Notional: relating to a notion or an idea

■

Arcane: secretive and not understood by many
The selection process was criticized as being arcane.
Esoteric: difficult to understand
The layman doesn't under esoteric articles.
*Synonyms: **abstruse, recondite** (complex and recondite data), **inscrutable, incomprehensible, unfathomable, indecipherable**
Hazy: unclear
The details of the incident are still hazy.
*Synonyms: **obscure, vague, dim, nebulous**, shadowy, blurry, fuzzy, muzzy, woolly, muddy, cloudy, murky
*Noun forms: haze, blur, dimness, nebula, fuzz, muzz
Abstract: purely theoretical and not having any physical existence
*Synonyms: **amorphous** (shapeless), conceptual, notional, metaphysical, philosophical, academic
Inexplicable: something that cannot be explicated (explained)
The inexplicable overnight appearance of red marks on his face.

■

Enigma: a mystery
Who killed John F. Kennedy will forever be an enigma.
*Adjective form: mysterious, enigmatic, cryptic
Cipher: a secret code
The military communicates in ciphers.
Decipher: to decode a secret coded message
*Synonym: encrypt
Encipher: to convert a plain into coded text
*Synonym: decrypt

■

Irony: a state of affairs that has turned out to be opposite to what one expects and is almost funny as a result
The irony is that after robbing the bank, the bank money was stolen from the robber's house.
Paradox: a seemingly contradictory statement
To blend in and yet stand out of the crowd is a paradoxical advice.
Dichotomy: a division into two mutually exclusive and incompatible parts

The dichotomy between science and obscurantism.

Oxymoron: a self-contradictory phrase
The title of 'Benevolent Dictator' is an oxymoron.
Conundrum: a confusing and difficult question
What is inside a black hole is a conundrum.
Quandary: dilemma, situation where caught between two tough choices
He was caught in a quandary as to which job offer to take.
*Synonyms: in two minds, on the horns of a dilemma, on the fence, torn between
Vacillate: to be indecisive
The seller did not like vacillating buyers who kept changing their minds about what they want.
*Synonyms: to **fluctuate**, to **waver**, to **oscillate**, to **dither**
*Adjective form: **irresolute, wavering**
Noncommittal: not committing oneself
The Nokia CEO was noncommittal and refused to confirm the rumoured release date of the new phone.

∎

Predicament: a problematic situation
The students found themselves in a predicament when they got lost in the forest.
*Synonym: **mare's nest**
Imbroglio: an extremely confused and complicated situation
He wrote an article to explain the entire imbroglio to the general public.
Powder keg: a dangerous or volatile situation
*Etymology: a powder keg is a barrel of gunpowder
Byzantine: extremely complicated
The byzantine civil procedure laws meant even a simple case took years to resolve.
*Pronounced as biz-aan-tine
*Etymology: this relates to the complex architectural style developed by the Byzantine Empire (the Eastern Roman Empire)

∎

Abbreviation: shortened version
The abbreviation of Defence Secretary is Def-Sec.
Acronym: shortened version formed by the initial letters
The acronym of Ministry of Defence is MOD.
Anagram: a word formed by rearranging the letters of another word; for example, 'Neo' from Matrix is an anagram of the 'One'

Annotation: a short explanatory comment
The new edition of the book had many useful annotations.
Notation: a system of graphic symbols used for specialized use writing for example musical notation

∎

Allegory: a story that has a hidden meaning, usually a moral or a political one
The famous allegory *Animal Farm* is written by George Orwell.
Parable: a short instructive story
There are many parables about saving for a rainy day.
Fable: a short instructive story but necessarily using animals
The fable of the rabbit and the tortoise.
Saga: an epic story

∎

Rumour: an unverified story of unknown source
*Synonyms: gossip, hearsay, tittle-tattle
Canard: a rumour intended to defame someone
Canards were spread to malign the character of the rape victim.
Grapevine: the circulation of rumours
He heard it on the grapevine that the company was about to hire a new CEO.
Bandy: to pass on; to toss about; exchange or casually discuss an idea
The media bandied about the wrong figure of coronavirus cases.

∎

Theme: the subject, topic, dominant and recurring idea
Honour is the main theme of any Army book.
*Adjective form: **thematic** (relating to a theme)
Décor: the style of the decoration of a room
Their new house had a Spanish décor.
*Pronounced as dey-kawr
Motif: design
The hotel used the Victorian Era motif in its decoration.
Leitmotif: the dominant and recurring design
The leitmotif of all his paintings was the beauty of nature.
Aesthetic: relating to beauty
His aesthetic taste was very refined.
*Pronounced as es-thet-ik

∎

Blueprint: a design plan
*Etymology: earlier on design prints were composed of white lines on a blue ground.
Playbook: a book containing a sports team's strategies and plays
Pilot project: an activity planned as a test or a trial
The state government decided to run a pilot project to gauge the public's reaction.
*Etymology: earlier, pilot did not mean the driver of an aircraft but meant 'to guide'.
Prototype: the first version of a product
The prototype of the iPhone was only 3 inches tall.
*Synonym: **mock-up**
Archetype: the typical example
Romeo is the archetype of romantic lovers.
*Synonyms: **paradigm, quintessence, template,** model
*Adjective forms: archetypal, quintessential, typical, representative, paradigmatic
Stereotype: an example that is widely held but oversimplified
The racially biased stereotype of the Africans as being savages.
Paragon: the perfect example
Einstein is a paragon of inventive thinking.
*Synonyms: **exemplar, epitome** (He was considered an epitome of honesty; *pronounced as ih-pit-uh-mee)
Personification: the embodiment of an abstract quality
Stephen Hawking is considered to be the personification of intelligence.
*Synonyms: **exemplification, manifestation, incarnation**

■

Apogee: peak; highest point
The movie *Gandhi* was the apogee of the career of the Ben Kingsley, the actor who played Gandhi.
*Synonyms: **summit, zenith, apotheosis, acme, crescendo, pinnacle, vertex**
Nadir: the lowest point
The expulsion from the Parliament on corruption charges was the nadir of his career.
Crest: the highest point in a wave
Trough: the lowest point in a wave

■

Symbolism: the use of symbols in art, literature, etc., to represent ideas

There is a lot of religious symbolism present in Leonardo da Vinci's paintings.
Tokenism: the practice of making small superficial gestures to show commitment to a large cause for gaining public admiration; for example, hiring of a few gay people to show the liberal culture of a company
Betoken: to signify
He wondered if the cold unmoving eyes of his manager betokened anger or boredom.
Typify: symbolize
The Occupy Wall Street movement typified the monetary angst of the new generation.
*Synonym: **emblematize**
Typecast: to assign an actor to the same type of role
The actress was type casted as always playing the doting mother on screen.
Pigeonhole: to forever assign into a particular category
The versatile writer detested being pigeonholed as a romantic author.
*Synonyms: compartmentalize, label, brand, tag
*Etymology: pigeonholes are small holes in a building for domestic pigeons to nest in; these also refer to letter boxes in a workplace or an organization.
Genre: a style or category of art, music or literature
Harry Potter novels fall within the genre of fantasy literature.
*Pronounced as zhahn-ruh
Ilk: type or kind
Him and all the politicians of his ilk are a danger to democracy.
*Etymology: from Old English *'ilca'* meaning alike

■

Metamorphosis: complete transformation
The metamorphosis of Marshall Mathers to Eminem is the stuff of legends.
*Synonyms: **transmutation, transfiguration**
Metanoia: a major spiritual conversion or change in lifestyle after such a spiritual conversion
*Etymology: Greek *'metanoein'* = change one's mind
Permute: to alter by rearrangement
*Noun form: permutation
Transpose: to exchange places
The mere transposing of a few words in the text made a huge difference in its readability.
Transcend: to take to a different level all together
The singer's soulful voice transcended the audience to a new plane.

Transmogrify: to completely transform the appearance into a funny or strange one
His teenage son transmogrified his room into a tropical jungle.

Translation: the conversion of text from one language to another

Transcribe: the conversion of spoken word to text

Transliteration: the conversion of text from one language to another but without giving the literal meaning and used only to help in pronouncing the word. Translation of the Hindi word '*Rashtra*' is nation and the transliteration is 'Rashtra'.

■

Anthology: a collection
The anthology of all the works of William Shakespeare was published on his hundreth birthday.
*Synonyms: **compendium, compilation, conglomeration, agglomeration**
Array: a large display or range of something
The library had a wide array of scholarly papers on the 'Basic Structure' doctrine.
Panoply: a large and impressive collection
The movie star showed the reporters his panoply of film awards.
*Plural: panoplies
Potpourri: a mixture
The band played a potpourri of hit songs.
*Synonyms: **medley, melange, miscellany, assemblage, assortment, amalgam**
Concoction: a mixture of various liquids; also means a false story
Shambles: a state of confusion, disorder and disorganization
The economy was in shambles.
*Adjective form: shambolic
*Synonym: **disarray** (The company was in disarray after the CEO quit)
Scrum: a disorderly crowd of people or things
*Etymology: scrum is an ordered formation of players in Rugby
Hotchpotch: a confused disorganized mixture, a mess
The play was a hotchpotch as the director was novice.
*Synonyms: **welter, mishmash, ragbag, farrago, snafu, topsy-turvy** (upside down).
Helter-skelter: in a hasty and disorganized manner
Everyone was running helter-skelter looking for the lost child.

*Synonym: **pell-mell** (They rushed pell-mell to the hospital)
Smorgasbord: a wide variety of food items served at a buffet
*Etymology: Swedish for *smörgås* (a slice of bread and butter) and bord (table)

■

Stockpile: a large stock of something
In the Cold War, both the US and USSR stockpiled weapons.
Hoard: a secret stock
During the prohibition, people hoarded alcohol.
*Synonyms: **stash, cache** (a cache of weapons; *pronounced as cash)
Trove: a collection of objects; for example, a treasure trove, which is a collection of valuable items.

■

Sundry: various
The salad had radish and sundry other vegetables.
Motley: varied in appearance
The motley crew consisted of people from all walks of life.
*Synonyms: diverse, assorted, **heterogeneous**
Variegated: colourful
The variegated fabric was the perfect choice for the dress.
*Pronounced as vari-ey-gated
*Synonyms: **polychromatic, many-hued, prismatic, kaleidoscopic, fluorescent, opalescent, iridescent**
Vivid: bright and colourful
The court artist painted a vivid portrait.
*Vivid also means producing powerful feelings; for example, the vivid memories of the accident.
Verisimilitude: the appearance of being true or real
The photos in the novel gave it a lot of verisimilitude.
Chequered: having a pattern in which there are alternating squares of different colours; marked by fluctuations of fortune; for example, a chequered career.
Particoloured: having two or more different colours
*Synonym: **pied**
Monochromatic: containing only one colour
Achromatic: without colour

■

Brindle: of yellowish-brown colour with streaks of other colour

He adopted the brindle pup off the street and gave it a loving home.

Dappled: marked with spots or rounded patches of a different colour than the surface

The black horse's sides were dappled with large white patches.

Flecked: marked with dots or small patches

The body of the white rabbit was flecked with grey patches.

Mottled: marked with multi-coloured spots and patches

The mottled body of the parrot made it look very attractive.

Piebald: having patches of black and white; for example, a piebald horse

Skewbald: having patches of brown and white

■

Speckle: small spot or patch, usually on the skin

He had black coloured speckles on his forehead.

*Synonym: **speck**

Freckle: a small patch of light brown colour on the skin, caused by pigment deposition

He had a light sprinkling of freckles on both his cheeks.

Blotch: a large unevenly shaped spot or patch, usually on the skin

His face had red coloured blotches.

*Adjective forms: blotchy, blotched

Splotch: a large spot or stain

The red wine which fell on her dress left a large red splotch.

*Synonyms: **splodge, blot**

Stripe: a long, narrow band of a colour which is different from the whole body, for example a zebra's black stripes

*Synonyms: **streak, striation**

Smudge: a blurred or smeared mark on the surface of something

The crime scene had a smudge of blood on the floor next to the body.

■

Blanch: to make white or pale by removing the colour

His face blanched when he heard the bad news.

*Synonyms: to **bleach**, to **blench**

Pale: light in colour, lacking the usual intensity of colour

His face looked pale because of the fever.

*Synonyms: **pallid** (He had a pallid complexion because of work stress), **pastel, pasty** (*etymology: having

the appearance of paste), **ashen, ashy** (*etymology: resembling ashes), **waxen, waxy** (*etymology: having an appearance like that of wax), **wan** (*pronounced as wawn), muted

*Noun forms: paleness, pallidness, **pallor**, wanness, ashen hue, pastiness

*Antonyms: bright, vivid, flushed, rosy, glowing, ruddy

Sallow: having an unhealthy looking pale yellow colour

His skin was sallow because of the jaundice.

*Synonym: **flaxen** (a flaxen-haired girl)

Stramineous: straw-colored; yellowish

*Etymology: Latin *'strāmen'* = straw

Etiolate: to make a plant pale by excluding light

The mushroom was etiolated as it grew in darkness.

*Pronounced as ee-tio-late

Albino: a person who has the hereditary inability to produce the skin colour pigment melanin and thus has pale skin, white hair and pink eyes.

■

Complexion: the natural skin colour, especially of the face

*Pronounced as kum-plek-shun

Swarthy: dark-skinned

*Synonyms: dusky, tanned

*Antonym: fair

*Pronounced as swawr-thee

Ruddy: having a healthy red colour

The child had a ruddy complexion.

*Synonyms: rosy-cheeked, **roseate** (*etymology: like a rose), **rubicund** (*etymology: from Latin *rubere* meaning 'be red')

*Antonym: pale

Brunette: a woman with dark brown hair

*Pronounced as broo-net

Blonde: a woman with golden yellow hair

Hoary: greyish white

His hair went hoary with age.

■

Epigraph: an inscription; a short quotation in the beginning of a book that gives an idea about the theme of the book

Epitaph: an inscription on a tombstone, in memory of the deceased

Excerpt: a short extract from a book

The newspapers published an excerpt from the book along with its full review by the critic.

Blurb: a short description of a book, written for promotional purposes
The president wrote a blurb for the much respected journalist's autobiography.
Primer: a basic level book used to serve as an introduction to a subject
Prologue: an introduction but which is separate from the main story
Epilogue: an ending chapter but separate from the main story
Foreword: a short introduction to a book, typically by a different person than the author and intending to shower praise on the book
Afterword: a concluding section in a book
*Synonym: **coda** (*plural: codas)
Exordium: the beginning or introductory part, especially that of a treatise, discourse, oration, etc.
Preface: an introduction which sets out the aim and scope of the book
*Adjective form: prefatory
*Synonym: **prolegomenon**
Peroration: the closing remarks of a speech, typically intended to make the audience very excited
Frontispiece: an illustration facing the title page of a book
Prelude: the introductory piece of a musical orchestra
Interlude: the interval in a musical orchestra
Segue: an uninterrupted transition from one piece of music to another or from one scene in a film to another
*Pronounced as seg-way

■

Manuscript: the first draft of a book which is not published
Typescript: text which is typed
Postscript: an additional remark placed at a text's end, as an afterthought
Subscript: numbers written below the line; for example $C_6H_{12}O_6$
Superscript: numbers written above the line; for example y^4

■

Semantics: the branch of linguistics and logic concerned with meaning; the exact meaning and implication of a word or phrase
He quibbled over the semantics of being called an intern or an unpaid volunteer.

Syntax: the arrangement of words to make a well-formed sentence
Pleonasm: the use of more words than are required to convey a meaning, typically done to add emphasis; for example, to see with one's own eyes
Ellipsis: the process of omission of text that is considered extra and is done with a set of three dots
*Plural: ellipses
*Adjective form: **elliptical** (a difficult to understand writing because of the heavy use of ellipsis).
Erratum: an error in printing or writing
*Plural: errata
Solecism: a grammatical mistake in speech or writing; for example, 'we is the experts'
*Pronounced as sol-uh-sizm
*Plural: solecisms
Malapropism: the mistaken use of a word, where the word so incorrectly used is similar in sound to the correct word and this is done usually with an intention to be amusing; for example, when someone tells their leader, 'Lead the way and we will precede'
*Plural: malapropisms

■

Corrigenda: a list of corrections of errors in a written publication
*Singular: corrigendum (pronounced as kaw-ree-jen-dum)
Recension: the revision of a literary work or the revised edition of the text so produced after such revision
*Pronounced as re-sen-shun
Retraction: the withdrawal of a statement earlier made
Retcon: to change past events of a storyline with newly introduced facts
The writers decided to retcon the backstory of Uncle Ben in *Spiderman 3*.

■

Append: to add something to the end of a written document
The author appended a short chapter to the main novel.
*Synonym: annex
*Noun form: appendage (the additional part which has been added)
Addendum: an additional material placed at the end of a book
Synonyms: **annexure, appendix** (*plural: addenda, annexures, appendices)

■

Codicil: an addition to a will
*Pronounced as cod-uh-sil
Charter: a written constitution
Covenant: a written agreement
Accord: a treaty; accord also means to grant someone power or status
Protocol: the official government procedure of dealing with highlight ranking officers and dignitaries
Modality: a particular procedure
The government was working out the modality of the free health to all scheme.
Rigmarole: a lengthy complicated procedure
They did not want the rigmarole of an elaborate wedding.
*Pronounced as rig-muh-roll
Champerty: an illegal agreement in which a third party agrees to finance a lawsuit to order to get a share of the winning sum or the disputed property if the suit succeeds
*Pronounced as shamperty

■

Missive: a letter
*Synonym: **epistle**
Dispatch: an official report; to send something off
The head quarter dispatched a new set of instructions for the agents in the field.
Obituary: a notice of a death, especially in a newspaper

■

Glossary: an alphabetical list of words, relating to a particular subject, with their brief explanation
*Plural: glossaries
Legend: a table on a map which explains the various symbols used
Lexicon: a dictionary
Thesaurus: a book that lists synonyms and antonyms of words
Bibliography: a list of books on a particular topic
*Plural: bibliographies

■

Cliff-hanger: a dramatic ending to a serial's episode, which leaves the audience in suspense and thus eager to watch the next episode
*Etymology: from the 1930s in which serial episodes ended with the characters in perilous situations such as hanging off the edge of a cliff
Spin-off: a by-product of a larger project; a show that develops from the characters from another show
The show Joey was a spin-off of Friends.

■

Chevron: a V-shaped line, worn typically on the uniform of an army officer
Chyron: brief text that is placed on the bottom part of the screen to explain a scene on a TV
Caption: brief text placed below a picture used to explain the picture
Subtitle: text placed on the bottom part of the screen to translate or transcribe what is being said
Rubric: a heading on a document; a category
The paper was filed under the rubric of policy proposals.
Scrip: a share or stock certificate; a receipt
Scroll: a roll of parchment or paper for the purposes of writing on it
Inscription: text which is inscribed (engraved onto a surface)
Docket: a list of cases waiting to be heard before a court
Dossier: a collection of documents
*Pronounced as daw-see-uh
Memorandum: a written message, especially in business or diplomacy

■

Summation: a sum total of things
The summation at the end of the meeting was that the sales department has to get more deals done.
Summary: a brief account of the main point
*Synonyms: **synopsis, precis, digest, gist, conspectus**
*Verb forms: summarization, encapsulation, abridgement, condensation, recapitulation
Crux: central point
*Synonyms: heart, core, **nub, nucleus, kernel, marrow, pith, the bottom line, purport**
Anecdote: a short amusing story about a real life incident
Narrative: a spoken or written account; a representation of a particular situation based on a particular viewpoint
Every party was trying to shape the narrative in their favour.
Discourse: discussion; debate
The discourse around illegal immigrants is very heated at the current moment.
Chronicle: a record of historical events
*Synonym: **annals**

Empirical evidence: information collected through observation and then used as evidence to prove or disprove a theory by the process of experimentation
*Etymology: Greek word *'empeiría'* = experience

■

Inference: a conclusion reached after reasoning
*Synonym: deduction
*Verb forms: to **infer**, to **deduce**
Conjecture: to guess; to draw a conclusion based on incomplete information
Everyone conjectured that it was the maid who stole the diamond.
*Synonyms: to **surmise**, to **speculate**
Punt: to gamble
*Noun form: punter (a gambler)
Reckon: to draw a conclusion of which one is sure of
Based on the traffic and time left, they reckoned that they would miss the movie.
Extrapolate: to draw a conclusion in one situation by assuming that results from another situation will also apply here
The scientists extrapolated the results from the experiments on mice to make medicines for humans.
Paraphrase: to reword a text written by someone else
The students paraphrased sections of the book to avoid plagiarism charges.
Plagiarize: to copy someone's work and pass off as one's own.
Rehash: to reuse old ideas without any significant improvement
The audience was getting tired of stale movies with rehashed scripts.

■

Expatiate: to speak or write in great detail about something
The scientist expatiated about the issue.
*Synonyms: **expound, explicate**
Expostulate: to express strong disagreement or disapproval or complaint
The board of directors expostulated with the CEO's decision.
Propound: to propose an idea or theory for others for consideration by others
When Galileo propounded the heliocentric model, he was decried as a heretic.

*Synonym: to **posit**
*Noun form: proponent
Pontificate: to express one's opinions in a very pompous and dogmatic manner
He pontificated about art as if he was Leonardo da Vinci.
Postulate: to assume something as the basis of a belief or theory
He postulated that the people were social creatures in his theory to explain the network effects of social media.
*Noun form: postulation, **supposition**
Predicate: to base something on
His theory on the spending habits predicated on people being rational actors.
Premise: the base of a theory or action
The scathing judgment on economic crimes was the premise for the government's new law against it.

■

Opine: to give one's opinion
The lawyer opined that he had no case.
Posit: to assert; to put forward
The psychologists posited the patient's frame of mind as destructive.
Descant: to talk at length about something
The TV pundits descanted on his true motives for running for office.
*Synonym: **hold forth** (The economics professor held forth on the causes for the 2008 economic crash)
Sound off: to forcefully express one's opinion
The activist sounded off to the press about the rampant corruption.
Trot out: to bring forward repeatedly, usually for approval or admiration
The party spokesperson trots out the same excuses every time.
Proffer: to bring forward for acceptance; to offer
He proffered another reason for buying a second car.
Perforce: by force; due to necessity
He had to, perforce, travel by train as he could not afford the expensive flight ticket.

■

Counterfactual: expressing facts that are opposite to what happened
Imagine the counterfactual if WWII had not happened.
Hypothetical: expressing facts that are supposed but did not necessarily happen Imagine the hypothetical situation if the US was invaded by China.

■

Homologous: having the same position and structure but different functions; for example, a seal's flipper is homologous with the human arm
*Noun form: homologue
Analogous: having the same function but having a different evolutionary origin, for example the wings of insects are analogous with the wings of a bird
*Noun form: analogue

■

Monologue: a long solo speech given by an actor in a play when this actor is in a conversation with others and then starts this speech
Soliloquy: a long solo speech given by an actor in a play as if there is no one around, to explore his/her deep emotions
*Pronounced as so-lilo-kwee
Oration: a formal speech
Declamation: a prepared speech for an occasion
Elocution: the skill of speaking very clearly both in content and expression
Allocution: a formal speech given to advise or warn
The students were bored of the daily allocutions by the principal about premarital sex.
Recitation: the act of repeating something aloud from memory
Rendition: a dramatic or musical performance: His musical rendition won him many accolades
Valedictory: a farewell speech

■

Reprise: to repeat a past performance
The show Joey was a spin-off of *Friends*, where Matt LeBlanc reprised his role as Joey Tribbiani.
Redux: brought back
With US and Russia fighting again, it was the Cold War redux.
*Pronounced as re-ducks
Encore: a repeat performance at the end of a concert because of audience demand: The audience demanded an encore.
*Pronounced as awn-core
*Etymology: French for 'still, again'
*Synonym: **curtain call**

■

Argot: jargon of a particular class
The argot of the candle maker's guild was inscrutable to others.
*Pronounced as argo
*Synonyms: **patois** (*pronounced as pat-wah), **parlance, dialect, vernacular**
Demotic: relating to the kind of language that is used by ordinary people in everyday conversation
The author used demotic idioms in his storylines.
Colloquial: casual and informal in expression
The audience loved his colloquial style of writing.
*Pronounced as kuh-loh-kwee-uhl
*Synonym: conversational
*Noun form: colloquialism (colloquialism means a colloquial word or phrase)
*Antonyms: literary, formal
Colloquium: an academic conference or seminar
*Pronounced as kuh-loh-kwee-uhm
Euphemism: a word that is used in place of another to softy and mildly express the original word, when the original word is considered as harsh or blunt
Non-performing asset (NPA) is a euphemism for a bank defrauder.
*Pronounced as you-fuh-mizm
*Synonyms: polite term, mild alternative
*Antonym: **dysphemism** (an unpleasant term used instead of a pleasant one; for example, using 'Looney Bin' in place of mental hospital)
Raconteur: an expert storyteller
He was a colourful raconteur.
*Pronounced as rah-kun-tur
*Etymology: French 'raconter' = recount
Rapporteur: a person appointed to compile and present reports to the governing body of an organization
The UN rapporteur filed his report.
*Pronounced as rap-oh-tur
*Etymology: French for reporter
Dialectic: the process of discovering the truth or solving a problem by debating the opposite theories through questions and answers. This dialectic method was originally used by Socrates to teach his students in ancient Greece.
Conflict between ideas and disagreement of views are a necessary part of a dialectic approach.
*Adjective form: dialectical
Anagnorisis: the critical moment in a novel or play where the central character recognizes or discovers a very important truth
Peripeteia: a sudden reversal of fortunes or turn of

events especially in a fictional literary work
*Pronounced as peri-puh-taya
*Plural: peripeteias
Picaresque: relating to a style of fiction writing which tells the adventures of a roguish, dishonest but an appealing hero
The picaresque adventure novel about Che Guevara in the jungles of Cuba
*Pronounced as pik-uh-resk
*Etymology: from Spanish *'Pícaro'* meaning rogue
Ratiocination: the process of logical reasoning
The famous detective Sherlock Holmes is an expert in ratiocination.
Syllogism: the process of coming to a particular conclusion by deduction from two given broad statements; for example, all horses are animals and all animals have four legs, which means that horses have four legs.
Induction: the inference of a general conclusion from specific instances; for example, if only two in a group are criminals then by inductive reasoning everyone in that group is a criminal
*Antonym: **deduction**

■

Pulpit: raised platform in a church where the preacher gives the sermons
Podium: a small platform where a person stands to deliver a speech
*Synonyms: **dais, rostrum**
Pedestal: the base on which a statue, column, etc. is mounted and this base serves as the support for the same
*Synonym: **plinth**
Lectern: a sloping desk where a person keeps their notes and delivers a lecture

■

Disquisition: a long essay discussing a topic in detail
Dissertation: a long essay on a particular subject written for a university degree
*Synonym: **thesis**
Monograph: a very detailed essay on a single specialized subject
Treatise: a very detailed book on a subject
*Pronounced as tree-tis
Tome: a large, heavy, scholarly book
Codex: an ancient manuscript that is bound to form a book rather than loose scrolls or pages

*Plural: codexes or codices
Omnibus: a volume containing several books which were published earlier
Magnum opus: the greatest work of an artist, writer, composer, etc.
'Lose Yourself' is Eminem's magnum opus.
*Etymology: Latin meaning great work
Screed: a long speech or text, usually complicated and tedious to read
The journalist wrote a scathing screed criticizing the mayor.
Breviary: a book containing the daily prayers and hymns that are to be recited in a church
*Pronounced as bree-vee-airy
*Plural: breviaries

■

Novella: a short novel
Graphic novel: a novel in comic-strip format
Manga: a Japanese comic or graphic novel aimed at adults
*Etymology: Japanese 'man' meaning 'rambling, aimless' and 'ga' meaning 'picture'

■

Prose: any written or spoken text
The prose was very brief.
Symphony: a grand musical composition involving the full orchestra
Sonata: a musical composition involving one or two instruments
Concerto: a musical composition for a musical concert
Libretto: the text of an opera
Adagio: a musical composition that is to be played very slowly
Staccato: a passage that is to be performed with short sharp sounds
Maestro: a distinguished conductor of classical music
Aria: a solo song in an opera performance
Rhapsody: a very emotional musical composition
*Adjective form: rhapsodic (very emotional: his singing was very rhapsodic)
Flautist: a flute player
Pianist: a piano player
Percussion: musical instruments played by striking the instrument by one's hands or a stick for example drums, bells, etc.
*Adjective form: percussive

■

Stanza: a group of lines that form part of a poem
*Synonym: **verse**
Chorus: a part of a song which is repeated after each verse
*Synonym: **refrain**
*Pronounced as korus
Choir: an organized group of singers, especially one that sings during church service *Pronounced as kwa-yur
*Synonym: **chorale**
Canto: a small section of a large poem
Couplet: a small poem
Cantata: a musical composition with one singer and multiple musicians
Allegro: a musical composition to be performed at a quick pace
Doggerel: a badly written poem
Madrigal: a musical composition to be performed by several singers without any musical instruments
Acappella: sung without any musical or instrumental accompaniment
*Etymology: Acappella comes from the Italian phrase *alla capella*, which means 'according to the chapel', and chapel here refers to the oldest church traditions of singing without music.

■

Ballerina: a female ballet dancer
Prima donna: the main female singer in an opera; a very egotistical female performer; a drama queen
*Synonyms: **leading lady, diva**
Soprano: a singer who hits very high tones
Protagonist: the central character in a novel, movie, etc.
Antagonist: the villain in a novel, movie, etc.
Thespian: an actor or actress
Minstrel: a medieval poet or singer, who performed for nobility
Troubadour: a French medieval poet who composed and sang mostly on the theme of courtly love and romance
*Pronounced as true-buh-dawr
Amphitheatre: an open air theatre with semi-circular seating

■

Ensemble: a group of performers who perform together
*Pronounced as on-sawm-bul
*Etymology: French in (in) = simul (at the same time)

Orchestra: a group of musicians who perform together
Choreography: the sequence of coordinated steps in a dance
Impresario: a manager or organizer of a musical concert, theatre, play, etc.

■

Amend: to make minor changes to a text
*Synonyms: revise, alter
Emend: make corrections to a text
*Synonyms: rectify, repair, fix
Emote: to portray emotion in a theatrical manner
Indite: to write, compose

■

Foresight: the ability to predict what will be needed in the future
The seasoned traveller had the foresight to keep extra money.
Forewarn: to warn someone well in advance
Foretell: to predict the future
The palm reader foretold of great riches in his future, which he gullibly believed. *Synonyms: to **forecast**, to **prophesize**, to **prognosticate**, to **divine**
*Noun form: prediction, prophecy, prognostication, divination
Forethought: careful planning for the future to avoid problems
The students had the forethought to book the hotel rooms.
*Synonyms: **far-sightedness, precaution, prudence**

■

Hindsight: the understanding of an event but only after it already occurred
With the wisdom of hindsight, he regretted his decision.
Afterthought: a later thought; a reconsideration
It was only as an afterthought that he decided to thank the hosts for the dinner.
Anticipate: to expect something
The police anticipated the crowd to go violent so they brought ample tear gas.
*Synonyms: **foresee, forecast**
Envisage: to form a mental picture about the desired future
The nation's founders envisaged a just and fair country.
*Synonym: **envision**

Intuition: a feeling about something without any conscious reasoning
Sherlock Holmes had an intuition as to who was the killer.
*Synonyms: hunch, sixth sense, feeling in one's bones, sneaking suspicion, funny feeling, gut feeling
*Verb form: to intuit (to know or understand by intuition)
Inkling: a hint
She did not give one inkling about her hurt feelings.
Unbeknownst: unknown; without someone's knowledge
Unbeknownst to the CEO, the Board had already decided to sell the company.
Advisement: careful consideration
The Minister took the petition from the protestors under advisement.

■

Premonition: feeling that something bad is about to happen
Days before she died, the old lady got a got a premonition about her death.
*Synonyms: **presentiment, foreboding**
Prescience: knowledge of an event before it occurs
*Synonym: **foreknowledge**
Prognosis: a doctor's opinion about the likely course of a disease
Presage: to be a sign of something bad which is about to come
The black clouds on the day of the ceremony presaged trouble.
*Synonyms: to **portend**, to **augur**, to **foreshadow**, to **forebode**, to **herald** (The blossoming of flowers heralded the coming of spring), to be an omen of
*Noun forms: sign, indication, portent, augury, omen, writing on the wall, **harbinger** (The dry leaves on the ground are the harbingers of autumn)
*Adjective forms: ominous, portentous, premonitory, prognostic, foreshadowing
Predestine: to be chosen in advance for a particular purpose
His admirers say that God predestined him to do great things in the world.
*Synonyms: **preordain, foreordain, predetermine**
Precursor: a forerunner
The League of Nations was a precursor to the UNO.
*Synonyms: **predecessor, antecedent**

■

Ancestor: a person from whom one has descended
His ancestors have been traced back to Southern Africa.
*Synonyms: **forebear, forefather, progenitor**
*Antonyms: **descendant, successor, scion**
Lineage: ancestry; ancestral background
He could trace his lineage back to the early settlers in America.
*Synonym: **pedigree**
Progeny: children
*Synonym: **offspring**
Genealogy: the study of ancestry
Gerontology: the study of aging
Geriatrics: the study of age related diseases
Senile: showing a decline in physical and mental strength due to old age
*Noun form: senility, **caducity** (*pronounced as kuh-dyu-city)

■

Senectitude: old age
*Etymology: from Latin *'senectus'* meaning old age
Senescent: growing old; aging
*Noun form: senescence
Anile: like a senile old woman
*Pronounced as ay-nile
*Noun form: anility

■

Pharaoh: an ancient Egyptian king
*Pronounced as fey-roh
Regent: the person appointed to rule a kingdom because the real king or queen is too young or incapacitated or absent
Regnant: reigning; ruling
All hailed the regnant queen.
Interregnum: the period between two reigns, where the King gives up the throne and his successor has not yet formally taken up the throne
*Etymology: from Latin, *'inter'* (between) + *'regnum'* (reign)
Heir apparent: the most likely heir to the throne
Coronation: the ceremony of crowning of a King or a Queen
Investiture: the ceremony of investing a person with honours or rank
*Pronounced as invest-ee-chur
Divestiture: the act of divesting; the action of selling off business interests or investments

*Pronounced as divest-ee-chur
Induct: to admit someone into a body or post with a formal ceremony

■

Sibyl: a woman in the ancient times who would give prophecies
Clairvoyant: a person who can see the future
*Pronounced as clair-voy-unt
*Synonyms: **psychic, prophet, seer, soothsayer, oracle, diviner,** fortune teller, crystal ball gazer
*Adjective form: prophetic, **oracular**
Druid: a priest in a pre-Christian era of the ancient celtic region (modern day Ireland) *Synonyms: wizard, **sorcerer**, diviner
Auspex: an augur in ancient Rome, who would interpret omens gleaned from the movement of birds
Magus: a Zoroastrian priest in ancient Persia (modern day Iran)
Messiah: a saviour
*Adjective form: messianic

■

Necromancy: the practice of talking to the dead to predict the future
Legerdemain: sleight of hand used to perform conjuring tricks
Prestidigitation: conjuring tricks performed for entertainment
Conjure: to cause a spirit or something to appear by a magic ritual
Incantation: a magical chant or spell
*Synonym: **invocation**
Alchemy: medieval era chemistry aiming to convert scrap metal to gold
Seance: a meeting in which people try to communicate with the dead through a medium or spiritualist
*Pronounced as sey-ahns

■

Intonation: the rise and fall of one's voice when speaking
*Synonym: **modulation**
Pronunciation: the correct way of saying the spelling of a word
Enunciation: to speak in a manner that is clear and audible to all

Diction: the style of pronunciation of a word
Accent: the distinct way in which people of a certain geography or social class pronounce a language
He speaks with a perfect French accent.
Twang: a distinct manner of pronunciation with a heavy nasal and ringing sound
His heavy twang, made it difficult to understand him.
Cadence: tone
The cadence of the Beyonce's voice is mesmerizing.
*Synonyms: **rhythm, tempo, tenor, timbre** (*pronounced as tam-ber; *homonym: timber [timber means wood; *pronounced as tim-bur])
Chord: a group of three or more musical notes played at the same time

■

Phonetics: the study of speech sounds
Phonemics: the study of the phonemes (the distinct units of sound in a particular language)
*Etymology: from Greek *'phonein'* meaning speak.

■

Philately: the collection and study of postage stamps
Numismatics: the collection and study of coins, paper notes, medals, etc.
Taxidermy: the art of cleaning, preparing and preserving the skins of animals and then stuffing and mounting them to give a lifelike effect

■

Amulet: an ornament to give protection against evil
Auspice: a prediction about the future made from observing the movement of birds
*Etymology: from Latin *'avis'* (bird) + *'specere'* (to look)
Totem: an object or animal believed to have spiritual or magical significance
*Synonyms: **fetish, juju**
Talisman: an object which brings good luck
*Synonym: lucky charm
Rune: a symbol with mysterious or magical significance
*Adjective form: runic (mystical, mysterious, magical; for example, the runic inscriptions on the cave)
Mascot: something that is meant as a token to bring good luck, used especially in sporting events

■

Babble: to talk nonsense

The local politician babbled all the way through his speech

*Synonyms: to blabber, to blather, to maunder, to piffle, to prattle, to prate, to ramble, to waffle, to warble, to twaddle, to drawl, to jibber-jabber, to yammer, to yak (yak also means a large domesticated ox), to yap

*Homonym: **bauble** (small worthless thing)

Rabble: lower class people (used as an insult)

*Synonyms: common folk, common herd, masses, **peasantry, hoi polloi, riff-raff, ragtag and bobtail**

*Antonyms: aristocracy, nobility, gentry

Garble: to mix up

Because of the storm, the messages were coming in all garbled.

*Synonyms: to muddle, to jumble, to scramble

Gibberish: nonsense talk

The infant only spoke gibberish.

*Synonyms: **balderdash, bunkum, hogwash, baloney, drivel, malarkey, gobbledygook, folderol, claptrap** (insincere and empty language aimed at securing claps from the public)

Ado: nonsensical fuss

There was much ado about nothing.

*Ado also means without wasting more time; for example, without further ado, the event began.

■

Multitude: a large number of people

Multitudes that suffered because of the water shortage.

*Synonyms: **bevy, throng, swarm, drove, assemblage**

Horde: a tribe of nomadic warriors

The Dothraki were a barbarian horde.

Phalanx: a group of people standing together very closely

*Plural: phalanxes, phalanges

*Etymology: a phalanx was a military formation from the Greek times, in which soldiers stood together to form a rectangle

Stampede: a sudden rush of panicked people moving together

The fire in the cinema hall caused a stampede.

Congregation: a group of people assembled for religious worship

*Synonyms: **parish, flock**

Troupe: a group of theatrical performers

*Synonym: **ensemble**

*Homonym: **trope** (a metaphor), **troop** (a group of army soldiers)

Legion: a large unit of army men

*Synonyms: **brigade, regiment, battalion, troop, squadron, platoon, contingent, corps, detachment**

Infantry: a troop of soldiers marching on foot

Cavalry: a troop of soldiers who fight on horseback

Cadet: a young trainee in the armed forces

Cohort: a group of people with same characteristics

The first all-female cohort to pass out of the academy.

*Synonym: batch

Chariot: a two-wheeled vehicle which is drawn by horses and was typically used for racing and warfare in ancient times

■

Cabal: a secret group

The cabal of dacoits hid in the ravines.

Coterie: an exclusive group of people

The politician would not listen to anyone but his coterie of friends and advisers.

*Pronounced as koh-tuh-ree

*Synonyms: **inner-circle, clique** (*pronounced as kleek)

Faction: a small group of people (inside a larger group) with a separate agenda of their own

Caucus: a faction inside a political party or legislative body

The caucus of black senators in the Senate decided to protest against systemic racism.

Corps: a group of soldiers

*Pronounced as core

Cadre: a small group of trained and qualified people, especially in a political organization, who can train others or perform a particular task

Syndicate: a group of individuals or organizations, coming together to promote a common interest

■

Surreal: bizarre; unreal; having a hallucinatory or disorienting quality

Every time he smokes marijuana, he enters a surreal world.

*Etymology: French surréalisme = 'sur' (beyond) + 'réalisme' (realism)

Uncanny: strange; mysterious; having a supernatural basis, especially in an unsettling way

He has an uncanny ability of foreseeing bad events.

*Synonym: **eerie** (the eerie midnight howl of the dog; *pronounced as eary)

Preternatural: beyond what is natural
The winter arrived with preternatural speed baffling scientists.
*Etymology: from the Latin phrase *'praeter naturam'* which means 'beyond nature'
Illusion: something you see but which is not actually there
*Synonyms: **mirage, hallucination, fantasy, chimera** (*pronounced as *ki-meera*; *etymology: in Greek mythology a chimera is a fire-breathing monster with a lion's head, a goat's body and a snake's tail)
Delusion: an irrational belief
The patient was suffering from delusions of persecution by the entire world.
Psychedelic: relating to drugs that cause hallucinations
The rockers would ingest psychedelic substances before their concert.
Pipe dream: an unattainable or fanciful plan or hope; a fantastical scheme
A world without borders will forever remain a pipe dream.
*Etymology: the dreams experienced by a person when they would smoke an opium pipe.
Fallacy: a mistaken impression
In *Game of Thrones*, Ned Stark laboured under the fallacy that people were loyal.
*Synonyms: misbelief, misconception, misapprehension
*Adjective form: fallacious

■

Disabuse: to correct someone's wrong impression
The headmaster disabused the pupil of his belief of being above the rules.
Dissuade: discourage
His friends tried to dissuade him from quitting his job.
*Synonym: to **deter**
*Antonym: persuade
Disillusioned: to be disappointed and unhappy after discovering the truth about someone, who one highly admired
He was a disillusioned man after seeing the corrupt side of the leader.
*Synonym: **disenchanted**
Dismay: a feeling of unhappiness and disappointment when things don't go as planned
Much to his dismay, he failed in one subject.
Distrait: distracted because one's mind is preoccupied with a problem

The parents worried as the child seemed distrait.
*Pronounced as dis-tray

■

Lore: a myth; a story based on fantasy
The lore of the Scottish Loch Ness Monster.
*Synonyms: **mythos**, folklore, folk tales, tales, legend
Mores: societal customs and conventions
*Pronounced as mo-reyz
Mythology: the study of myths

■

Poltergeist: a ghost which causes violent disturbances such as throwing around of objects
*Pronounced as polter-gaa-ist
Spectre: a visible ghost which does not have a particular shape
Apparition: a ghostlike image of a person
*Synonyms: **phantom, phantasm, wraith** (*pronounced as ray-th)
Ghoul: an evil spirit which feeds on dead bodies
Gremlin: an evil mythical creature
*Synonyms: **goblin, hobgoblin, gnome,** leprechaun, troll, elf, pixie, kelpie
Sprite: an evil fairy
*Synonym: Imp
Banshee: an evil female spirit which appears before a death in the family
Bogeyman: an imaginary evil being that carries away naughty children
Werewolf: a person who, as per folklore, changes into a wolf whenever there is a full moon
*Synonym: **lycanthrope** (*etymology: from Greek *'lykánthrōpos'* = *'lýkos'* [wolf] + *'ánthrōpos'* [man])
Valkyrie: the handmaiden of the God Odin in Scandinavian (Norse) legend
Mermaid: a mythical half-human and half-fish sea creature
Minotaur: a half-human and half-bull monster in Greek mythology
Cyclops: a one-eyed giant monster in Greek mythology

■

Taboo: a societal prohibition; for example, the taboo in society about premarital sex
Anathema: a socially repugnant practice
Racial discrimination is an anathema in modern society

Boycott: to stop buying something or interacting with someone as a punishment or protest
A new movement started to boycott foreign goods.
Ostracize: to exclude from society
The wilful defaulter was ostracised from the investor community.
*Synonyms: blackball, blacklist, cast out
Pariah: a social outcast
The people of the village treated him like a pariah because of his liberal views.
*Synonym: **persona non grata**
Exile: to expel someone out of their own country as a political punishment
The old President was exiled after the military coup.
*Synonym: **banish**
Excommunication: the official exclusion of someone from the church

■

Emigrate: to move out of one's own native country
Immigrate: to move into a non-native country
He emigrated from Mexico and immigrated into the US, in search of a high paying job.
Migrate: to move from one place to another in the same country
The intense rural migration is putting a strain on the city's resources.
Expatriate: a person who lives outside their native country
Repatriate: a person who has returned back to live in their native country
Diaspora: the group of people living outside their own country
The Indian diaspora in the US is very close knit.
Indigenous: local; the original inhabitants of a land before the arrival of the colonists
*Synonyms: native, **aboriginal**
Denizen: residen; inhabitant
The denizens of the pub loved to drink beer.
Populace: the residents of a particular area
Demographic: a particular section of a population or relating to a particular section
The easy to use phone was popular with the older demographic.
Miscegenation: interbreeding between people of different races

Accede: to agree to someone's wishes (The management acceded to the demands of the striking workers); also means to attain office or title (The prince acceded to the throne and became the king); also means to formally join a group
Bulgaria acceded to the European Union in 2007.
*Pronounced as ak-seed
*Noun form: **accession** (*pronounced as ak-session)
Concur: to be of the same opinion
The judge wrote a concurring opinion along with the main judgment.
*Noun form: **concurrence**
Assent: to approve
The Bill received the presidential assent and became a law.
*Antonym: **dissent**
Approbate: to officially approve
The Secretary wrote a letter approbating the contract.
*Synonym: to **sanction** (sanction also means a penalty; for example, the US imposed sanctions on Iran for violating the trade agreement)
Imprimatur: an official approval
The ambitious health insurance plan for the public got the president's imprimatur.
Ratify: to sign and make a treaty, contract, etc., officially valid
The US has still not ratified the Kyoto protocols on global warming.
Endorse: to publicly declare support
Many local leaders endorsed his candidature for the post of the president.
Accredit: to officially sanction
Only accredited journalists were allowed to enter the briefing room.
Veto: to legally reject a proposal
The committee vetoed the extra expenditure for the construction of a new parking lot.
Dictate: to authoritatively give a command
Stipulate: to give a specific condition, which must be fulfilled

■

Vow: an oath; a pledge; a promise; an attestation
Avow: to openly admit or declare
He avowed his support for the local party leader in the upcoming elections.

*Noun form: **avowal**

Aver: to formally state or declare

He averred that he was innocent and was being framed by his enemies.

*Noun form: averment

*Synonym: to **asseverate** (He asseverated his intentions to run for president)

Deposition: the giving of testimony under oath in court or such sworn testimony so given

The prosecutors relied on the deposition of the expert.

Adumbrate: to outline but not in great detail

The candidate adumbrated his policy proposal of free college for all.

*Synonym: to sketch

Delineate: to outline but in great detail

The Finance Minister delineated the country's new tax plan in his budget speech.

*Pronounced as de-lini-ate

Demarcate: to set the boundaries of something

He demarcated his property with fences.

Delimit: to determine the boundaries of something

The two countries entered into an agreement to delimit the new border.

■

Intercede: to mediate

The Pope tried to intercede between the two warring leaders.

*Synonym: to **interpose**

Intervene: to become a party in a matter though not directly involved

The country objected to the UN intervention into their local issues.

Interloper: an intruder

The court branded him as a meddlesome interloper.

*Synonyms: encroacher, trespasser, infiltrator

Interlocutor: a person who takes part in a dialogue

Meddle: to interfere in others affairs

*Synonyms: to butt in, to pry, to poke

Officious: the quality of being irritatingly aggressive and interfering when offering one's help when no one asked for it

The stranded couple yelled at the officious bystander, who kept offering help.

*Pronounced as offi-shus

Solicitous: concerned and eager to help

He was always very solicitous about his grandmother's health.

*Pronounced as soli-sit-us

■

Busybody: a trouble maker

Scandalmonger: a person who spreads malicious and maligning rumours

Muckraker: a person who looks for dirt on others

Mudslinger: a person who throws defamatory false accusations on others

Tattler: a gossiper

*Synonym: **quidnunc** (*pronounced as kwid-nik)

Tattletale: a child who reveals the secret activities of other children

*Synonyms: **talebearer, telltale**

Eavesdropper: someone who listens into other people's conversation

Voyeur: someone who likes to secretly watch other people's private lives

■

Turncoat: a traitor; a person who commits treason (the act of betraying one's own country)

*Etymology: in earlier times a military traitor would wear his coat inside out to hide the badge of his army

*Synonyms: **Quisling** (*etymology: a Norwegian leader named Vidkun Quisling, collaborated with the Nazis during World War II, betraying his country), **Judas** (*etymology: Judas was one of the Twelve Apostles of Jesus Christ and he betrayed Jesus by revealing his identity to the crowd who had come to crucify him)

Defector: a person who has abandons their camp and joins the enemy

Deserter: a member of the armed forces who runs away from duty

Stool pigeon: a police informer

*Etymology: hunters would fix a fake pigeon to a stool to use as a decoy

*Synonyms: snitch, nark, fink, informant

Fugitive: a person who is running from the legal authorities

Insurgent: a rebel; revolutionary

In Cuba, Fidel Castro led an armed insurgency against the US-installed puppet government.

*Synonyms: **mutineer, agitator, renegade, desperado, outlaw**

*Antonym: loyalist

Insurrection: a violent uprising against a government

*Synonyms: **rebellion, revolt, uprising, mutiny, insurgence, sedition**

Insubordination: the refusal to obey orders from an authority, especially in the military
The Major was court-martialled on insubordination charges.

Guerrilla: a member of a small rebellious group fighting against a larger formal Army: Ho Chi Minh used Guerrilla tactics in the Vietnam War
*Synonyms: underground fighter, irregular soldier, resistance fighter.

Marauder: a raider; looter
In *Game of Thrones*, the Dothraki hordes were known as savage marauders.
*Synonyms: **plunderer, pillager, ravager, reaver, highwayman, buccaneer** (buccaneer also means a pirate), robber, freebooter, bandit, brigand, rustler

Depredation: an act of attacking or plundering
The wheat was stored in the silo to protect it from the depredations of mice and weevils.

■

Instigate: to urge someone to commit a crime
*Synonym: **incite**

Suborn: to induce a witness to give false testimony and commit perjury

Actuate: to motivate
The crooks were actuated by greed.

Foment: to incite violence against an authority
He was hanged for fomenting the mutiny.
*Synonyms: **ferment**, spark off, trigger off

Rabble-rouser: someone who stirs up emotions and prejudices of the public, typically for political reasons
The rabble-rouser caused a riot by whipping up hysteria in the locals.

Soapbox orator: someone who makes unwanted and uninvited public speeches
*Etymology: such people would use large soap boxes to stand on and deliver their speeches

Demagogue: a political leader who wants to get votes by appealing to people's fears and prejudices rather than talking about development
*Pronounced as dem-uh-gawg

Demigod: an inferior God as he or she is the child of a God and a mortal; also refers to a person who is a man who is greatly admired or respected

Demimonde: a person of questionable reputation
*Pronounced as demi-mond

*Etymology: literally meaning 'half-world' in French. Demimonde were a class of women in nineteenth century France who had low social standing because of their sexual promiscuity.

Firebrand: a person with radical or revolutionary thinking
As he was a political firebrand, no party wanted to associate with him.

Agent provocateur: a secret agent hired to provoke a person to commit a crime and thus ruin their reputation
*Pronounced as agent: pruh-vok-uh-tur
*Etymology: French for 'inciting agent'

■

Infidel: a person who doesn't believe in a particular religion
The self-declared aim of the terrorist groups is to wipe out infidels everywhere.
*Synonyms: **heathen, idolater** (a person who worships idols and regarded by as infidel as many religions ban idol worship), **pagan** (*etymology: Latin *'paganus'* meaning civilian that is not enrolled in the army of Jesus Christ)

Apostate: someone who renounces their religion
*Noun form: apostasy

Atheist: someone who doesn't believe in God

Agnostic: someone who has not taken any position on God and wants proof for either God's existence or non-existence

Pantheist: someone who worships many Gods

Proselyte: a new convert to a religion

Evangelist: a person seeks to convert others to Christianity by preaching the word of God
*Synonyms: **missionary, gospeller, proselytizer**

Apostle: a strong advocate of a cause or belief
Friedrich Hayek is the most famous apostle of the free-market economics.
*Etymology: in the Bible, the apostles were the 12 original disciples of Jesus Christ

Disciple: an ardent follower
Plato was a disciple of Socrates.

Lobby: to seek to influence a legislator on a particular issue
The fossil fuel lobby scuttles all attempts at solving climate change.

Clout: influence, especially in politics or business
The veteran politician had a lot of clout in the government.

Espouse: to adopt and support a cause or belief

He espoused the cause of free and good quality health care for all.
*Antonyms: reject, oppose

■

Mortician: a funeral director
*Synonym: **undertaker**
Pall-bearer: the assistant to the funeral director
Embalmer: someone who preserves human bodies by treating them with chemicals to stop decomposition
Pall: a cloth, usually made of velvet, used for spreading over a coffin; also means a dark cloud of smoke or dust.
*Pronounced as pawl
Hearse: a vehicle used for conveying the dead person to the place of burial

■

Inter: to bury
The martyred soldier was interred with the military honours.
*Synonyms: to **entomb**, to **inhume**
*Antonym: disinter
Exhume: to dig out something buried in the ground like a corpse
*Synonyms: to **disinter**, to **unearth**
*Antonym: inhume
Inurn: to place in an urn, like someone's ashes after cremation
*Etymology: an urn is a vase used for storing the ashes of a cremated person
Cremation: the burning of a dead body to its ashes as a funeral rite
Sepulture: burial
*Pronounced as sep-uhl-cher
*Etymology: Latin *'sepelīre'* = to bury)
*Synonyms: interment, entombment, inhumation

■

Tomb: an underground burial chamber
*Synonyms: **crypt, mausoleum, catacomb, sepulcher** (*pronounced as sep-uhl-ker), **undercroft, ossuary**
Tumulus-an ancient burial mound
*Synonym: **barrow**
*Pronounced as tumuli
Shrine: a holy place with an association to a revered person
Tabernacle: a place of worship for Christians

Vault: an underground storage room
*Synonym: **cellar**
Casket: a coffin
Sarcophagus: a stone coffin

■

Anarchist: someone who wants to spread anarchy (lawlessness)
Nihilist: someone who believes in nihilism, the philosophy that all social and religious order should be rejected
*Etymology: Latin *'Nihil'* = nothing

■

Filial: related to son or daughter
Thor had filial respect for Odin.
Familial: relating to family
Conjugal: relating to marriage
*Synonyms: marital, **matrimonial, nuptial, connubial**

■

Communion: sharing of thoughts and emotions
He went to the woods to have a communion with Mother Nature.
Catharsis: the process of releasing pent up emotions
The crying provided much needed catharsis for his anguish.
*Pronounced as kuh-thar-sis
Dote: to excessively adore or bestow fondness
He doted on his son.
Platonic: close in relations but not sexual
They never got married as they had a purely platonic relationship.
Infatuation: a short-lived but intense and passionate attraction for someone
He developed an infatuation with his classmate.
*Synonym: **smitten** (He was smitten with the new girl in the class)
Paramour: a lover, especially the illicit partner of a married person
Spouse: a person's husband or wife
Bachelor: an unmarried man
Play Cupid: to attempt to set two people up together in a romantic relationship
*Etymology: this refers to Cupid, the Roman God of love
Unrequited: unreturned

He was agonising over his unrequited love.
Jilted: rejected
The jilted lover kept bothering her with endless calls.

■

Elope: to run away in order to get married
He eloped with his girlfriend when her father said no to their union.
Betroth: to formally engage someone to be married
Affiance: a pledge to marry
*Pronounced as uh-fy-uns
Banns: a notice announcing an intended marriage, read out on three successive Sundays in a church to give opportunity for objections
Trousseau: the clothes, linen, etc., collected by a bride for her marriage
*Pronounced as troo-soh
*Etymology: in French *'trousse'* means bundle

■

Virago: a domineering and bad-tempered woman
*Synonyms: **termagant** (*pronounced as tur-muh-gunt), **shrew, vixen** (vixen also means a female fox), **harridan, gorgon**
Hag: a witch
Crone: an ugly old woman
Ogress: a female ogre
Henpeck: to bully or intimidate one's husband or boyfriend
Cuckold: the derogatory term for a husband of a sexually cheating wife
Uxorious: having excessive fondness for one's wife and being overly submissive to her
*Etymology: In Latin *'uxor'* means wife
Trophy wife: a derogatory term used for a young and attractive wife used as a status symbol for an older and unattractive but very wealthy husband
Gold-digger: a woman who marries a man for his money and not love
Jezebel: an immoral, shameless and wicked woman

■

Convoke: to call together or summon a meeting or an assembly
The president convoked an emergency meeting of the cabinet
*Synonym: **convene**

*Antonym: disperse
Conclave: a private meeting
Quorum: the minimum number of members required to be present for a meeting to be legally valid
*Pronounced as kwo-rum
Parley: a meeting between opposing parties to negotiate a settlement
Powwow: a meeting to discuss something important
Palaver: to discuss at length something which is completely unimportant
Hobnob: to socially mix with people of high status
Schmooze: to chat idly and gossip

■

Comrade: a friend; a colleague; a fellow member of an organization
Camaraderie: friendship; comradeship
Compatriot: a fellow citizen, a fellow countryman or woman
Confidante: a close friend
*Synonyms: **companion, crony, bosom friend, kemosabe** (*pronounced as chemo-saa-be; *etymology: kemosabe is from the Native American dialect)
Confrère: a fellow member of a profession; an office colleague
The CEO discussed the proposal with his with confreres.
*Pronounced as con-frair
Consort: the spouse of a reigning monarch; also means to associate or socialize with someone
He was hanged for consorting with the enemy.
Consigliere: a trusted advisor in a Mafia organization
*Pronounced as kawn-sil-ee-ary
*Etymology: Italian for member of the council
Wingman: a close friend who helps and protect
*Etymology: in Air Force, a wingman is a pilot who supports and protects the lead pilot
Kinship: blood relationship
The brothers were bound by kinship.
Rapport: close relationship
The student developed a good rapport with his thesis advisor.
*Pronounced as ra-pawr
Sibling: a brother or sister
Brethren: a body of brothers referred to as collectively
Fraternity: brotherhood
Sorority: sisterhood; a society for female students in a university or college; *Pronounced as so-rawr-ity
Fealty: allegiance; loyalty

Loki had no fealty towards his brother Thor.

Propinquity: closeness

Geographical propinquity should not be the only reason for choosing a college.

*Synonyms: **proximity**, nearness

Consanguinity: relationship by descent from the same ancestor

Consanguinity is a ground for annulment of marriage.

Patriarchy: a system of society where the eldest male is the supreme authority in the family and women are arguably considered to be powerless.

*Related word: patriarch (the male head)

*Antonym: **matriarchy**

■

Impiety: lack of piety or reverence or respect

The grandchildren's impiety shocked the devout grandfather.

*Synonyms: **irreverence, godlessness**

*Adjective form: **impious**

*Antonyms: reverence, piety, faith

Blasphemy: obscene talk or actions against God

Defacing an idol in a temple is blasphemy and punishable in many countries.

*Synonyms: **sacrilege, profanity**

*Adjective forms: blasphemous, sacrilegious, profane

■

Heretic: someone who holds belief that are contrary to the established religious order

Nicolaus Copernicus was branded a heretic for saying that the earth revolves around the sun.

*Synonyms: **iconoclast, nonconformist, unorthodox, heterodox thinker**

*Antonyms: orthodox, conformist, believer

*Noun form: **heresy** (Copernican theory was branded as heresy)

Bohemian: a socially unconventional person who is involved in the arts

*Synonyms: beatnik, hippy, avant-gardist, free spirit

Idiosyncratic: someone with unconventional behaviour that some would label as weird

His idiosyncratic behaviour got him the label of 'weirdo' in office.

*Synonyms: bizarre, odd, quirky, **zany, eccentric, outlandish,** unconventional, uncommon, irregular

*Antonyms: ordinary, conventional

*Noun form: idiosyncrasy, peculiarity, quirk, eccentricity, oddity, **foible**

Maverick: a very unconventional and independent minded person

Bernard Sanders is considered as the most maverick senator in the US.

■

Subversive: seeking to overthrow an established system or institution

In China, Mao Zedong had thousands executed for publishing subversive material against his government.

*Synonyms: disruptive, troublemaking, insurgent, insurrectionary

*Verb forms: to subvert, to disrupt

Supplant: to put something in place of what is already there

The domestic products were supplanted by the cheap Chinese imports.

Supplicant: an applicant who requests a higher authority for some relief

In *Game of Thrones*, Queen Daenerys Targaryen heard the supplicants at her Pyramid Court.

*Etymology: Latin *'supplicantem'* = to plead humbly

■

Implore: to request someone

The student implored the teacher for a deadline extension.

*Synonyms: to **beseech**, to **supplicate**

Importune: to bother someone repeatedly with requests

The child importuned his parents to buy him the latest toy.

*Adjective form: importunate (annoyingly persistent: the parents were fed up with the importunate demands from the children for toys)

Entreaty: an earnest request

The teacher declined his entreaty for an extension.

*Synonym: **adjuration** (His adjuration for parole was denied)

Solicit: to ask someone for something

The junior associate solicited advice from his senior colleague.

Canvass: to ask for votes

During election time, the politicians go about canvassing in their area.

*Homonym: **canvas** (a coarse cloth used as a surface for oil painting)

Coax: to persuade someone gently yet persistently

Cajole: to persuade someone with flattery and praises

Prod: to poke someone with a pointed object like a stick or a finger so as to get them to move or do something

Nudge: to gently encourage someone to do something

Exhort: to strongly encourage or urge

The Constitution exhorts us to be model citizens.

*Synonyms: to call on, to enjoin

*Adjective forms: exhorting; encouraging, **hortatory** (a hortatory speech to the students to work hard)

Goad: to annoy someone into action

The wife goaded the husband into cleaning the store room.

*Synonyms: to nag someone (The mother nagged her daughter to get married), to get on someone's back

Galvanize: to energize into action

The crowd was galvanized by the inspiring speech.

*Synonyms: jolt into action, impel forward, stir, spur

Tantalize: to tease or torment someone with the promise of something that is usually unobtainable

The brochure had tantalizing images of the beach.

Arouse: to excite; to awaken; to evoke a feeling or emotion

His strange behaviour aroused the guard's suspicions.

*Synonym: **rouse** (The crowd was roused by his powerful speech)

Heady: having an exhilarating or exciting effect

In the heady days of his youth, he thought that nothing was impossible.

Embolden: to make someone feel bold

The racist speech of the politician emboldened the mob.

*Synonym: hearten

*Antonym: dishearten

Behove: to be necessary for someone to do something due to moral, ethical or legal reasons

It behoves the legislators to pass urgent laws when the situation in the country demands it.

*Synonyms: to be obligatory for, to be **incumbent** on (It is incumbent on the court to hear both the sides before passing a judgment)

*Behove also means to befit; for example, it does not behove a civilized society like ours to not punish animal cruelty.

■

Itinerant: a person who travels from place to place

He joined a group of itinerant traders who sold spices along the silk route.

*Pronounced as i-tinuh-runt

*Synonyms: **peripatetic, wayfaring,** travelling, roaming

Vagrant: a homeless person who makes living by behind for money

*Synonyms: drifter, vagabond, beachcomber

■

Tact: the skill of dealing sensitively with difficult situations and people

He possessed excellent social tact and thus got the job of Chief PR officer.

Discreet: careful in handling something to avoid embarrassment or maintain secrecy

The whistle-blower Edward Snowden very discreetly gathered evidence of the snooping by the US government.

Discrete: separate; distinct

The puzzle has six discrete parts.

*Synonyms: **disparate, disjunct, disjoined,** detached, unattached, disconnected

Discreet: careful in one's actions or speech so as to not reveal any confidential information or saying something offensive

The CEO was very discreet and did not give out any extra information.

*Antonym: indiscreet

Discretion: the quality of being discreet (The CEO exercised a tremendous discretion and did not reveal anything); the freedom to decide as per one's own judgment (It was the sole discretion of the player to play for any team)

*Antonym: **indiscretion** (the quality of not being discrete)

Discretionary: available to someone to use as per their choice and without having to take permission from anyone

The officer was given a lot of discretionary powers.

■

Visceral: coming from instinct or the gut rather than intellect or the brain

The bigot had a visceral reaction to their inter-faith marriage.

*Etymology: relating to the viscera (organs in the abdomen like the stomach)

Dispassionate: impartial and reasoned; not influenced by passion

The judge dispassionately evaluated the evidence.

Biased: being in favour of someone and not completely fair

*Synonyms: prejudiced, predisposed, partial, **tendentious** (The Facebook page of the tendentious blogger had millions of views daily; *pronounced as ten-den-shius; *etymology: showing a definite tendency or bias)

■

Reactionary: opposing progressive reforms
Some politicians still have reactionary attitudes toward female empowerment.

Orthodox: strictly conforming to the traditional beliefs
The Christian orthodoxy in US strongly decries abortion.

*Synonyms: **conservative, stodgy, doctrinal**, conformist, conventional, traditional, observant, devout, fogey

*Antonyms: unconventional, unorthodox, **heterodox**, nonconformist

Doctrinaire: seeking to impose a doctrine in all circumstances even if not practically feasible
The doctrinaire politicians wanted a tax cut even if it meant a record deficit.

*Synonyms: **dogmatic**, unyielding, rigid, inflexible

*Antonyms: liberal, flexible, open-minded

Insular: unaccepting of any views outside one's own belief
He was not liked because of his insular attitude.

*Synonyms: **blinkered, parochial, provincial, bigoted, entrenched**, dogmatic, petty-minded, close-minded, illiberal, intolerant

*Antonyms: broad-minded, tolerant

Partisan: an ardent and intolerant supporter of a cause
His partisan supporters blocked the traffic to demand his release from jail.

*Synonyms: **zealot, devout, adherent, fanatic, votary**

Rabid: irrationally extreme in belief or support of something
He made incendiary speeches to rile up his rabid base.

*Synonyms: **fanatical**, overzealous, extremist, maniacal, fervent

*Etymology: affected with rabies

Fetish: an excessive and irrational devotion to something
The fetish among young graduates over the size of the salary cheque.

Sectarian: concerning a sect; rigidly following the doctrines of one's own sect

In civilized democracies, sectarian violence has no place.

*Synonyms: **factional, cliquish** (*pronounced as cleekish), **clannish**

Xenophobic: hater of foreigners
Many foreign Chinese students are subjected to racial slurs by xenophobes.

*Synonyms: racist, ethnocentrist

Fissiparous: causing fissures
We must not let the fissiparous forces win.

*Etymology: from Latin *'fissus'* which means to split

Divisive: dividing; tending to cause disagreement and hatred among people Immigration is a highly divisive issue.

*Synonym: **schismatic** (causing schisms)

*Antonym: unifying

■

Revert: to return to a previous state
Two days after the scolding, the child reverted to his naughty self.

*Noun form: **reversion**

Recidivism: the tendency of a convicted criminal to again commit a crime

Relapse: the deterioration in a person's health after a temporary improvement

Regress: to move in a direction opposite to progress
The government introduced many regressive policies.

*Synonyms: **retrogress, retrograde**

*Antonym: progress

*Etymology: in Latin *'Retro'* means back

■

Syncretism: the mixture of different cultures and religions
We live in a syncretic society and must equally respect everyone.

Pluralism: a system where people of different faiths, sects, etc. peacefully coexist in society

Cosmopolitanism: an ideology which says that all human beings belong to one large community and not divided on different lines

■

Pontifical: acting arrogantly as if superior to others
Everyone was tired of him, acting all pontifical, after he came back from graduation from Oxford.

*Etymology: relating to the Pontiff (Pope) in the Roman Catholic Church.
*Pronounced as as pon-tif-i-kuhl
*Synonyms: cocksure, cocky, self-important, proud, condescending, patronizing, smug, brash, vain, **vainglorious** (He liked to vaingloriously boast about his wealth), **haughty, conceited, snobbish, stuck-up, pompous, egotistical, supercilious** (*pronounced as super-silly-us), **scornful, contemptuous, disdainful, overweening**, overbearing, high-handed, full of oneself, **bumptious**
*Antonyms: humble, plain, simple, ordinary, modest, unassuming
*Noun forms: pontificality, arrogance, **hubris** (*pronounced as hyu-bris), haughtiness, **hauteur** (*pronounced as hoh-tur), **vanity**, conceit, contempt, scorn, snobbery, pomposity, superciliousness, disdain, condescension;
*Antonyms of the noun form: humility, humbleness, modesty
Narcissist: someone who has excessive admiration of oneself
*Pronounced as nar-suh-sist
Egoist: a very self-centred person; an arrogant and conceited person
*Antonym: altruist
*Synonyms: **egotist, egocentric, egomaniacal**
Hypocritical: having double standards
He was hypocritical as he would scold non-veg food eaters but himself gorge on hamburgers.
Sanctimonious: act morally superior to others
The media questioned the politician caught in the sex scandal about his sanctimonious speeches on morality.
*Synonyms: **sententious, self-righteous,**
holier-than-thou
Puritanical: having a very strict moral attitude especially about matters related to sex The puritanical mother as shocked to hear stories about premarital sex.
*Synonyms: **prudish, Victorian, strait-laced**, prim and proper, niminy-piminy, prissy, mimsy

■

Peremptory: dictatorial and arrogant; bossy
The team was tired of him acting peremptory and dictating orders to everyone but not doing any work himself.
*Synonyms: **imperious, high-handed, autocratic, dictatorial, despotic, domineering, overweening,**

overbearing, (in law) not open to appeal or challenge, final (The judgment of the Supreme Court is peremptory)
Pretension: a claim to be something that one is not, in order to impress others
His friends were tired off his literary pretensions after he attended summer school in Cambridge on Classic English Literature.
*Synonyms: airs, posing, posturing, affectation, **pretence** (Mahatma Gandhi spoke without any pretence of being morally superior to others)
*Adjective form: **pretentious** (Pretentious means pretending to be smart and clever; for example, most moviegoers do not read the reviews of pretentious film critics), **affected** (He put on an affected English accent upon his return from Cambridge)
*Verb form: pretend, **purport** (He purported to be a wine critic to impress his date. Purport also means the essence of a document or speech; for example, no one understood the purport of his monologue).
Ostentation: the conspicuous and pretentious show of wealth with the aim of showing off
The ugly design of the businessman's house reeked of ostentation.
*Synonym: **flamboyance**
*Adjective form: ostentatious, flamboyant
*Antonym: modesty
*Verb form: to **flaunt**, to parade
Putative: generally considered or reputed to be
He was considered as the putative leader of the team, even though someone else held the title of captain.
*Synonyms: assumed, evident, prima facie, reputed, seeming
Pretext: an excuse
The doctor used the pretext of medical emergency when asked about not sterilizing the surgical scalpel before the operation.
*Synonyms: ostensible reason, supposed grounds
Alibi: a defence where one says that they were elsewhere when the crime took place
Poseur: a person who pretends and behaves affectedly to impress others; *Pronounced as poser

■

Bluster: to speak in a loudly and arrogantly to intimidate or bully someone;
*Etymology: bluster means the loud roar of the wind
Braggadocio: a boasting person
*Pronounced as brag-uh-doshio

*Adjective form: braggadocian
*Synonyms: **braggart, boaster, Gascon**
Gasconade: to talk boastfully and extravagantly
He gasconaded to his friends about his latest foreign trip.
*Pronounced as gas-cun-ade
Loudmouth: a person who talks too much and brag a lot
*Synonyms: **windbag, blow-hard**
Blabbermouth: a person who talks a lot and gives out more information than he or she should
Motor-mouth: a person who just doesn't stop talking
Vaunt: to excessively praise and boast about something
The indigenous people liked to vaunt the achievements and glories of their civilization.

■

Fudge: to manipulate figures and data
The scientists were accused of fudging the data.
*Synonyms: to distort, to doctor (The video was doctored)
Falsify: to alter a document and thus make it false in order to deceive
He falsified his income records to evade tax.
*Noun form: falsification
Fabrication: a false story
His fabrication of being unwell was exposed when his boss caught him in a café.
*Etymology: fabricate means to manufacture
*Synonyms: **concoction, piece of fiction, fib, contrivance**
Forgery: making a copy of something, usually a work of art, signature or currency note
*Etymology: forge means to make a metal object like a sword by heating the metal and then beating it into shape with a hammer
Counterfeit: a copy of something fraudulently made to pass off as an original
There were many counterfeit iPhones floating around.
*Synonyms: **knock-off**, fake, lookalike, dummy, bogus, sham, **spurious** (Many villagers died by consuming spurious medicines), **phony**/phoney (The crook sold him a phony Rolex watch)
*Antonyms: authentic, genuine
Contraband: smuggled goods
*Synonym: **bootleg** (*etymology: smugglers used to hide bottles of illegal liquor in their boots)
Replica: a duplicate of an original artwork produced under the permission of the original creator
Facsimile: an exact copy, especially of written material

*Pronounced as fac-simi-lee
*Synonym: **clone**

■

Dope: to take or administer performance enhancing drugs
Lance Armstrong admitted to doping and was stripped of his Tour de France titles.
Debase: to degrade; to devalue; to cheapen
Critics say that cheap movies debase the true value of cinema.
Vitiate: to tarnish; to blacken; to blemish
The corruption scams vitiated the investment climate.
*Synonyms: **mar, deface, defile, despoil**
Contaminate: to make something impure
*Synonym: to **taint**
*Antonyms: to purify, to purge, to cleanse
Adulterate: to reduce something in quality by adding another substance
The grain was adulterated by adding gravel and other such tiny stones.
Alloy: to debase or reduce in value by intermixing another substance of inferior quality
His enthusiasm was alloyed by the bad news that came.
Tamper: to make unauthorized alterations
The security locks of the bank were tampered by an insider to allow in the thieves.
Sabotage: the destruction or obstruction of something for military advantage and usually done by insiders
The tanks sabotaged by the local engineer who had been paid off by the foreign power.

■

Self-effacing: a modest person, someone who effaces (erases) him/herself so as to not attract attention towards oneself
Despite being a three-time president, he was known for his self-effacing demeanour.
Self-deprecating: to be modest by making jokes on oneself
His self-deprecating humour made his junior associates relaxed in his company.
Self-abasing: self-punishment in order to atone for sins
*Synonyms: **self-abnegating, self-sacrificing**
Self-flagellation: to criticize oneself extremely harshly
*Etymology: self-flagellation is the act of whipping oneself as part of a religious ritual to do penance for sins committed

Self-loathing: hatred of oneself
After being very rude to his parents, he experienced an episode of prolonged self-loathing.
Self-pity: excessive pity for oneself
He kept wallowing in self-pity but refused to take any action to remedy the situation.
Self-styled: to use a title or description that one has given themselves
The self-styled Godman took advantage of the devotee.
Self-immolation: the action of setting oneself on fire, usually to protest
The protest was accompanied by a few cases of self-immolation.

■

Brusque: short and abrupt
The partner was always brusque in talking to the juniors.
*Pronounced as brusk
*Synonyms: **curt, terse, gruff,** rude
Blunt: straightforward and to the point
He said a blunt no to the request.
*Synonyms: undiplomatic, plain-spoken, forthright, point-blank
Succinct: short and brief
In competitive exams it is best answer in simple and succinct sentences.
*Pronounced as suk-sinkt
*Synonyms: **laconic** (*pronounced as luh-konic), **pithy, concise,** compact, condensed, crisp, to the point, short and sweet, synoptic
*Antonyms: **verbose** (a verbose speech), **prolix** (a prolix account of the meeting), lengthy, long-winded

■

Verbiage: verbose piece of writing
*Pronounced as vur-bee-ij
Padding: unnecessary writing added to increase the length of a text
Convoluted: Having many curves and turns
The movie was panned by the critics because of its convoluted and inscrutable story line.
*Synonyms: **tortuous, sinuous, serpentine, labyrinthine** (maze-like)**, meandering, undulating, gnarled** (gnarl means a knot on a tree; *pronounced as nahrl)**, knotty** (full of knots)**, intertwined** (twisted together), winding, windy, curving, curling, coiling, **circuitous, roundabout, tortuous,** tangled, twisted, snaking, zigzagging

*Antonyms: simple, straightforward
Cursive: writing in which the characters are joined
After learning to spell, the school children started to practice cursive writing.
Discursive: unfocussed writing which randomly moves from one topic to the next
Digress: to deviate from the main point
The moderator brought the debaters back on point after they digressed.
*Noun form: digression
*Synonyms: **diverge,** depart, drift, stray, ramble, wander
Straggle: to wander about in a scattered fashion
The tourists straggled around the monument.
*Homonym: **straddle** (to sit on something with one leg on each side of that object; for example, the actor was seen straddled on a horse posing for the cameras)

■

Loquacious: talkative; outgoing
The loquacious child was good company during the long and boring plane journey.
*Pronounced as loh-kway-shus
*Synonyms: **garrulous** (*pronounced as gar-uh-lus), **voluble,** chatty, extroverted *Antonyms: shy, **taciturn, reticent,** reserved, introverted
Tight-lipped: staying quiet so not to disclose anything
The officials remained tight-lipped about the cause of the accident.
*Synonyms: close-mouthed, unresponsive, to keep mum, unforthcoming, cagey
Mealy-mouthed: not straightforward
The student gave mealy-mouthed excuses for coming late to the class.

■

Lucid: expressed very clearly; easy to understand
The author wrote a lucid account of his time in the army.
*Synonyms: intelligible, comprehensible, **pellucid,** crystal clear
*Antonyms: unclear, muddled
Coherent: able to speak clearly and logically
Despite the head injury, he was still coherent.
*Antonym: incoherent
*Synonyms: reasoned, rational, sound
Eloquent: fluent
Dr Martin Luther King Jr gave very eloquent and moving speeches.
*Synonyms: **expressive, articulate**

*Antonym: inarticulate

Grandiloquent: pompous in style or language
The grandiloquent speeches of Hitler got the masses excited for whatever draconian policy measures he would come up with.
*Synonyms: **bombastic, magniloquent**

Oratory: the art of formal public speaking, especially in an eloquent manner
The prime minister is well known for his powerful oratory.
*Adjective form: oratorical
*Related word: orator (public speaker)

Rhetoric: language, whether spoken or written, designed to have a very persuasive impact but insincere in nature and lacking any meaningful substance
The public got swayed by the politician's rhetoric and voted him to power.
*Pronounced as ret-er-ick
*Adjective form: rhetorical
*Related word: rhetorician (an expert in the art of rhetoric)

Hyperbole: an exaggerated statement which is not meant to be taken literally
The product was marketed with hyperboles like it will make you lose your mind. *Pronounced as hyper-buhlee
*Plural: hyperboles
*Synonyms: overstatement, overplaying
*Antonym: understatement

Puffery: exaggerated praise, especially when done in advertising
Marketers use a lot of puffery to boost their sales.
*Plural: pufferies

Perorate: to speak at length
He perorated against the government policy.
*Perorate also means to bring a speech to a close with a formal conclusion.

■

Avant-garde: pioneering
He was known as an avant-garde music composer, who always produced innovative soundtracks;
*Pronounced as uh-vahnt-gahr
*Synonyms: revolutionary, innovative, inventive, trendsetting, trailblazing, spearheading, groundbreaking, pathbreaking
*Etymology: from French 'avant' (before) and 'garde' (guard)

Vanguard: a group of pioneering people: He was a proud member of the vanguard in the modern music industry
*Etymology: vanguard is the front line of soldiers in an advancing army

Forefront: the front line; the most important place
The chronic floods brought the issue of global warming to the forefront.

Cutting edge: the latest and the most advanced stage in the development of a field The researcher worked on the cutting edge of artificial intelligence.

Seminal: strongly influencing later developments
Newton's seminal work on gravitation laid the foundation for modern physics.
*Etymology: seminal means related to semen.

Germinal: providing material for future development
The show had several germinal characters that later got their own spin-offs.
Germinal also means in the earliest stage of development.
*Etymology: Latin 'germen' = sprout, bud

Pave: to cover a ground with flat stones, bricks, tiles, etc., to make it firm and level for walking
The Newton's pioneering work paved the way for modern scientific research.
*Noun form: pavement (a path so formed by paving)

■

Perimeter: the boundary of an area or object; also means the length of such a boundary
He installed a security fence along the perimeter of the garden.
*Synonyms: **border, bounds, confines** (The students were told not to leave the confines of the school)

Periphery: the outer limits or edge of an area or object
Small townships started to develop on the periphery of the main city.
*Pronounced as peri-fery
*Adjective form: peripheral
*Synonym: **fringe** (No one except the activists cared about the marginalized who live on the fringes of the society)

Contour: the outline that represents the shape or boundary of something
The portrait artist studied the contours of his face.

Verge: edge
He was on the verge of getting fired because of his latest mistake.
*Synonyms: **margin, brink, rim, borderline**

Frontier: a border that separates two countries
International human trafficking knows no frontiers.

*Frontier also means the limit of understanding, knowledge or achievement in a particular field.

Extremity: the furthest or extreme point of something
The forest lies on the northern extremity of the state.
*Extremity also means the hands and feet or fingers and toes; for example, he started experiencing numbness in his extremities.

Terminus: the final point of something; the ending point in space or time
*Plural: terminuses
*Synonyms: last stop, the end of the line, final station
*Adjective form: terminal (He was in the terminal stage of the disease)

Outskirts: the outer parts of a city
He lived on the outskirts of the city.

Outpost: a small military camp that is located at a distance away from the main camp of the army to guard against a surprise attack
*Plural: outposts

Purlieu: the area surrounding another place
The tourists loved the beautiful purlieus of Paris.
*Pronounced as pur-lyu
*Plural: purlieus

Suburb: a small residential district lying just outside a city
*Plural: suburbs

Cusp: the dividing line between two very different things, where the transition between these two very different things or states happens
There was a special lecture for all the teenagers on the cusp of adulthood.

Horizon: the limit of a person's knowledge
He wanted to travel the world to expand his horizons.
*Etymology: the line at which the surface of the earth of the sky seems to meet

Purview: the scope or sphere of influence
The purview of the tax legislation was only limited to domestic transactions and not international ones.
*Synonyms: **ambit, jurisdiction**

Remit: the work or area of activity officially assigned to be dealt with by an individual or organization
Remit also means to send money to someone.

Parameter: a measurable factor which defines the condition of something
As per the latest blood report all his parameters like blood sugar level were normal.
*Synonym: **metric** (The company diligently monitored its sales metrics like monthly sales and daily inbound queries)

Parameter also means the boundary within which a work must be done; for example, the newspaper routinely crossed the parameters within which the media should work.

■

Realm: domain; kingdom
In *Game of Thrones*, Jon Snow wanted to the guard the realm of men from the White Walkers.
*Pronounced as relm

Turf: someone's personal territory
The drug dealers did not like any outsider selling on their turf.
*Synonyms: domain, province, preserve

Ambience: the atmosphere of a place
The café had a nice ambience.

Bailiwick: a person's sphere of authority or area of interest
The CEO considered product design as his own bailiwick.
*Etymology: bailiwick is the district or jurisdiction of a bailie or bailiff

Ken: the range of one's knowledge or understanding
You are dealing with matters way outside your ken.

Precinct: an area with clear and set boundaries; a city district
*Pronounced as pre-sinkt

Occident: the countries of the West, especially Europe and America
*Pronounced as oksi-dent

Orient: the countries of the East, especially countries in East Asia like China

Clime: a place with a particular climate
After the long winter, everyone wanted to visit the sunnier climes of California.

Environs: surroundings
Everyone loved the pristine environs of California.

Biome: an area with a particular climate and floor and fauna that can survive in that climate only
The tropical rainforests are a complex biome.

Habitat: the natural environment of a plant, animal, etc.
Monkeys live in a forested habitat and cannot survive in a desert.

Milieu: a person's social and cultural surroundings
He came from a very rich milieu.
*Pronounced as mil-yoo
*Plural: milieus

Locale: a place or locality associated with a particular event or circumstances

The locale for the Batman movies is the crime-ridden Gotham City.
*Pronounced as lo-kal
Expanse: a wide and uninterrupted area of something
Birds should fly freely in the vast expanse of the sky.
*Synonyms: **tract, swath** (The British colonized large swaths of land. Swath also means a broad strip)
Vicinity: the area surrounding a particular place
There are several hotels in the immediate vicinity of the airport.

■

Vista: a pleasing view
The tourists loved the sea facing vistas.
Spectacle: an event meant for visual impact
The fight between judges was an awful spectacle.
Panorama: an unbroken view of the entire area
The Tower offers a panoramic view of the city.
Bird's eye view: an overview of a situation
Topography: landscape
*Synonym: **terrain**
Scenery: great looking landscape
Paragliding offered tourists a close look of the mountain scenery.
Picturesque: visually attractive
The picturesque landscape of California brings tourists from all over the world.
*Synonym: scenic

■

Diorama: an exhibit with three-dimensional figures arranged to depict a scene
The museum has some amazing dioramas.
Montage: a short video of various clips joined together
The tribute ceremony showcased a montage of the actor's best performances; *Pronounced as mon-tazh
Vignette: a brief moving account or sketch
The artists produced a touching vignette of life as a refugee.
*Pronounced as vin-yet
Tableau: a group of models representing a scene
*Pronounced as tab-loh

■

Portrait: the painting of a person, usually focussing on the person's head and shoulders
Portraiture: the art of making portraits

Mural: a painting made directly on a wall
There is a famous mural of Nelson Mandela in Johannesburg, South Africa.
Mosaic: a picture made with coloured pieces of glass, stone, etc.
Frieze: a horizontal decorative band, painted or sculpted from stone, placed at the top of a wall near the ceiling
*Pronounced as freez
*Plural: friezes
Al fresco: in the open air
We enjoyed the al fresco lunch on the café balcony.
*Etymology: Italian for 'in the fresh'
Chandelier: a large decorative light, suspended from the ceiling with many branches with bulbs or candles on it
*Pronounced as shan-duh-lee-uhr
Tapestry: a thick piece of cloth with intricate designs and patterns used to hand on a wall for decoration
Tassel: a group of short threads held together at one end, used as a hanging decoration on curtains, furniture, etc.
Graffiti: writing and drawings scribbled illegally on a public wall

■

Embellish: to decorate something
The room was embellished with paintings from the famous artists
*Synonyms: **adorn, dress up**
Embroider: to decorate a cloth by sewing patterns on it
Garnish: to decorate or embellish food, usually with a small quantity of other food items
He garnished the soup with chopped coriander.
Spangle: to decorate a cloth by adding metal pieces
The Star-Spangled Banner is the national anthem of the United States.
Weave: to form a length of something by twisting together various threads
The students weaved a fanciful story to explain their coming late to class.
*Synonyms: to braid, to interlace, to **entwine** (twine means thread)

■

Continuum: a spectrum; a continuous sequence in which the adjacent elements have only a slight difference but the elements at the opposite ends are direct opposites; for example: he could not place himself on the conservative-liberal continuum.

*Pronounced as contin-you-uhm
*Plural: continua
Matrix: the complex environment or point from which something develops or originates
The fertile floodplain of the Indus River was the matrix for the Indus civilization.
*Matrix also means a mould
*Plural: matrices or matrixes
Lattice: a grid like structure, consisting of wood or metal strips joined together in a diagonal pattern with square empty spaces in the middle and used as a fence or screen or support for creeping plants
*Pronounced as lat-is
*Plural: lattices
*Synonym: **trellis, treillage** (*pronounced as tray-lij)
Reticulation: a netlike pattern, a pattern consisting of lines interlacing each other like a net
*Adjective form: reticulated
*Related word: reticulum (a netlike structure or a fine network; *plural: reticula)
Filigree: delicate jewellery made from twisted and interlaced gold or silver wires
*Pronounced as fili-gree
*Plural: filigrees

■

Scrawl: to hurriedly write something
The boss scrawled his signature on the proposal just before boarding the flight.
*Synonym: scribble
Stipple: to draw or paint by making numerous small dots
His stippling skills made him famous in the art world.
*Pronounced as stip-ul
Doodle: to draw something absent-mindedly

■

Ecclesiastical: related to the Church
The Pope is the head of all the ecclesiastical affairs in the Vatican.
*Synonyms: priestly, ministerial, clerical, prelatic, canonical, parsonical
Ecumenical: relating to a group of Churches of all denominations
The ecumenical committee had members from all denominations.
Sacerdotal: relating to priests
Immanent: pervasive as in God being present everywhere and in everything
God is immanent in every object of the universe.
Cardinal: a high-ranking person in the Roman Catholic Church; cardinal also means of the greatest importance
The cardinal rule in personal finance is to live below one's means.
*Synonyms: **paramount, fundamental, elemental**

■

Holy Trinity: the Godhead formed by the unity of Father, Son and Holy Spirit as per Christian doctrine
Eucharist: the ceremony which commemorates the Last Supper of Jesus Christ in which bread and wine are consecrated and consumed
*Synonyms: **Holy Communion, Lord's Supper, Mass**
*Pronounced as you-ka-rist
Epiphany: a sudden and important realization
When the apple fell on Newton's head, he got an epiphany that led to theory of gravity.
*Etymology: in Christianity, the epiphany refers to a realization that Jesus Christ is the Son of God and is celebrated as a Christian festival on 6 January
Christen: to give a baby a Christian name at baptism
Catechism: a book which contains the main teachings of Christianity in the form of questions and answers, used in religious education with the teacher asking the questions and the students giving the answers in unison
Baptism: a Christian religious ceremony where a person is immersed in water or holy water is sprinkled on their forehead. This symbolizes purification and admission to the Christian Church; this is usually done with newborn babies and is followed by 'Christening', which involves giving the baby a Christian name.
*Verb form: to **baptize**
Yuletide: the Christmas season
*Pronounced as yuul-tide
Purgatory: as per the Roman Catholic Christianity, this is a place where the souls of the repentant sinners are sent after death for punishment and after undergoing such punishment, the souls are purified and then go to heaven
*Pronounced as purg-uh-tawry
Limbo: a place outside heaven and hell, where some souls (like unbaptised infants) reside
*Etymology: from Latin 'limbus' meaning edge
*Limbo also means an uncertain or transitional state situation; for example, they kept his visa application in limbo for months before finally rejecting it.

Nirvana: a state in Buddhism where there is no desire, suffering or sense of self and one is freed from the cycles of rebirth and death; the attainment of this stage is the final goal in Buddhism
*Etymology: from Sanskrit *'nirva'* (extinguished) = *'nis'* (out) + *'va'* (blow)

■

Adjutant: a military officer who is an assistant to a senior officer
Envoy: a diplomat
*Pronounced as on-voy
Underling: a person who is subordinate to a more senior person
Understudy: a person in theatre who learns another actor's role in order to be a backup in case the main actor is unavailable due to sickness, etc.

■

Proctor: a disciplinary officer or invigilator at a university
Provost: the head of a university
Preceptor: a teacher
Docent: a university teacher; a guide in a museum, art gallery, etc
Lector: a lecturer in a university; a preacher in a church
*Plural: lectors
Emeritus: retired from active service but allowed to retain the title of one's office as sign of an honour, especially when retired from a university teaching position
He became professor emeritus of law when he retired.
*Related word: **emerita** (a female emeritus)

■

Clergy: the body of all people in the Christian Church
Laity: the body of lay people; the body of people who are not clergy
Cleric: a religious leader, especially a Christian or Muslim one
Rabbi: a Jewish priest
Prelate: a member of the Clergy
*Synonyms: **parson, chaplain, rector, vicar, bishop**
Pastor: a preacher
Pontiff: the Pope
Chaplain: a member of the clergy attached to a private chapel

Archbishop: a very high-ranking bishop
Archangel: a very high-ranking angel
*Pronounced as ark-angel
*Synonym: **seraph** (*pronounced as ser-uf)
Coadjutor: a mid-level bishop who assists a more senior Bishop
Deacon: a member of clergy ranking below a priest
Acolyte: a person assisting a priest in a religious service
Synod: a council of top members of a clergy
Diocese: the jurisdiction of a bishop
Pronounced as dahy-uh-seez
Archdiocese: the diocese of an archbishop
Cathedral: the principal church of a diocese
Basilica: a large Roman medieval building, typically used as a church
Pew: a long bench with a back, placed in rows for churchgoers to sit
Homily: a lecture given for teaching morals
Homiletic: the art of preaching
Sermon: a religious talk; based on a passage from the Bible, usually given during a church service
Daven: to pray, to recite religious prayers, especially used in Judaism
Miracle: an extraordinary event that is considered as a work of God
Nightmare: a frightening dream

■

Semite: a Jewish person
Good Samaritan: a helpful person
*Etymology: in one of the parables told by Jesus, a Samaritan (resident of Samaria) came to help a dying Jew on the roadside and that was especially compassionate because Jews and Samaritans were generally considered as enemies

■

Abbey: a monastery where monks or nuns live
*Pronounced as ab-ee
Abbot: a man who heads an abbey of monks
Abbess: a woman who heads an abbey of nuns
Seminary: a training institute for priests and nuns
Conservatory: a training institute for musicians
Monastery: the religious house where monks live
Nunnery: a convent; community of nuns living together
Friary: community of friars (monks) living together
Yeshiva: a training institute for Rabbis (Jewish priests)
Synagogue: a Jewish temple

Chapel: a small church or a separate room in a church used for worship.
Cemetery: a burial ground
Crematorium: place where bodies are cremated
Cloister: a covered walkway in a monastery
Capitol: a building which houses the legislature

■

Crèche: a day care centre for babies and kids
*Pronounced as kresh
Dormitory: a college hostel

■

Sanctuary: a safe place; a nature reserve
*Synonym: **haven**
Hermitage: the house of a hermit (a recluse person)
Abode: a place of residence
*Synonym: **dwelling**
Observatory: a place with a telescope for observing the planets and stars

■

Sanatorium: a nursing home for the sick
Solarium: a glass-enclosed room where one can sit and soak in the sun rays for tanning or to recover from illness
Infirmary: a hospital
Commissary: a food store in a military base, prison, etc.
Apothecary: a medicine shop
*Synonym: pharmacy
Hospice: a nursing home for the terminally ill
*Pronounced as hos-pis
Asylum: a mental hospital; political refuge granted to an alien person

■

Sacrosanct: sacred: The freedom of speech in a democracy is sacrosanct
*Synonyms: holy, pious, **hallowed** (The hallowed pitch of Lord's Cricket Ground in London), **consecrated, sanctified, blessed**
Sanctum sanctorum: the most sacred of all places
No one except the head priest was allowed to go into the sanctum sanctorum.
Sacrament: a religious ceremony in Christianity
*Synonyms: rite, ritual, **liturgy** (*pronounced as lit-er-jee; *plural: liturgies)

Scripture: holy text
Obsequy: a funeral rite or ritual
*Pronounced as ob-si-kwee
*Plural: obsequies
*Synonym: **exequy** (*pronounced as ek-si-kwee)
Gospel: the teachings of Jesus Christ
Carol: a religious folk song
*Synonyms: **hymn, canticle, chorale**
Psalm: a holy song in Christianity
*Pronounced as saam
Rosary: a type of a prayer in which the name of God is repeated many times, a string of beads used for counting during these prayers
Litany: a long Christian prayer
Litany also refers to a long list of unpleasant things; for example, the company received a litany of complaints from angry customers
Doxology: a hymn or liturgical expression to praise God
Plaint: an official complaint against someone in the court of law
*Adjective form: plaintive (complaining, sad)
Grievance: an official complaint
Jeremiad: a list of woes
No one paid attention to the jeremiads of street preacher.
*Etymology: this refers to 'Lamentations of Jeremiah' in the Bible

■

Consecrate: to declare something as holy
The old building was consecrated by the Vatican and made into a Church.
*Synonyms: to **sanctify**, to **bless**, to **hallow**
Desecrate: to deface a religious thing
The temple was desecrated by hooligans who smeared the walls with spray paint.
Venerate: to revere
The Star of David is venerated by the Jews.
Ordain: to appoint someone to a high post in the clergy
He was ordained Bishop.
*Synonym: to **anoint** (He was anointed as a Vicar)
Defrock: to strip a clergy member off their ecclesiastical status
Canonize: to officially declare a dead person to be a saint
Mother Teresa was canonized in 2016 by Pope Francis.
Beatify: the preliminary step in canonizing someone
Mother Teresa was beatified in 2003 by Pope John Paul II.

*Pronounced as bee-at-uh-fy

Beatitude: a title given to top dignitaries in a Clergy (His Beatitude, Your Beatitude)

*Etymology: from Latin *'beatus'* meaning blessed

Benediction: a blessing

*Synonym: **benison**

Malediction: a curse

*Synonyms: **anathema, execration, imprecation**

Oblation: an offering made to God during worship

■

Pedantic: excessively concerned with minor details during teaching

The students disliked the pedantic teacher who cut full marks on small errors.

Didactic: to teach others about morals while acting superior

Gandhi made sure not to come across as preachy or didactic.

Pedagogue: a strict or pedantic teacher

*Pronounced as peda-gawg

Pedagogy: the method and practice of teaching

The students liked the relaxed and open pedagogy of young teacher.

*Pronounced as peda-go-jee

Anagogy: a spiritual interpretation, especially of scriptures like the Bible

*Pronounced as ana-go-jee

*Plural: anagogies.

*Also written as anagoge

Martinet: a strict disciplinarian

The hostel was run by a martinet person who gave heavy punishment for minor things.

*Synonym: **drill sergeant**

Matron: a senior female nurse; a woman in-charge of a boarding school

Stickler: a person who unyieldingly insists on something

The judge was a stickler for procedure.

Taskmaster: a tough boss who makes the employee do a lot of hard work

Highbrow: an erudite person who acts all superior to others

The politician was criticised for being highbrow when he called the middle class as 'Cattle Class'.

*Synonyms: **pedant, snob**

Patrician: an aristocrat or nobleman

*Synonym: **grandee**

Plebeian: belonging to the lower class

He faced a lot of discrimination because of his plebeian background.

*Pronounced as pli-bee-uhn

*Synonyms: **proletarian, baseborn, subaltern**

Bourgeois: belonging to the middle class

*Pronounced as bor-zhwah

Rarefied: elite

The rarefied atmosphere of the Golf Club.

Crème de la crème: the top of the field

The crème de la crème of Russian Ballet dancers performed at the musical event.

Literati: a group of scholarly people who are interested in literature; a group of intellectuals

*Related word: **literatus** (a member of the literati)

■

Gentility: the aristocracy; a feeling of social superiority

Genteel: refined and polished

He had a very genteel upbringing.

Gentry: the people of good social standing; the class of people just below nobility

*Synonyms: high society, the **haut monde** (French for high world; *pronounced as oh mond), the county set

Gentile: not Jewish

The gentile escaped the Nazi persecution.

■

Secede: to formally withdraw from membership, especially from the membership of a federal union

The Southern States seceded from the United States of America.

*Pronounced as si-seed

*Synonym: break away from

*Noun form: secession (*pronounced as si-session)

Segregate: to separate; to isolate

The Civil Rights Act of 1964, was brought in the US to end racial segregation

*Synonyms: to **seclude** (The hermit lived a secluded life), to **sequester** (The jury was sequestered)

Solitude: the state of being alone

He liked to get up early in the morning to enjoy a few hours of uninterrupted solitude.

Polarize: to divide a group into opposite camps

The election rhetoric aimed to polarize society on the basis of religion.

Quarantine: the separation of an infected person from others to prevent the spread of the disease

Cordon: the separation of a place by a line consisting of policemen
The crime scene was cordoned off from the general public.
Subsume: to absorb a smaller entity within yourself
In US, when the Pentagon was formed, it subsumed many smaller military departments.
*Synonyms: to **assimilate**, to **co-opt**
Nexus: a connection
The report exposed the criminal nexus.
Enclave: a small area (inside a large territory) whose residents are culturally distinct from the large territory
The Chinese enclave inside San Francisco is called Chinatown.
Ensconce: to settle in a safe and comfortable place
The child was ensconced in his mother's arm.
*Pronounced as en-skons
Enshrine: to put something in a shrine, with the aim of preserving it forever Democratic values are enshrined in our Constitution.
Entail: to involve something as a necessary part or consequence
The heavy repairs of the house will entail a considerable amount of spending.

■

Simmer: to cook just below boiling point
Their disagreement with each other simmered for months and eventually boiled over at the party.
Smoulder: to burn slowly with smoke but no flame
There was a smouldering pile of garbage at the corner of the road.
Scald: to cause burn injuries
Chengiz Khan used to kill his traitors by pouring scalding hot oil on them.
Scathe: to harm
Peter Quill was heavily scathed in the spaceship crash.
Sear/Sere: dry and withered
The oppressive heat seared the vineyards.
*Synonym: **parch**
*Homonym: **seer** (a sage)
*Homonym of parch is **perch**, which means the high nest of a bird
Shrivel: to wrinkle and contract due to lack of moisture
Scorch: to burn something
The ship's exterior was scorched by the heat.
Singe: to burn but only superficially
The blast singed his eyebrows.

Char: to burn partially so as to blacken the surface
The charred remains of the dead body were found at the site of the arson attack.

■

Sweltering: hot and humid
The students detested the open-air assemblies in the sweltering July heat.
*Synonyms: steamy, sticky, **sultry, muggy, stuffy, torrid**
*Homonym: **welter** (a mess)
Dank: cold and humid
There was a dehumidifier in the dank wine cellar to prevent the wine from spoiling.
*Synonyms: **damp, musty, clammy**

■

Gelid: icy; frozen
They went skating on the gelid pond.
*Pronounced as jelid
*Synonym: **hyperborean** (*etymology: from Greek *'Huperboreos'* = *'huper'* [beyond] + *'boreas'* [north wind])
Sledge: a vehicle, mounted on runners (kind of skis) or having a flat smooth bottom surface, pulled by draught animals and used for conveying loads or passengers over snow
*Synonyms: **sled, sleigh** (*pronounced as slay), **toboggan, bobsled, bobsleigh, coaster, luge** (*pronounced as loozh)
Rink: an enclosed area of ice used for skating, ice hockey, etc.

■

Stygian: unlit; very dark
The exploiters went inside the stygian cave.
*Synonyms: pitch-black, pitch-dark, **dusky, dim**, shadowy
Murky: questionable; shady
He had a murky past.
*Synonyms: **dubious, louche** (*pronounced as loosh)
Turbid: muddy
The turbid river suffered from severe pollution.
Limpid: completely clear and transparent
The limpid water of the Bahamas attracted a lot of tourists.
*Antonyms: **opaque**, muddy, turbid

Translucent: semi-transparent
He wore a translucent shirt that showed his large belly.
Flimsy: very light and thin; feathery
The flimsy walls did not provide any privacy.
*Synonyms: **gossamer-like** (The gossamer-like curtains were practically see-through; *etymology: gossamer is the filmy substance spiders excrete to weave their webs), **diaphanous** (She wore a diaphanous gold dress to the dinner), **gauzy** (She wore a gauzy top to the party; *etymology: light and thin like a gauze), sheer (She wore sheer nightgown)
*Antonyms: thick, opaque

■

Morbid: gruesome
King Joffrey had a morbid fascination of torturing his enemies
*Synonyms: **grisly, ghastly, gory, ghoulish, grotesque** (*pronounced as grow-tesk), **macabre** (*pronounced as muh-kah-bruh)
Horrendous: shocking and horrifying
The Rwandan Genocide in 1994 saw some hideous war crimes being committed by the Hutu tribe.
*Synonyms: **heinous, atrocious, appalling, terrible**
Hideous: horrifyingly ugly
In Avengers, Thanos sent hideous Chitauri Army to invade Earth.
*Synonyms: **unsightly, monstrous**
Repugnant: disgusting
In a civilized society cannibalism (man eating man for food) is considered repugnant.
*Synonyms: **abhorrent, abominable, obnoxious, despicable, detestable, deplorable, contemptible, beyond the pale, odious, execrable, loathsome, revolting, repulsive, reprehensible vile, nauseating,** foul, nasty, sickening, scurvy, noxious
Sordid: shocking and morally wrong
The sordid sex scandal rocked the government.
*Synonyms: **seedy, seamy, unsavoury**
Squalid: dirty; filthy
The squalid hotel was no place to stay.
*Synonyms: **grubby, grimy** (grime means dirt), **grungy** (grunge means dirt), **mucky** (muck means waste), **slummy**
*Noun form: **squalor** (They lived in squalor and filth), squalidness, grubbiness, muckiness
*Antonyms: clean, hygienic
Squeamish: easily sickened or disgusted
She was always very squeamish about cockroaches.

■

Obsolete: outdated
Nokia 3310 is obsolete in front of the iPhone.
*Synonyms: **outmoded** (like outmoded customs like Sati), ancient, **antiquated, anachronistic, quaint, archaic**, outworn, behind the times, passé (Old-fashioned-Bell-bottom pants are passé; *pronounced as pa-say)
*Antonyms: contemporary, current, modern
Antediluvian: belonging to the time before the Biblical deluge (flood)
The antediluvian practices of the barbarians.
*Etymology: 'Ante' means before and 'diluvian' is the adjective form of the deluge
*Synonyms: **primordial, primitive, primeval** (*pronounced as prime-evil) *Antonyms: postdiluvian.
Anachronism: something that belongs in the era bygone
Sending letters by post, instead of emailing, is considered an anachronism.
*Etymology: from Greek 'ana' (backwards) and 'khronos' (time)

■

Contemporary: belonging to the same time period
The actions of king Nero were recorded by the contemporary historian Tacitus.
*Synonym: **coeval** (*pronounced as co-evil: the beginning of Baseball in US is coeval with the invention of the telephone)
*Adjective form: **synchronous, contemporaneous** (Pythagoras was contemporaneous with Buddha)
*Noun forms: contemporaneity (The quality or state of being contemporaneous or contemporary), contemporaneousness, synchronicity
Coterminous: having an equal scope
Both the earthquakes were coterminous with respect to the amount of damage they both caused.
Contiguous: sharing a common border
The Arabian Sea is contiguous with the Indian Ocean.
*Synonyms: adjacent, adjoining, bordering
Abut: to be adjacent to something
My garden abuts his vineyard.
Imminent: about to happen
The National Security Advisor warned the Prime Minister that an enemy attack was imminent.
*Synonyms: **impending**, proximate

*Antonym: **remote**
Proximate: close, especially in terms of time or space
They rushed the accident victim to the most proximate hospital.
Unison: when multiple people speak simultaneously
The students said yes in unison when the teacher asked if they wanted a holiday.
Lockstep: a way of marching (especially in the US) where people march as close together as possible
The duo marched in lockstep.
The pharma company raised the prices in lockstep with those of foreign competitors.

■

Penchant: a strong preference or special liking for something
He has a penchant for fine wine and antique cars.
*Pronounced as pen-chunt
*Synonyms: leaning, bent, **predilection** (He has a predilection for classical music), **affinity** (He has an affinity for mathematics)
Proclivity: a strong tendency or natural inclination to do something
He was rewarded by his boss for his proclivity for hard work and meticulousness.
*Synonyms: **propensity** (He was taken to a counsellor to sort out his propensity for violence and fighting), **predisposition** (He has an irritating predisposition to correct other people's mispronunciation)
Predisposition: apart from proclivity, predisposition also means the tendency to suffer from a particular disease
Research shows that children inherit a predisposition to mental diseases from their parents.
*Synonyms: **susceptibility, proneness, miasm** (*pronounced as my-az-um)

■

Antipathy: hostility; hatred
Karl Marx's writings showed his antipathy to capitalism.
*Synonyms: **aversion, antagonism, animosity, animus, abhorrence, loathing, repugnance, odium**, enmity
*Antonyms: liking, **affinity, rapport**, goodwill, friendship
Acrimony: bitterness
There was nothing but acrimony between the bride and the mother-in-law.

*Synonyms: **resentment, rancour**, ill-will, bad-blood
*Adjective form: acrimonious, rancorous, **jaundiced**
Malevolence: desire to hurt or annoy someone
*Synonyms: **spite, malice**
*Antonym: **benevolence**
No love lost: dislike
There was no love lost between the enemies.
Falling-out: when relations between two people end because of a disagreement
The allies had a falling-out.
*Synonyms: **estrangement, severance, alienation, detachment, separation**
Nemesis: an enemy
*Synonyms: **foe, adversary**, opponent
Rival: a competitor
*Synonyms: contestant, contender, challenger

■

Collaborate: to work together
Alliance: a close association
Concordat: an alliance; an agreement
Rendezvous: a meeting
*Pronounced as rahn-duh-voo
Liaison: the cooperation between different bodies and agencies to achieve a common goal
The liaison between local police and the FBI is crucial to nab gangsters.
*Pronounced as lee-ey-zawn
*Verb form: to liaise

■

Throttle: to choke someone
*Synonyms: strangle, **strangulate, garrotte** (*pronounced as guh-rot)
Suffocate: to kill someone by depriving them of air
*Synonyms: to **stifle**, to **asphyxiate**
*Noun form: suffocation, stiflement, asphyxia
Smother: to kill someone by covering their nose and mouth
Gag: to something put into a person's mouth like a piece of cloth to prevent speech
The robbers gagged him with a kitchen cloth.
Muffle: to cover something to reduce the loudness of the noise
The attacker put his hand on her mouth to muffle the screams.

■

Wholesome: conducive to moral or general well-being
The clean wholesome show could be watched by the entire family together.
Winsome: charming
He made everyone at ease with his winsome smile and pleasant disposition.
*Synonyms: **charismatic, prepossessing, fetching, engaging**, attractive, appealing, delightful
Endearing: inspiring affection and love
The child had an endearing face.
*Synonyms: adorable, cute
Enrapture: to make someone super excited and full of joy
The football star enraptured the crowd as soon he came on stage.
*Etymology: in theology, rapture means the transporting of devout believers to heaven at the Second Coming of Jesus Christ
Enthral: to captivate or charm someone
The crowd was enthralled by his virtuoso performance.
*Etymology: Old English 'thræl' means slave
*Synonyms: to **enchant**, to **engross**, to **mesmerize**, to **bewitch**, to **bedazzle**, to **spellbind**, to **woo over** (used gifts to woo her over), to **rivet** (The actor gave a riveting performance; *etymology: a rivet is a short metal pin that holds two metal plates together)
*Antonyms: to bore, to repel
Intrigue: to arouse the curiosity
His ideas intrigued the investor.
*Synonym: to **fascinate**
Regale: to entertain someone with amusing talk
The grandfather regaled the children with his stories from the war.

■

Amicable: friendly, polite and good natured
After months of fighting, everyone just wanted an amicable settlement between Tony Stark (Iron Man) and Steve Rogers (Captain America).
*Synonyms: **affable, amiable, convivial, genial, personable, jovial**, likeable, good-natured, good-humoured, cordial, polite, harmonious, warm, **comradely**, neighbourly, welcoming, **hospitable**
*Antonyms: unfriendly, hostile
Benign: gentle and kind
The benign old lady ran the animal welfare NGO.
*Synonyms: warm-hearted, affectionate, compassionate, caring

Innocuous: not harmful; not offensive
He got unreasonably upset at what was a mere innocuous question.
*Synonyms: **anodyne** (anodyne also means non-controversial), **unobjectionable, unexceptionable**
Hospitality: the very friendly and warm reception of friends and guests
He was famous among his circle of friends for his hospitality.

■

Congenial: like-minded
Ted always provided Ed with congenial company
*Synonyms: **compatible, kindered, simpatico** (a simpatico relationship)
Comport: to be in agreement and harmony
The findings of the latest study do not comport with accepted theory in the field.
*Synonyms: to conform, to fit, to match, to agree with
*Noun form: **comportment, conformity, compatibility, consonance, congruity/congruence** (His explanation is congruous with his earlier statements), accordance, harmony
Coincide: occur at the same time
The book's release coincided with a recession.
*Synonyms: simultaneous, **concurrent** (There were three concurrent book fairs going on in the city)
*Coincide also means to correspond in nature; for example, the interest of the company and the employees do not always coincide and that is why we have layoffs.
Correlate: to have a connection but that does not necessarily mean a causal link
For example, high amounts of radiation from cell phones correlates to brain damage in the user. It means that if there is high radiation then the chances of brain damage are high. But that does not mean that cell phone radiation necessarily causes brain damage as there might be causes for such brain damage such as the tendency of cell phone users to stay up late at night on social media or watching YouTube.
Dovetail: to join together
The teacher told the student that all parts of his essay must dovetail together to form a cohesive whole.
*Etymology: in carpentry, a dovetail is kind of a joint in the shape of a tail of a dove (a triangle) used to connect two boards of wood
Tally: to correspond
The signatures in the attendance sheet did not tally with

the names.

*Tally also means the score or to make an entry in a register.

Apposite: appropriate; relevant

At the launch event, reporters were told to ask only apposite questions and no personal questions.

*Synonyms: suitable, apt, befitting, **germane** (The comment was not germane to the issue), **pertinent** (The lecture was pertinent to our current times), **felicitous** (a felicitous phrase), **apropos** (the objection was apropos)

*Antonyms: **inapposite**, **extraneous** (irrelevant), immaterial, beside the point

Symbiosis: an interaction between two living organisms which benefits both of these organisms

For example, the symbiotic relationship between the oxpecker and the water buffalo, where the oxpecker feeds on the ticks on the buffalo's back and the buffalo gets rid of parasites

*Plural: symbioses

*Related word: **symbiote** (The organisms living in a symbiotic partnership, for example the buffalo and the oxpecker, are both symbiotes)

■

Attune: to harmonize

Even after the Cold War, the interests of East and West are still not attuned.

Attune also means to adjust or accustom or acclimatize: New doctors are not attuned to making quick decisions.

Acclimatize: to become accustomed to a new climate; to acclimate: He had no trouble at all in acclimatizing to college life.

Calibrate: to check the readings of an instrument with another instrument; to adjust something as per the situation

The politician decided to calibrate his speeches and make them less aggressive.

■

Idyllic: peaceful and calm

He always wanted an idyllic life in the countryside.

*Synonyms: **halcyon** (*pronounced as hal-see-un), serene, Arcadian

*Antonym: hellish

*Noun form: **idyll, Arcadia**

Balmy: like a balm (pleasant and soothing)

He wanted to relax in the balmy winds of California.

*Synonyms: **clement** (The clement weather made for fun sight-seeing), **soothing**

*Antonyms: harsh, wintry, inclement

Quaint: charmingly old-fashioned

The quaint village was a popular tourist destination for city dwellers.

Utopia: an imaginary place where everything is perfect

*Synonyms: paradise, heaven on earth, Garden of Eden, Shangri-La, **Elysium, nirvana**

*Antonyms: **dystopia,** hell on earth

Riviera: a coastal region

Hamlet: a small village

■

Poignant: evoking sad feelings

The poignant movie about the Nazi concentration camp survivors brought made everyone cry.

*Pronounced as poi-nuhnt

*Synonyms: touching, moving, affecting, **heart-rending, heart-breaking, tear-jerking**

*Noun form: poignancy, **pathos** (The pathos of the movie on trafficking was strong & everyone cried; *pronounced as pey-thos)

Bathos: an anti-climax where things from the sublime to the ridiculous

*Pronounced as bey-thos

Mawkish: overly sentimental

The movie's mawkish script was lambasted by the critics.

*Synonyms: **maudlin** (a maudlin poem), **cloying** (a cloying love song), **saccharine** (a saccharine ballad; *pronounced as sack-ur-in)

*Noun form: mawkishness, **schmaltz**, saccharinity, maudlinness

Lachrymose: tears inducing; something that makes one cry

The lachrymose account of the plight of undertrials moved the judge.

Evocative: arousing strong emotional feelings

The evocative lyrics of the song about death made everyone's eyes well up.

*Synonym: **emotive**

Provocative: arousing sexual feelings

The adult rated movie had many provocative dance scenes.

*Synonyms: **seductive, titillating**

■

Scintillating: bright and shiny
The jewellery at the wedding fair was scintillating.
*Synonyms: **glossy, gleaming, glittering, glistening, coruscating**, twinkling, sparkling, flashing, shimmering
Resplendent: glowing; radiant
She looked resplendent in the Versace dress.
*Synonyms: **refulgent, effulgent, lustrous, luminous, lucent**
Incandescent: emitting light as a result of being heated
Electricity was needed for heating the filament in the incandescent lamp.
Noctilucent: shining at night
For example, high-altitude noctilucent clouds
*Pronounced as noktah-lusent

■

Glimmer: a faint light
Finally, there was a glimmer of hope.
Shimmer: a soft light
The shimmer of moonlight.
Lustre: a soft shine coming from a surface
The lustre of the freshly washed car in sunlight.
*Synonyms: **sheen, patina, gloss**
Glint: a quick flash of light
She noticed the glint of gold in his teeth.
Glisten: to shine because the surface is wet and is reflecting light
The pond glistened in the sunlight.
Gleam: to shine because the surface is well polished and is reflecting light
The crockery gleamed under the overhead lights.

■

Ember: a small piece of glowing coal in a dying fire
Cinder: ashes; a small piece of partially burnt coal or wood
Soot: dark black substance, formed by the incomplete burning of coal, etc.
Pyre: a heap of wood and combustible material
He visited the funeral pyre.
Bier: a frame on which a coffin or corpse is laid before burial or cremation

■

Amber: orange-ish yellow resin that covers fossils
Auburn: of reddish-brown colour (like henna)
She had auburn hair.

Azure: sky-blue colour
Crimson: a purplish red colour
Scarlet: a bright red
*Synonym: **vermilion**
Mauve: a pale bluish purple
*Pronounced as mohv
Hazel: golden-brown colour
Tawny: of yellowish-brown colour
Tabby: of grey or brownish in colour with dark stripes (for example, a tabby cat)
Taupe: a brownish-grey colour
Teal: a dark greenish-blue colour
Turquoise: a greenish-blue colour
The turquoise waters of the pond.
*Pronounced as tur-koiz
Tint: slight colour
He wore rose-tinted glasses.
*Synonyms: **tinge, hue**

■

Gaze: a steady look
He turned his gaze to question paper.
Gape: to look at someone with one's mouth wide open in amazement
The tourists gaped at the tall skyscrapers.
Gawk: to stare at someone openly and stupidly
He was reprimanded for gawking at the new girl in the class.
Glance: a quick look
He glanced around to see if his boss was around.
Glimpse: a partial view
He glimpsed his boss's shadow outside the gate.
Squint: to look at something with eyes partially closed as there is strong light coming from the direction of the object
Descry: to catch sight of something; to notice something after careful observation
He descried two suspicious figures outside his room window.
*Synonyms: to **discern**, to **espy** (The captain espied dry land 10 miles ahead; *pronounced as is-pie; *verb tenses: espy, espies, espied, espying)
Peep: to take a quick look at something especially through a small opening like a keyhole
Peer: to look with great concentration
He peered through his office curtains to see the protestors.
Peer also means a person of the same age and status: his peers were jealous of his academic ability.

Leer: to look at someone sexual and unpleasant way
*Synonym: **ogle**

■

Glean: to collect slowly bit by bit and with a lot of effort
The detective gleaned the thief's whereabouts from Uber records and call logs.
Garner: to gather
The leader garnered support from his allies.
Accretion: accumulation
*Synonyms: amassment, accrual, augmentation
Increscent: gradually growing
The increscent moon in the night sky.
Increment: an increase or addition, especially on a fixed scale
He did not receive a salary increment this year.
*Adjective form: incremental
Collate: to collect and compile data
His report collated news reports from many different sources into a single easy to read prose.
Cull: to pick a few from a large quantity
He culled the best cases to present to the judge as precedents.
Cull also means to reduce the population of a wild animal by selectively killing them.

■

Graphic: giving clear details
He gave a graphic account of the shooting.
Stark: sharply clear
The position of the two camps were in stark contrast to each other.
*Synonyms: **blunt, bald, bare**
Explicit: stated clearly without any room for confusion
The editors wanted his explicit approval for using his pictures in their book.
*Synonyms: **clear-cut, crystal clear**
*Antonyms: **implicit, tacit** (Tacit means understood or implied without being clearly stated: the two parties reached a tacit understanding to form an alliance)

■

Ambiguous: open to interpretation
Ambiguous clauses make a contract tough to enforce.
*Synonym: **equivocal**
*Antonym: **categorical**
Ambivalent: having mixed feelings

The critics had an ambivalent reaction to his latest movie.
Ambidextrous: someone who can use right and left hands equally well

■

Verdant: covered with grass
His mansion had a verdant lawn in the front.
Fecund: highly fertile
The child's fecund imagination.
*Synonyms: **prolific, inventive**, productive, creative
Barren: an infertile land
Arid: a land that is barren because of very low rainfall
Desolate: an uninhabited place which gives a very gloomy feeling

■

Dreary: dull and boring
The executive was not looking forward to another dreary Monday morning.
*Synonyms: **drab, dingy**
Bleak: gloomy
The future of the convicts looked bleak.
*Synonyms: dark, **dour** (The captain's dour look depressed the other shipmates), **dismal** (the dismal forecast), **glum** (wore a glum expression), **grim** (The future looked grim), **sombre** (the sombre atmosphere at the funeral), **saturnine** (the saturnine setting of a cremation)
Lacklustre: lacking any vitality
The actor was criticized for another lacklustre performance
*Pronounced as lack-luster
*Synonyms: colourless, **listless**, lifeless, unanimated
Insipid: lacking flavour; boring
The insipid conversation made her sleepy.
*Synonyms: **vapid, prosaic, banal** (He was tired of his boring and banal life)
Tepid: only slightly warm; half-hearted
The movie got a tepid response.
*Synonym: **lukewarm**
*Antonyms: enthusiastic, passionate
Tedious: long, slow, boring and tiring
Making sugar from sugarcane is a tedious process.
*Synonyms: **monotonous** (monotonous existence), **mind-numbing** (mind-numbing job), **humdrum** (humdrum routine), **mundane** (boring and mundane lives), **wearisome** (wearisome journey)

Drudgery: menial hard labour
The maid detested the drudgery of domestic tasks.
*Synonym: **donkey work**
Drone: to speak in a dull and monotonous tone
The boring old professor droned on for hours about the types of domes in medieval architecture.
Chore: a routine household task like cooking or cleaning
Errand: a short trip to deliver or collect something typically groceries

■

Travail: burdensome work
Everyone must do their fair share of travails that life brings with itself.
Tribulation: hardship; suffering
No one wants to suffer life's trials and tribulations.
*Synonyms: **plight, ordeal, adversity**, agony, trauma, torment.
Crucible: a very testing and difficult situation
Not many understand the plight of students in the crucible.
*Pronounced as cruu-suh-buhl
Affliction: a disease
He was undergoing treatment for a painful affliction of the heart.
*Synonyms: **ailment, malady**
Symptom: a physical or mental feature in a patient which is an indicator of a disease
For example, high fever and joint pain is a symptom of malaria.
Syndrome: a group of symptoms that occur together. Also means a predictable pattern of behaviour
The classic 'the deadline is close' syndrome of project managers.
Scourge: someone or something that causes great suffering
The scourge of corruption on our nation.
*Synonyms: **plague, bane, menace, blight**
Pestilence: a widespread disease that causes definition
Many doctors were sent in to stop the advance of the pestilence.
Infestation: the presence of a large number of pests
There was a locust infestation at the farm.
*Verb form: to infest
Hazard: a danger or risk
There are many hazards in a sea voyage.
*Synonyms: **pitfall, peril, jeopardy** (He put his safety in jeopardy)

Mishap: an unfortunate accident
The group suffered through many mishaps during their journey.
*Synonyms: mischance, misadventure

■

Toil: to work extremely hard
The labourers toiled through the night to meet the deadline.
*Synonyms: to **plough** away, to **plod** away, to **exert**, to **slog**
Eke out: to make a living by a lot of hard work
They somehow managed to eke out a living by farming on that barren land.
*Pronounced as eek-out
Endeavour: to try very hard to achieve something
The NGO endeavoured to provide cheap medicines to the poor.
*Noun forms: **venture, undertaking**

■

Unpropitious: indicating a low chance of success; unfortunate
The minister did not want the swearing in ceremony at an unpropitious time.
*Synonyms: **inauspicious**, ill-fated, ill-omened
*Antonyms: auspicious, propitious (*pronounced as pro-pish-us), fortunate
Inopportune: inconvenient or inappropriate
He met me at an inopportune time as I was busy preparing for a meeting.
Untoward: unexpected
No one wanted an untoward incident at the wedding
*Synonyms: unanticipated, unforeseen, unpredicted
Inexpedient: impractical
Always sending clothes for dry-cleaning instead of just washing at home is inexpedient.
*Antonyms: **expedient** (The party dumped the loud-mouth minister because of it was politically expedient; *noun form: expediency), **pragmatic** (Politics involves making pragmatic choices and not always the ideal ones; *noun form: pragmatism)
Impolitic: unwise
Not consulting before investing is an impolitic strategy.
*Synonyms: **imprudent, injudicious,** ill-advised, misguided
Fortuitous: occurring by chance and not design

The movie star recounted his break after fortuitous meeting with the producer at a café.
*Pronounced as for-two-it-us
*Synonyms: lucky, fortunate, **providential, adventitious** (adventitious encounter in the market led to a love affair)
Serendipitous: occurring by accident
Alexander Fleming's serendipitous discovery of Penicillin earned him a Nobel Prize.
*Noun form: serendipity
Coincidence: when two unconnected events occur but seem connected
It was pure coincidence that they both wore the same dress to the wedding.
*Synonym: **happenstance**
Fortuity: a chance event
*Synonyms: **serendipity, fluke**
Providence: the care and guidance of God
The group believed in both providence and preparation.
*Homonym: **provenance** (the place of origin; a record of ownership used as a certificate of authenticity)
Hapless: unlucky; unfortunate
The hapless victims of the earthquake.
Jinx: to bring bad luck on someone
He jinxed him by sneezing as soon as he went out of the door.

∎

Wretched: miserable
The street children lived a wretched life.
Synonyms: **abject, pathetic, pitiful**, piteous, pitiable.
Lugubrious: sad and depressed
The student wore a lugubrious look after he failed in his exams.
*Pronounced as low-gyu-bri-us
*Synonyms: **dejected, despondent, downcast, crestfallen, melancholic, morose, woebegone, forlorn, doleful, dolorous, sullen**, sorrowful, mournful, anguished, distressed, despairing, dispirited, heavy-hearted, downhearted, mirthless, joyless, cheerless
*Noun forms: lugubriousness, **doldrums**, dejection, despondency, melancholy, dismalness, sadness, misery, woe, anguish, wretchedness, heavy-heartedness, despair, dispiritedness
Inconsolable: someone who is grief-stricken and not able to be consoled
*Synonyms: **disconsolate, devastated, distraught**
Mourning: feeling of intense sorrow after losing someone

*Synonyms: **plaintive, grieving, sorrowing**
Plangent: loud and mournful
The movie's plangent background score made everyone cry.
Lament: to regret
The student lamented not studying enough for his exams.
*Synonyms: to **rue**, to **bemoan**, to **bewail**
Contrite: feeling guilty and sorry for one's wrong actions
*Synonyms: **remorseful, repentant, penitent,** self-reproachful
*Noun form: **contrition, remorse, repentance, penitence**, self-reproach, guilt
*Antonyms: uncontrite, unrepentant, remorseless, impenitent, unapologetic
Atone: to make up for one's sin
The sage told the King that he must build one hundred shelters for the poor to atone for his sins.
*Synonyms: to **expiate**, to **make amends**
*Noun form: atonement, expiation
Penance: punishment inflicted upon oneself to show how sorry one is for committing a sin
He paid penance for his misconduct by volunteering.
Redeem: to make up for the faults and bad aspects
The overall disappointing movie was redeemed by its stunning climax.

∎

Commiserate: to express sympathy with someone over their loss
*Synonyms: to offer **condolences**, to **condole** with
Solace: comfort in the time of misery or grief
He turned to religion for solace during the bad times.
*Pronounced as sol-is
*Synonym: **consolation** (The main consolation for him was that everyone at the office also got laid off due to the recession; *verb form: console)
Succour: aid or assistance during hard times
The NGO offered succour to the tsunami victims by providing shelter and food
*Pronounced as suker

∎

Commonplace: not unusual; commonly occurring
Kidnappings were a commonplace occurrence in Colombia.
Mediocre: ordinary

The movie was a run-of-the-mill romantic comedy.
*Synonyms: **pedestrian** (a piece of pedestrian writing), **nondescript** (He owned a nondescript house), **bog-standard** (He bought a cheap bog-standard phone), **plain vanilla** (He wore plain vanilla clothes), unexceptional
Quotidian: daily
He hated wading through the quotidian traffic.
Hackneyed: unoriginal; overused
The audience started getting tired of the hackneyed superhero movies.
*Pronounced as hak-need
*Synonyms: **trite** (boring trite jokes), **clichéd** (The movie was full of clichéd dialogues; *pronounced as cle-shayd), **derivative**, unimaginative, stale, worn out, **sequacious** (*pronounced as si-kway-shus)
Platitude: a moral saying that is been used so much that it is now boring
The principal bored the students with platitudes about honesty.
*Synonyms: **cliché, truism, banality, bromide**

■

Poise: balanced
The match was beautifully poised with both sides having excellent batting and bowling departments.
Poise also means dignified behaviour.
Precarious: likely to fall because of not being securely held in place
The car was lodged precariously on the cliff's edge.
*Antonyms: safe, secure
Undulate: to move in a wave like motion
The undulating roads of the countryside.
*Synonym: **to billow** (Her dress billowed in the wind)
Flail: to swing wildly
Flailing arms are a sign of drowning.
*Synonym: **to thrash** around
Flounder: to struggle clumsily and awkwardly
The novice swimmer was floundering even in the shallow end of the pool.
*Synonym: **to bumble**
Grope: to search blindly by using one's hands
He groped for his keys in the dark.
Grope also means to touch someone inappropriately without their consent; for example, he was accused of groping the new intern.
*Pronounced as grohp
Writhe: to make twisting and squirming movements in pain

During the epileptic attack, they found him writhing on the floor in pain.
*Pronounced as rithe
*Synonyms: to **spasm**, to **convulse**

■

Gait: a person's manner of walking
He had an uneven gait after the injury.
Ambulatory: able to walk-the patient was ambulatory soon after the surgery
Perambulator: a pram (the push cart for babies)
Somnambulate: to sleepwalk

■

Boulevard: a wide street lined in a town meant for casual walking
Arcade: a shopping centre; a covered passage with arches on both sides
Colonnade: a row of evenly spaced columns supporting a roof
Esplanade: a long and wide walkway, typically next to a sea, for people to walk on for pleasure
*Synonym: **promenade**
Thoroughfare: the main road of a town
Tarmac: a road or airport runway
Turnpike: a road on which a toll is collected at a toll gate
Kerb: the stone lining that forms the edge of a pavement and this lining separates the pavement from the road
Aisle: a passage between rows of seats for example in a theatre, plane, etc.
*Pronounced as ahyl
*Homonym: **isle** (a small island)
Wayside: the sides or edge or a road
Due mismanagement, the company fell by the wayside.

■

Prance: to walk around with a bold, arrogant and self-important behaviour
He pranced around after winning.
*Synonyms: to strut, to swagger
Flounce: to walk around with anger
He got so angry in the meeting that he got up and flounced out of the conference room.
Stomp: to walk around with loud and heavy steps to show anger
Stamp: to bring down one's foot heavily and noisily on

the ground, in order to crush something

The dictator vowed to stamp out all his critics.

Trample: to step or walk heavily on something and crush it

He accused the autocrat of trampling on the civil liberties of the citizens.

Amble: to walk at a relaxed pace

The couple ambled in the park: to **stroll,** to **saunter,** to **traipse** (*pronounced as trayps)

Canter: the slow walk of a horse

Flit: to move swiftly

The bees flitted from one flower to another.

Stride: to walk quickly

The soldiers strode into the town.

Scurry: to move quickly with short steps

The tourists scurried for cover when it began to rain.

*Synonyms: to scamper, to scuttle, to scoot

Streak: to quickly run

The cat streaked across the lawn to get away from the dog.

*Synonyms: to dash, to sprint, to bolt, to dart, to gallop, to hotfoot

Slalom: to ski

Good lawyers slalom through a regulatory minefield.

*Pronounced as slah-lum

*Etymology: slalom is a downhill ski race.

Wade: to walk but with a lot of effort

He waded through the swamp to get to dry land, after his boat broke down.

Trudge: to walk slowly and heavily because one is really tired

He trudged up the stairs after a tiring day.

*Synonyms: to tramp, to drag oneself

Trundle: to slowly roll along

Carts trundle across the market every day.

Clamber: to climb with great difficulty, typically using both feet and hands

He clambered out of the ditch.

Lumber: to move in a slow and heavy way

The overloaded truck lumbered past the parked car on the highway.

Lumber also means to cut trees.

Limp: to walk with difficulty, usually because of a leg or foot injury

He limped out of the car.

*Synonym: hobble

*Antonym: to stride

Tread: to walk with careful steps

The thief tread lightly to avoid detection.

Waddle: to walk with short steps rocking from side to side

The ducks waddled across the pavement to get to the pond.

Gallivant: to move around from place to place, looking for pleasure

He quit his job to gallivant around the countryside.

*Synonym: to **gad** (He was last seen gadding around with his girlfriend in France)

Rove: to wander

He spent his time roving around in shopping malls.

Traverse: to travel through

The explorers traversed through the Arctic.

■

Lunge: to suddenly move forward with arms outstretched, usually done to attack someone

He lunged at the pickpocket to stop him from running away.

*Synonym: to **pounce**

Careen: to move very fast and in an uncontrolled way

The bank robber's getaway car came careening around the street corner.

*Synonym: to **hurtle** (The car hurtled towards the edge of the cliff)

Veer: to abruptly change direction; to suddenly deviate

The debate quickly veered off course when the personal attacks started.

*Synonym: **swerve** (The truck driver swerved in order to avoid hitting the motorcyclist)

■

Hover: to float in the air

The plane hovered above the airport for an hour because of poor visibility.

Levitate: to rise into the air and then float

The crowd clapped as the magician levitated his assistant twenty feet above the stage.

Gyrate: to rapidly rotate or move in a circular pattern

The helicopter blades started to gyrate during take-off.

*Synonyms: to spiral, to whirl, to twirl, to swirl, to pivot, to whir (The ceiling fan whirred; *pronounced as wur)

Centripetal: moving towards the centre

*Etymology: from Latin *'centripetus'* (centre-seeking) = *'centri'* (centre) + *'petus'* (seeking).

Churn: to stir vigorously

The milk was churned to make butter.

Roil: to make a liquid muddy by stirring up the sediments

The heavy wind roiled the sea.

Torque: a force that causes rotation

The new engine of the bike had massive torque power.

*Pronounced as tawrk

Whorl: a pattern of concentric circles; a circular arrangement of leaves, flowers, etc.

*Synonym: **verticil** (*pronounced as verti-sil)

Helix: a spiral; a shape where a curve moves like a line wrapped around a cylinder

*Plural: helices

■

Plonk: to set down heavily or carelessly

He plonked the cup on the table.

Plunge: to dive down into something

The economy plunged into crisis when the markets crashed.

*Antonym: escalate

Plummet: to drop down at a very fast rate

The value of the Yen compared to the dollar plummeted.

*Synonyms: to fall headlong, to nosedive

Swoop: to rapidly move downwards through the air

The eagle swooped in on its prey.

Submerge: to drown underwater

The flood submerged the houses.

Rappel: to move down a steep slope (like a rock face) by using a rope

Rebound: to bounce back after hitting something hard

The price of gold rebounded during the gifting season.

*Synonyms: **ricochet** (The bullet ricocheted off the wall; *pronounced as rik-uh-shey), **recoil** (The gun recoiled after firing and hit his shoulder), **kickback**

■

Ascend: to move up

*Noun form: **ascent, ascension** (Obama's ascension to the post of the US President was stunning)

Descend: to move down

*Noun form: **descent, descension**

Acclivity: an upward slope

*Synonyms: **gradient** (The path becomes tough as the gradient increases), incline, steepness, slant

Declivity: a downward slope

■

Avuncular: uncle-like

His boss treated him with an avuncular affection.

Aquiline: eagle-like; the quality of someone's face when it is hook-shaped like an eagle's beak

His aquiline features made him a much sought after model.

*Synonym: **angular**

Askance: sideways (The spy quickly looked askance to see if he was being followed); with a look of suspicion (The younger generations looked askance at the old traditions)

Oblique: indirect

He made an oblique comment on her dress at the party.

Athwart: from side to side of something

The welcome mat was placed athwart the entrance door.

Askew: tilted

The wind knocked his hat askew.

*Synonyms: skew, crooked, at an angle, slanted

Lopsided: with one side smaller than the other

The villain's lopsided smile meant that he just got an evil idea.

*Synonym: **asymmetrical**

Rugged: having an uneven surface

The car trip on the rugged road gave him back pain.

*Synonyms: rocky, craggy, scraggly

*Antonym: smooth

Jagged: spiky

The mountain climber got cuts on his legs because of the jagged edges of the rocks.

Pitted: having many pits (holes) on its surface

The pitted roads of the city are a blemish on the record of the municipality.

*Synonyms: **indented, pockmarked** (Pockmarks are the scars left by a pimple on a person's face)

Puncture: a small hole like in a tyre caused by the penetration of a sharp object

*Plural: punctures

Perforated: something with small holes on its surface

The edges of the stamps are perforated for easy tearing.

*Verb form: perforate

Precipitous: extremely steep

His fall from grace was precipitous after the sex scandal broke out.

*Pronounced as pre-sipi-tus

*Etymology: of the nature of precipices

*Synonyms: **vertiginous, meteoric** (His rise to fame was meteoric after his debut album dropped)

■

Echelon: a level of rank

He moved up the echelons of power in the government.
*Pronounced as esh-uh-lon
*Synonyms: **tier, rung**
Firmament: the heavens; the galaxy
He was a star in the firmament.
Pantheon: a group of the most respected and important in a field
He quickly entered the pantheon of the all-time greats.
Hierarchy: a system of ranking
*Pronounced as hey-ur-are-key
Stratum: a level or class to which people are assigned to as per their status in society
*Plural: strata
*Verb form: to stratify (to classify)
Gradation: a series of grades or degrees
Graduated: graded
A tax code provided for a graduated tax system
Gamut: the complete range
The audience felt the gamut of human emotions, from grief to joy, in the Steven Spielberg movie.

■

Ram: to push your way through
He rammed his way into the party.
Hurl: to throw something
They hurled abuses at each other.
*Synonyms: to **lob** (They lobbed grenades at each other), to **fling**
Heave: to lift something very heavy
They heaved the old sofa above their head and then threw it in the garage.
Haul: to drag something very heavy
They hauled the bed across the room.
Lug: to carry something very heavy
They lugged the box down the stairs.
Hoist: to raise something using ropes and pulleys
The President hoisted the national flag on Independence Day.
Foist: to impose someone or something unwelcome
His enemy foisted a lot of false cases on him.
Levy: to impose a tax, fee, fine, etc.
An excise duty was levied on all goods.
Tote: to carry
He toted the books from the library to his room.
*Pronounced as toht
Stow: to load; to pack
He stowed his luggage into the boot of the car.
Flout: to openly disregard something

He frequently flouted traffic rules by not wearing a helmet.
*Synonym: to **defy**
*Antonym: to observe
Brandish: to wave something in the air, usually a weapon to scare people
The rioters brandished knives and swords.
*Synonym: hold aloft

■

Projectile: an object that is propelled through the air, usually as a weapon
The soldiers wore helmets to protect their heads from enemy projectiles.
Payload: the part of an aircraft's load that yields payment
For example, the passengers or the cargo.
Pod: a detachable self-contained unit on an aircraft
The superhero fled from the spacecraft using the secret escape pod.
Fuselage: the main body of an aircraft to which the wings are attached
*Pronounced as few-su-laazh
Propulsion: the act of pushing forward
Propellant: something that is used to propel (push forward)
*Etymology: propellant is a mixture of fuel and oxidizer, used for propelling a rocket
Trajectory: the path followed by a projectile when moving through air
Orbit: the path followed by spacecraft or celestial objects like planets
The Earth orbits the Sun.
Headwind: a wind that blows in the direction opposite to the travel of an object (from head to the tail) and thus opposes forward motion and decreases the object's speed
*Antonym: **tailwind**
Headway: progress or forward movement, especially when the situation is difficult The ship made little headway because of the storm on the sea.

■

Hangar: a large building with an expansive floor area, used to house an aircraft
*Pronounced as hanger
Helipad: a small area meant for the take-off and landing area for helicopters
Hippodrome: an arena meant for horse races and other public events

Aerodrome: a small airport

■

Loop: a circle
Noose: a loop made with a rope by knotting the rope at one end
Lasso: a rope with a noose at one end, typically used for catching cattle
*Synonyms: **lariat, riata**

■

Diadem: a headband (usually jewelled) worn as a crown by royalty
*Synonyms: **circlet, chaplet, coronet**
Tiara: a jewelled headband worn on above a woman's forehead
Festoon: a chain of flowers or ribbons, hung in a curve for decoration
Wreath: a circular arrangement of flowers and leaves, used for decorating or laying on a grave
*Pronounced as reeth
*Synonyms: garland, lei
Wreathe: to encircle
The python wreathed his body.
*Pronounced as reeth
*Synonyms: to **girdle**, to **cincture**

■

Wrest: to snatch away something from a person's grasp
He wrested the remote away from his younger brother.
Prise: to forcefully open something by using a lever
The policeman prised open the car door after the accident.
*Pronounced as prize

■

Panhandle: to beg on the streets
Manhandle: to physically handle someone very roughly
The star was manhandled by the crowd.
Frogmarch: to force someone to walk forward by holding their arms from behind
The policeman frogmarched him into the station with handcuffs.

■

Jostle: to push and bump against each other

The metro riders jostled for breathing space during the rush hour.
*Synonym: **hustle**
Vie: to compete eagerly
The players were vying for the captain position
*Synonym: **jockey** (*etymology: jockey is the rider of a racehorse)
Grapple: to wrestle
He liked to grapple with tough unsolved problems.
Bustle: excited activity and movement
He was not used to the hustle and bustle of city life.
*Synonym: hustle
Bristle: to be overflowing with something
The concert hall was bristling with excited fans.
*Synonyms: **teem** (The crime scene was teeming with police officers), **brim** (The club hall was brimming with energy)
*Bristle also means a short hair on an animal's skin (*synonyms: whisker, hackle).

■

Debacle: a major and humiliating failure
The 2008 crash is considered as the greatest financial debacle in US history.
*Synonym: **fiasco**
Setback: a major reversal or stop in the progress of something
The fight between the ambassadors was a major setback for the peace talks.
*Synonym: hitch
*Antonym: breakthrough (a major step forward)
Blunder: a careless mistake
The student made many blunders in his maths exam.
*Synonyms: error, fault, slip, **oversight** (oversight also means supervision; *synonym of oversight and supervision: superintendence)
Gaffe: an embarrassing mistake
He apologized to the crowd for the gaffe of farting on stage.
*Pronounced as gahf
*Synonyms: **pratfall, faux pas** (*pronounced as faw-pa; *etymology: French for 'false step').
Botch: to make a mess of things
The doctor botched up the operation and had to pay millions in damages to the patient.
*Synonym: to **bungle**

■

112

Pine: to miss

The wife pined for her soldier husband to return.

*Synonyms: to **long** (He longed to go back to his home country), to **yearn** (He yearned to have a home cooked meal), to **yen** (There is no use yenning for the simple old times)

*Noun forms: pining, longing, yearning, yenning

Nostalgia: a sentimental longing for the past

Everyone nostalgically remembers their childhood days.

*Synonym: **wistfulness**

*Adjective form: nostalgic, wistful

Reminisce: to remember happy past incidents

At the reunion, the friends reminisced their good old college days.

*Pronounced as remi-niss

Mope: to wander aimlessly because of being sad

The jilted lover spent his time moping about the house.

*Synonym: to **sulk**

Brood: to think worry and think deeply about a problem

*Synonyms: **fret about, agonize over**

Brood also means a family of just born young animals.

Pensive: engaged in deep thought

His parents wondered why he was always in a pensive mood.

*Synonyms: reflective, contemplative, broody

■

Drape: to cover with a cloth

The caskets were draped in the nation's flag.

Swathe: to wrap

The body of the mummy found in Egypt was swathed in bandages.

*Synonym: to **swaddle**

*Homonym: **swath** (a broad strip)

Shroud: to envelop something to make it unclear

The event was shrouded in mystery.

*Synonyms: to **cloak**, to **veil**

*Noun forms: shroud (a covering cloth), **cloak** (a loose outer garment), **cape** (like Superman's cape), **veil** (a cloth used by women to cover their face), **stole** (a shawl)

Tuck: to push the loose edges of garment into a closed space so to hide things or make them appear tidy

He tucked his shirt into his trousers before the meeting.

Tarp: a tarpaulin sheet, a large piece of waterproof plastic, used as a cover

Upholstery: soft and padded textile that is used to cushion and cover furniture like armchairs and sofas

*Pronounced as uh-pol-stuh-ree

Quilt: a decorative cover for a bed that is stitched in an ornamental pattern

Duvet: a comforter used to keep warm while sleeping, consisting of two layers of fabric stitched together with a cotton filling

*Pronounced as do-vey

Garb: clothing

The actress liked to be photographed garbed in traditional dresses.

*Synonyms: **apparel, raiment, habiliment, vesture**

Attire: formal clothing

The actor was attired in a black three-piece suit.

Wardrobe: a person's entire collection of clothes

His wardrobe would even put a prince to shame.

■

Integument: a natural covering, for example skin or shell

Incrustation: a crust or hard coating on the surface of a body

Rind: the tough outer skin of a fruit, especially citrus fruit like orange

Fleece: the woolly covering of a sheep or goat

*Pronounced as flees

Plumage: a bird's covering of feathers

*Pronounced as plu-mij

Moult: to shed old feathers, hair or skin for the purpose of making way for the new growth of the same; it is also written as olt

*Synonym: to **cast off**

Slough: to shed off (usually a layer of dead skin)

*Pronounced as sluff

■

Purvey: to supply

They were purveyors of wooden furniture.

Furbish: to renovate

The newly furbished house looked great.

Furnish: to provide

The couple wanted a fully furnished flat to rent.

Burnish: to polish by rubbing

He was looking to burnish his reputation so he took on the tough case.

*Synonym: to **buff up**

Varnish: to coat something to make it shiny

The accused insisted that he was telling the unvarnished truth.

*Synonym: to **overlay**

Veneer: a thin covering of fine and high-quality wood applied on top of a coarser and lesser quality wood for decorative purposes
He hid his corruption under a veneer of respectability.
Patina: a green or brown coloured film produced on the surface of bronze because of oxidation
He carries the patina of civility to fool everyone.
Inlay: to insert something into another's surface
The designer inlaid small gold coins into the wooden panel.
*Synonym: to **embed**
Glaze: a shiny coating
The muffin was glazed with hot butter.
*Synonyms: **enamel, lacquer** (*pronounced as lack-er), **shellac**
Emblazon: to conspicuously display something
The name of the new officer in-charge was emblazoned on the office entrance.
Redound: to greatly contribute to
His latest court victory redounded his reputation in the legal circles.
Emboss: to stamp a design on a surface
His freshly printed gold-embossed visiting card impressed one and all.
Engrave: to carve a design onto a surface
*Synonyms: to **inscribe,** to **etch** (usually done on glass with a needle), to **chisel**
Wrought: produced by beating into shape by hammers; for example, gold or silver items
Wrought also means elaborated, embellished and not crude (His lyrics are well-wrought and deeply emotional; *pronounced as rot)
Gouge: to make a hole in a surface
The eagle gouged his eye out.
*Pronounced as gouj
Gouge also means to overcharge by over-pricing.
Gild: to cover thinly with gold leaf or gold paint; for example, gilded cutlery
*Pronounced as gild and not jild
*Homonym: **guild** (an association of professionals or traders)
Gilt-edged: having a gilded edge, usually refers to a book whose pages are gilded, for example a gilt-edged invitation card
Gold-leafed: printing in which the text on the paper is printed using gold leaf (a thin sheet of gold)

■

Philology: the study of languages as a combination of literary studies, history, and linguistics
Epigraphy: the study of inscriptions
*Etymology: in Greek *'Epi-graphē'* literally means 'on-writing'
Iconography: the study or interpretation of icons (images and visual symbols)
Calligraphy: the art of producing decorative handwriting
Graphology: the study of handwriting; for example, for the purposes of inferring a person's character
Phraseology: the choice of one's words

■

Arable: land that is fertile and suitable for growing crops
Agrarian: related to agriculture
Riparian: related to the banks of a river
The right to fish is a part of the riparian rights of the local people.
Rustic: rural
The ladies fell for his rustic charm.
*Synonyms: **bucolic** (*pronounced as byu-kolic), **pastoral**
Sylvan: relating to woods and forests
*Etymology-from Latin 'silva' = wood

■

Fodder: food (like dried hay or straw) for livestock
Ranch: a large cattle farm
Barn: a large building on a farm used to store grains or house livestock
*Synonym: a **shed**
Silo: a tall tower on a farm used to store grain
Commune: a settlement which is typically on a farm where people share possessions and responsibilities

■

Tillage: the preparation of land for growing crops
Fallow: to leave a piece of land without any cultivation for it to regain fertility
Plough: to turn over soil and then make furrows (lanes) in it to sow seeds
 *Synonym: to **plod**
Reap: to gather ripened crops
The catering company reaped the benefits of the juicy multi-year supply contract.
*Synonym: to **harvest**

114

Yield: the amount produced after an agricultural or industrial activity

The yield was low due to lower-than-expected rainfall.

*Synonym: harvest

■

Canine: relating to dogs

Feline: relating to cats

Bovine: related to cattle

Equine: relating to horses

Equestrian: relating to horse riding

Feral: relating to wild and ferocious animals

Bestial: relating to beasts

Diurnal: during the day

Dogs are diurnal animals.

Nocturnal: during the night

Owls are nocturnal animals.

Marsupial: mammals that carry their young inside a pouch in the mother's belly; for example, Kangaroos

Avian: relating to birds

There was an outbreak of avian flu.

Swine: related to pigs

Serpent: a large snake

Rodent: the class of mammals that comprise of animals like rats, mice, squirrels, etc.

Primate: the class of mammals that comprises animals like monkeys, apes, etc.

Simian: relating to apes or monkeys

*Noun form: simianity

Mammal: a warm-blooded vertebrate animal, with hair or fur, giving birth to live young and secreting milk for nourishment; for example, humans and dogs

Amphibian: a cold-blooded vertebrate animal that has gills at young stage and lungs at adult stage

For example, frogs and toads

Reptile: a cold-blooded vertebrate animal that lays eggs; for example, snakes

Quadruped: an animal which has four feet

Ungulate: a hoofed mammal

*Etymology: Latin *ungula* meaning 'hoof'

Pachyderm: a large mammal with thick skin like elephants, rhinoceros, etc.

Invertebrate: an animal lacking a spine (backbone) for example worms, octopus, etc.

The politician was criticized as being invertebrate and never standing up to his corrupt colleagues.

*Antonym: **vertebrate**

*Etymology: **vertebra** is each of the small bones that together form the spine

*Plural: **vertebrae** (*pronounced as vur-tuh-brey)

Crustacean: the group of animals such as crabs, lobsters, shrimps, etc.

*Pronounced as cruh-stey-shun

Arachnid: the group of animals such as spiders and scorpions

*Pronounced as uh-rack-nid

Arthropod: the group of invertebrate animals such as insects, arachnids or crustaceans

Barnacle: a very tenacious person

*Pronounced as bar-nuh-kul

*Etymology: a barnacle is a small sea creature that attaches itself to surfaces like ship bottoms and rocks

Gnat: an insignificant and irritating person

*Etymology: a small fly that bites

*Pronounced as nat

*Plural: gnats

Gadfly: an irritating person

*Etymology: gadfly is a fly that bites livestock

Minnow: an insignificant person

*Pronounced as min-oh

*Etymology: a minnow is a small freshwater fish

Mite: a small spider like parasite; plural noun

*Pronounced as might

*Plural: mites

*Synonym: tick

Beeline: a straight line between two places

*Etymology: this refers to the supposed straight line that a bee makes when it returns to the hive

Mongrel: a mixed breed animal or one whose breed cannot be determined

Parasite: an organism that lives off another organism (known as the host) by taking nutrients from the body of the host and thus harms the host

Vermin: wild animals that are considered as harmful to crops, danger to farm animals and people and may carry diseases, like wild boars

Vector: an organism that is a carrier of a disease and transmits the disease to other organisms

For example, the female anopheles mosquito is one of the most capable vectors of Malaria

Draught animal: a strong animal that is used to draw heavy loads like a cart or to the plough the field

For example, a bullock is a draught animal used to draw a bullock cart

*Pronounced as draft and not draut

Milch animal: an animal that is kept for producing milk, for example a cow

*Pronounced as milch

■

Eunuch: a castrated man; an ineffectual person
*Pronounced as you-nuhk
Hermaphrodite: an organism having both male and female reproductive organs
For example, an earthworm
Androgyne: a person having both masculine and feminine characteristics
*Pronounced as andro-jaa-in
*Etymology: From Greek 'androgunos' = 'andr' (man) + 'gunē' (woman)

■

Fowl: a domesticated bird kept for its eggs or flesh, for example chicken or turkey
*Synonym: poultry
Ewe: a female sheep
*Pronounced as you
Ram: a male sheep
Lamb: a young sheep
Sow: an adult female pig
*Pronounced as saa-oh
Hog: a domesticated pig reared for slaughter
Fawn: a young deer, especially not a weaned one
Runt: the smallest and weakest youngling in a litter
Mice: plural form of mouse.

■

Foal: a young horse, mule, etc., whose age is less than one year
Filly: a young female horse
Colt: a young male horse whose age is less than four years
Mare: a fully matured female horse
Stallion: a fully mature male horse used for breeding
Bronco: a wild or semi-tamed horse of the western US

■

Matador: a bullfighter
Toreador: a bullfighter on horseback
*Pronounced as tawr-eh-dor
*Synonym: torero
Banderillero: a matador's assistant
*Pronounced as banduh-ree-air-oh
*Synonyms: **capeador, picador**

Rodeo: a public exhibition in North America, which serves both as a sport and public entertainment, where cowboys ride broncos and rope in calves

■

Arboretum: a botanical garden made especially to cultivate trees
Aviary: a large enclosure for keeping birds
Apiary: a place where bees are kept
Aerie: a nest on high altitude, for the aerie of an eagle
*Pronounced as airy
It is also written as **eyrie** (*pronounced as eaa-ree).
Menagerie: a collection of wild animals kept in captivity for exhibition
*Pronounced as muh-naj-uh-ree
Kennel: a small shelter for a dog
Trough: a water or food feeding rack for animals
*Synonym: manger; trough also means the lowest point of a wave
*Antonyms: crest, peak
Corral: an enclosure for livestock on a farm
*Pronounced as kuh-rahl
Paddock: a small field or enclosure where horses are kept, usually near a racetrack for horses to be displayed before a race
*Plural: paddocks
Byre: a cowshed
*Pronounced as bah-yuhr
Bivouac: an encampment made with tents
The soldiers decided to setup a bivouac in the jungle and rest for the night.
*Pronounced as biv-oo-ack
Greenhouse: a room, with the glass roof and walls to trap in the sun's heat for growing plants that need warmth
*Synonym: glasshouse

■

Bonsai: the art of growing artificially dwarfed trees and shrubs in a tray, typically for ornamental purposes
*Pronounced as bon-zai
*Etymology: from Japanese 'bon' (tray) and 'sai' (planting)
Ikebana: the Japanese art of flower arrangement
*Pronounced as ee-kay-bahna
*Etymology: from Japanese 'ikebana' (living flowers) = 'ikeru' (keep alive) + 'hana' (flower)

■

Terrestrial: relating to land

Subterranean: underground; secret

Seismic: relating to earthquakes or other such vibrations of the earth

*Pronounced as size-mik

Aquatic: relating to water

Arboreal: relating to trees

Aerial: relating to air; for example, an aerial view of the city

Astral: relating to the stars

*Synonyms: **stellar** (stellar also means excellent, outstanding), **sidereal** (from Latin 'sider' meaning star)

Supernal: relating to the sky or the heavens

*Synonym: **celestial**

Spatial: relating to space

The spatial distribution of population shows clustering in the towns and cities.

*Pronounced as spay-shial

Hibernal: relating to or occurring in winter

Nautical: relating to the sea, navigation, ships, sailors, etc.

The compass is the most important nautical equipment.

*Synonyms: **naval, maritime**

Pelagic: relating to the open seas or oceans

The book was on the pelagic wanderings of the sailor.

*Pronounced as puh-laj-i

*Synonym: **thalassic**

■

Brooke: a small stream of water

*Synonym: **rivulet**

Ford: a crossing in a river where the water is shallow

Delta: the change in a measurable and certain quantity

Shoal: a low lying sandbank on the shore of a sea which becomes visible when the water is low; shoal also means a large number of fish

Cay: a small low island or a bank of sand and coral

*Plural: cays

Tombolo: a sandbar that joins an island to the mainland or to another island

*Etymology: from Italian meaning 'sand dune'

Catchment area: the area served by an institution

The hospital provides free medical facilities to the people living in its catchment area.

■

Grassland: an area covered with grass where cattle are taken to graze

*Synonyms: **prairie** (*pronounced as pray-reeh), **savannah** (*pronounced as suh-van-uh), **meadow, pasture**

Swamp: waterlogged land unfit for cultivation

*Synonyms: **slough, bog, marsh, morass** (*pronounced as mo-ras), **quagmire** (*pronounced as kwag-my-ur)

All these words also mean a complex and hazardous situation.

Bayou: a marshy outlet of a lake or river

Thicket: a dense group of bushes or trees

*Synonym: **copse** (*pronounced as cops)

Hedge: a row of bushes or small trees that form a boundary; hedge also means to safeguard oneself against loss on an investment by making other transactions to balance or compensate for this risky investment

Coppice: an area where trees are grown and regularly cut back to the ground to provide wood and stimulate regrowth

*Pronounced as cop-is

Grove: a small forested area

*Homonym: groove (a cut in a metal or an established routine)

Wilderness: a wild and uncultivated area like a jungle

Badlands: large tracts of land that are heavily eroded and uncultivable

Boondocks: a remote sparsely populated rural area, which is far away from the main cities

*Synonyms: **boonies**, outback, backwoods, back country

■

Bale: a large bound bundle of hay, cotton, etc.

*Synonym: **truss** (truss also means a cluster of flowers growing on single stalk; *plural: trusses)

Tuft: a small bunch or cluster of feathers, hair, thread, etc.

Tussock: a clump of growing grass

Tendril: a thin, leafless organ of a climbing plant that grows in a spiral form and attaches itself by twining around an object to support the plant

Timber: trees grown for commercial use

Timber also means the wood so produced ready for commercial use, after the cutting of such trees.

Briquette: a small block of compressed coal dust or charcoal as fuel, usually for barbecuing

*Pronounced as brick-et

*Plural: briquettes

■

Twilight: evening time when there is semi-darkness
Dusk: sunset
Dawn: sunrise

■

Suave: gentlemanly
All the ladies swooned over his suave mannerisms.
*Synonyms: **urbane**, **debonair**, polished, refined, cultured, courtly, courteous, civil, sophisticated, **genteel**, decorous
Svelte: thin and graceful
The hostess of the party was svelte and sophisticated.
*Pronounced as svelt
Courtesy: polite words or actions
Doctors never take fees from other doctors as a matter of professional courtesy.
*Synonym: **politesse** (*pronounced as poly-tess)
Chivalry: courteous behaviour, especially from a man towards a woman
It is considered by some chivalrous to stand when a woman enters a room.
Decorum: dignified and decent behaviour; good manners
The hotel expected all its diners to maintain decorum and not talk loudly.
*Synonyms: **poise**, **grace**, **civility**, **etiquette** (*pronounced as eti-ket)
Aplomb: self-confidence or self-assurance, in a difficult situation
The chairperson of the committee presided over the heated proceedings with aplomb
*Synonym: poise
*Antonyms: gaucherie, gaucheness

■

Fiend: a wicked person
Hooligan: a rowdy guy
*Synonyms: **lout, vandal, ruffian, brawler**
Brute: a savage person
*Synonyms: **barbarian, ogre**
Boor: a uncivil and bad-mannered person
*Synonyms: **oaf, philistine, Neanderthal** (*etymology: the Neanderthal are an extinct subspecies of humans who inhabited Europe and parts of Asia in the prehistoric times; *pronounced as nee-ander-thawl)
*Adjective form: boorish, oafish, **uncouth** (*pronounced as un-kooth), **churlish, coarse** (literally meaning rough in texture), **gruff** (literally meaning rough like a

gruff voice), rude, impolite, uncultured, discourteous, ungallant, unchivalrous, indecorous
Tartar: a savage and ill-tempered person
*Etymology: Tartar was a member of the combined forces of the Mongols and Turks who, under Genghis Khan, conquered Asia and Eastern Europe in the thirteenth century.
Trollop: a derogatory term for a woman who has many sexual partners
Troglodyte: a person who lives in a cave; a hermit; a person who chooses to remain ignorant or old-fashioned
Luddite: a person opposed to technological change
*Etymology: Luddites were an organization of English textile workers in the nineteenth century who destroyed textile machinery because they feared that the machines were taking away their jobs. This movement was named after Ned Ludd, a fictional apprentice who allegedly smashed machines in protest.
Opportunist: a person who takes advantage of opportunity, while abandoning all moral principles and ethical concerns
He was an opportunist who would change political parties just before every election.
Carpetbagger: a political candidate who seeks to win an election in a constituency where he or she has no prior connection
*Etymology: Carpetbaggers are referred to the residents of North US who went to the South US (states like Texas) to profiteer from the reconstruction after the Civil War in the 1860s. Carpetbag refers to the bag they carried, which was usually made of cheap carpet fabric.
Egalitarian: a person who believes that everyone in society should be treated equally
*Etymology: from French *'egal'* meaning equal

■

Demeanour: a person's outward behaviour, such as body language and facial expressions
*Pronounced as dee-mean-er
Disposition: a person's general character or mental nature
*Synonyms: attitude, **temperament**, **temper**
Trait: a distinguishing characteristic of one's personality
Patience is his most admired traits.
*Synonym: **attribute** (Sensitivity is best attribute)
Stance: the viewpoint of a person towards something
The politician's drastic stance on death penalty sparked a major public debate.

*Synonyms: outlook, standpoint, perspective

∎

Obstinate: stubborn; refusing to change one's mind despite persuasion
The obstinate seller refused to even negotiate the price with the buyer.
*Synonyms: **adamant, obdurate, refractory, intransigent, intractable** (intractable also means unmanageable; for example, the intractable problem of global warming), **mulish, pig-headed**, unyielding, inflexible, unbending
*Antonyms: yielding, amenable (amenable also means open to suggestions: he was amenable to the idea of moving to another town)
Recalcitrant: someone who has a stubbornly uncooperative towards authority and discipline
The recalcitrant children just wouldn't listen to their teacher.
*Pronounced as re-cal-si-trunt
*Antonym: obedient
Recrimination: counter accusation
The public was tired of the squabbling and recriminations between the government and the opposition
Remonstrate: to forcefully protest
We remonstrated against the tax hike.
Picket: a person who stands outside the site of a protest (like a factory) and persuades others (other workers or customers) to not enter that place

∎

Impudent: rude, arrogant, disrespectful
The impudent young kid was disliked by the teachers.
*Synonyms: **impertinent, insolent, pert, cheeky**
*Noun forms: impudence, impertinence, insolence, **effrontery, gall** (*pronounced as gawl), cheekiness, nerve, pertness
Upstart: a person who has recently gained importance and has let that get to his/her head and thus become rude and arrogant
Parvenu: a person who has recently gained wealth and fame but not yet become refined and cultured and ostentatiously displays their wealth
*Pronounced as pahr-vuh-noo
*Synonyms: **vulgarian, nouveau riche** (*pronounced as noo-voh reesh), **arriviste** (*pronounced as ayr-ee-veest)

∎

Obstreperous: noisy; rowdy; difficult to control
The teacher complained to the principal about the obstreperous students.
*Pronounced as ubs-trep-uh-rus
*Synonyms: **unruly, clamorous, boisterous, raucous** (*pronounced as raw-kus), **rambunctious** (The rambunctious child was difficult to handle; *pronounced as ram-bunk-shus), **lumpen**
Ruckus: a chaotic situation
The angry students created a ruckus.
*Synonyms: **commotion, bedlam, mayhem, pandemonium, hurly-burly**
Tantrum: a sudden burst of anger and frustration, typically done by a kid
*Synonym: **hissy fit**
Paroxysm: a sudden burst of intense emotions
The flight delays sent the passengers into a paroxysm of rage.
*Pronounced as par-awks-ism
Furore: an outcry of public anger
The not guilty verdict raised a furore over the powerful getting away with murder.
*Pronounced as few-rawr
Fracas: a noisy physical fight between people
The police had to break up the fracas in the street.
*Pronounced as frak-ah
*Synonyms: **brawl, affray, scuffle, tussle, melee** (*pronounced as may-lay), **free-for-all, skirmish, scrimmage** (*pronounced as skrim-ij), **clash**
Slugfest: a fist fight
*Synonym: **fisticuff**
Altercation: a noisy verbal fight between people
*Synonyms: quarrel, **squabble, shouting match, contretemps**, war of words, wrangle, spat, tiff
Contentious: controversial
*Synonyms: disputable, debatable
Dissension: a major and angry disagreement
*Synonyms: conflict, **strife, discord, dissonance, disputation, contention**
*Antonym: harmony
Disaffection: a feeling of dissatisfaction and annoyance: There was disaffection among the soldiers.
*Synonyms: **disgruntlement, discontent**
*Antonyms: contentment, satisfaction
Exasperation: the feeling of being upset or annoyed because of results not showing
The teacher was exasperated as the children would not settle down.
*Synonym: **frustration**

■

Bicker: to quarrel about minor things
The couple bickered about who moved the remote from the table.
*Synonyms: to **squabble**, to spar
Spar: to quarrel; to argue
The couple sparred over their joint finances.
Spar also means to train for boxing by making the motions of boxing but without actually landing any heavy blows on the sparring partner.
Duel: a fight between two persons, fought with deadly weapons to settle a private quarrel
*Pronounced as dual
*Homonym: dual (double)
Bout: boxing or wrestling match; a short spell of intense activity or a short period illness
He was suffering from a bout of malaria.
Derby: a horse race; an important sporting event
*Plural: derbies
Tourney: a tournament, especially a medieval joust
*Plural: tourneys
Pugilist: a boxer

■

Caw: the harsh and grating sound made by a crow
Coo: the soft and murmuring sound made by a pigeon
Chirp: the short and sharp sound made by a bird
Caterwaul: the wailing of a cat
Croak: the deep hoarse sound made by a frog
Cackle: a loud and harsh laugh (the cackle of a witch)
Crackle: a series of short and sharp cracking sounds
The crackling of the burning wood in the bonfire.
Creak: to make a harsh, high-pitched sound, especially when made by wooden objects when they are moved or pressure is applied on them
*Homonym: creek (a small inlet of water into a land)
Cluck: to make a short and low sound to express concern or disapproval
The mother clucked at her plan to go to California.
Clack: to make quick sharp sounds
The clacking keyboard.
Clatter: a continuous rattling sound
The clatter of the heels on the floor.
Clink: sharp ringing sound like when glass is struck
The clinking of champagne glasses at the party.
Clang: loud noise made especially by metals
The alarm bell started to clang when the air raid started.

Clangour: loud noise created by banging
The clangour at the factory.
Clamour: loud noise created usually by people shouting
The clamour in the Parliament made an unseemly sight.
*Synonyms: **din, racket, uproar, rumpus, brouhaha, babel, hubbub, hullabaloo, tumult**
Clapper: the metal part which strikes the bell to make the sound
Cacophony: a discordant mixture of sounds
The cacophony of city traffic.
Chime: the short melodious ringing sound made by a clock
The clock chimed midnight.
*Pronounced as chime and not kime
Croon: to sing in a low and soft voice
Trill: to make a low vibratory sound
The phone line trilled when he called her landline.
Jangle: to make a ringing metallic sound
The keys jangled in his keychain.
Jangle also means to make someone uncomfortably excited.
Grunt: to make a low and short guttural (coming from the stomach) sound, like the kinds a pig makes
Gurgle: to make a bubbling sound like when water comes out of a bottle
Rustle: to make a soft, muffled sound like that caused by the moving of leaves in the wind
Squawk: the harsh noises made by birds like seagulls
Squeal: a loud, piercing, high-pitched noise
The injured dog squealed in pain.
*Synonyms: **shriek** (She let out a shriek), **screech** (tires screeching), **squall** (the baby squalling), **wail** (the child's wailing), **yelp** (a young girl yelping in pain), **howl** (a mother howling over a loss), **blare** (sirens blaring)
Squelch: a soft sucking sound made such as the sound made when walking on wet mud
He could hear the squelch of their boots in the mud.
Snort: to make a sudden loud sound by forcefully breathing in through one's nose to express indignation or derision or when excited or frightened
Ululate: to howl or wail like a dog to express sadness
She started to ululate when she heard the bad news.
*Pronounced as youl-youl-ate
Bray: the loud, harsh cry of a donkey or mule
The hungry mules suddenly started braying.
Whinny: the gentle, high-pitched noise made by a horse
*Pronounced as vine
*Synonym: **neigh** (*pronounced as ney)
Hoot: the low, wavering musical sound made by an owl

Honk: the loud and harsh sound made by a car horn

Toot: the short, sharp sound made by a trumpet, horn, whistle, etc.

Toll: the sound produced by the striking of a bell

Thrum: a continuous rhythmic sound
The thrum of the guitar strings.

Strum: to play a stringed instrument (like a guitar) by running one's fingers gently across the strings

Plectrum: a small and thin piece of plastic or metal that is worn on one's finger to pluck the strings of a musical instrument like a guitar

Pitter-patter: the sound of quick taps or steps
The pitter-patter of the children's feet in the house.

■

Dulcet: pleasant sounding
He remembered the dulcet voice of his grandmother.
*Pronounced as dul-sit
*Synonyms: soothing, sweet-sounding, **mellifluous, euphonious** (*pronounced as you-phoni-us)**, mellow, honeyed, tuneful, melodious**

Sonorous: capable of giving out a deep, ringing sound
The sonorous alloy was used to make wind chimes and bells.
*Synonyms: **resounding, resonating, reverberating, orotund** (*pronounced as awr-uh-tuhn)**, pealing, booming, rumbling**

Resound: to echo
The voice of the opera singer resounded throughout the theatre.
*Synonyms: to **reverberate**, to **resonate**, to **peal** (The alarm began to peal)

Bellow: to shout
The contestants bellowed during the debate.
*Synonyms: **yell, bawl, holler**

Baritone: a heavy adult male voice
The performer sang in a rich baritone and impressed the judges of American Idol.

Stentorian: loud and powerful
The actor had a stentorian voice.
*Synonyms: booming, roaring

Strident: rough and harsh sounding
The singer's voice became strident after years of non-stop smoking.
*Synonyms: **grating, raspy, jarring, shrill, gruff, husky, hoarse, gravelly, guttural, croaky**

■

Carillon: a set of bells, usually hung on a tower and used to play a tune
Carillon also means a piano type instrument but in which bells are used to make the sound.
*Pronounced as car-uh- lawn
*Plural: carillons

Tocsin: an alarm bell
*Pronounced as tok-sin

Peal: the loud ringing of bells
*Pronounced as peel
*Plural: peals (His idea was met with peals of laughter)
*Synonym: **tintinnabulation**

Gong: a large metal disk, usually made of bronze, originally of Asian origin, which produces a loud sound when struck and thus used as a signal

■

Oblivion: the state of being unconscious or unaware
The popstar produced on hit and then faded into oblivion.
*Adjective form: oblivious (The minister seemed oblivious to the negative effects of the new law)
*Adverb form: obliviously
*Antonyms: cognizant, aware, conscious

Amnesia: a partial or total loss of memory, caused by a brain injury, shock, etc.
He suffered from amnesia after the car accident.
*Pronounced as am-nee-zhia
*Adjective form: amnestic
*Related word: amnesiac (a person affected by amnesia; *pronounced as am-nee-zheeak)

■

Cognizance: knowledge or awareness
The CEO was not cognizant of the latest developments in the field.
*Adjective form: cognizant, aware, **privy** (After leaving the job, he was no longer privy to the inner workings of the company. Privy also means a toilet)

Apprise: to inform
The army chief apprised the Defence Minister about the latest attack.
*Homonym: **appraise** (to assess something's value)

Insight: accurate and deep understanding on an issue

Perception: one's own interpretation
*Synonym: **discernment**

Incisive: sharp and direct to the point with clear and analytical thinking

His incisive comments impressed the professor.
*Synonyms: **keen, acute**, piercing, penetrating
Astute: clever, showing quick wit and good judgement
The astute investor made solid profits during the bull-run
*Synonyms: **canny, shrewd**, prudent
*Noun form: astuteness, canniness, prudence, **acumen, acuity**
Perspicacious: keeping a sharp eye on things; observing details; having keen insights on a field
The perspicacious real-estate investor had a good eye for property.
*Pronounced as purse-pi-kay-shus
*Synonyms: **perceptive, percipient, discerning, observant, insightful**.
*Noun form: perceptiveness, perspicaciousness, perspicacity, discerningness

■

Knoll: a small hill
*Pronounced as nol
*Synonyms: **mound, dune, hummock**
Ridge: a hill; an elevation of land formed when the land folded up due to two opposing tectonic plates pushing against each other
Furrow: a wrinkle or fold on one's face
His furrowed eyebrows.
Pleat: a fold in a garment
He wore pleated pants.
Crease: a line produced in a garment by folding it

■

Kink: a sharp twist or curve in something that is usually very straight
There were many accidents at that spot because of the kink in the road.
Arch: a shape which is like a bow (a symmetrical curve)
He arched his eyebrow whenever he got surprised.
Crescent: shaped like a half-moon or a semicircle
The crescent sand dunes in the desert.
*Pronounced as kre-sent
*Synonym: sickle-shaped
Elliptic: oval shaped
Orb: a spherical object or shape
Oblong: a shape in the form of a rectangle with semi-circular ends
Tesseract: the four-dimensional analogue of a cube
Cardioid: a heart-shaped curve

Ovoid: egg-shaped
Sigmoid: S-shaped
Cuboid: cube shaped
Naviform: boat-shaped
*Synonym: **navicular**
Stelliform: star-shaped
*Pronounced as stel-uh-form

■

Pore: tiny opening in a surface; for example, the pores in our skin
Orifice: a hole; an opening especially in the body for example the nostril or the anus
*Pronounced as ori-fis
Chink: a narrow gap or hole
There was a chink in his armour.
*Synonyms: **aperture** (*pronounced as app-er-cher), **crack, cranny**
Crevice: a narrow gap in a wall
The thief escaped through a crevice.
*Pronounced as krevis
Cavity: a small hole or chamber
He got his tooth cavity filled up.
Cavern: a large cave
Crater: a large bowl-shaped hole on the earth's surface, caused by a blast
Rut: a track on the ground made by repeated passage of vehicles
Pit: a large hole in the ground
Pothole: a hole in a road, usually caused by rains
Sinkhole: hole in the ground caused by water erosion
Groove: a long narrow cut in a metal; an established routine
He got back in his groove after some time off.
*Homonym: **grove** (a small forested area)
Void: an empty space
He filed the void created by the loss with alcohol.
*Synonyms: **vacuum, vacuity**
Vacant: empty; unoccupied
Many of the job openings are still vacant because of the low salary on offer.
*Noun form: vacancy
Lacuna: a gap especially in a piece of text
The court filled the lacuna in the law by issuing guidelines.
*Plural: lacunae, lacunas
Indentation: a depression or hole on the surface of something

His shoes left an indentation on the wet mud.

Quarry: a large pit from which stones, etc. are extracted

Gorge: a steep and deep valley; gorge also means to overeat (The kids gorged on the cake)

*Synonyms: **ravine, canyon, gully, chasm, gulf**

Shaft: a vertical tunnel

The mine shaft got flooded due to the rains.

Trench: a long and deep depression on the ocean bed

The explorers went to study Mariana Trench in the Pacific Ocean.

Abyss: a deep bottomless hole

His money wasting habits led him to the abyss of bankruptcy.

■

Fissure: a long, narrow opening formed by the cracking and splitting of the earth due to seismic activity

Rift: a crack or split

Money problems led to a rift in their relations.

*Synonym: **schism** (*pronounced as skizm)

Cleave: to split; to tear apart

The disagreement threatened to cleave the party into two rival camps.

*Synonyms: to crack open, to lay open, to **sever**, to **splinter**, to **rend**, to **rive**, to **rupture**

*Noun forms: cleaving, rupture, severance, separation, disjuncture, fission

*Antonyms of the noun form (i.e. antonyms of cleaving and severance): joining, **fusion, amalgamation, conjugation**, merger, integration

Cleft: split into two

Cleft lip is a common issue with new born kids.

*Synonyms: **cloven, bisected**

Asunder: apart

The unhappy families tore the couple asunder.

Splinter: a small sharp piece that has broken off from the larger piece of wood, metal, glass, etc.

*Synonyms: **sliver, shard, chip**

■

Plume: a cloud of smoke

The thick black plumes of pollution coming out of the factory.

Nimbus: a large rain cloud

Halo: the circle of white light above the head of a saint or an angel, showing their holiness

*Synonyms: **corona, aureole** (*pronounced as awr-ee-ohl)

Aura: a spiritual field emanated by a person that tells their nature

The heroine had an aura of superstardom around her.

Vibe: the general feeling of a person or place

She picked up bad vibes from the new guy at the office.

■

Vagary: an unexpected and unexplainable change in a situation

The meteorologists could not explain the vagaries of the weather.

*Pronounced as vay-gur-ee

*Synonym: **fluctuation**

*Plural: vagaries

Vicissitude: change of circumstances; the ups and downs

He was unable to handle the vicissitudes of the stock market.

*Pronounced as vi-sisi-tude

Volatile: ever-changing

The political situation just after the coup was very volatile.

*Synonyms: inconstant, unstable, turbulent, fluctuating, fluid, mutable, **protean** (artificial intelligence is a protean subject), fitful, wavering

*Antonyms: stable, constant

Volatile also means easily evaporated at normal temperatures; for example, Benzene is a volatile solvent.

Labile: changing often and easily

She was drawn to emotionally labile bad boys.

*Labile also means easily broken down (The labile proteins disintegrated quickly when exposed to heat)

*Pronounced as label

*Synonym of labile with respect to changing often: **mercurial, quicksilver** (He has a quicksilver temper; *etymology: quicksilver is mercury's common name)

Capricious: moody and unpredictable; given to sudden and unexplainable changes of mood or mind

He had a tough time working with his capricious boss.

*Synonyms: **fickle, whimsical** (The princess had a whimsical nature; *etymology: whim means sudden and unexplainable change of mood or mind: she bought the expensive purse on a whim)

Capricious also means erratic and volatile (The coastal town had very capricious weather)

Erratic: unpredictable

His erratic work schedule started to affect his health.

Flux: continuous change

After the military coup, the whole government structure was in a state of flux.

■

Influx: an arrival of a large number
The country was not ready to accommodate the heavy influx of refugees.
Efflux: material that is flowing out
The routing for the jet efflux also needs to be considered.
Advent: the arrival of an important person or thing
With the advent of the internet, global communications became much easier.
Effluent: liquid waste that is discharged into a water body
*Synonyms: **sewage, effluvium, discharge, sludge, slime**
Emission: gases that are discharged as a result of commercial activity
Defecate: to discharge faeces from the body
*Pronounced as defi-cate
*Noun form: defecation, bowel movement
Faeces: bodily waste matter discharged through the anus; dung
*Pronounced as fee-sees
*Synonym: excrement
Excrete: to expel the waste products caused by metabolism
The liver excreted the by-products into the blood
*Synonym: **egest**
Secrete: to produce and discharge a substance
The job of the pancreas is to secrete insulin to control the sugar levels in the body.
Ejaculate: to eject semen from the body at the moment of sexual climax
Incursion: a sudden yet brief attack
The army was prepared to handle the enemy incursion into our country.
Excursion: a short fun trip
They went on an excursion to the zoo.
*Synonyms: **outing, jaunt**
Junket: an extravagant trip by government officials on taxpayers money with the aim for doing official work but the real reason being enjoyment
Ingress: entry
Measures to stop the ingress of illegal immigrants
Egress: exit
The passengers want a quick egress after the long flight.

■

Resurgence: revival
Everyone in the West is worried about the resurgence of divisive forces like Nazism.
Resurrection: the coming back to life after death
Some Russians want the resurrection of the old Soviet Empire.
*Pronounced as rez-uh-rek-shun
*Etymology: In the Bible, Jesus Christ was resurrected after being crucified.
Rejuvenation: the process of restoring something to a younger state
There are many government programmes for the rejuvenation of the river.
Renovation: the process of restoring something that is old and broken, back to a good condition
*Synonyms: **refurbishment, revamp, facelift**
Resuscitation: the act of reviving someone from unconsciousness
The medical workers successfully resuscitated the drowning victim.
*Pronounced as ri-sus-ee-ta-shun
*Verb form: to resuscitate
Rehabilitation: the act of restoring someone to health or normal life
Jails should have good rehabilitation programmes for the convicts.
Recuperate: to recover from illness
The patient recuperated in the ICU after the surgery.
*Synonyms: **convalesce** (*pronounced as con-va-less)
*Antonym: deteriorate
Recusal: the withdrawal by a judge from a case due to possible conflict of interest
*Verb form: to recuse
Renaissance: this is the period of revival of arts, science and literature in Europe in the fourteenth to sisteenth centuries, which started after the end of the Dark Ages (fifth to fourth centuries)
*Pronounced as ren-ay-saans
Reconnaissance: a quiet exploration done by the military to get information on the enemy area
*Pronounced as ri-con-uh-suns
*Synonym: **recce** (*pronounced as rek-ee)
Reiterate: to repeat something for added emphasis
The news anchor reiterated the negative impacts of air pollution.
*Noun form: reiteration
Iteration: the process of making a newer version of a product, improving upon its prototype (first version)

Apple iPhone XR is the latest iteration of the iconic smartphone.

Rehash: to reuse old ideas and material again without any improvement or addition The song writer was criticized for rehashing his old songs.

■

Embark: to go on board a ship, aircraft, etc.
He embarked at Mumbai for his holiday cruise to Singapore.
*Antonym: disembark
Commute: the daily travel from one's home to work place and back
Expedition: a journey undertaken for a particular purpose like academic research or exploration
The scientists went on an expedition to Africa.
Voyage: a long journey by the sea or space
Vasco da Gama reached Africa after an arduous voyage.
*Synonym: **odyssey**
Trek: a hike; a long journey on foot
He went on a mountain trek.
Safari: an expedition to see animals in the wild.
Sojourn: a temporary stay
During his sojourn in Paris, he visited the Eiffel Tower.
*Pronounced as soh-jurn
Peregrination: a long wandering journey, especially the one made on foot
He visited many villages during his peregrination in Tibet.
Pilgrimage: a journey to a holy place
Quest: a search or pursuit
He was always on a quest for knowledge.
Crusade: a campaign
He is on a campaign to wipe out corruption.

■

Sortie: a short flight by a single military plane
The pilot flew three sorties into the enemy territory to gather military intelligence.
Debrief: to question a soldier, astronaut, etc., on the return from a mission to get useful intelligence and assess the result of the mission
Deploy: to move and station troops for military action
The troops were deployed to the border.
Marshal: to gather and assemble a group of soldiers
The Army General marshalled his troops to prepare for the attack on the enemy.
Martyr: a soldier killed on the battlefield

Muster roll: an official list of soldiers in a military unit
Defenestrate: to throw someone out of a window
Ceasefire: a temporary stoppage of fighting
*Synonyms: **truce**, suspension of hostilities, **armistice**
(*pronounced as ahr-muh-stis)

■

Junta: a military group that rules a country by force
Militia: a military force that consists of civilians and developed in order to supplement a regular army
*Pronounced as mili-shia
Para-military: a military force that is organized like an army but performs civil functions
Gestapo: the Nazi secret police
*Pronounced as gus-taapo
Storm trooper: a member of the Nazi paramilitary

■

Skewer: a long piece of wood or metal used during a barbecue; to intensely question someone (The Home Minister was skewered by the journalists)
Lance: a long spear, typically used by knights in jousting
Pike: a spear used by foot soldiers in the infantry
Javelin: a light spear thrown in a competitive athletic sports
Harpoon: a very large spear used to catch whales
Trident: a three-pronged spear
Pitchfork: a farm instrument with a long wooden handle and two sharp metal tips, used for lifting hay.
Bayonet: a long knife-like blade attached to the muzzle of a rifle, used in hand to hand combat
Prong: a tip; each of three projecting pointed parts of a fork
A trident has three prongs.
*Synonym: **tine**
Prickle: a small thorn
Barb: a sharp point near the tip of an arrow or fish hook
They traded barbs.

■

Hatchet: a small axe
Tomahawk: a small axe as used by the Native Americans
Machete: a sword used in Central America
*Pronounced as muh-shet-ee
Dagger: a knife with a pointed blade, usually used for stabbing

Scalpel: a small knife used by surgeons

Sickle: an agricultural tool which consists of a semi-circular blade mounted on a short handle used for cutting grain, grass, etc.
*Plural: sickles

Scythe: an agricultural implement consisting of a long, curving blade fixed to a long wooden stick used for cutting grass
*Pronounced as saa-ith

Shank: a makeshift knife, made of a razor blade on a toothbrush handle

Lancet: a small two-edged knife used in surgery
*Pronounced as lan-sit

Cutlass: a short slightly curved sword used by sailors and pirates

Sabre: a heavy sword, slightly curved and having only one sharp edge, typically used by soldiers on horses
*Pronounced as say-bur

Katana: the sword used by Japanese samurai

■

Sheath: the cover for a knife or a sword
*Synonym: **scabbard**

Holster: the holder for a gun, usually made of leather and worn on a belt

Pommel: the rounded knob on the end of the handle of a sword

■

Baton: a thin wooden stick used by an orchestra conductor or a thick wooden stick used by a patrol officer
*Synonym: staff

Cane: a walking stick; a stick used as an instrument for punishment

Wand: a thin wooden stick used by magicians for conjuring spells

Sceptre: an ornamental staff (stick) carried by royalty and usually made of gold
*Pronounced as sep-ter

Bludgeon: a thick wooden stick used in a fight
*Pronounced as bluj-un
*Synonyms: **club, cudgel** (*pronounced as kuj-uhl), **truncheon**

Mace: a thick wooden stick with a spiked metal head used in a fight

Boomerang: a curved piece of wood that looks almost like an 'L' that returns to the owner due to its aerodynamic construction if it doesn't hit the target and was traditionally used by Australian Aborigines for hunting (The alcohol ban boomeranged on the government as it lost all the tax revenue)

■

Artillery: large guns, usually mounted on vehicles, used in warfare
*Synonyms: heavy weaponry, **cannonry**

Munition: materials used in war, such as weapons and ammunition
*Synonym: **armament**

Ammunition: a supply of bullets and shells

Ordnance: military supplies like guns and bombs; large guns mounted on wheels; the branch of government dealing with such military equipment

Arsenal: the collection of weapons or military equipment or the place where such a collection is stored
*Plural: arsenals
*Synonyms: **armoury** (*plural: armouries), arms depot, arms cache, ordnance depot

Ballast: heavy material like gravel, etc., placed in a ship to give it stability

Catapult: an old time military machine that worked on lever and ropes for throwing large stones, etc., at the enemy
*Synonym: **trebuchet** (*pronounced as tre-boo-shay)

Shrapnel: the fragments of a bomb (like the shell or nails) that are thrown out by the explosion

Whip: a strip of leather cord on a handle used to flog someone

Archery: the sport of shooting at targets with a bow and arrows

Archer: a person who shoots with a bow and arrow
*Synonym: bowman

Quiver: an archer's case for holding his or her arrows

■

Pennant: a small triangular flag
*Synonyms: **pennon, streamer, guidon**

Banderole: a long narrow flag
*Synonyms: **banner, bannerol**

Ensign: a military flag that indicates the nationality
*Synonym: **jack**

Burgee: a triangular flag which has the emblem of a sailing club or yacht

Bunting: flags and colourful festive decorations like

draperies and streamers, usually in the colour of the national flag

Gonfalon: a banner, hung across a bar or a beam, used in a religious procession
*Pronounced as gon-fuh-lun

Oriflamme: an ensign or banner that serves as a rallying point in battle
*Pronounced as ori-flahm and not ori-flame
*Plural: oriflammes
*Etymology: from Old French when the red coloured banner of St Denis (with golden flames drawn inside it) was carried by early French Kings as a military ensign and from Latin *'aurum'* (gold) + *'flamma'* (flame)

Sigil: a seal or a symbol
*Pronounced as sij-il

Insignia: a military badge or distinguishing mark of office or honour in the military
The General wore a green khaki uniform with insignias on the collar.
*Pronounced as insig-nia
*Synonyms: **crest, emblem, seal**

Regalia: the emblems of royalty such as the crown or sceptre

Fatigues: non-military menial tasks that soldiers are supposed to perform, many times as punishment such as cooking or cleaning
Fatigues also means the soldier's uniform (typically made of khaki) for such fatigue duty.

∎

Freight: goods transported by various means like train, ships, etc.
*Pronounced as frayt
*Synonyms: **cargo, consignment**

Merchandise: branded products that promote something like a movie, etc.

Ware: articles offered for sale
He hawked his wares at the traffic crossing.
*Synonym: commodity
*Plural: wares

Chattel: a movable item which is the personal property of someone

∎

Pail: a bucket

Receptacle: container
*Synonym: **repository** (repository also means a storehouse; for example, the law school topper was a repository of all things legal)

Coffer: a large strongbox to store money; the financial reserves of an organization
Corporate donations filled up the coffers of the political party.

∎

Hawk: to carry about and offer goods for sale by shouting in the streets
Hawk also means a person who always pushes for war in foreign policy.

Peddle: to try to sell (usually small items) by going from place to place
Peddle also means to advocate something (The radio host was slammed for peddling outlandish conspiracy theories)
*Homonym: **piddle** (to urinate: the puppy piddled on the new carpet)

Tout: to try and sell something by directly approaching the potential buyer and being very persistent. It also means to promote or publicize something (He was touted as the next big thing in music)

Huckster: a door-to-door salesman; an aggressive salesperson; it also means a person who uses showy methods to win votes

Costermonger: a person who sells fruits and vegetables on the streets from a handcart
*Pronounced as coster-monger

Colporteur: a salesman of religious books, newspaper, literature, etc.; a book peddler;
*Pronounced as kawl-porter

Porter: a person employed or hired to carry the luggage of travellers at railway stations, airports, etc.
*Synonyms: baggage carrier, baggage bearer

Skycap: a porter at an airport

Redcap: a porter at a railway station

∎

Easel: a wooden frame which holds the painting, while the artist does the drawing, colouring, etc.
*Pronounced as ee-zul

Canvas: a coarse cloth used as a surface for oil painting
*Homonym: **canvass** (to ask for votes: he canvassed for votes during the election)

Palette: a thin board on which an artist lays and mixes colours
*Pronounced as pal-it

*Homonym: **palate** (the roof of the mouth; the sense of taste: he was known for a very sensitive palate which could distinguish between all types of wines; *pronounced as pal-it)
Decal: a sticker where the design is transferred to a surface using heat

■

Dilettante: a person who develops an interest in an area (like the arts) but in a non-serious way and only for amusement
*Pronounced as dili-tahnt
*Synonyms: **dabbler, tinkerer**
*Antonym: professional
Marionette: a puppet
*Pronounced as marion-et
Silhouette: a shadow; a dark outline of something as seen against a lighted surface
*Pronounced as siloo-et
Pirouette: the act of spinning on one foot, usually done with the other foot touching the knee of the leg of the spinning foot
*Pronounced as piloo-et
Guillotine: a machine with a heavy blade which drops down and used for beheading people
*Pronounced as gil-uh-teen

■

Carousel: a merry-go-round at a fair
It also refers to the conveyor system at an airport which brings the luggage from the plane to the passengers.
Anvil: a heavy block made of iron with a flat top, on which heated pieces of metal are kept and then beaten into a desired shape with a hammer
Foundry: a workshop or factory for casting metal
Derrick: the framework over an oil well, which holds the drilling machinery
Gallows: a wooden structure, consisting of poles, used for the hanging of criminals
*Synonym: **gibbet** (*pronounced as jib-it)
Scaffold: an elevated wooden platform used earlier for hanging criminals but now used for holding workers during the erection of a building
Turret: a small tower, usually occupied on top by a guard with a rifle
Pylon: a tower used for guiding aviators or carrying wires
Tenterhook: a hook used to fasten cloth on a tenter (a drying frame)
*Related phrase: **on tenterhooks** (to be in state of suspense: the student was on tenterhooks waiting for the exam results)

■

Suite: a set of rooms
*Pronounced as sweet
Ghetto: the slum area of a city, usually inhabited by racial minorities
Tenement: an overcrowded apartment complex in a poor neighbourhood
Hutment: a group of huts
Hovel: a small and dirty house
Shack: a hut or a cabin
*Synonym: **shanty**

■

Telegenic: having a physical appearance that looks great on television
*Synonym: **videogenic**
Photogenic: having a physical appearance that looks great in photos
Autotelic: an activity where the purpose of doing is in the activity itself
For example, autotelic people are driven by the desire to accomplish the work in itself and not by money.
*Etymology: Greek, *'self'* (autos) + *'telos'* (goal)
Autodidact: a self-taught person

■

Dowdy: unstylish and unfashionable, especially when referring to a women
They mocked her dowdy appearance.
*Synonyms: **frumpish, frumpy**
Slovenly: untidy and messy
His slovenly appearance irritated his boss.
*Synonyms: shabby, scruffy, **unkempt, slatternly, dishevelled, bedraggled, tousled**, rumpled, frowzy, ill-groomed
Tatterdemalion: a person in tattered, ragged and dirty clothes
Slattern: a dirty, untidy woman
Ragamuffin: a child in ragged and dirty clothes
*Synonym: **urchin**
Waif: a homeless and neglected child
*Pronounced as weyf

Guttersnipe: a badly behaved child who is dirty and badly dressed, belonging to the slums
*Synonym: **street urchin**
Scamp: a lovable and mischievous child

■

Chic: stylish; fashionable
She was wearing a chic designer hat.
*Pronounced as sheek
*Synonyms: **natty** (a natty black blazer), elegant
Dapper: neat and tidy; smart in appearance, usually used for complimenting a man's appearance
He looked very dapper in a dark black three piece suit.
*Synonyms: handsome, **spruce, dashing**, well groomed
Raffish: disreputable and nonconformist in an attractive way
The actor's raffish behaviour attracted many young girl fans.
*Synonym: **rakish**
Comely: good looking, usually used to compliment a woman's appearance
The comely young actress caught the producer's attention.
*Synonym: **prepossessing**
*Antonyms: ugly, unprepossessing
Seemly: decent; decorous; proper
He was seemly dressed for the party.
*Synonyms: fitting, in good taste
*Antonyms: unseemly, unbecoming
Gorgeous: very beautiful
*Synonym: stunning
*Pronounced as gor-jus
Pulchritude: beauty, especially of a woman's
The model's pulchritude brought her millions in advertising contracts.
*Pronounced as puhl-kri-tude
Panache: a stylish and confident way of carrying oneself
The famous actor has a lot of panache that leaves everyone in awe of him.
*Pronounced as puh-naash
*Synonyms: **flair, élan** (*pronounced as ey-laan), **poise**
Posh: related to the upper class, very stylish
He lives in a posh locale
Swanky: very stylish and expensive
The mogul had a fleet of swanky cars.
Faddish: fashionable but soon will become outdated
Faddish diets don't work.
*Etymology: a fad is a temporary craze among people

Vogue: the current trend; the latest fashion
Superhero movies are in vogue right now.
*Pronounced as vohg

■

Fop: a man who is excessively concerned with his clothes and appearance
*Synonym: **dandy**
Preen: to make a lot of effort in dressing up very nicely and then admire one's appearance
Teenagers like to preen in front of the mirrors for hours.
*Synonyms: to **primp**, to **prink**
Ornate: overly decorated; excessively embellished
The ornate office design was aimed at giving an impression of enormous wealth.
*Synonyms: **rococo** (rococo furniture), **curlicued** (having decorative curls in design), **florid** (florid speech), **flowery** (flowery writing), **baroque** (baroque cutlery; *pronounced as buh-rohk)
*Etymology: baroque refers to a highly ornate and extravagant style of architecture and arts in the seventeenth and eighteenth centuries Europe
*Antonyms: **austere**, plain, simple
Tacky: of cheap quality
The bride to be did not like the tacky designs.
*Synonym: **kitschy** (*pronounced as kichy)
Garish: showy; flashy; tasteless
She wore a garish dress to stand out in the party.
*Synonyms: **gaudy, tawdry, trumpery, meretricious** (*pronounced as meri-trish-us; *etymology: in Latin *'meretricius'* means related to a prostitute and *'mereri'* means to be hired)
Bedizen: to dress up or decorate in a tasteless manner; to adorn gaudily
The dictator's uniform was bedizened with many large gold medals.

■

Bespoke: custom made
He bought a costly bespoke three piece suit.
Draper: a textile fabrics seller
Clothier: a clothes seller
Outfitter: a shop selling clothes
Haberdasher: a person who sells men's furnishings such as shirts, ties, gloves, socks, hats, etc.
Milliner: a person who makes and sells women's hats
Seamstress: a female tailor

Seamless: smooth and continuous; without any seams
*Etymology: seams means stitching; *synonym of seams: **sutures** (meaning stitches)
Sartorial: relating to tailoring and style of dressing
His sartorial workmanship got him many customers.
Hemline: the level of the lower edge of a garment like a skirt
The office had a policy that the hemlines must be below the knee.

■

Braid: women's hair woven together
*Synonym: **plait**
Tress: a long lock of a woman's hair
*Plural: tresses (Rapunzel had long golden tresses, which the Prince used to climb up the tower)
Mane: the thick long hair which grows on the back or around the neck of an animal like a horse or a lion
*Plural: manes
Coiffure: a person's hairstyle
*Pronounced as kawf-your
*Etymology: from French 'coiffer' meaning 'arrange the hair'
Toupee: a man's wig, a small patch of artificial hair used to cover a bald spot
*Pronounced as too-pay
*Synonym: **hairpiece**
Torsade: an artificial plait of hair
*Pronounced as tor-sayd
Tonsure: the act of shaving the head
*Etymology: tonsure is the act of shaving the top of a monk's head before entering the religious service
Scalp: the skin covering the head, excluding the face
Alopecia: baldness
*Pronounced as alo-peshia
Pomade: a scented ointment or oil for the hair or scalp

■

Copywriter: a person who writes the text of advertisements
Copyeditor: a person who edits a manuscript for publication
Compositor: a person who arranges the text and pictures of a book
Draughtsman: a person who makes detailed technical plans or drawings
Draftsman: a person who drafts legal documents
Drover: a person who drives cattle from one place to another
Dustman: a person who is employed to empty out the trash cans
Forester: a person employed to be in charge of a forest
Fruiterer: a fruit seller
Rubber tapper: a person who collects the latex from a rubber tree
Furrier: a fur seller
Tanner: a person who makes leather from animal hides
Mason: a peon who does stone, tile and cement work
Glazier: a person who fits glass onto windows and doors
Joiner: a person who constructs the wooden components of a building
Lumberjack: a person who is employed to cut trees; a logger
Steeplejack: a person who climbs tall structures to carry out repairs
Surveyor: a person who examines the condition of land and buildings
Emcee: a master of ceremonies; a person whose job is to introduce performers in a television or stage show
*Synonym: **compère** (*pronounced as kom-pair; *plural: compères)
Ventriloquist: an entertainer who performs with a wooden dummy and who speaks with near zero lip movement so that it seems that voice is coming from the dummy and not the ventriloquist
*Pronounced as ven-trilo-kwist
Frogman: a person who swims under water for the purpose of salvaging, police or military operations, scientific exploration, etc.
Foreman: a supervisor at a factory or construction site. Foreman also means the presiding member of a jury, who speaks on behalf of the others.

■

Vocation: a person's occupation, job or profession
Avocation: a hobby
Graveyard shift: a work shift from midnight to eight in the morning
Moonlight: to secretly have a second job which begins at night after the end of the day shift of one's regular job
The cop moonlighted as a private security officer at a local nightclub.

■

Dabble: to casually take part in an activity
The mogul dabbled in politics.

Dalliance: a brief involvement with something in a non-serious way

The famous actor quickly ended his dalliance with politics.

*Pronounced as dal-ee-uns

Dalliance also means a casual sexual relationship.

Foray: to get involved in a new activity for a short time

The footballer forayed into acting before getting back to sports.

Spree: a period of extreme and unrestrained activity

The killer went on a killing spree and shot twenty people before the police gunned him down.

Tinker: to casually repair something or make minor adjustments

As a child he loved to tinker with his computer.

*Synonym: to **fiddle**

Tweak: to improve a system by making small adjustments to it

*Antonym: **overhaul** (Overhaul means to fix something by completely taking it apart: the entire criminal justice system requires massive overhaul)

Twiddle: to twist or move something purposelessly when one is nervous

The revenue was going down but the sales staff just twiddled their thumbs.

■

Jester: a joker, especially one that would perform at a medieval court

*Synonyms: clown, **buffoon**

Harlequin: a mute comic character in a pantomime, typically masked and dressed in a colourful diamond-patterned

*Pronounced as har-luh-kwin

Courtier: an advisor to a king or a queen

*Synonym: **aide**

Courtesan-a prostitute with high class clients

*Synonyms: **harlot, strumpet**

Concubine: a mistress

Geisha: a Japanese professional hostess, who entertains men with dance and song but not sexual acts

*Etymology: Japanese *'geisha'* (entertainer)

Bordello: a whore house; a house of prostitution

*Synonyms: **brothel, bagnio** (*pronounced as ban-yo)

■

Cortège: a ceremonial procession

For example, a funeral cortège

*Pronounced as cor-tayzh

Convoy: a fleet of vehicles accompanying someone for protection

For example, a police convoy that travels with a head of state.

Cavalcade: a formal procession with people walking, on horseback and riding in vehicles

Motorcade: a procession of motor vehicles, carrying a prominent person

■

Escort: a person who accompanies someone to look after them

*Synonym: **chaperone** (*pronounced as shap-uh-rohn)

Man Friday: a male personal assistant

*Etymology: In Daniel Defoe's novel *Robinson Crusoe*, the eponymous hero calls his servant as Man Friday

*Synonym: **valet** (*pronounced as va-ley; a valet is also the attendant who parks the cars of the patrons of a hotel, restaurant, etc)

Butler: the chief manservant of a house

Lackey: a male servant

*Synonym: flunky (also written as flunkey)

Factotum: a person employed to do small tasks

*Synonyms: odd-job man, **dogsbody** (*etymology: Sailors in the British Royal Navy were fed vary bad food including a pudding made of boiled peas. This pudding was referred to angrily by the sailors as 'Dog's breakfast' and the junior officers who prepared this dish were called 'Dogsbody')

■

Entourage: a group of people attending or surrounding a very important person

The famous actress travelled with an entourage of twenty people.

*Pronounced as on-trazh

*Synonym: **retinue** (*pronounced as ret-noo)

Posse: a group of friends

He had a large posse.

*Pronounced as pos-ee

Groupie: a young woman who follows a rock band on tour, often engaging in sexual relations

*Pronounced as groo-pee

*Plural: groupies

■

Vassal: a lord in a feudal society, who received land from the king in return for his allegiance and military service to the king

Fiefdom: a territory under the complete control of someone

*Etymology: fiefdom originally meant the estate controlled by a feudal lord

Serf: a slave

Servitude: slavery

*Synonyms: **enslavement, bondage, serfdom**

Indentured labour: bonded labour

*Etymology: indentured means bound

Beholden: obligated

The government was beholden to corporate interests because of their large donations.

*Synonyms: indebted, bound

■

Usher: someone employed to show people their seats in a cinema hall

Steward: a flight attendant

*Synonym: cabin attendant

Custodian: a person who has the responsibility of taking care of something

The government is the custodian of the public funds.

Curator: the custodian or keeper of a museum

Conservator: a person who has the responsibility of taking care of cultural or environmental things like historical buildings and forests

Chauffeur: a person employed to a drive

*Pronounced as show-fer

Janitor: a person employed for cleaning like sweeping, mopping, etc.

■

Leeway: freedom to move

The strict deadlines meant no leeway for error.

*Synonyms: margin, **latitude, slack, breathing space, elbow room**

Leisure: free time meant to relax

No one has time for leisure these days.

Furlough: a leave of absence

He went to his hometown during his furlough.

*Pronounced as fur-loh

Sabbatical: a paid leave given to a university teacher or other worker to study and research

*Pronounced as suh-ba-tik-uhl

Respite: a short break

The rains provided a much needed respite from the oppressing summer heat.

Reprieve: the postponement of a punishment

The lawyers were able to secure reprieve from the court just before the hanging.

Remission: the reduction in the punishment or the severity of a disease

The judge ordered remission of the sentence by two years because of mitigating circumstances such as good behaviour.

Commutation: the changing of a punishment from a severe to a less severe one

The Judge orders commutation of his jail term to mandatory community service

*Verb form: to commute

Abeyance: in a state of suspension

The talks were in abeyance till the time the troops were not withdrawn from the border.

Moratorium: a temporary prohibition

The president called for a moratorium on all racial violence.

Hiatus: a pause or gap in activity

He took a hiatus from his career.

*Synonyms: interval, intermission, **recess, halt** (The factory manager halted the production as the raw material finished)

Lull: a temporary period of quiet

There was lull in the fighting between the brother and the sister because of the holiday.

Cessation: the end; stoppage

Nicotine chewing gums patches help in the cessation of smoking.

*Synonyms: **termination, abatement**

Standstill: a situation in which all movement has stopped

Because of the heavy rains, the traffic came to a standstill.

Impasse: a situation in which no progress is possible due to a major disagreement

*Pronounced as im-pass

*Synonyms: **deadlock, stand-off**

Gridlock: a major traffic jam

Dead-end: a situation where no more development can happen

*Synonyms: **blind alley, cul-de-sac** (*pronounced as kuhl-duh-sak; *etymology: from French meaning 'bottom of a sack')

Stalemate: a draw

The match ended in a stalemate.

*Synonym-dead-heat

Sinecure: a job where there is very little work involved but good societal status and pay

The judge lobbied for a post-retirement sinecure.

*Pronounced as sign-ee-cure

*Etymology: Latin *'sine cura'* (without care)

Supersession: the act of replacing one person with another, especially when a junior officer replaces a senior one

Superannuation: the retirement of an employee

Demit: to leave office after the expiry of the tenure

■

Exalt: to raise to a higher rank

The success of the movie exalted him to the status of a megastar.

*Synonyms: to **elevate**, to **aggrandize** (The patriarch purchased the massive house to aggrandize the family's status)

Ennoble: to give someone a noble rank or to confer on someone the title of nobility

The Queen ennobled him as a Knight.

Lionize: to treat someone like a celebrity

Athletes are lionized in the press.

*Synonyms: to glorify, to **fete** (fete literally means a large celebration; *pronounced as feyt)

*Antonyms: **vilify**, condemn

Idolize: to praise and revere excessively as if worshipping an idol of a God

The fans idolize the football star.

*Synonym: **hero-worship**

Valorize: to lend valour to something

We must not valorise extra-judicial killings.

*Etymology: valour means bravery

Swoon: to be overcome with admiration and adoration

The young fan girls swooned over the movie star.

Deify: to worship as a God

The young child was deified because of his resemblance to the deity.

*Synonyms: revere, venerate

*Antonym: to **demonize**

*Homonym: **edify** (to teach someone and improve them morally or intellectually: the teacher told the chatty student to edify the class)

■

Acclaim: to praise very enthusiastically in public

Ben Kingsley was widely acclaimed for his portrayal of Gandhi.

*Synonyms: to **laud** (He was lauded in the press), to **extol** (The Mayor extolled the virtues of the police officer), to **hail** (The actor was hailed in the media), to **rave** about

*Antonym: to criticize

Applaud: to show praise by clapping

The audience applauded the amazing performance by Jennifer Lawrence.

*Noun form: **applause, ovation** (Eminem received a standing ovation)

Adulate: to excessively praise

Despite a mediocre performance, he was adulated in the press.

*Noun form: adulation

Commend: to formally praise

The soldier got a medal commending his bravery on the battlefield.

*Noun form: commendation

Commemorate: to remember and pay respect

The monument commemorates the fallen soldiers.

*Synonym: to pay homage to

Felicitate: to congratulate

The topper was felicitated by his coaching institute in a glittering ceremony.

Plaudit: praise; admiration

The news channel received plaudits for its sustained coverage of the pollution crisis.

*Synonyms: **acclaim, acclamation, accolade, laurel, kudos**

Homage: a special honour shown publicly

The musician paid homage to his mentor at the award ceremony.

*Pronounced as hom-ij

Paean: a song praising someone

*Pronounced as pee-uhn

Encomium: a speech praising someone

The president delivered an encomium for the fallen soldiers.

*Synonym: **panegyric**

Testimonial: a written statement testifying to someone's character

Blandishment: praise meant to persuade someone to do something

*Synonyms: **flattery, cajolery, wheedling, blarney**

■

Eulogy: a mournful speech to remember and honour

someone who has died
*Pronounced as yoo-luh-jee
*Plural: eulogies
*Verb form: eulogize

Elegy: a mournful poem to remember and honour someone who has died
*Pronounced as el-uh-jee
*Verb form: elegize (*pronounced as el-uh-ijze)
*Synonyms: **funeral poem, burial hymn, lament, threnody**

Dirge: a mournful song to remember and honour someone who has died
*Pronounced as durhj
*Plural: dirges

Requiem: the Mass (Christian ceremony) to honour and pray for the souls of the dead
Requiem also means the music played at such a Mass.
*Pronounced as reck-wee-uhm
*Plural: requiems

Coronach: an Irish or Scottish funeral song
*Pronounced as coro-nakh

Monody: a mournful poem to remember and honour someone who has died, sung by a single actor in a Greek tragedy

■

Bust: a sculpture of a person's head, shoulders and chest, usually made in honour of someone

Effigy: a roughly made model of a person, usually made in order to be damaged as a protest against that person
*Pronounced as eff-ee-jee

Mannequin: a dummy of a person used to display clothes in a shop
*Pronounced as mani-quin

■

Metamorphosis: a complete transformation
The actor underwent a metamorphosis from a non-entity to an international celebrity.
*Verb form: metamorphose
*Synonyms: **transmutation, transfiguration**

Morph: to transform an image using software
*Etymology: morph comes from Greek *'morphe'* which means shape

Mould: a hollow container used to give shape by putting molten liquid metal inside it
The swordsmiths poured molten steel into the blade shaped mould to make the sword.

*Synonyms: **cast, die, matrix**, frame

Chassis: the base frame of a car on which the body of the car is supported; the skeleton of a car
*Pronounced as shas-ee

Undercarriage: the wheeled framework under a plane which supports the plane on the ground and is retracted when not in use

■

Ledge: a cliff; a small horizontal surface protruding from a wall

Ledger: a book of accounts

Lodge: a small house
Lodge also means to be firmly fixed into something (The pollution particles get lodged in our lungs; *synonyms: **wedge**)

Leverage: to use something in order to gain advantage from it
He leveraged his skills as an orator to start a litigation practice.

Harness: a piece of equipment which consists of straps, belts, etc. by which a horse is fastened to a cart
*Harness also means to control something in order to utilize it.
For example: we should harness tidal energy to produce electricity.

■

Abortive: something which failed to produce the desired results
The leader of the abortive coup was arrested and executed.
*Synonym: **vain** (His performance went in vain as his team ultimately lost the match)

Futile: pointless
It was futile trying to reason with him as he was very mulish.

Efficacy: effectiveness; the ability to produce the desired results
His efficacy as a bail lawyer was well-known with a near hundred percent success rate.
*Pronounced as effi-kusy
*Adjective form: **efficacious, effectual** (*antonyms: ineffectual, inefficacious)

■

Overarching: comprehensive; all-embracing

The overarching principle in the fast food industry is speed.

Catch-all: a term that encompasses a wide variety of things

'Mental-problems' is a catch-all term that can mean different things.

■

Contemplate: to deeply think about something

*Synonyms: **ponder, mull over, brood over, cogitate** (*pronounced as koji-tate) **ruminate** (*etymology: rumination is the action of chewing the cud by cows)

Conscience: a person's moral sense of right and wrong

Conscious: having awareness of something, especially of one's surroundings

He was still conscious after falling on his head.

*Antonyms: unconscious, **insensible**

Conscientious: meticulous; paying great attention to detail

He conscientiously did his math homework.

*Conscientious also means controlled or influenced by one's conscience (He was a conscientious judge who did not let any biases affect him)

*Pronounced as con-she-en-shus

Subconscious: that part of the mind which one is not fully aware but influences our thoughts and actions

Unconscionable: unreasonable; something that offends the conscience

He repeatedly committed the unconscionable act of adultery.

■

Reflex: instinctive; performed without conscious thought and as an automatic response to a stimulus

Some people sneeze as a reflex reaction when exposed to dust.

*Synonyms: conscious, deliberate

*Adverb form: reflexively (All the members reflexively dismissed the new proposal)

Stimulus: something that evokes a reaction

Our brains are very sensitive to auditory stimuli.

*Plural: stimuli

Cue: a signal for action

He took his cue from the host's unwelcoming voice and politely left the party.

*Plural: cues

*Synonym: prompt

*Etymology: in theatre, a cue is a signal for an actor to begin the performance

Subliminal: something that affects our mind but we are not able to actively notice it: an example of subliminal advertising is the Amazon logo which has an arrow pointing from 'A' to 'Z', indicating their large product range

Patent: obvious; clear and plain

Unless there is a patent irregularity, a trial court order should not be reversed.

*Synonyms: **apparent, manifest, glaring**, self-evident

*Antonyms: hidden, clandestine

Latent: existing but not yet active or apparent

The doctors were worried about latent genetic diseases in the baby.

*Synonyms: **dormant, quiescent** (*pronounced as kwee-es-unt), inactive

Blatant: bad behaviour done openly and without any shame

The politician blatantly lied to the press.

*Synonyms: **flagrant** (a flagrant violation of the law), **brazen** (He brazenly broke the law), **egregious** (an egregious abuse of the law; *pronounced as ee-gree-jeus)

Clandestine: secret

The killers held five clandestine meetings before the mission.

*Synonyms: **covert** (covert operations), **furtive** (furtive glances), **surreptitious** (surreptitious payments from the contractors to the local politician; *pronounced as sur-up-tish-us), **stealthy** (stealthy military missions)

*Antonyms: **overt** (done openly), unconcealed

Conspicuous: something that kept or done in plain sight to attract attention

He placed his trophies conspicuously on the class table.

Salient: the most important and striking

The salient feature of the phone was its 50 megapixel camera.

*Noun form: salience

Substantive: related to reality and facts and thus very important

The gun was the first substantive piece of evidence unearthed by the investigators.

Cynosure: centre of attention

The heroine was the cynosure of all eyes as soon as she walked into the party.

*Pronounced as sign-o-sure

Limelight: public attention

*Etymology: limelight was a type of stage lighting used

in theatres produced by heating quicklime (calcium oxide)

Evince: to show clearly; to reveal
The dumb answers by the candidate evinced his lack of knowledge on policy matters.
*Antonym: conceal

■

Slink: to move quietly to avoid detection
The cat slunk in to the house looking for milk.
*Synonyms: to **tiptoe**, to **creep**
Skulk: to keep out of sight
The stranger skulking outside their office building aroused the staff's suspicion.
Lurk: to hide somewhere waiting for the right moment to attack
The killer was lurking in the shadows, waiting for her to come out of the house.
Loom: to appear in a large and an unclear form and seem threatening
The pirates loomed out of the darkness.
Prowl: to move about in a stealthy way, usually looking for prey or to steal something The cat prowled the empty streets at night in search of food.

■

Confide: to tell someone a secret
He confided in his mother.
Divulge: to reveal someone's secret
He would never divulge any secret.

■

Ephemeral: something that lasts for a very short time; short-lived
Fashion is ephemeral but class is permanent.
*Pronounced as efem-rul
*Synonyms: **evanescent, transitory, transient, temporal, fleeting,** momentary
*Antonyms: long-lived, permanent
Ethereal: delicate and refined; light and airy (like ether)
Everyone complimented the ethereal bride.
*Pronounced as eh-thi-ree-ul
Ineffable: too extreme that it can't be described in words
The ineffable pain of the soldier's widows.

■

Extant: still existing; surviving
There are only four extant copies of the first edition of the Superman comic.
Existential: relating to existence
The party was facing an existential crisis as it secured only 50 seats in the last national elections.
Erstwhile: former
The erstwhile CEO of the company was jailed for fraud.

■

Tangible: something that can be touched and felt because it has a physical presence
The company purchased tangibles like machinery for setting up its factory.
*Synonyms: touchable, **palpable**, concrete
Intangible: something that cannot be touched and felt because it does not have a physical presence
The company hired the lawyers to secure intangibles like patents and trademarks.
*Synonyms: **impalpable, incorporeal** (*pronounced as in-kawr-poh-real)
Corporeal: relating to a person's body
Schools have banned corporeal punishment for children like slaps and cane strikes.
*Pronounced as kawr-poh-real
*Homonym: **corporal** (a mid-level officer in the army)
Somatic: physical; relating to the body and not the mind
The doctor did a check-up of the patient's somatic and psychological symptoms.
*Etymology: Greek *'soma'* meaning body
*Antonym: psychic (mental)

■

Deft: a very light and delicate touch
If only the US had preferred deft touch diplomacy over all-out war in Iraq.
Sleight of hand: expert skill in the usage of one's fingers
Magicians fox audiences with their sleight of hand.
*Pronounced as slight and not slate

■

Caress: to gently touch to show affection or love
He caressed the furry back of his dog.
*Pronounced as cuh-res
Fondle: to touch sexually

■

Insinuation: a hint or a side remark meant to slander someone

He was tired of all the insinuations that he embezzled the company funds.

*Synonyms: **innuendo, allusion, imputation**

Double entendre: a double meaning phrase, usually sexually indecent

*Etymology: from seventeenth century French meaning double understanding

*Pronounced as double-awn-tawn-druh

Undertone: an underlying feeling; hidden meaning; secondary meaning

Today's advertisements have a sexual undertone to them.

*Synonyms: **undercurrent, overtone, subtext**

Overture: a proposal

She was discomfited by her boss's sexual overtures.

Feeler: a tentative proposal which is sent to gauge someone's opinion

The president sent out feelers to the opposition asking for a compromise.

Connotation: the underlying or secondary meaning of a text as opposed to its literal or primary meaning

The word 'home' has a denotation of an abode and connotation of a place of love.

Denotation: the literal or primary meaning of a text as opposed to its underlying or secondary meaning

Subtle: very delicate and fine, and hence difficult to describe

Only a linguist can recognize the subtle differences in the tones of the local dialects.

Nuance: a subtle difference in meaning; a fine distinction

With all the yelling on TV debates, the nuances of the problem are lost.

Nicety: a subtle yet important detail

The lawyer was worried that his client did not understand the niceties of law and would end up in jail.

Punctilio: a fine point of conduct or procedure

The judge insisted on following the punctilios of court procedure and practice.

*Pronounced as punk-tili-oh

*Etymology: from Spanish *'punto'* meaning a point

*Adjective form: punctilious (punctilious means very attentive to details or punctilios: the manager was punctilious in providing every amenity for the guests)

■

Sift: to put a powdery substance through a filter or sieve so as to remove unwanted lumps

We sat all night sifting through the data.

Winnow: to blow air through grain to remove the chaff (seed shells)

It is difficult to winnow out the facts from the chaff of fake news.

Scrutinize: to very carefully and deeply analyse

The prosecutors scrutinized the call logs.

*Synonym: to **assay** (pronounced as a-sey)

Appraise: to assess the quality or value of something

The appraisal of evidence is a crucial aspect of a judge's job.

*Noun form: appraisal

Audit: an official inspection of an organization's accounts

Gauge: to measure something

Scientists tried to gauge the level of unexpected rainfall last year.

*Pronounced as gayj

Fathom: to measure the depth or to understand something

He did not fathom the seriousness of the situation.

*Etymology: a fathom is a unit of length which is equal to 6 feet, and used mostly in nautical measurements

Peruse: to very carefully and deeply read

The judge perused the affidavit.

*Synonym: to **pore** (He pored over volumes of history books for his class project on the independence movement)

*Noun form: perusal

Parse: to break something into its smaller components

The video editors parsed the full movie to take out the juicy parts to make the trailer.

Ferret: to discover information through careful investigation

The inspector swore to the ferret out the truth.

*Etymology: a ferret is a kind of a cat used for catching rabbits

Forage: to search for food

The birds foraged for insects.

Scavenge: to search for and collect something which is usable, from discarded waste

He sold glass bottles scavenged from the garbage.

Delve: to systematically investigate

The inspector delved deep into the matter to look for the truth.

Dissect: to methodically cut up a body in order to study its internal parts

We carefully dissected the judgment to understand its conclusion.

*Homonym: to **vivisect** (to dissect a body while the person is still alive)

Excavate: to unearth

Archaeologists excavated the tomb in Egypt.

Rummage: to hurriedly and unsystematically look for something

He rummaged through his cupboard looking for his favourite shirt.

Ransack: to hurriedly and unsystematically look for something and cause damage to the place

The thief ransacked the house looking for money.

■

Faculty: the mental power inherent in a person; also means a department of a major field of study in a university or the teachers in such a department

Rote: mechanical repetition without any analysis of its meaning

The children learned poem by rote.

Mnemonic: a memory aid

A common mnemonic in biology for the 10 organ systems of the human body is 'NICER DRUMS' which expands to 'Nervous, Integumentary, Circulatory, Endocrine, Respiratory, Digestive, Reproductive, Urinary, Muscular, Skeletal'.

Heuristic: mental shortcuts used to solve problems in a rough and ready way

For example, a common heuristic is social proof (if everyone is using something then that thing should be of good quality).

Rule of thumb: a broadly accurate principle

For example, when in doubt then always gift cash in a wedding

*Etymology: brewers once tested the temperature of a batch of beer by dipping their thumb into the brewing vat

■

Histrionic: melodramatic behaviour aimed to attract attention

The director angrily told the actress to cut out the histrionics.

*Synonym: theatrics

Optics: the way in which the public perceives a political act

The optics of the nuclear deal was very favourable to the government.

■

Salon: barber shop or beauty parlour

*Pronounced as sa-lon

Saloon: a public room meant for a particular purpose (the dining saloon of the ship)

*Pronounced as suh-loon

Saloon also means a bar.

Boutique: a small shop that sells fashionable clothes and accessories

Emporium: a large retail store that sells a vast wide variety of goods

Lounge: a public room meant for people to sit and relax

■

Bassinet: a basket with a hood over one end, used as a baby's bed

Boudoir: a woman's bedroom

*Pronounced as boo-dwaah

■

Softball question: a deliberately asked easy question

Pliant media always asks softball questions to the powerful politicians

*Etymology: softball is an easier version of baseball, where the match is played on a smaller field and the ball is softer than an actual hard baseball

Closed-ended question: simple yes or no question

For example: Is blue your favourite colour?

Open-ended question: a question in which the answer is not a simple yes or no but requires you to give your opinion with reason

For example: Why is blue your favourite colour?

Leading question: a question that leads to a particular answer

For example: The prosecutor asked the psychologist, 'Didn't the defendant appear uncontrollably angry?' The non-leading question would be: 'In your opinion, what was the mental state of the defendant?'

Loaded question: it is a question that is loaded with an unjustified assumption like a presumption of guilt

An example of a loaded question is: So, when did you stop beating your wife?

■

Criterion: a standard by which something is judged

One of the criterions to run for elections is being a citizen of US.

*Plural: criteria, criterions

Norm: standard; convention

The newly inducted officers were expected to stick to strict norms of discipline.

Benchmark: something which is used as a reference point

*Etymology: a benchmark is a surveyor's mark which is cut into a wall or a pillar and is used as a reference point in measuring altitudes

Touchstone: something which serves to measure quality of others

The Supreme Court tested the new law on the touchstone of established constitutional doctrines.

*Etymology: Touchstone is a black quartz stone that is used for testing the purity of gold and silver by observing the colour of the mark which the metal makes when rubbed up against the touchstone.

Gold standard: something of such top quality that it serves a reference for measurement of the quality of others

The iPhone is the gold standard for mobile phones.

*Etymology: earlier, the value of a currency was defined in terms of the amount of gold for which the currency could be exchanged

Yardstick: a standard used for comparison and measurement

Number of hours put in office is not the only yardstick to measure an employee's performance.

*Etymology: a yardstick is a yard long (a yard is three feet) rod, with inch wide markings and is used to measure cloth, etc.

Litmus test: a conclusive test

The final exam was the litmus test of his course preparation.

*Etymology: a litmus test is used in chemistry to test a liquid's acidity or alkalinity using litmus

*Synonym: **acid test** (*etymology: this refers to the use of nitric acid to test the authenticity of gold)

∎

Lightning rod: a person or a body that attracts all the criticism from the public to divert the public's attention away from the real problem

The coal factory owners created a 'Cheap Energy Council' as a lightning rod to distract the public from the problem of global warming.

*Etymology: It is a metal rod placed on top of a building to divert lightning into the ground.

Mother lode: the principal source of something

The investigators hit the mother lode of hidden financial data.

*Etymology: Mother lode refers to the main collection of metal in an ore and lode is a variant of the word 'load'

Lodestone: something which attracts another thing

Scandalous YouTube videos are a lodestone for comments.

*Etymology: a lodestone is a piece of magnetite (a natural rock mineral which has magnetic properties)

Cornerstone: a central feature on which something (like a policy) is based on

Cleaner energy was the cornerstone of the politician's election pitch.

*Etymology: cornerstone is the foundational stone which forms the base of a corner of a building by joining two walls

*Synonym: **keystone** (The central stone placed at the top of an arch that joins the whole thing together)

Bedrock: the fundamental principle on which something is based on

Trust is the bedrock of any relationship.

*Etymology: bedrock is the solid rock underlying loose deposits such as soil or alluvium

*Synonyms: **substratum, substructure**, understructure

Linchpin: a person or thing which is vital to an organization

Good quality nurses are the linchpin of the hospital services.

*Etymology: a linchpin is a pin that passes through the end of an axle to keep the wheel from falling off

Centrepiece: an item that is intended to be the focus of attention

Healthcare reforms were the centrepiece of his Obama's presidency.

*Etymology: a centrepiece is an ornament placed in the middle of a dining table

Wellspring: an abundant source of something

Universities are a wellspring of innovative ideas.

*Etymology: in Old English, 'wiellspring' meant an actual water spring or fountain

Mainspring: the driving force

Necessity is the mainspring behind innovation

*Etymology: mainspring is the spring which makes a clock work

Mainstay: something on which everything else depends on

Agriculture is the mainstay of the rural economy.

*Etymology: mainstay is the main rope that is used to support the mast on a ship

Hallmark: a distinctive feature

A fruity smell is the hallmark of good wine.

*Etymology: hallmarks were marks stamped on articles of gold or silver by the British examining offices, certifying their purity

Tell-tale sign: an outward sign

The lipstick marks on his shirt was a tell-tale sign of an affair.

■

Face-saver: something that provides an honourable exit

As a face-saver, he preferred to resign rather than getting fired from his job.

Failsafe: a backup plan

They hid some cash in the garden as a failsafe in case their house got robbed.

Salvage: to rescue and retrieve a wrecked ship or any of its cargo from the sea

The divers salvaged a box of jewels from the shipwreck.

Contingency: a provision made for a possible future event

They stocked up on groceries as contingency in case of a hurricane.

Redundancy: a useless item; a component inside a machinery that is used as a backup in case the main components fail

The generator had a redundancy switch in case the main switch malfunctioned.

■

Totem Pole: these are wooden poles used by Native Americans with carvings of their important leaders, etc. Higher the position on the totem pole, meant more important the leader.

Pole position: the most favourable position at the start of a race

*Etymology: in horse and motor racing, the fastest qualifying rider or driver would be placed in the most advantageous position in the oval race track

Pecking order: a hierarchy of status

*Etymology: peck means the bite of a bird with its beak; pecking order refers to the social hierarchy seen in chickens, where the most dominant chicken gets the first right over the food

■

Walled garden: a garden enclosed by high walls

In tech, this means a restricted range of services to which only paying users are allowed into.

Paywall: a metaphorical wall which allows only the entry of the paying subscribers of a tech service or website

Ivory tower: a state of privileged seclusion from the ground level realities

Academics are criticized for living in ivory towers and writing papers without any ground knowledge.

*Etymology: in the Christian tradition, ivory tower is used as a symbol for noble purity and referred to the Blessed Virgin Mary

■

Sounding board: a person with whom one shares their ideas, in order to get feedback

The young mayor used his father as a sounding board for many of his bold ideas.

*Etymology: a sounding board is a thin sheet of wood placed inside musical instruments to increase the sound produced

Launchpad: a platform from which something can be launched

American Idol is a great launchpad for a singing career.

*Etymology: a launchpad is the area from which rockets are launched

Springboard: something that supplies the impetus to a change

The economic spending plan was meant to springboard the economy out of a recession.

*Etymology: it is a flexible board used by divers and gymnasts to gain added speed and height when jumping into the swimming pool

Bully Pulpit: a position that allows you to speak to a large audience on an important social issue

*Etymology: This term was coined by US President Theodore Roosevelt, who referred to the office of the US President as a 'bully pulpit'. At that time, the word bully meant 'wonderful'. Pulpit is a raised platform in a Church where the pastor delivers his sermons.

■

Proxy: a person authorized to act on the behalf of another; something used to indicate the value of another

Fancy watches are a proxy for wealth.

Surrogate: a substitute

For many people, reading books about famous tourist

destinations is a surrogate for actual travel to those places.

Bellwether: something that indicates a trend
California is bellwether for US politics as the individual states vote the way California does.
*Etymology: a bellwether is the leading sheep of a flock and has a bell around its neck

Cross section: a small group that represent a large group
The survey completed by a cross section of the voters showed deep discontentment.
*Etymology: a cross section is the surface that is exposed by a straight cut made perpendicular to the object's axis

∎

Man of letters: a scholarly man
Pen-pusher: a person with a clerical job
Sparring partner: a boxer employed to spar with another boxer for the purposes of training
*Etymology: to spar in boxing means to train by actual boxing in the ring but not land any heavy blows to avoid injury
Straight shooter: a person who gives his/her honest opinion in a straightforward manner
Ambulance chaser: a derogatory term used for personal injury lawyers
*Etymology: Earlier, some lawyers would pursue victims in ambulances and hospitals, encouraging them to sue.
The Grim Reaper: the imaginary character who personifies death
He looks like a skeleton, wears a long black hooded cloak and carries a scythe.

∎

Hark back: to return to an earlier point or thought
He loves telling stores that hark back to his college days.
*Etymology: hark is a hunting term that means to listen
It is also written as harken back.
Piggyback: to a ride on someone's back and shoulders
The telephone company managed to enter remote villages by piggybacking off the mobile towers built by the government.

∎

Common refrain: a phrase that is often repeated, especially in poetry
'Every vote counts' is a common refrain in politics.

Focal point: a centre of interest or activity
The famous singer was the focal point of attention at the party.
*Etymology: in optics, a focal point is the point at which rays converge after refraction or reflection

Freudian slip: an unintentional slip of the tongue that is said to reveal the person's subconscious feelings and hence give a glimpse into their true nature
*Etymology: named after the famous Austrian psychoanalyst Sigmund Freud, who is considered as the founder of psychoanalysis

Ticker tape parade: a parade held to celebrate a victory
*Etymology: originally this was a celebratory parade where large amounts of shredded paper was thrown from the buildings to the road carrying the victor and the paper so used was the thin tape paper on which stock reports were printed

Trial balloon: a statement issued in advance to test the reaction of the people
The government's statement on increasing the tax rates was a trial balloon to gauge the public's reaction.
*Etymology: it is a small balloon that is sent before a manned flight to check the wind direction and strength

∎

Baptism by fire: an introductory experience that is a severe ordeal, for example when a soldier's first experience in the military is the exposure to enemy fire on the front lines

Righteous indignation: an angry reaction to perceived injustice or mistreatment
*Etymology: in Christian doctrine, righteous indignation is considered the only form of anger which is not sinful; for example, the famous incident when Jesus drove the money lenders out of a temple.

∎

Glass ceiling: a non-merit related upper limit beyond which one cannot advance in a profession, especially affecting women and minorities
Choppy waters: troublesome and uncertain times
*Etymology: water is choppy when there are a lot of small waves on it because of a wind blowing, which makes it tough to navigate
Skid row: a run-down part of a town that is inhabited by vagrants and alcoholics
*Etymology: this expression came into being in the

Great Depression in the US where residents of the 'skid row' referred to someone who was slipping down in society and thus was 'on the skids'

Pearly Gates: the gates of heaven
*Etymology: this refers to the description of the New Jerusalem in the Bible which states 'The twelve gates were twelve pearls, each gate being made from a single pearl'.

Event horizon: the point of no return
They reached the event horizon in the contract negotiation and now could not back out.
*Etymology: it is the boundary around a black hole beyond which no light can escape

Washout: a disappointing failure
The movie was a washout at the Box Office.
*Etymology: an event that is spoiled by heavy rainfall

Watershed moment: a turning point
Graduating from college is a watershed moment in the student's life.
*Etymology: a watershed is a geographical area which sends water to rivers and is formed by a chain of mountains
*Synonym: **inflection point** (The collapse of Lehman Brothers was an inflection point in the US economy;
*etymology: an inflection point is a point on a graphical curve where the curve drastically changes direction)

Twilight zone: an ill-defined zone which is in the middle of distinct conditions and having some features of both
After drinking, he entered the twilight zone between fantasy and reality.
*Synonym: grey zone

End of history status: the status when a society reaches its pinnacle economically and socially

∎

At full tilt: at top speed
*Etymology: tilting was another word for jousting and full tilt means to move at full speed on the horse
Post-haste: very quickly, ASAP (as soon as possible)
They went to the hotel post-haste to meet his favourite actor.
*Etymology: in the sixteenth century, 'haste, post, haste' was used to inform the couriers that a letter was urgent
Breakneck: dangerously fast
He was driving his bike at breakneck speed before the accident.

∎

Tunnel vision: to focus only on a single aspect and ignore all others, as if one is travelling in a tunnel and can only see what is directly in front
Myopic vision: to be short-sighted and not see the long run
*Etymology: myopia is an eye disease in which a person can't see distant objects clearly as they become blurry
*Antonym: **visionary**
Navel-gazing: the activity of spending too much time thinking about one's own problems and thoughts
The movie perfectly captured the navel-gazing of politicians who ignore the problems of the country.
*The word also means excessive analysis of a single issue while ignoring the big picture.
Second-guess: to criticize someone after the decision has been taken and one has the benefit of hindsight
The committee second-guessed the actions of the pilot but it had no idea about how tough the situation.

∎

Stop-gap: a temporary solution but not a permanent fix to a problem
Workaround: a solution to a problem
The students found a workaround for cheap potato chips by ordering directly in bulk from the company.

∎

Pet peeve: an annoyance for a person, which in itself might not be very irritating to others but is very irritating for this particular person
For example, a teacher's pet peeve is messy handwriting.
*Synonym: pet hate
Killjoy: someone who deliberately kills the joy of others
His father acted like a killjoy by cancelling the party.
*Synonyms: **spoilsport, party pooper**
Buzzkill: someone who has the effect of dispiriting others
Nobody invited him to parties because he was a buzzkill and kept irritating people.
Sourpuss: a person who is always grouchy and in a bad mood

∎

Peace offering: a conciliatory gift
Climb down: a withdrawal from a position earlier taken in a negotiation
Landslide victory: an electoral victory where one

candidate receives an overwhelming majority of the votes

*Etymology: the term comes from geology, where a landslide takes down everything along its path

Slam-dunk: to win decisively

The presentation was a slam-dunk and they got the contract.

*Etymology: slam-dunk comes from basketball when a player thrusts down the ball down the basket to score a point emphatically

■

Lemming syndrome: to blindly follow everyone even if it results in one's destruction

*Synonyms: **herd mentality, bandwagon effect**

*Etymology: A lemming is a type of a rat that lives in the Arctic. Lemmings migrate out of an area when the population becomes large and sometimes they jump off a cliff in a large herd, all together, into water and drown because of the mistaken belief that the waters below the cliff are swimmable.

Stockholm syndrome: feelings of trust or affection developed by the captive towards a captor

*Etymology: This comes from the 1973 Stockholm Bank robbery where the hostages developed affection for their captors.

Writer's block: a condition in which a person is not able to think clearly and creatively and thus not be able to proceed with writing.

■

Holy Grail: something that is eagerly pursued or sought to be achieved

Nuclear fusion is the holy grail of the clean power industry.

*Etymology: As per legend the Holy Grail is the cup used by Jesus Christ at the Last Supper before he was crucified and this cup is supposed to have mystical powers.

Hail Mary: a last ditch effort

The party gave out cash sops to the farmers in a Hail Mary attempt to win them over before the elections.

*Etymology: Hail Mary is a prayer by Christians to the Virgin Mary.

Kingdom come: the end of time

The speed at which they work, the project won't be completed till kingdom come.

*Etymology: this refers to the phrase 'Thy kingdom come' in the Christian Lord's Prayer meaning a time when the kingdom of God with all its peace and justness arrives on earth

■

Voir dire: the cross examination of a witness by a counsel

*Etymology: French *voir* (true) + *dire* (to say)

*Pronounced as vaah-dear

Volte-face: a complete U-turn in a one's position

*Etymology: Latin volvere (to roll) + facies (face)

*Pronounced as volt-fahs

Via media: a compromise

Both parties were looking for a via media.

*Etymology: Latin for 'the middle road'

Viaduct: a kind of a bridge

■

Bugle call: a loud tune played on a bugle (a bugle is a trumpet like instrument) usually done on a military base to announce the start of the day

Clarion call: a strong demand for action

The General's clarion call urged the soldiers to fight until the end.

*Etymology: a clarion is a medieval horn

Rallying cry: a phrase that is used to gather people in support of an idea

'Meat is Murder' is a rallying cry for vegetarianism.

*Etymology: rally means to reunite after a setback, in order to continue fighting

Death Knell: a warning about the end of something

Arrival of Amazon was the death knell for local retailers.

*Etymology: death knell is a bell tolled to announce a death; knell means the sound of a bell when rung

Marching orders: the official notice of dismissal from a job

*Synonyms: **walking papers, pink slip** (*etymology: pink slip comes from the early twentieth century where pink paper was used to write such dismissal notices)

Polestar: a guiding principle

*Etymology: polestar is a bright star that can be seen in the sky in the northern hemisphere when one looks directly toward the north

*Synonyms: **North Star, lodestar**

True north: the real North (direction wise) as per the earth's axis and not the magnetic North

■

Rib-tickler: a very funny story
*Etymology: something that evokes a lot of laughter as if one is being tickled in the ribs by someone's fingers
Tear-jerker: a very sad and sentimental story
*Etymology: a soda-jerker (a soda fountain) which is used to dispense cold drinks in a diner
Potboiler: a movie or book that is artistically very mediocre but caters to popular taste and thus gets good financial returns
*Etymology: something done solely to put food on the table and keep the pot boiling
Boilerplate: clichéd writing
The politicians hid behind nationalistic boilerplates after the new taxation policy proved to be a disaster.
*Etymology: boilerplates are rolled steel plates that are used for making boilers

■

Cash cow: a business that is a steady source of income
Money-spinner: a thing that brings in solid profit
The Harry Potter movies were a money-spinner for the studio.
Gravy train: an opportunity to make a lot of money with very little effort
He went to Dubai to get on the gravy train of betting on cricket matches.
Meal ticket: a person used by another as a source of regular income
*Etymology: a meal ticket is a coupon that gets the holder a free meal
Mom-and-pop shop: a small family run business
Brick-and-mortar store: an actual physical offline store as opposed to an online shop
*Etymology: mortar is a mixture of lime, cement, sand and water, which is used to bind the bricks together when constructing a building
Fly-by-night operators: untrustworthy business people
*Etymology: untrustworthy business people run away (flee) as soon as it is dark.
Bait-and-switch: the illegal tactic of baiting buyers by advertising good quality or well-priced goods but then substituting them at the last minute with inferior quality or expensive goods
*Synonyms: to **fob off**, to **palm off**
Bootstrap: to run a startup with minimal existing resources before looking for outside funding

*Etymology: bootstrap is a cloth loop sewn at the top of the back side of a boot, which is pulled to put the shoe easily on the foot
Sweatshop: a workshop, typically manufacturing clothes, with horrible working conditions and very little pay
*Etymology: in the mid-1800s, small garment manufacturers or middlemen (called sweaters) would run these shops (sweatshops) with horrible work conditions and low pay
Going concern: a business that is operating and making a profit
Deep pocket: having extensive financial resources
Mint condition: pristine condition; without any imperfections
The painting was in mint condition as it was very carefully locked in the vault.
*Etymology: a coin factory is called a 'mint', hence in coin collecting 'mint condition' meant a coin in excellent condition, just like a fresh coin leaves the mint

■

Crony capitalism: an economic system in which the government favours its cronies (such as industrialist friends or large donors) with policies like tax breaks or lucrative government contracts
*Etymology: crony means friend
Nepotism: the favouring of family members over other more deserving and meritorious candidates
Old boy network: a system where men use their power to favour their school or college friends

■

No-brainer: something that requires no mental effort
Buying the heavily discounted mobile during the Christmas sale was a no-brainer.
Non-issue: a topic of no importance
Skin colour is a non-issue.
Non-starter: a plan that has no chance of succeeding
The CEO rejected the new sales plan, calling it a non-starter.
Nonentity: an unimportant person
He did not get the ticket to contest the elections as the party viewed his as a political non-entity.
*Synonyms: small fry, lightweight
*Antonym: heavyweight

■

Boo-boo: a small mistake
The young accountant made a boo-boo in the totalling of the receipts.
Pooh-pooh: to dismiss something as foolish
Until recently, acupuncture therapy was pooh-poohed by the medical community.
Tom-tom: to boast about something
The government tom-tommed the one percent increas in the GDP.
*Etymology: a tom-tom is a drum of Asian origin played with one's hands
Tut-tut: to express disapproval or annoyance or disdain
His Uncle tut-tutted the disorderliness of his room.
*Etymology: tut-tut is used in writing to represent the sound which one makes when one touches the top of their mouth with their tongue to show disapproval
*Synonym: **tsk-tsk** (The fashion critics tsk-tsked over the model's new outfit)
Nitty-gritty: the practice details
The student wanted to find out the nitty-gritty of hostel life before he left for college.
Wishy-washy: indecisive; weak and watery
The candidate gave wishy-washy answers when asked about his stand on death penalty.
*Synonym: **namby-pamby** (The scholar's writing was criticized as namby-pamby because he did not take a strong stand on any issue)
Shilly-shally: to act indecisively; to be hesitant
The government was rebuked for shilly-shallying on the action against wilful defaulters.
Hanky-panky: unethical or illegal behaviour; improper sexual relations
The CEO said that there was no hanky-panky going on at the company.

∎

High-handed: arrogant; haughty; using power without consideration for others
The factory workers were tired of the CEO's high-handed approach.
Heavy-handed: clumsy; using excessive force
The residents were tired of the heavy-handed approach of the local police.
Moral high ground: to be morally superior to others
He was tired of his elder brother taking the moral high ground after every mistake he made.

∎

Flag-bearer: someone who openly promotes an idea
*Etymology: a flag-bearer carries the flag at a ceremonial event
*Synonym: **torchbearer**
Cheerleader: an enthusiastic and vocal supporter
*Synonym: **trumpeter**
Propaganda: biased or misleading information aimed to promote a particular ideology
Pamphleteer: someone who writes pamphlets and other sub-standard propaganda material
Mouthpiece: a media organization that publishes propaganda for a political party
*Etymology: mouthpiece is that part of a musical instrument which has to be put inside the mouth in order to play the musical instrument
Spin doctor: a spokesperson (usually of a political party) whose job is to give a favourable interpretation to seemingly negative events; also known as **spinmeister** (*pronounced as spin-mahi-ster; *etymology: from the German *word 'meister'* meaning master)
Apologist: a person whose job is to defend controversial things
Votary: an ardent supporter
*Etymology: votary means a person, like a monk or nun, who has taken the vows to dedicate their life to religion
Revisionist history: history that is rewritten to suit a particular agenda
Echo chamber: an environment where only supportive opinions are just repeated and opposing views are not allowed
The president lived in an echo chamber and ignored the media's views.
*Etymology: an echo chamber is a room used in broadcasting as it echoes sound (amplifies and reflects)
Rubber stamp: to approve automatically without due application of mind
The role of the Supreme Court is not to just rubber stamp the decisions of the government.
*Etymology: a rubber stamp is a small device with a name, date, etc., which you press onto an ink pad and then onto a document.

∎

Lapdog: a person or an organization under the control of another
The lapdog media kept quiet.
*Etymology: lapdog is a small pet dog
Watchdog: a person or an organization that closely

monitors the activity of another

A vibrant democracy needs many watchdog organizations.

*Etymology: a watchdog is a dog kept to guard private property

Ombudsman: an official appointed to investigate complaints

*Etymology: Ombudsman is Swedish for 'legal representative'

∎

Yellow journalism: tabloid journalism; sensationalist journalism

*Etymology: the term is from the 1890s where newspapers would resort to sensationalising news and use yellow ink to drive up sales

Gotcha question: a question that is deliberately posed to make a politician answering to that question look dumb and stupid

For example, if a journalist asks a question which was specifically decided between them to be asked later.

*Etymology: gotcha is a contracted form of 'got you'

Media buying: the buying of advertising space from a media company; an example of media buying are front page advertisements in newspapers which we see everyday

Media buying does not mean paid journalism.

Reportage: the journalistic reporting of events

CNN was lauded for its reportage of the Gulf War in the early 90s.

Bulletin: a short summary of the daily news

The viewers really liked the news channel's evening bulletin as it was always crisp and clear.

Stringer: a reporter who is retained on a part-time basis

Scrivener: a drafter of documents; a notary

Scribe: a professional copyist; a journalist; a Jewish recordkeeper

Tabloid: a newspaper which carries sensational stories and no real news

Paparazzo: a freelance photographer who hounds celebrities to get their photographs

*Plural: paparazzi

Puff piece: an article in the media that is very complimentary about someone or something

By-line: a line in a newspaper which states the name of the writer of the article, usually placed right below the article heading

*Homonym: **beeline** (A beeline is a straight line between two places)

∎

Broad Church: a group that embraces a wide variety of views

*Etymology: this refers to a party in the Church of England which favours a broad and liberal interpretation of Anglican rituals

Rainbow Coalition: a coalition of people who come from very diverse backgrounds: socially, economically, ethnically, etc.

Ginger Group: a very active group within a political party that pushes for stronger action

*Etymology: the practice of 'gingering' where ginger was rubbed on a horse's backside so that it would carry its tail high

Young Turk: a young person who wants radical change

*Etymology: a member of the radical party in the Ottoman Empire (modern day Turkey), which carried out the 1908 revolution and deposed the Sultan and ushered in an era of multi-party democracy for the first time in Turkey's history

Splinter group: a small group that has broken away from the main party

∎

Kitchen cabinet: a group of unofficial advisers to a political leader

*Etymology: this comes from President Andrew Jackson was criticised for listening more to his trusted friends than the official US Cabinet

Parlour cabinet: the group of official advisers to a political leader

*Etymology: a parlour is the room in the front of the house to meet guests

Shadow cabinet: an unofficial cabinet formed by the opposition to act as counterpart of the official government cabinet and formed for expertise in criticising the government policies and ready alternative policy prescriptions

∎

Nerve centre: the control centre of an organization

Nodal agency: an agency that is deputed to execute a government project and to coordinate with other agencies for the execution of these projects

The Ministry of Environment is the nodal agency for tackling pollution.

*Etymology: a node is a point in a plant stem from which leaves emerge

Synapse: the point between two nerve cells, where the electrical signals are received and transmitted
*Plural: synapses
*Adjective form: synaptic

■

Uncle Sam: the personification of the American government, shown as a tall thin bearded man, wearing a blue coat, red-and-white trousers and a hat
John Bull: the personification of a typical Englishman, usually shown as a stout farmer wearing hats and boots

■

Payola: a bribe for the promotion of a product in the media
Kickback: a bribe given to a sanctioning officer; such a bribe is usually in the form of a percentage of the economic value of the project

■

Mountie: a member of the Royal Canadian Mounted Police (Mounted police is the police which patrols on horsebacks)
*Plural: mounties
Centurion: a commander of a century (a century is a company of 100 soldiers in the ancient Roman army)
Sentinel: a guard
Sniper: a person who shoots others from a hiding place at a large distance from the target with the help of long-range rifles
*Synonym: sharpshooter
Sleuth: a detective
*Pronounced as slooth
Beefeater: a ceremonial guard at the Tower of London in England
*Etymology: the Grand Duke of Tuscany, who visited the Tower in 1669, said that these guards should be called beefeaters because they ate a lot of beef

■

Guilt trip: to induce someone to do something by making them feel guilty about a past mistake
Honeytrap: a tactic where a victim is seduced into a compromising sexual situation and then blackmailed into divulging sensitive information

Fault line: a divisive issue that can have serious consequences
Religion is the great fault line of modern politics.
Faustian bargain: to make deal with corrupt people to gain something
*Etymology: as per German legend, Faust was a scholar who traded his soul to the devil in exchange for knowledge and power
*Pronounced as fow-stee-un and not fow-shun
Supine policy: when a person or organization is too cowardly to act against something wrong
*Etymology: supine means to lie down on the ground with one's face upwards
Conspiracy of silence: a conspiracy to keep quiet about a crime
The prime minister entered into a conspiracy of silence and shielded his corrupt coal minister to protect the government.

■

Gubernatorial: relating to a governor
Arnold Schwarzenegger won the 2003 California gubernatorial election and became the Governor of California.
*Etymology: from Latin *'gubernator'* meaning governor
Plebiscite: a direct vote by the people on an important issue
*Pronounced as pleb-e-site
*Synonym: **referendum**
Suffrage: the right to vote
Modern democracies have universal adult suffrage.
*Pronounced as suf-rij
*Synonym: **franchise**

■

Machismo: aggressive masculine pride
The misguided young boys displayed their machismo by eve-teasing girls.
*Pronounced as mah-chiz-mo
*Synonym: male chauvinism
Chauvinism: aggressive patriotism to the point of hatred of other nations
Chauvinism also means blind devotion to any cause or group.
*Pronounced as shaw-vun-ism
*Adjective form: chauvinist

Jingoism: aggressive patriotism to the point of hatred of other nations and also support for a warlike foreign policy; belligerent chauvinism

Hawk: a person who always pushes for war in foreign policy instead of diplomacy

*Antonym: **dove**

War-mongering: the policy of encouraging of war among nations instead of diplomacy

*Antonym: **pacifism**

■

Parthian shot: a parting shot; a devastating blow delivered right at the end

*Etymology: this was a military tactic used by the Parthians (ancient Iranian people) where the archers while pretending to retreat on the horses would turn their bodies back to shoot at the enemy

Pyrrhic victory: a victory that is virtually a defeat because the victor suffered extensive and irreparable damage in the pursuit of this victory

*Etymology: this term originates from the King Pyrrhus of Epirus, whose army suffered massive casualties in defeating the Romans in 280 BC.

Trojan Horse: a person or thing that joins an organization with the aim of destroying it from the inside

*Etymology: Trojan means related to Troy. When Greece invaded Troy they were unsuccessful in getting through the high Trojan walls, so they pretended to leave and left a giant wooden horse. The Trojans took the horse inside their city as a symbol of victory but it was hollow and had Greek soldiers hidden inside it who then destroyed Troy.

Damocles sword: a danger which is close by

He worked under a lot of pressure with the Damocles sword of termination always hanging above his head.

*Etymology: As per Roman myth, Damocles was a courtier to the King Dionysius and said that the King was very fortunate. The King then told him to sit on the throne for one day. Damocles agreed but the King placed a large sword above his head, attached to the ceiling by a single hair from a horse's tail. Damocles then understood all the dangers the King faced.

Achilles heel: a vulnerable point

Algebra is the young student's Achilles heel.

*Etymology: When the mythical Greek hero Achilles was a baby, his mother dipped him in the River Styx to protect him from all injuries but she held him by one of his heels while dipping him and the river water did not touch that heel, thus making it his weak spot and

eventually Achilles was killed by an arrow that hit his heel.

Icarus flew too close to the sun: to be reckless and not know one's limits

*Etymology: in Greek myth, Icarus fell after flying too close to the sun because his wings melted (as they were made of wax and feathers) despite being warned by his father, Daedalus, who gave him the wings.

Cross the Rubicon: to commit yourself to a course of action with no option of going back

*Etymology: in 49 BC, Julius Caesar crossed the Rubicon, a stream that separated the province of Gaul from Rome, to wage civil war.

Open Pandora's box: to create a major problem

*Etymology: In Greek mythology, the God Zeus gave Pandora (the first woman) a box with strict instructions to not open it. Pandora's curiosity however got the better of her and she opened the box and out came all sorts of evils.

Hold out an olive branch: to extend an offer of peace and reconciliation to end a dispute

*Etymology: An olive branch is an emblem of peace in the Bible. For example, a dove brought an olive branch to Noah to signal that God was no longer angry and that the floods would stop.

Fig leaf: something used to hide an embarrassment

The government used the fig leaf of 'national security' to ban the movie.

*Etymology: the leaf of a fig tree is often used to conceal private parts in paintings and sculpture

Caesar's wife must be above suspicion: the associates of public figures must not even be suspected of any wrongdoing

*Etymology: The ancient Roman King Julius Caesar divorced his wife Pompeia just because she was suspected of wrongdoing despite there being no evidence against her.

■

Sieg Heil: the Nazi salute

*Pronounced as sig-ha-ill

*Etymology: from German *'sieg'* (victory) and *'heil'* (hail), a common chant in Nazi Germany

Revanchism: the policy to recover lost status

Hitler pursued a revanchist policy to regain the lost glory of the old German Empire.

Irredentism: the policy to recover lost territory

■

Blue-ribbon panel: a panel of experts appointed by a government to study a subject and give recommendations
*Etymology: blue ribbon refers to the first prize ribbon given to the smartest students in a science fair
Blue-chip: a company which is well established and whose stock is a reliable and less risky investment
Apple is a blue-chip company.
*Etymology: in gambling, blue chips are the chips with a high value
Gilt-edged: stocks that are very reliable and give high returns
Pink slip: the official notice of dismissal from a job
*Etymology: in early twentieth century where pink paper was used to write such dismissal notices
White-shoe firm: a professional services firm (like a law firm, accounting firm, etc) that represent the top level companies
*Etymology: wealthy upper class students in Ivy League colleges used to wear white shoes
White-collar worker: a worker who works in an office environment like a lawyer or accountant
*Etymology: white dress shirts of male office workers common in the early nineteenth and twentieth century offices of western countries
Blue-collar worker: a worker who performs manual labour like working in manufacturing, mining, construction, etc.
*Etymology: industrial workers wear blue denim jeans and blue coloured shirts, as the blue colour of the clothes concealed the dirt and grease on the worker's clothing
Pink collar: a worker who works in service industry, for example waiters, salespersons etc.
*Etymology: earlier pink collar referred to jobs which were usually held by women but now the phrase encompasses all service jobs
Green-collar worker: a worker who works in the environmental sector, like environmental systems engineers, green building architects, etc.
Red Tape: excessive government regulation
*Etymology: in the eighteenth century where red coloured tape was used to bind official documents and files
Redlining: This refers to institutional racism where some districts in the US were marked red, which meant that no investments would be done in these areas because they were deemed too poor and risky. Predominantly, these redlined districts were populated by black people.

■

Body politic: this is a metaphor in which the people of a society or a nation are considered together as a human body
Communal and corrupt politicians are painful pimples on our body politic. *Synonym: **polity**
Realpolitik: politics based on practical concerns rather than principles
Focussing on 'winability' of a candidate over his criminal record is an example of realpolitik.
*Pronounced as rey-ahl-poh-li-teek

■

Colleague: a co-worker in an office
Collegial: marked by good relationships between colleagues
The environment in the office was collegial and everyone was nice to each other.
Collegium: a body of colleagues
Collegiate: relating to a college

■

Constabulary: a body comprising of constables
Citizenry: a body comprising of citizens
Studentry: a body comprising of students
Commissionerate: the staff and office of a local commissioner
Collectorate: the staff and office of a district collector
Commentariat: a body comprising of news commentators
Directorate: a body comprising of directors
Electorate: the body comprising of voters
Professoriate: a body comprising of professors
Protectorate: a state that is protected by another
With the China-Pakistan Economic Corridor, Pakistan has become a protectorate of China.
Governorate: an administrative division of a country which is headed by a governor, especially in Arab countries like Egypt
Magistracy: the staff and office of a local magistrate
Bureaucracy: a body comprising of bureaucrats
*Etymology: bureau comes from French *'baize'* meaning a coarse cloth, used as a desk cover

■

Apparat: the governing body of a communist political party
*Pronounced as aa-per-aat

Apparatchik: a loyal member of the communist political party
*Pronounced as aa-per-aa-chik
Commissar: an official of the Communist Party who is responsible for political education
Kompromat: Russian for compromising material
Politburo: the executive committee and chief policy making body of a Communist Party
*Etymology: Russian for 'political bureau'
Gulag: a soviet era prison camp
*Pronounced as goo-laag

■

Entente Cordiale: a situation where there are cordial and peaceful relations between two nations
*Pronounced as on-taunt cordi-aaal
*Etymology: the Entente Cordiale was a series of agreements signed in 1904 between the United Kingdom and France that established peace
Détente: the relaxation of tensions between two nations through diplomacy
*Pronounced as de-taunt
*Etymology: French *'détente'* = relaxation
Entente: an informal friendly understanding
France wanted an entente with England after the war.
*Pronounced as on-taunt
*Etymology: French for understanding
Modus vivendi: an informal arrangement between two nations where they don't fight each other
*Etymology: Latin phrase that means 'mode of living'

Rapprochement: resumption of friendly and harmonious relations, especially between two nations
Hectic diplomatic efforts led to a rapprochement between the feuding nations.
*Pronounced as rap-rosh-mahn

■

Introspection: the act of looking within oneself to analyse one's own emotions and feelings
He spent every morning doing some quiet introspection.
*Synonym: **soul-searching**
Retrospection: the act of looking in the past to analyse events in one's own life
In moments of retrospection, his grandmother would tell him stories about her childhood days.

■

Vicious cycle: a chain of events where one problem leads to other problems and these problems make the original problem worse
For example: people caught in the vicious cycle of poverty, don't have money for good education and thus don't get good jobs and stay in poverty
Virtuous cycle: a chain of events where one good thing leads to other good things and these good things make the original good thing better
For example, some people get caught in the virtuous cycle of exercise, feel good because of the exercise and thus want to eat better and look better and because of the good looks want to exercise more.

DIFFERENCE BETWEEN SOME COMMONLY CONFUSING WORDS

Justiciable vs Justifiable: Justiciable means conforming to the law of the land like the constitution; for example, the new law made by the government was proved justiciable in the Supreme Court. Justifiable means something which can be justified. For example: His action of hitting the other person was justifiable as he was exercizing the right to self-defence.

Judicious vs Judicial vs Juridical: Judicious means showing good judgment. Judicial means relating to courts of law or judges. Juridical means relating to jurisprudence (the study of law).

Liberalism vs Libertarianism: Liberalism is the philosophy of being open, tolerant and progressive. Libertarianism is the philosophy emphasising the liberty of the individual, with minimum intervention by the State.

Reoccur vs Recur: Reoccur means occur (happen) once again and recur means to happen again but regularly: the rain reoccurred two hours after the first showers; the town gets recurring annual rainfall of 20mm per annum.

By default vs By design: By default means using the standard pre-selected option provided. By design means deliberately choosing one option out of the several offered. Some people use Internet Explorer as their browser by default, while some use Chrome as their browser by design.

Efficiency vs Efficacy: Efficiency is the ability to produce the desired outcome with minimal wastage of any input items like energy, money, time etc. Efficacy is the power to produce the desired outcome. For example, the hammer is efficacious in driving a nail into a wall but the hammer is not as efficient as an electric nail gun.

Malfunction vs Dysfunction: Malfunction is the failure to function. Dysfunction means functioning but not properly. For example, if the liver of a person is not working then it is malfunction. But when the liver produces extra cells and causes cancer, then that is dysfunction.

Hypothesis vs Thesis: A hypothesis is a statement that is proposed as an explanation to a phenomenon, which is then tested with experiments to prove if it is correct or incorrect. A thesis statement is a short sentence that encapsulates the main point of an essay or research paper. A thesis is also the dissertation written by a student to obtain his or her university degree.

Exponent vs Proponent: An exponent interprets or explains something in great detail. A proponent advocates a cause or belief.

Dissenter vs Dissident: A dissenter is anyone who dissents (disagrees) with a particular point of view while dissident is a person who formally opposes the current political group in power.

Intuition vs Instinct: Intuition is a gut feeling and instinct is a tendency or reaction that you are born with. For example, when you meet a new person you have an intuition if this person is good or bad. But when this person throws a glass of water at you then your instinct is to move away to avoid the water.

Psychopath vs Sociopath: A psychopath is a person who derives pleasure in the pain of others. A sociopath is a person with little or no conscience. The sociopath won't care if he or she hurt another person, but this sociopath will not hurt someone to derive pleasure out of it. For example: the Joker from Batman is a psychopath as he enjoys hurting other people and derives pleasure in their pain. But Sherlock Holmes is a sociopath. Sherlock Holmes won't care if he hurt someone by being rude to them but Holmes would certainly not derive pleasure in seeing this person being upset. Holmes would be rude in order to shoo this person away but the intention would never be to derive happiness out of this shooed away person's pain and hurt.

Avenge vs Revenge: To avenge is to punish someone who did a wrong with the aim of serving justice; revenge is more personal than just dispensing justice. It is more about causing damage in return for the harm caused to you.

Substantive vs Substantial: Substantive refers to quality and substantial refers to quantity. For example, investment bankers on Wall Street get substantially higher pay than teachers but teacher's contribution to society is much more substantive.

IMPORTANT WORD ROOTS

Word root and meaning	Etymology
Ante: before	From Latin *'ante'* meaning before
Anthro: relating to humans	From Greek *'anthropos'* meaning human being
Anglo: relating to England	From Latin *'Angli'* which referred to the Germanic people who settled in Great Britain in the post-Roman period
Miso: hatred	From Greek *'misos'* meaning hatred
Amor: love	From Latin *'amor'* meaning love
Philo: love	From Greek *'philos'* meaning love
Logy: study	From Greek *'logia'* meaning study
Poly: many	From Greek *'polus'* meaning many
Pole: seller	From Greek *'poles'* meaning seller
Panto: all	From Greek *'pant'* meaning all
Post: after	From Latin *'post'* meaning after, behind
Omni: all	From Latin *'omnis'* meaning all
Oli: few	From Greek *'oligoi'* meaning few
Mega: large	From Greek *'megalo'* meaning large
Mono: single	From Greek *'monos'* meaning sole
Cracy: rule	From Greek *'kratos'* meaning rule
Cide: kill	From Latin *'cida'* meaning killer
Mancy: prediction or foretelling	From Greek *'manteia'* meaning divination (divination means fortune telling)
Mania: madness	From Latin *'mania'* meaning madness
Phobia: fear	From Greek *'phobos'* meaning fear
Graphy: writing	From Greek *'grapho'* meaning writing
Hypo: below	From Greek *'hupo'* meaning under
Hyper: above	From Greek *'huper'* meaning over
Endo: internal	From Greek *'endon'* meaning within

Word root and meaning	Etymology
Exo: external	From Greek *'exo'* meaning outside
Ecto: outer	From Greek *'ektos'* meaning outside
Ento: inside	From Greek *'entos'* meaning within
Entomo: relating to insects	From Greek *'entomon'* meaning insect
Homo: same	From Greek *'homos'* meaning same
Hetero: different	From Greek *'heteros'* meaning other
Gen: relating to birth or production	From Greek *'genes'* meaning born
Derma: relating to the skin	From Greek *'derma'* meaning skin
Gastro: relating to the stomach	From Greek *'gaster'* meaning belly
Entero: relating to the intestines	From Greek *'enteron'* meaning intestine
Thermo: relating to heat	From Greek *'thermos'* meaning hot
Cryo: relating to cold	From Greek *'cryo'* meaning cold
Baro: relating to pressure	From Greek *'baros'* meaning weight
Phon: relating to sound	From Greek *'phonein'* meaning speak
Vore: relating to an eater	From Latin *'vorare'* meaning to devour or eat
Phag: relating to eating	From Greek *'phagein'* meaning to eat
Dipso: relating to drinking alcohol	From Greek *'dipsa'* means thirst

Oeno: relating to wine	From Greek *'oinos'* meaning wine	**Fratri**: relating to brother	From Latin *'frater'* meaning brother
Onio: relating to buying	From Greek *'onios'* meaning for sale	**Sorori**: relating to sister	From Latin *'soror'* meaning sister
Biblio: relating to books	From Greek *'biblion'* meaning book	**Uxori**: relating to wife	From Latin *'uxor'* meaning wife
Bellum: relating to war	From Latin *'bellum'* meaning war	**Gamy**: relating to marriage	From Greek *'gamos'* meaning married
Machy: fighting	From Greek *'machia'* meaning battle	**Gyny**: relating to women	From Greek *'gune'* meaning woman
Demo: relating to people	From Greek *'demos'* meaning people	**Andry**: relating to men	From Greek *'andr'* meaning man
Psepho: relating to elections	From Greek *'psephos'* meaning pebble or vote In ancient Greece, people would cast votes using pebbles	**Fili**: relating to son or daughter	From Latin *'filius'* meaning son and *'filia'* meaning daughter
Auto: relating to self	From Greek *'autoteles'* meaning self	**Avunculi**: relating to uncle	From Latin *'avunculus'* meaning maternal uncle
Dei: relating to God	From Latin *'deus'* meaning God	**Nepoti**: relating to nephew	From Latin *'nepos'* meaning nephew
Theo: relating to God	From Greek *'theos'* meaning God	**Zoo**: relating to animals	From Greek *'zoion'* meaning animal
Hagio: holy	From Greek *'hagios'* meaning holy or saintly	**Phyto**: relating to plants	From Greek *'phuton'* meaning plant
Pluto: relating to wealth	From Greek *'ploutos'* meaning wealth	**Lacto**: relating to milk	From Latin *'lact'* meaning milk
Aristo: relating to the nobility	From Greek *'aristos'* meaning best	**Pisci**: relating to fish	From Latin *'piscis'* meaning fish
Strato: relating to the army	From Greek *'stratos'* meaning army	**Ovo**: egg	From Latin *'ovum'* meaning egg
Kakisto: relating to the worst	From Greek *'kakistos'* meaning worst	**Xeno**: relating to foreigners	From Greek *'xenos'* meaning stranger
Klepto: relating to thieves	From Greek *'kleptes'* meaning thief	**Neo**: new	From Greek *'neo'* meaning new or young
Regi: relating to the king	From Latin *'rex'* meaning king	**Natal**: relating to birth	From Latin *'natalis'* meaning birth
Sui: relating to oneself	From Latin *'sui'* meaning one's own	**Necro**: relating to dead bodies	From Greek *'nekros'* meaning corpse
Parri: relating to parents	From Latin *'parens'* meaning parent	**Sen**: old	From Latin *'sen'* meaning old
Patri: relating to father	From Latin *'pater'* meaning father	**Ger**: relating to elderly people	From Greek *'geras'* meaning old age
Matri: relating to mother	From Latin *'mater'* meaning mother	**Geronto**: relating to old people	From Greek *'gerontos'* meaning old man
		Paleo: old	From Greek *'palaios'* meaning ancient
		Paedo: relating to children	From Greek *'paid'* meaning child

Paedia: education	From Greek *'paideia'* meaning child-rearing, education	**Chrono**: relating to the time	From Greek *'chronos'* meaning time
Iatric: doctor	From Greek *'iatros'* meaning healer	**Retro**: relating to the past	From Latin *'retro'* meaning backwards
Ochlo: relating to crowds	From Greek *'okhlos'* meaning crowd	**Prospec**: relating to the future	From Latin *'pro'* meaning forward and *'specere'* meaning to look
Nycto: relating to the dark	From Greek *'nyktos'* meaning night	**Ergo**: relating to work	From Greek *'ergon'* meaning work
Photo: relating to light	From Greek *'phos'* meaning light	**Somn**: relating to sleep	From Latin *'somnus'* meaning sleep
Diu: day	From Latin *'dies'* meaning day		
Nocti: night	From Latin *'nocti'* meaning night		

IDIOMS

THEME-WISE BATCHING

- **An easy victory**: easy meat, cakewalk, easy canter
- **A near miss**: narrow squeak, close call, by a nose, by a whisker, by the skin of the teeth
- **To surrender:** cave in, show the white flag, lay down one's arms, lay down and die
- **To reverse one's opinion:** do a U-turn, do an about-turn, do a 180 degree
- **Take the problem head-on**: grasp the nettle (*etymology: nettle is a plant which has hairs growing on its stems and these hairs inject toxins into the skin of anyone who touches them. But if the stem is grasped firmly and in the direction in which the hairs are growing then hairs get pushed flat and do not penetrate the skin and thus do not inject any poison), to grab the bull by the horns, to take the bit in the mouth
- **To rebel against authority**: to kick over the traces, to kick against the pricks
- **To irritate someone**: get under someone's skin, get on someone's nerves, rub up the wrong way, ruffle someone's feathers, make someone's hackles rise (*etymology: hackles are the hairs on an animal's back, which rise when it is angry; *synonym of hackles: bristle)
- **To anger someone**: drive one nuts, det a rise out of someone, make one's gorge rise, make one's dander rise, make one's back rise, make one's Irish rise, make one's hackles rise
- **To be very angry**: with one's hackles up, in high dudgeon, huff and puff, hopping mad, go into a lather, go spare, have kittens, fly off the handle, foam at the mouth, froth at the mouth, breathe fire and smoke, go into a huff, beat one's breast, blow one's top, go ballistic, lose it, fly into a volcanic rage
- **To scold someone**: haul someone over the coals (My father hauled me over the coals for not doing the homework on time), rake someone over the coals, haul someone on the carpet, to read the riot act, to give a tongue-lashing, give a dressing down
- **To fire someone from their job**: give someone their cards, give the pink slip
- **To get a light punishment for a major offence**: to get a rap on the knuckles, to get a slap on the wrist
- **Futile activity**: fool's Errand, fool's game, mug's game, game not worth the candle (*etymology: this relates to an occupation that is so fruitless that it isn't even worth the price of a candle to create enough light to partake in it)
- **Useless items**: amount to a hill of beans, fool's gold (*etymology: the name given to iron pyrites, which looks a little like gold but is worthless), mare's nest (*etymology: Mare is a female horse and does not make a nest. So, if someone found a mare's nest it means something mythical and of no value. Mare's nest also means a confused state as in referring to a rat's nest with lots of entangled items strewn together)
- **Trinkets:** bits and bobs, odds and ends
- **An ostentatious display meant to show off**: pomp and show, ceremony and show, ceremony and spectacle, pageantry
- **To trick someone**: to put one across, to put one over, to lead someone up the garden path, to throw dust in someone's eye, to put wool over someone's eyes (*etymology: This idiom relates to the wigs commonly worn by judges in the eighteenth century. A judge fooled by a lawyer was said to have his wig pulled over his eyes), to buy a pig in a poke (*etymology: This refers to a trick in the Middle Ages when meat was so scarce that clever shop keepers would sell some low quality meat in a poke (bag) instead of the expensive meat)
- **Doubtful story**: cock and bull story, a likely story
- **Not realistic**: pie in the sky, castles in the air, all moonshine (false promises)
- **When something is very clear and apparent**: as plain as a pikestaff, as plain as the nose on one's face, sticking out like a sore thumb, right under one's nose,

staring one in the face, writ large, written all over someone, as clear as day, as plain as day

- **To improvise:** play it by the ear (If we go into the meeting unprepared, we'll have to play everything by ear; *etymology: this refers to being able to play a piece of music after just listening to it a few times), make it up as one goes along (No one knew how the game was played so they made up the rules as they went along)
- **To hide or explain away an issue:** to paper over, to gloss over
- **Smooth talker; Glib; fawning; servile:** silver tongue, smooth tongue, oily tongue, soft soap, brown nose, apple polisher
- **Disreputable or bad member of an honourable family:** bad egg, black sheep
- **To use power to unethically gain advantage:** to feather one's own nest (The minister feathered his nest through his connection with big businesses), to line one's pockets
- **To be caught unexpectedly or unprepared:** caught on the wrong foot, catch somebody on the hop (The early winters caught the farmers on the hop as they were not prepared for it. *Etymology: The hop is a flower used to brew beer and in old times hop-picking was an activity that men often did after making an excuse to get off from work and sometimes their employers would discover their lies and catch them quite literally picking hops)
- **To confess:** to come out clean, to make a clean breast (After months of lying about the money, I decided to make a clean breast of it and tell the truth. *Etymology: The 'breast' here refers to one's heart and this idiom means to confess and clean one's heart of impurity)
- **In close association:** hand in hand, hand in glove
- **To not react:** not bat an eyelid, not turn a hair
- **To be under the control of someone:** under someone's heels, under someone's thumb, dance to the tune of someone
- **To bring someone under control:** rein in, reel in (*etymology: like a fish is reeled in with a fishing rod after getting caught), bring someone to heel, pull on a leash
- **To be the one in charge:** rule the roost, wear the pants in the house (*etymology: this idiom refers to the 1500s, when women only wore skirts and wearing pants meant masculine authority)
- **To not have a stake in the outcome of an event:** to not have any dogs in the fight, to not have any horse in the race
- **To win over the audience by making them laugh wildly:** knock then in the aisle, to make someone roll in the aisles
- **To spoil someone's plans or create an impediment in the plans:** to put a spoke in wheel (*etymology: this refers to the use by carters, of an extra spoke or bar which could be thrust between the spokes of a wheel to serve as a brake), to put a spoke in someone's guns (*etymology: in the seventeenth century, to disable a cannon, one would drive a spike, or large nail, into the touchhole), throw a monkey wrench into the works, gum up the works, throw the spanner in the works, to put sand in the wheels
- **Unnecessarily create drama:** to kick up a fuss, to kick up a dust, make a song and dance about it
- **To create a huge hue and cry about something:** to scream bloody murder, to scream blue murder (*etymology: long time ago in France, the Christians did not want to take the name of God in vain, so rather than saying *'Mon Dieu!'* [My God!], they said *'morbleu'* as *'bleu'* means blue in French and rhymes with *Dieu* [God], making it a handy way to avoid the problem)
- **To quibble:** to split hair, wrangle over an ass's shadow (*etymology: This refers to a Greek story where a traveller hires an ass [donkey] to get to his destination. Soon it becomes unbearably hot and the traveller gets off the donkey and sits in the shadow cast by the animal. The owner asks the traveller for extra money as the amount he has paid allows him to sit on the donkey, but not in its shadow. Both then start fighting and the scared ass runs away, leaving the two men without any shade whatsoever)
- **To talk about unpleasant events from the past:** rake over the ashes/rake up the ashes, open up old wounds, dig up bones, bring up the dead, raise the buried
- **To be a coward:** faint-hearted, spineless, lily-livered, chicken-livered, pigeon-hearted, yellow belly
- **To be very scared:** white as a ghost, white as a sheet, have one's heart in one's mouth, seen a ghost, blood drained from her face
- **Causing great horror:** blood-curdling, spine-chilling, hair-raising
- **To be very sad:** have one's heart in one's boots, to be down in the mouth
- **To be very happy:** jumping for joy, walking on air,

in seventh heaven, on cloud nine, over the moon, on top of the world, tickled pink, beside yourself with joy, pleased as punch

- **To be very tough and sturdy**: tough as boots, tough as nails
- **To be a very clumsy person**: like a bull in a china shop, butterfingered, ham-fisted, ham-handed, heavy-handed, cack-handed, flat-footed
- **To be demented or act crazy**: out of one's mind, as mad as a hatter (*etymology: earlier on, in some parts of England, mercury was used in the hat making process and the workers over there would get dementia because of mercury poisoning), as mad as a March hare (*etymology: this refers to the unpredictable antics of the European hare [a kind of a rabbit] during the March breeding season)
- **To be full of energy**: be bright-eyed and bushy-tailed, be full of beans
- **To take rest**: take the weight of one's feet, take the load off one's feet, rest one's oars, catch forty winks (*etymology: This idiom refers to the Thirty-nine Articles, written by the Church of England in the sixteenth century. These articles contained the rules that a person must agree if they wanted to become clergymen. They were very lengthy and tedious to read, and it was said that a man after reading these Thirty-nine Articles had to take forty winks)
- **To work very hard**: work one's fingers to the bone, work like a Trojan (*etymology: as per legend, the Trojans were a hard-working and industrious people), work like a dog, work day and night, exert oneself, keep at it, keep one's nose to the grindstone, grind away, burn the midnight oil
- **To be very troubled or in a tough situation**: bog down, hard-pressed, with one's back to the wall, in a tight corner, in a tight spot, pinned against the wall
- **To be in a precarious situation**: hanging by a thread, hanging in the balance, on a slippery slope, on thin ice, touch-and-go, built on sand
- **To mess up or ruin something**: make a pig's ear of something, muck it up, run something to seed
- **To be involved in too many things so that one can't concentrate and do any of them well**: have too many irons in the fire, have one's finger in too many pies, spread oneself too thin
- **To wait for something and while away time**: to cool one's heels (Jack cooled his heels in the holding cell till his wife posted bail), to kick one's heels (*etymology: this refers to the toe shuffling and foot tapping that people do when they get impatient while waiting for something)
- **To bide one's time and wait for a better opportunity**: play the waiting game (The crocodile plays the waiting game and then when the deer approaches the pond, he attacks it), tread the water (He's just treading water here until he can find another job)
- **To talk informally and have a fun chat**: shoot the breeze, chew the fat (*etymology: derived from a practice by Native Americans of chewing animal hides during their spare time and the British farmers chewing on smoked pork)
- **To act haughty**: queen it, to act like a stuffed shirt, give oneself airs
- **To be appointed as a royal advisor**: to take silk, to take to purple
- **To treat with contempt**: to snap one's fingers, to treat as beneath one's notice, to talk down, turn up one's nose, cock a snook (He refused to accept his award, cocking a snook at the film industry; *etymology: 'cock' here means to lift up and 'snook' means snout. So, cock a snook means to lift up one's nose with one's thumb and waggle one's fingers as a gesture of disrespect or derision. It is the same as thumbing one's nose to make fun of someone)
- **Exactly right**: on the nose (His estimate that they would consume 23 boxes was on the nose. *Etymology: as if so accurate that it hits exactly on the nose to inflict maximum damage), on the beam (*etymology: as if exactly right on the beam balance while measuring)
- **Make lots of money**: make a bundle, make a pile, make money hand over fist
- **Easy way of earning money:** make money for old rope (Babysitting is money for old rope if the children go to sleep early. *Etymology: earlier ropes were made from hemp and had a limited lifespan but one could sell these used and worn out ropes to ship-makers. These ship-makers would use these old ropes in waterproofing their ships and hence by selling old used ropes that are worthless one could make easy money), make money for jam (*etymology: this is an World War II British Army expression and refers to the low monetary value of jam as it was present in huge quantities in the diet of soldiers)
- **To be broke**: Stony broke, out at the elbows (*etymology: This idiom refers to the elbow patches on the clothes of poor people)

- **To be very poor:** live hand to mouth, keep body and soul together, be hard up, in straitened circumstances, hard up, unable to make ends meet, on one's beam-ends, down and out, pauperized, without a penny to one's name, without two farthings (*etymology: a farthing is a former British monetary unit equal to a quarter of a penny), as poor as a church mouse, without a sou (*etymology: a sou is a small value French coin), without two pennies to rub together

- **To waste something good on someone who doesn't appreciate it**: caviar to the general (*etymology: caviar is picked fish eggs of a large fish like sturgeon, eaten as a delicacy), cast pearls before swine

- **To tip someone:** oil the knocker, cross palm with silver

- **To try to do something new**: have a bash at something, have a smack at something, try a hand at it, try one's luck

- **Secretive:** hole and corner (hole and corner policy), cloak and dagger (A lot of cloak-and-dagger activity was involved in the appointment of the director)

- **To be flooded**: up to one's ears, up to one's eyes

- **When the situation becomes critical**: the fat is in the fire, if it comes to the pinch, when the balloon goes up (The balloon went up last Friday when the scandal became public; *etymology: the phrase comes from World War I when the British artillery sent up a balloon to signal that firing was about to begin)

- **A dangerous situation:** treacherous waters, choppy waters, sticky wicket

- **The worst in a series of negative events**: take the cake, take the biscuit

- **The excess supply of a product in the market:** drug on the market (Right now, smartphones are a drug on the market), glut on the market

- **To have an issue to sort out with someone:** have a bone to pick with someone, have an axe to grind with someone

- **To be engaged in a dispute or fighting with each other**: cross swords, lock horns, be at each other's throats, be at loggerheads, on a collision course, no love lost, bad blood, daggers drawn

- **To beat up someone**: to beat someone black and blue, to knock the living daylights out of someone

- **To put someone through a tough examination to check their worth:** put someone through the wringer (*etymology: a wringer was a hand operated machine in old times which was used to dry out wet clothes after washing them. It consisted of two rollers through which wet clothes went and then these clothes would come out much drier but also looking beaten), put someone through the mill

- **A decisive test to check a quality or a claim**: acid test, litmus test (*etymology: this phrase comes from chemistry when a test for acidity or alkalinity is done using litmus)

- **To try every possible course of action to accomplish a task:** move heaven and earth, leave no stone unturned

- **To come up to standard**: pass muster (*etymology: this is from the 1500s where in the military, a muster meant a military review), come up to scratch, fit the bill, meet the case

- **To not be irreplaceable:** not the only fish in the sea, not be the only pebble on the beach (Every team member needs to remember that they are not the only pebble on the beach), another cog in the machine

- **To be of average quality:** nothing to write home about, dime a dozen (*etymology: a dime is an American coin that is worth 1/10th of a US Dollar), no great shakes, run-of-the-mill

- **To be better than others:** to be cut above the rest, to be head and shoulders above the rest

- **To be careless and do something risky:** throw caution to the wind, to tempt fate

- **To be caught in equally bad choices:** between the devil and the deep blue sea, between a rock and a hard place, being between Scylla and Charybdis (*etymology: Scylla and Charybdis were mythical sea monsters in Greek mythology as noted by the famous writer Homer in his book *Odyssey*)

■

To marry above oneself: to marry someone of a higher social standing

Go in the family way: to be pregnant

Patter of tiny feet: the noise of children running about in the house

Second childhood: senility (mental infirmity as a consequence of old age)

Latchkey kid: a child who returns from school to an empty home because the parents are at work and opens the house with a key given to him/her

■

Teething troubles: short-term problems encountered in the early stage of a project
*Etymology: this refers to the discomfort that children go through when their teeth first come out
Growing pains: short-term problems encountered by an organizations when they start to become big or expand
*Etymology: this refers to the pain in the limbs and joints of children during growth spurts

■

Alive and kicking: in good healthy condition
Art imitating life: a creative work that is based on a true story; for example, a movie that is based on a real person
Larger than life: having a very flamboyant appearance or behaviour
Movie stars always appear larger than life to their loyal fans.

■

Hang on like grim death: to hold onto something very tightly
When he found a great tea stall near his office, he hung hold onto it like grim death.
To turn in one's grave: an idiom used to express that had a concerned person been alive then this person would be utterly shocked and disappointed
The late founder of the company would be turning in his grave to see its directors' shamefully stealing money from the company reserves.
From cradle to grave: when something affects the entire life of a person
He lived in the same town from the cradle to the grave.

■

Give up the ghost: to die or to stop putting efforts
She'd been trying to get an acting role but without success and was about to give up the ghost.
Ghost town: a deserted town that was economically thriving but now completely abandoned

■

Bucket list: a list of things that a person wants to do in their lifetime
Kick the bucket: to die

*Etymology: a person who wants to commit suicide by hanging would stand on a bucket, put their head in the noose and then would kick to the bucket to suspend him/herself in the air

■

Pass the buck: to shift the responsibility to someone else
*Etymology: A buck is an object in a poker game which is placed in front of a person to serve as a reminder for whose turn it is to be the dealer.
Buck stops here: to take full responsibility
*Etymology: US President Harry Truman said that the president must take full and final responsibility for everything in the country.

■

Take something with a pinch/grain of salt: to listen to something with scepticism and not blindly believe in it
Worth one's salt: worthy of one's pay
*Etymology: in early days when there was no refrigeration, salt was the primary method of preservation of food and hence salt was considered as very valuable
Salt of the earth: a person having a great reputation

■

Cast a long shadow: to have considerable influence
The dictator cast a long shadow over every aspect of the country.
Living in the shadows: receiving little attention because someone else gets all the attention
Tom was a good lawyer, but he was always in the shadow of his famous father.
Hog the limelight: to take more attention than one deserves at the cost of others

■

Steal someone's thunder: to take away the effect of someone's speech by saying the same thing before them
Storm in a teacup: big fuss over a trivial matter
Flash in the pan: something that draws a lot of attention for a short time
Keep the pot boiling: keep the matter alive to gain benefit

■

Take a French leave: take an off from work without permission
*Etymology: In eighteenth century France, it was customary to leave a party without saying bye to the hosts
Be out on the tiles: to party a lot
When the Naval officers came on shore they went out on the tiles.
Bunch of malarkey: bunch of nonsense excuses
When he goofed up, he gave his dad a bunch of malarkey.
Take a rain check: this is an expression said to someone when refusing an invitation but saying that one would like to accept the invitation at a later time
*Etymology: rain check is a ticket to a sporting event where the holder is allowed to re-enter on a later day as the event was cancelled due to rain

■

Hell for leather: to go really fast
He completed the long journey in record time by traveling hell-for-leather.
Like the clappers: very fast
The thug ran like the clappers when the policeman came.
*Etymology: reference to the clappers of bell
Go at it hammer and tongs: to do something, especially to argue, with a lot of energy or violence
They went at the problem hammer and tongs.
*Etymology: The origins lie in blacksmithing, where tongs are used to hold the hot iron as it is given shape by hammering.
With might and main: with great force and valour
Make the dust fly: to work in a very vigorous manner
Get down to brass tacks: to come to the main point
Clear the decks: to get out of the way
All hands on deck: a signal used on a ship to call all crew members on the deck to solve an emergency situation

■

Long in the tooth: an old person
*Etymology: this idiom refers to the practice of ascertaining the age of a horse by measuring the length of its tooth and longer the teeth means older the horse
Lie through one's teeth: to boldly lie to someone
*Etymology: a liar will laugh while telling a lie so that he/she can show that he/she is completely calm and relaxed so as to signal that there is no deceit going on
Wailing and gnashing of teeth: to show off anger or irritation

The poor attendance caused wailing and gnashing of organizer's teeth.
Fight tooth and nail: to oppose with full vigour
The trade union vowed to fight the oppression tooth and nail.
Armed to the teeth: heavily armed with deadly weapons
*Etymology: pirates would hold a knife between their teeth and guns in their hands and hence this idiom means to carry the maximum number of weapons possible

■

Bring a knife to a gunfight: to come to a fight severely underequipped
Not the sharpest knife in the drawer: to be stupid or mediocre
The boss described him as not the sharpest knives in the drawer.
Cut the air with a knife: a situation which is very tense and a major fight can start anytime
The first team meeting after the humiliating loss in the World Cup was so tense that one could cut the air with a knife.
Like a hot knife through butter: very quickly and easily
The newly developed laser can cut through rock like a hot knife through butter.

■

Back into the harness: back doing one's job
I don't look forward to getting back into the harness after the vacations get over.
*Etymology: This expression alludes to work horses being harnessed
In double harness: to be married
*Etymology: a double harness is a harness used for a pair of horses
Give someone a fair crack of the whip: to give someone a reasonable opportunity to do something
Jack was upset because he was not given a fair crack of the whip and was fired from his job just three days after joining.

■

Cut the Gordian knot: to solve a very complex problem in a simple way
*Etymology: In ancient Greece, an intricate knot was tied by King Gordius and an oracle declared that the person who would untie the knot would rule Asia. Alexander

the Great just cut it with his sword and thus untied it.

Hobson's choice: a take it or leave it choice

*Etymology: Thomas Hobson, a stable owner in sixteenth century England, used to rotate the use of his horses and for that he told his customers to use the horse he offered or to leave.

Occam's razor: the simplest answer is usually the right one

*Etymology: English philosopher William of Ockham (c. 1287-1347) propounded this idea, which refers to the cutting away of unnecessary material

Catch-22 situation: an impossible situation where one can't succeed due to contradictory options

An example of this is a condition which states that to get a nomination for an award one must be a member of a particular society but only a past nominee can be a member of that society.

*Etymology: Joseph Heller coined the term in his 1961 novel *Catch-22*.

Cornelian dilemma: a dilemma in which someone gains and losses something in both the choices that are presented

*Etymology: French writer Pierre Corneille wrote a play where the main actor has to choose between his love or to take revenge for his family's death caused by his lover's father. If he loves his wife then he can't kill her father (and thus fail in taking revenge) and if he kills her father then he will lose his love.

Zero-sum game: a situation in which one can win only by causing a loss to the other person

Competitive exams are a zero-sum game.

*Etymology: This term comes from game theory of mathematics where the sum of the gain of one person and the loss of the other person, totals to zero as both are of the same value but the gain is positive and the loss is negative.

■

To talk shop: to talk about business especially at social events where such talk is out of place

To talk through one's hat: to talk nonsense

*Etymology: this refers to the emptiness of the hat atop one's head

To beggar description: to be so magnificent that mere words are not enough to describe the magnificence

The play's stage set was so elaborate and awesome that it beggared description.

■

Throw down the gauntlet: to issue a challenge

*Etymology: gauntlet is a metal glove used as armour in a sword fight and in medieval England a gauntlet-wearing knight would challenge a fellow knight to a duel by throwing one of his gauntlets on the ground

Take up the gauntlet: to accept a challenge

Running the gauntlet: a form of punishment

*Etymology: a form of physical punishment wherein the defaulter is to run between two rows of soldiers who repeatedly strike him

■

To be in the wrong: to make a mistake

Be for the high jump: to be read for major penalty

She'll be for the high jump when her mother finds out she's been missing classes.

To take the rap: to take the blame

He refused to take the rap for the crime as he was not even in town that night.

Carry the can: to take the blame or responsibility for one's mistake

*Etymology: in the military, a person who had made a mistake was given the punishment of fetching a container of beer for the other soldiers.

Wear sackcloth and ashes: to show that one is very sorry for something one did wrong

After having apologized enough, he wondered aloud how long must he wear sackcloth and ashes before he would be forgiven.

*Etymology: earlier, clothes made of sackcloth (a kind of a rough cloth) were worn by the Jews in religious ceremonies to show remorse

To take one's medicine: to accept punishment

To pocket one's pride: to swallow one's pride and accept mistakes

Laughing on the other side of one's face: to experience a humbling reversal of fortunes

After not studying and just partying, he was laughing out of the other side of his face when he found out that he had failed

Chickens come home to roost: to face the consequences of one's mistakes

*Etymology: chickens roam on a farm all day but when the sun goes down they all return to the safety of their henhouse to rest/roost

Cross to bear: a burden that one must put up with

The serious illness of the child was a cross to bear for the whole family.

*Etymology: this idiom refers to the cross carried by Jesus to his crucifixion

A millstone around one's neck: a problem or responsibility that one has all the time, which prevents one from doing what they want

He remained debt free as he did not want a millstone around his neck.

*Etymology: a millstone is a large stone that is very heavy

Albatross around one's neck: a burden which a person has to carry to signify repentance for a past sin

The tag of a traitor was an Albatross around his neck as he left the army without permission.

*Etymology: This idiom comes from the poem 'The Rime of the Ancient Mariner' by Samuel Taylor Coleridge, in which the sailor, who shoots an albatross, has to carry the burden of the bird hung around his neck as a punishment for his sin.

Monkey on my back: a persistent and irritating trouble

Breathe down someone's neck: to monitor someone too closely, causing discomfort and irritation

His boss was always breathing down his neck with the demands for constant email updates.

With bated breath: in a state of suspense, anticipation, excitement, etc., as if one is holding their breath in

With bated breath we watched the final over of the cricket match.

■

Take a hard line with someone: to be firm with someone

The manager takes a hard line with people who show up late.

Throw the book at someone: to make as many criminal charges as possible against an offender

The prosecutor threw the book at the drug peddler and made sure he spent his entire life in jail.

Give a curtain lecture: a private reprimand given to a husband by his wife

Pull someone to pieces: to criticize very harshly

Pick/puncture holes in: to find fault with

■

Fall to my lot: to succumb to destiny

After the death of his brother, it fell to her lot to take care of his children.

Throw in a lot with someone: to join someone

He's reluctant to throw his lot with a young company that may not even survive the next year.

■

Fool for one's pain: to do a thankless job

I was a fool for my pain to host my ungrateful relatives for dinner.

Not getting a sausage: thankless work

■

Think aloud: to speak whatever is on one's mind

Think nothing of it: to not apply mind on something and just ignore it

With malice aforethought: having criminal intentions

He attacked the child with malice aforethought and hence was given the maximum sentence.

■

Let the cat out of the bag: to reveal a secret by mistake

Give the game away: to reveal a plan or strategy

■

Keep one's own counsel: to keep one's thoughts and plans to oneself

Bite one's tongue: to stop oneself from being frank and not say what one is really feeling

Her conservative mother had to bite her tongue when she introduced her new biker boyfriend.

Hold one's peace: to keep quiet in spite of strongly wanting to give one's opinion: He held his peace because he did not want to ruin the family dinner

Closed book: something or someone about which one knows nothing

Playing one's cards close to one's chest: to not tell anyone one's plans

Hide one's light under a bushel: to conceal one's good ideas or talents

He was advised to not hide his light under a bushel and share his opinions openly with other people.

*Etymology: a bushel is a bowl

Beat around the bush: to speak evasively or to waste time

*Etymology: In earlier times, hunters would hire men to beat the area around bushes with sticks in order to flush out the birds hiding in them. But these men carefully avoided hitting the actual bushes because they might hit something dangerous like a hornet's nest and that would mean the end of the hunt

Man of a few words: a person who doesn't speak much

162

Swallow one's words: to retract one's statement
The politician had to swallow his words after the fact checking proved that his claims were false.
Sweet nothings: affectionate but meaningless words spoken to express one's love
At the college party, a lot of couples were spotted whispering sweet nothings to each other as they danced to the music.

■

Come to blows: to start physically fighting
Come to grief: to end badly or sadly
His career as a lawyer came to grief after he became involved with gamblers.

■

Straight and narrow: to behave honestly
Up and up: honourable and trustworthy
Not kosher: socially unacceptable
*Etymology: Kosher foods are those that conform to Jewish dietary regulations

■

To be on the fiddle: to be involved in illegal activities
If he's not on the fiddle then how did he afford the huge house in the posh part of town?
*Etymology: this is related to Emperor Nero, who famously played the fiddle [a violin] while Rome burned and hence refers to corruption and dishonesty
To play second fiddle: to be someone's subordinate or play a minor role to someone
He was sick of playing second fiddle to the lead actor as he thought that he was a much better performer.

■

To run in the same groove: to be in good relations
Hand to hand: travel from hand to hand
The book travelled from hand to hand until it got back to its owner.
Hands down: undisputedly
All hands to the pump: a call for everyone to get to work
Turn a hand: to help out
Not do a hands turn: to not help out
Serves one turn: to help out fully and fulfil one's duty
To come with a cap in hand: to beg for money

Pass the hat around: to collect money from a group of people

■

Keep the wolf from the door: to earn enough to keep poverty away
Make both ends meet: to earn just enough money to pay for all living expenses
Live hand to mouth: to earn just enough money that whatever one earns is spent on paying for living expenses like buying food
Having a thin time: to experience a difficult period
Be on the breadline: to be very poor
*Etymology: In the US, during the great depression in the 1920s, the breadlines were poverty stricken people standing in a line waiting for free food provided by the government.
Cut coat according to cloth: to live according to one's means
Scrimp and save: to be very frugal
If it comes to the pinch: a financial emergency
Open up the purse strings: to spend money with a free hand
Pay off old scores: to take revenge
Cut corners: to take shortcuts to save time or money
The painter cut corners by applying only a single coat of paint.
*Etymology: in driving, to avoid taking a turn in the road, one could just go straight across the road and thus cut off the corner to save time by shortening the distance

■

Draw a blank: to not get a response
I asked him about Sam's financial problems, and I just drew a blank
Cut no ice: to have no effect
Her excuses cut no ice with the teacher.
Not give currency to something: to not give credence to something
Water off a duck's back: criticism that has no effect on the recipient

■

Make hay: turn a situation to one's advantage
The environmentalist lobby made hay of the nuclear plant accident.

Make hay while the sun shines: to take advantage of a brief opportunity while it is still there

Hang onto someone's coattails: gain success by association than effort

He got a big government post by hanging onto the coattails of the leader of his political party.

*Etymology: coattail is the rear flap of a man's coat

Hanker after: to eagerly want something

■

On the sauce: a drunk

On the wagon: a teetotaller (a person who doesn't consume alcohol)

*Etymology: In the US, the Salvation Army used to tour the slums in a wagon picking up drunks and delivering them to sobriety.

Fall of the wagon: to start drinking alcohol again

Wet one's whistle: to have an alcoholic drink

Have one over the eight: to drink excessively

*Etymology: the presumption being that an average man can safely drink eight beer glasses

Hair of the dog: an alcoholic drink taken to cure a hangover

*Etymology: This idiom comes from the expression 'hair of the dog that bit you' because, in ancient times, it was said that if a dog were to bite you, then putting the dog's hair into the wound would heal it because of the belief that 'like cures like'.

■

Let off the hook: to pardon someone or let them escape from blame

The sham investigation let the accused off the hook.

Can't hack it: unable to do the job

I thought delivering groceries would be an easy job, but I just can't hack it.

Know a hawk from a handsaw: to be able to tell the two things apart

*Etymology: in Shakespeare's *Hamlet*, where he wrote, 'Of course I know which twin is which, I know a hawk from a handsaw, after all!'

Not see the wood from the trees: to not understand the main point as one is preoccupied with minor details

He did see the woods from the trees because he focussed on door paint when the lock was broken.

■

Keep an open house: to welcome and entertain friends at all times

Kill somebody with kindness: to be too kind to someone

Strange bedfellows: unlikely allies; often used in the phrase 'politics makes strange bedfellows'

*Synonyms: **unholy alliance, odd couple**

■

To a fault: to do something so well that it almost seems excessive and hence one could say that a fault is committed

He was so nice that people called him being polite to a fault.

To a nicety: with great exactness or accuracy

■

In the same vein: along the same line

In the same breath: very similar

He is a relatively new rapper but his name has been mentioned in the same breath as Eminem

Paint with the same brush: to say that everyone has the same bad qualities

When one swimmer uses banned substances, all the other swimmers get painted with the same brush.

Tarred with the same brush: having the same characteristic

He and his brother are tarred with the same brush as both are scoundrels.

In broad brush strokes: to describe something in general terms and not in detail

In one fell swoop: to do all and at once

He fired everyone and reduced the salary expenditure to zero in one fell swoop.

*Etymology: fell means fierce and swoop refers to how a bird of prey like an eagle swoops down from the sky to catch its prey on the ground in one quick swift move

■

Go out like a light: to sleep very quickly

According to your own lights: behave as per your own wishes.

Make light of something: not to take something seriously

See the light of day: to come into existence into the world

After years, finally, his novel was published and saw the light of day.

Light at the end of the tunnel: an indication that the end of the difficult situation is near

■

For a tune/For a song: to get something very cheap
Can't carry a tune in a bushel basket: lacking musical ability
I don't know why he is in the choir as he can't carry a tune in a bushel basket. *Etymology: the person is so bad at singing that they can't carry a weightless thing like a tune in a basket
Have a frog in one's throat: to have a cough
It isn't over till the fat lady sings: the final outcome cannot be assumed until the matter finally concludes
*Etymology: this refers to the usually overweight female singers in an opera who would sing only at the climax

■

One jump ahead: to stay one move ahead
Steal a march on someone: to get an advantage over someone by acting before they do
Our rival company managed to steal a march on us by bringing out their product ahead of ours.
*Etymology: derived from the military manoeuvre of moving troops secretly, in order to gain an advantage
Stand on ceremony: to insist on completing all formalities

■

Knock someone sideways: to shock someone
The news of her brother's death knocked her sideways.
Knock them dead: to win over an audience
Knocking down doors: to investigate or search for something very thoroughly

■

Run rings around someone: to have much more skill or ability than someone else
Can't hold a candle to someone: to not be able to measure up to someone
Jeff can't hold a candle to Jeb when it comes to athletics.
*Etymology: apprentices used to hold candles to light the work that a master artist was doing and hence the person who held the candle has a lower level skill set
To carry the torch: to lead and be successful
To carry the torch for someone: to be in love with someone who is not in love with you

*Etymology: the Greek and Roman custom of the wedding torch where in a wedding procession the bride used to carry a torch lit by the fire in her own house and to light the hearth of her new home

■

Put a sock in it: to rudely tell someone to keep quiet
Put the kibosh on someone or something: to veto someone's plans
*Etymology: Kibosh comes from Gaelic *'caidhp bháis'* meaning 'coif of death' or cloth of death. It was the headgear which a judge would wear when pronouncing a death sentence or the covering pulled over the face of a dead body when a coffin was closed and put in the ground.
Put the mockers on something: to prevent something from happening
His parents decided to stay in on Saturday night, which put the mockers on his party plans.
*Etymology: mockers was an twentieth century Australian slang term meaning jinx or bad luck
Stick one's oar in: to interfere or give opinion when it is not asked for
The CEO scolded the new recruit for sticking his oars in the CEO's work.
To blackball something: to veto
The committee blackballed my idea.
*Etymology: Blackballing refers to the traditional form of secret ballot, where a white ball constitutes a vote in support and a black ball signifies opposition.

■

Help a lame dog over a stile: to help people who are in difficulty
Dog in the manger: someone who keeps something not because they need it but just to prevent others from having it
*Etymology: this refers to the infamous 'dog in a manger' in Aesop's fables, who occupies the manger (an open box from which farm animals eat) not because he wanted to eat the hay inside the manger but wanted to stop other animals from eating
Can't teach an old dog new tricks: this means that it is difficult to teach new stuff to an outdated person because this person is so used to doing things the old way that they are now very resistant to change
In the doghouse: to be in trouble

He is in the dog house because he forgot his wedding anniversary.

Dog-eat-dog world: a ruthless competitive landscape where people would even harm others to be successful

Lie doggo: to hide

*Etymology: It is a practice in Australian slang to add 'o' after a word and the rationale here being 'to lie low, like a dog in hiding'.

Barking up the wrong tree: to mistakenly pursue a matter at the wrong forum or with the wrong person

■

Keep on a short leash: to exercise a lot of control over someone

Straining at the leash: trying to get free

The restless dog was straining at the leash.

Yank someone's leash: to say something annoying in order to get this person to overreact

■

Make a pig's ear of something: to mess up some task

Pig's breakfast: a total mess

Pig headed: to be very stubborn

Guinea pig: a person used as a subject for experimentation

The pharmaceutical company used the homeless as guinea pigs to test new drugs.

*Pronounced as gini-pigs

*Etymology: a guinea pig is a small rodent found in South America that was used for lab experiments

When pigs fly: something will never happen

*Etymology: something has the same probability of happening as pigs flying

Put lipstick on a pig: to make cosmetic changes to something to make it more attractive

The car salesman would put lipstick on a pig by washing the car thoroughly and waxing it so that it shines.

Mutton dressed as lamb: this is a derogatory phrase used primarily in the United Kingdom, for an older woman who tries to dress up like a young girl

She embarrassed her children because she looked like mutton dressed as lamb.

Wolf in sheep's clothing: a dangerous person pretending to be harmless

No one trusted her because she was a wolf in sheep's clothing and would try to steal credit.

*Etymology: from Aesop's fable, about a wolf dressing up as a sheep and also from the Bible, where Jesus warns of 'false prophets in sheep's clothing but inwardly they are ravening wolves' (Matthew 7:15)

Save somebody's bacon: to save someone's job

Bring home the bacon: to earn money, particularly for one's family

*Etymology: bacon was the staple meat of the working class

Bust my chop: to annoy someone with nagging and criticism

*Etymology: bust means to hit and chop refers to meat chops that were the fashionable sideburns in the 60s

Babe in the woods: a naive person in a dangerous environment

■

Earn one's chops: to learn a skill

*Etymology: chops is a standard expression denoting technical skill in Jazz

Earn one's stripes: to do something to merit a higher position

Cut one's teeth: to gain experience or sharpen one's skill

He cut his teeth in the 90s working as the assistant to the editor.

*Etymology: cutting of teeth refers to the teeth of a baby first appearing as they cut through the gums

Learn the ropes: to learn the basic details of something, especially one's job

The new recruit was assigned a mentor to help him learn the ropes.

*Etymology: new recruits on a ship had to learn how to tie knots and work with the ropes that moved the sails of a ship

■

White elephant: something that is a headache to keep and maintain

His father-in-law gave him a Rolls Royce, but it's a white elephant as he can't afford the high cost of maintaining it.

White horse: brave and heroic person

White whale: a goal that is one's life's obsession

*Etymology: This is a reference to the book *Moby Dick*. The main character in the book chased the white whale (Moby Dick) for a really long time but never caught him.

White as snow: having a very fair complexion

■

To be as sick as a parrot: to be very sad

Jack was sick as a parrot when he heard Manchester United had lost the match. *Etymology: *'psittacosis'* is a disease which affects parrots but can be spread to humans

To be up with the lark: to get up early in the morning

*Etymology: lark is a small bird that sings in the early morning

Cock of the walk: a person who acts as if he is more important than other people

He acts like the cock of the walk around the office.

Cuckoo in the nest: someone who don't belong in the group

For Jack, his step father was a cuckoo in the nest.

*Etymology: This refers to the practice of European cuckoos to lay their eggs in other birds' nests as they do not build nests of their own. The baby cuckoo is then raised by parents of a different species along with their own offspring.

Canary in the coal mine: an early indicator of potential danger or failure

The presence of native fishes is very much the canary in the coal mine for the health of a river.

*Etymology: a canary is a kind of small yellow coloured bird and miners took caged canaries into coal mines to warn of methane gas as the canaries die in the presence of methane gas

Count one's chickens before they are hatched: to celebrate a win before the final outcome

He was warned to not count his chickens before they hatch, yet he tweeted out acceptance speech before the final result.

Foul one's own nest: to harm one's own interests

Feather in one's cap: an achievement to be proud of

*Etymology: This refers to the custom of Native Americans where warriors add a new feather to their head-gear for every enemy slain.

Empty nest syndrome: the sad feelings which parents have when their children grow up and leave home

To egg on: to incite or urge someone to do something

*Etymology: This idiom has nothing to do with an actual egg but comes from an Old Norse word, *'eggja'*, which means to edge.

Have an egg on one's face: to suffer a public embarrassment

The CEO had egg on his face after it was revealed that the company's new smartphone did not have any 4G capability nor WiFi.

To bring one's eggs to a bad market: to go to the wrong people for help

To walk on eggshells: to be extremely cautious about one's words or actions so as not to upset someone

The tiniest thing irritated his wife so he had to walk on eggshells whenever he was in the house.

Wind beneath my wings: to call someone supportive and helpful

Take someone under one's wing: to give someone help and protection

The experienced lawyer took the new recruit under his wings.

*Etymology: this refers to how a hen gathers her chicks under her wing

The bird has flown: when something untoward has occurred

As the crow flies: in a straight line

Have bats in the belfry: to be crazy

*Etymology: a belfry is the top part of a church tower

Blind as a bat: to be completely blind

■

Bee in the bonnet: to obsessively think a lot about something

The problem was like a bee in my bonnet.

*Etymology: 'bonnet' is a kind of hat

The bird and the bees: this refers to sex education, especially when taught informally to teenagers

*Etymology: in the song called *Let's Do It* (1928), Cole Porter said, 'And that's why birds do it, bees do it / Even educated fleas do it / Let's do it, let's fall in love'. This idiom uses sexual behaviour in animals to explain sex without referring to human emotions.

■

Bird has flown the coop: when someone escapes captivity

The prisoner flew the coop at the first opportunity.

*Etymology: a coop is a cage or a pen in which poultry is kept

To let the fox guard the henhouse: to give the duty of guarding a valuable asset to someone who is likely to steal it or abuse the power

Lunatics are running the asylum: when the least capable people are running an organization and then naturally disaster ensues

■

Pull a rabbit out of the hat: to do something surprising, which seemed impossible at the start
*Etymology: This is a reference to the magician's trick of pulling a live rabbit out of his hat.
Go down the rabbit hole: to enter into a problematic and strange situation
He went down the rabbit hole of narcotics addiction and that ruined his career.
*Etymology: this refers to how Alice started her adventures by going down a rabbit hole in the famous book *Alice in Wonderland* by Lewis Carroll

■

Kick the can down the road: to avoid or delay dealing with a problem
Sweep under the carpet/rug: to hide a problem rather than dealing with it
Bury one's head in the sand: to hide and thus ignore a problem rather than dealing with it head on
*Etymology: An ostrich is believed (incorrectly) to hide its head in a hole in the ground when it sees a threat.

■

Play ducks and drakes with something: to squander away something
*Etymology: Ducks and drakes is an English pastime of throwing stones on the surface of water to make them bounce and now it refers to just waste away something like throwing away rocks.
Take to something like a duck takes to water: to learn to do something very easily and naturally
She took to singing just as a duck takes to water.
To break the duck: to start something
*Etymology: based on the cricket term 'duck' meaning zero runs, so to break the duck means to start scoring
A fine day for ducks: a bad weather day
*Etymology: refers to the fact that ducks don't mind rain due to the coating on the feathers
A duck in a thunderstorm: person who thinks he is fine but is actually in a bad position
*Etymology: Ducks, due to the coating on the feathers, are impervious to rain but not to the lightning.
Dead duck: a person or a thing that is surely going to fail (The marketing campaign was a dead duck because it was prepared in English for a Chinese audience); a person who is about to get in a lot of trouble
Have one's ducks in a row: to be well prepared in case some trouble comes up

*Etymology: this phrase refers to how a mother duck leads her ducklings in a single and orderly file.
Swan Song: the last amazing performance before death
*Etymology: refers to the legend that while they are mute during the rest of their lives, swans sing beautifully and mournfully just before they die
Black swan: this is a metaphor which means that just because one has not something doesn't mean that it does not exist
For example, it was known as a fact that all swans are white and everyone proved that by pointing to all the swans who happened to be white in colour until finally one day a black coloured swan was spotted and the entire swan colour theory crumbled.
Wouldn't say boo to a goose: a very shy person
Jack is not cut out to be a politician as he wouldn't even say boo to a goose.
What's sauce for the goose is sauce for the gander: this signifies that the same rules apply to everyone

■

Old trout: an old irritable person
Neither fish nor fowl: something that can't be categorized
Loaves and fishes: benefits or rewards of doing some work
Give a sprat to catch a mackerel: a small price to pay in the short-term to obtain a long-term gain
*Etymology: a sprat is a small fish and a mackerel is a much larger fish
A kettle of fish: a mess
*Etymology: the mess of bones, head and skin that is left in the kettle (a metal utensil) after the fish has been eaten
Pot calling the kettle black: to criticize someone for a fault which the criticizer him/herself has

■

Change horses in midstream: to make major changes in the middle of the task
Lock the stable down when the horse bolted: to take care after the loss has already occurred
Look a gift horse in the mouth: to not question the value of a gift
*Etymology: this idiom refers to the practice of ascertaining the age of a horse by measuring the length of its tooth
Horses for courses: something that one says to convey that it is important to choose the right people for

particular activities because everyone has different skills

*Etymology: a British horse racing expression urging someone to stick to the thing he knows best.

Hold one's horses: to wait a moment and not rush into something

From the horse's mouth: information directly from the concerned person

*Etymology: in horse racing, a horse is the best person to give a tip on which is the best horse to bet on

Dark horse: a competitor about whom very little is known and who goes on to surprisingly win

*Etymology: this idiom from the world of horse racing, where a dark horse was the one about whom the gamblers did not have any information about and thus were wary about betting on it

Underdog: a competitor who everyone thinks has very little chance of winning

David was considered an underdog in front of Goliath.

A camel's nose under the tent: this idiom means that a small act can lead to a huge problem later on

*Etymology: an Arabian proverb which says that if a camel is allowed to get its nose inside of a tent then it will surely enter the tent and that will result in the dismantling of the tent

■

Meat and potatoes: the basic and essential aspects

The club's meat and potatoes remain the classical singers.

*Etymology: meat and potatoes are the main part of a dinner

Bread and butter: a person's livelihood or main source of income

Stock-in-trade: goods in stock necessary for carrying on a business

A charming smile is the salesman's stock in trade.

■

Run with the hare and hunt with the hounds: to support both sides of a dispute

Fight like cat and dog: to argue violently all the time

Rain cats and dogs: to rain heavily

*Etymology: from the Greek expression '*cata doxa*', which means 'contrary to experience or belief'.

To have a cat and dog life: to have an unhappy married life

Lead a dog life: to live a tough labour filled life

Die a dog's death: to die in a bad way and not acknowledged

■

Have kittens: to get extremely worried, upset or angry

She nearly had kittens when she found out that she may get fired from her job.

*Etymology: in the dark ages, women would get worried that instead of giving birth to a human baby, they would instead give birth to kittens because of a curse of a witch (who are usually pictured with black cats)

Like a cat on a hot tin roof: to be nervous or restless

He has been like a cat on a hot tin roof all day, waiting for the test results to come in.

No room to swing a cat: no room to move

*Etymology: a cat was a whip used in the British Navy, so no room to swing a whip means to be in closed confined quarters

To have nine lives like a cat: to have talent or luck for getting out of bad situations

*Etymology: legends say that cats have nine lives due to their keen senses and agility and thus they avoid death in dangerous encounters

Land like a cat on its feet: to be lucky and survive a difficult situation

Cat got one's tongue: to have nothing to say in reply

When the cat's away, the mice will play: when the authority figure goes away, those under the command will have fun

There's more than one way to skin a cat: there are many different ways to solve a problem

Curiosity killed the cat: excessive inquisitiveness can be dangerous

*Etymology: from Shakespeare's *Much Ado About Nothing*: 'What, courage man! what though care killed a cat, thou hast mettle enough in thee to kill care.'

■

On the prowl: to be actively looking for something, especially when looking for a sexual partner

He has been on the prowl for a new car ever since he got a huge salary hike.

Once bitten twice shy: to be extra cautious and avoid something or some person after being previously hurt by this thing or person

After losing a lot in the stock market, she swore to stick to bonds. As they say, once bitten, twice shy.

Keep tabs on something: to monitor something very carefully
The CEO kept tabs on all departments of the company.

■

Donkey's years: very long time
They had not met in donkey's ears.
Talk the hind leg off a donkey: to talk a lot
That girl can talk the hind leg off a donkey.
*Etymology: donkeys are regarded as strong and sturdy animals but this person can talk so much that even they can't tolerate it

■

Elephant in the room: this refers to a problem that everyone is aware of but no one wants to talk about
How to address the reckless actions of the CEO was the elephant in the room at the management meeting.
800-pound gorilla: this refers to an entity that is very dominating because of its sheer size and strength
Facebook is the 800-pound gorilla in the social media industry.

■

The blind leading the blind: the incapable leading the incapable
Lead up a blind alley: to lead someone to a dead end
To be led by one's nose: to force someone to go somewhere
She led her husband by the nose to go see the opera.
*Etymology: this is based on the way that a cow is sometimes led by rope attached to a ring in its nose

■

Not for all the tea in China: to not agree, whatever be the reward
Do anything for a consideration: to do anything for money
To pick something up for a song: to buy something very cheaply
Bill of fare: the menu of a restaurant

■

Be like a bull in a china shop: to be very clumsy
He is like a bull in a china shop and thus he was not allowed near the glass antiques.

To be ham handed/ham fisted: to be clumsy and inept
The government's ham-handed efforts to fix the problem only made it worse.

■

All bets are off: an idiom said to suggest that no one has any idea about what will happen in the future
Hedge one's bets: to place bets in such a way by which one minimizes the risk
For example, a high risk bet is balanced with two low risk bets.

■

Sound as a bell: in perfect condition
Clean as a whistle: extremely clean or free of any incriminating evidence
Bells and whistles: the non-essential items added to a product to make it more appealing
*Etymology: in a bicycle, the main features are the quality of the frame, tyres, etc., and bells and whistles are only added for attraction

■

It's an ill wind that blows nobody any good: something bad that results in good for someone
The huge storm destroyed the town but gave good business to the reconstruction companies so it was an ill wind that blew nobody any good.
In the wind: to run away or it can refer to rumours circulating
Straws in the wind: something that shows what might happen in the future
There were straws in the wind that suggested a market crash was likely.
To clutch at straws: to hope for help in something unlikely
He is hoping that the new medical experimental treatment will help him but everyone thinks that he is clutching at straws.
To scatter to the four winds: to scatter in all directions
Get a second wind: to regain energy after getting tired
Get wind of something: to get an idea of what is about to happen
The police got wind of the illegal drug deal.

■

Pet project: a project that one undertakes to do out of interest and not as a duty, for example a hobby

Labour of love: an activity that is hard work but one does it because it is enjoyable

He prefers to paint the baby's nursery himself because for him it is a labour of love.

Labour of Hercules: something that requires immense effort

Plough a lonely furrow: to work without help from others

He is happier in isolation, ploughing a lone furrow.

*Etymology: furrow is a long, narrow trench made in the ground by a plough for planting seeds

Sisyphean Task: a pointless task, which one must do over and over again, without any reward

He soon learned that trying to impress his rude boss was a Sisyphean task.

*Pronounced as sis-uh-fian task

*Etymology: Sisyphus (*pronounced as sis-uh-fuhs) was a Greek king who offended the gods because of his clever schemes and as punishment he was sentenced to spend eternity rolling a huge boulder up a hill. This task was obviously very difficult but also repetitive and fruitless as when he did manage to roll the boulder up the hill, it would just roll down again from the other side.

■

Dead beat: totally exhausted

He was dead beat after working the 12-hour shift at the factory.

Deadbeat: a lazy and negligent person

She had a hard time getting any alimony from her divorced deadbeat husband.

Dead heat: a stalemate; a tie

Dead letter: a law that is in effect but no longer enforced

Dead loss: a loss that cannot be salvaged

Caught dead to rights: to be caught red-handed

■

To work on the land: to work as a farmer

Live off the land: to live by eating only the food that one produces

Live off the fat of the land: to live abundantly

He won a million dollars in the lottery and is now living off the fat of the land.

Lay/lie of the land: the general state of affairs

Parish-pump: local politics

The government should not get distracted by the parish-pump narrative and instead focus on the national agenda.

■

Chicken feed: a small amount of anything, especially of money

Shoestring: a very small amount of money

The government prepared a shoestring budget for the education sector.

■

Great and small: persons of all ranks or degrees

Ragtag and bobtail: the lowest social class

As common as muck: a lowly person

The common run: the average or usual type of something

His nightly debate is definitely better than the common run of television news shows.

Small fry: an insignificant person

Rank and file: ordinary members of a group and not the leaders

*Etymology: the rows and columns of soldiers, drawn up for a drill are called 'ranks' and 'files' and then these are led by officers

Every man jack: every person

Man on the street: the everyday lay person

Low man on the totem pole: a low ranking person

■

To hold water: to be valid, sound and logical

To keep in watertight compartments: to keep completely separate

The editorial and the marketing teams in a newspaper must be placed in watertight compartments.

Watertight case: a case or an argument without any loopholes or weakness

Water under the bridge: this refers to events that occurred a long time back and are not important anymore

The Professor accepted the apology from the student for past bad behaviour calling it water under the bridge.

Tread the water: to bide one's time

He's just treading water here until he can find another job.

Test the waters: to get an idea of people's opinion before taking an action

He tested the waters before announcing his run for the presidency.

Go through fire and water: to go through a severe trial to prove something
Set the Thames on fire: to do something remarkable

■

Stir the blood: to generate interest
Stir one's stumps: to become active
After wasting time, he finally stirred his stumps and posted his CV on the Internet.

■

Hot and bothered: to get uncomfortable
Grin and bear: to tolerate something irritating
Bear Garden: a noisy place
Good and chattels: someone's private belongings
Common-or-garden: commonplace; ordinary
He just wanted a common-or-garden bike and nothing fancy like a Harley Davidson.
Cut the cackle: cut the nonsense and come to a point
Cock and bull story: a made-up story
Kill or cure: to either completely solve the problem or completely fail
Make or mar: to either fix or ruin completely
Peak and pine: to long for something a lot
Meek and mild: someone who is very non-confrontational
With might and main: with great force and valour
Rough and ready: crude, unpolished or hastily prepared but sufficient for the purpose
Rough and tumble: a situation without formal rules and order
Scissors and paste: a cut-copy-paste job from various sources
Ways and means: various methods and devices to accomplish a goal
Wit and wisdom: combination of brains and quick thinking
Nuts and bolts: the practical details
Leaps and bounds: rapidly
His business grew by leaps and bounds.
Dribs and drabs: in small scattered amounts
Dribs and drabs of gossip kept regularly flowing from the party office.
Thick and fast: rapid and in huge numbers
After the press conference the questions from the journalists came in thick and fast.
Through thick and thin: to stay with someone through the good times and the bad

Hem and haw: to be unsure and take a long time in deciding
*Etymology: In old days, hem meant to clear one's throat to get someone's attention (like saying ahem) and haw is a sound that signifies hesitation.
Betwixt and between: neither here nor there
The movie seems betwixt and between—neither a drama nor a documentary.
Fits and starts: to do something in an on and off manner and not consistently
She must work on her master's thesis regularly and not in fits and starts.

■

Milk and honey: prosperity and abundance
Economists think that the next 20 years will be a time of milk and honey.
Chalk and cheese: two things that are completely different from each other
Bread and butter letter: a thank you letter especially for hospitality received
Poison pen letter: an anonymous letter with abuses
Cakes and ale: the good life
High days and holidays: festive days

■

In twos and threes: in small numbers
People are coming to see the exhibition in twos and threes.
At sixes and sevens: to be very confused
Janus was at sixes and sevens when it came to filing her taxes.
Dressed to the nines: to be dressed up ornately
Do one's daily dozen: to do one's daily routine tasks
Baker's dozen: an amount totalling to 13
*Etymology: in the medieval era to avoid the penalty for less bread weight per piece, the bakers started giving an extra loaf when selling a dozen

■

At the eleventh hour: at the last possible moment
Beat the clock: to be on time
Clock in: to begin work
He was a punctual office worker and always clocked in on time.
*Etymology: in many workplaces there are special clocks that punch the time on the employee's time card

when they enter and leave
Clock out: to end work
He clocked out early yesterday.
Clean someone's clock: to thoroughly defeat someone; to physically beat up someone
The young tennis player cleaned the much more experienced player's clock.
*Etymology: this idiom originated in the US military where 'clockface' was the slang for someone's face

■

Shanks's pony/Shank's mare: to walk on foot to one's destination
*Etymology: It is said that this idiom is derived from an individual called Shanks, who manufactured lawn-mowing machines and one such horse-drawn mower had no seat so the driver had to necessarily walk behind it.
Walk ones leg off: to walk a lot
Walk a mile in his shoes: this idiom means that before judging someone, one must experience their lives and problems to fully understand them

■

Adam's ale: water
*Etymology: this is a reference to the only drink available to Adam in the biblical traditions
Not know from Adam: to not know who the person is
*Etymology: refers to Adam, the first man made by God as per the Bible
Snake in the grass: a treacherous person
*Etymology: this refers to the serpent in the Bible, who deceives Eve into eating the forbidden fruit

■

Play fast and loose with something: to treat someone or something in a careless way The reporter told the politician to stop playing fast and loose with facts.
Blow hot and cold: to alternate between moods and be unpredictable
Blink the fact: to ignore something

■

Counsel of despair: an action to be taken when all else fails
It was a counsel of despair to declare bankruptcy to prevent the foreclosure.

Counsel of perfection: ideal but unrealistic advice
Take counsel: to discuss a problem with a trusted person
Lend an ear: to listen sympathetically and patiently
He always lends an ear to his teammates when they get stressed at the office.

■

Pick someone's brains: to talk with someone and gain information
Brainstorm: to hold a group discussion to produce solutions to a problem or ideas for a project
Rack one's brains: to struggle to recall something or find a solution
He racked his brain but could not remember the name of his boss's wife.
Put on one's thinking cap: to think very hard, especially when trying to find a solution to a problem
The sales manager put his thinking cap on to figure out why the sales were declining.
Rake over old ashes: to revive old unpleasant memories
He told his wife to not rake over old ashes and focus on the disagreement at hand.

■

Hare-brained: crazy; rash; reckless
The villain has a hare-brained plan to conquer the world.
Scatter-brained: disorganized
He played the role of the Scatter-brained scientist in the movie.
Feather-brained: silly
The children had a feather-brained plan.
Half-baked: unplanned
His half-baked attempt to steal landed him in jail.

■

Raise one's eyebrows: to show disapproval
Cast/run one's eye over: to quickly look at something
The student requested the teacher to cast an over his essay and provide feedback.
To keep half an eye on something: to watch something or someone without giving them all one's attention
To keep one's eyes on the prize/main chance: to remain focussed on the main mission despite the distractions
Keep one's eyes peeled: to be very vigilant and alert
The security guards kept their eyes peeled while loading the ATM.
Eyes darting from one side to another: to quickly look

around oneself as if one is very nervous and looking for answers

See something from the corner of one's eye: to see something but not very clearly

Have eyes in the back of one's head: to be able to see things outside the scope of one's vision

He never dared open his Facebook account at work because his boss seemed to have eyes in the back of his head.

Turning a Nelson's eye: to ignore undesirable information

The government should not turn a Nelson's eye to people's suffering.

*Etymology: This idiom is attributed to Admiral Horatio Nelson (a British Naval Commander, 1758–1805). He was blinded in the eye during combat. Later on, during the Battle of Copenhagen (1801), he received a tactical order through the waving of flags. Nelson disobeyed the order by lifting his telescope to his blind eye and said, 'I have a right to be blind sometimes. I really do not see the signal.'

■

Eyes glaze over: to become bored

The student's eye glazed over whenever the professor started his lecture.

Roll one's eyes: to become annoyed or angry

The teacher rolled his eyes whenever the student gave excuses for not completing his homework.

Rub one's eyes: to be in disbelief

Roving eyes: a tendency to flirt

Glad eye: to look at someone in a way that conveys one's sexual interest

When he entered, the fan girl batted her lashes and gave him the glad eye.

Eyesore: an ugly thing, especially a building

To eyeball: to stare at someone

■

Tongue-tied: to be dumbstruck and speechless

Cross-eyed: to be confused

Wide-eyed: to be inexperienced and naive; to be in awe

The young boy from the small town roamed the streets of New York all wide-eyed.

Glassy-eyed: to be bored

Misty-eyed: to be teary eyed

Doe-eyed: having large innocent-looking eyes

Starry-eyed: to be naively idealistic

Shifty-eyed: to appear dishonest because of avoiding eye contact

Blue-eyed boy: the favourite of someone in power, often used disparagingly and hence got the choicest assignments

The young officer was the blue-eyed boy of the governor.

*Etymology: The term was first recorded in a novel by PG Wodehouse in 1924

■

Earshot: audible range

He waited for the teacher to move out of earshot before he started mimicking her.

Earful: a long and hard scolding

The teacher gave the student an earful for mimicking her.

Mouthful: hard-hitting statements, a tongue-twister (a long word or phrase that is difficult to say)

The principal gave a mouthful to the student about mimicking and disrespecting teachers.

■

Itchy palm: to be always wanting money

The waiters at that restaurant have itchy palms and don't do a good service without a large tip.

Dab hand: to have manual dexterity

Putty in one's hands: to be easily influenced by another person

*Etymology: putty is a thick clay-like paste that is used to affix glass sheets to window frames

Light fingers: to have nimble fingers especially with a tendency to steal

Sticky fingers: someone with a tendency to steal

Pull one's finger out: to get ready for action

*Etymology: This idiom comes from the arena of naval warfare where a small amount of gunpowder was put in the ignition hole of the cannons and to keep this powder dry and ready for the launch, a crew member would jam their finger in the ignition hole, only to take it out when it was time for ignition.

Burn one's fingers: to suffer a bad result as consequence of one's actions

Have a finger in every pie: to be involved in several different activities at the same time

The CEO was always pressed for time because had a finger in every pie of the company.

■

To bear the palm: to win a reward
*Etymology: earlier on palm leaves were used to signify victory
To win spurs: to earn the skill and recognition
To carry the day: to win
To carry the torch: to lead successfully
To bell the cat: to accomplish a very tough task
*Etymology: This refers to the Aesop's fable, The Mice in Council, where a group of mice were terrorized by a cat and one of them suggested that a bell be placed around the cat's neck to warn of its arrival.
Uncrowned king or queen: the unofficial leader of the area
Cushy number: an easy task
Put the flags out: this idiom is sarcastically said when one is surprised at a victory or an outcome
When Mary was done washing the clothes, her brother yelled to put the flags out.

■

To pip someone at the post: to narrowly win
To give someone the pip: to irritate someone or make them depressed
*Etymology: earlier, it used to mean to give someone a disease as pip also refers to a disease in the poultry industry but now it means just to irritate someone or make them unhappy

■

Act up: to misbehave or malfunction
The teacher got irritated when the children started to act up in the class.
Put on an act: to fake or pretend
To impress his friends he put on an act of coming from wealth when in reality he was stony broke.
Pull a disappearing act: to not to be seen when needed
The support technician pulled a disappearing act whenever the Internet went down.
Act the goat: to behave in a silly way in order to make people laugh
To cut a caper: to play a prank
*Etymology: caper means a prank or a crime plan
Make an exhibition of oneself: to make a fool out of one self, sometimes to get attention

■

Shot in the arm: to get encouragement and help

The return of Ronaldo was a shot in the arm for the Club's title hope.
*Etymology: this refers to the positive effects of injecting medicines, as in the US a 'shot' is slang for an injection
Shoot from the hip: to react without due consideration and thought; to speak rashly and recklessly
The president liked to shoot from the hip.
*Etymology: shooting a handgun immediately after taking it out from its holster near the hip and thus sacrificing accuracy for speed
Joined at the hips: when two people are so close that they are considered to be inseparable as if joined at the hip

■

Roll up one's sleeves: to prepare to do a lot of hard work
Elbow grease: this refers to working hard at manual labour
A little bit of elbow grease and we will have the house cleaned up in no time.
Legwork: work that involves a lot of travelling for collecting information
The police chief was very impressed by the legwork put in by the detectives.
Spadework: ground work
The junior completed the spadework for the senior lawyer by doing the preliminary research on the issue.
*Etymology: spade (also called a shovel) is a metal tool used for digging up the earth

■

Flesh and blood: an actual, living person; a human and thus having flaws and imperfections
My own flesh and blood: one's own blood relation
Ask for one's pound of flesh: to demand an exorbitant payment in return of a loan or favour
The local goons came asking for their pound of flesh from the local businessman for destroying his rival's shop.
*Etymology: In Shakespeare's *The Merchant of Venice*, the moneylender Shylock demanded he be paid the pound of flesh as a return for a loan.
Blood in the water: a sign that there is now is a good time to attack someone as a weakness has been exposed
*Etymology: when a swimmer is wounded and bleeding in the sea, the sharks pick up the smell and attack
Blood is thicker than water: family comes first before anyone

He sided with his sister in the fight with the neighbour, even though his sister was at fault because he strongly believed that blood was thicker than water.

■

Make one's hair curl: to scare someone
Make someone's flesh crawl: to cause disgust
Thorn in one's flesh: a constant source of irritation

■

Run a mile from something: to avoid something
Run a mile a minute: to run really fast
Run circles around someone: to outperform someone

■

Near the knuckle: bordering on obscene
His jokes were always near the knuckle and could not be heard with family around.
Beyond the pale: unacceptable
Because of Tom's rudeness, he's considered beyond the pale and thus never invited to parties anymore.
*Etymology: 'pale' refers to a paling fence and an area outside the fence is considered unsafe
At the back of beyond: a remote place
Lunatic fringe: the fanatical and extremist members of a society

■

Heads will roll: people will be dismissed from their job
If the sales don't improve then heads will roll.
*Etymology: when someone was decapitated in medieval times, their heads would fall and roll on the ground
To heap coals of fire on someone's head: to do good for someone
*Etymology: This refers to a custom in oriental villages, where a young member of the village would put a container full of hot coals on top of his head and distribute them to all the households in the village so that they could start the fires in their homes. This was considered a great job in the winters as the heat from the coal would keep this person warm and hence by extension this idiom means to bless someone.
Wires crossed in the head: to be confused
Touch one's forelock: to show respect to someone higher than oneself

*Etymology: forelock is the lock of hair that falls on the forehead
Chew the cud: to ruminate and think over something very deeply
Go belly up: to go bankrupt

■

Tongue-in-cheek: appearing to be serious when actually joking
He gave a tongue-in-cheek explanation of why the sun was yellow, suggesting that God bought yellow light bulbs on sale.
*Etymology: When one puts one's tongue in one's cheek, it induces a wink. A wink is a clear indication which suggests that what one is saying is meant to be a joke. The opposite of this is to speak 'with a straight face' which indicates seriousness.
Speaking with a forked tongue: to speak duplicitously, that is to say one thing and mean something else
*Etymology: a snake has a forked tongue
Cheek by jowl: side by side; close together
The pedestrians had to walk cheek by jowl along the narrow streets.
*Etymology: jowl is a word for the loose flesh by the lower jaw, which is very close to the cheek

■

Keep one's chin up: to stay positive and cheerful in a difficult situation
Take it on the chin: to accept misfortune courageously
*Etymology: this is a boxing term meaning to take an uppercut punch directly on the chin and then still stand straight
Keep a stiff upper lip: to display great control of emotions when facing adversity
*Etymology: the trembling of the upper lip is a sign of weakness

■

Put one's neck on the line: to put oneself at great risk
Stick one's neck out: to speak boldly on an issue knowing that it may bring a lot of criticism and anger
Breathing down the neck: to supervise someone very closely to the point they feel that they start feeling discomfort
Neck and neck: to be level in a race or competition

The two teams were neck and neck in the points table.
Nip and tuck: a cosmetic surgical operation

∎

Grind the faces of the poor: to exploit the poor
Make a wry face: to grimace, that is to make an ugly twisted face to show disgust
Fly in the face of: to openly go against what is convention or standard
The opinion of the rabble rouser flies in the face of the facts.

∎

Cut off one's nose to spite one's face: a self-destructive over-reaction to a problem
To have one's nose out of joint: to be irritated or get offended
*Etymology: Although a nose cannot actually come out of a joint like an arm, but this refers to how a person has a grumpy look on their face when they get upset.
Rub someone's nose in it: to remind someone of their mistake repeatedly to the point of irritating the other person
Thumb one's nose: to show disrespect
*Etymology: to place a thumb upon the tip of the nose and wiggle one's fingers
Hard-nosed: practical, realistic and no-nonsense
He was a hard-nosed businessman who always negotiated very hard for the best deal.
*Synonym: **down to earth**
*Antonym: **quixotic** (unrealistic, impractical and unworldly; *etymology: resembling the fictional character Don Quixote, who possessed these characteristics)

∎

Knee jerk reaction: to react quickly but without thought
The rising unemployment requires long term solutions and not knee jerk reactions.
*Etymology: knee jerk came from the physical reflex of a person when a doctor hits their knee with the small doctor's hammer
Hold feet to the fire: to put someone in tremendous pressure to get them to comply
*Etymology: this refers to the ancient form of torture where one's feet were placed near a fire to extract the truth out of them

Cold feet: to become nervous and lose confidence
He developed cold feet days before his marriage.
Feet of clay: a great person but with some flaw
Even Abraham Lincoln had feet of clay.
*Etymology: In the Bible, the Prophet Daniel interprets a dream which King Nebuchadnezzar had, where he saw a giant idol made of precious metals but this idol's feet were made of clay. The prophet Daniel told the King that the clay feet made the idol vulnerable and that the dream signalled the breaking apart of his empire. This idiom has now come to mean an unexpected flaw or vulnerability in a hero or an admired person.
Have two left feet: to be a very awkward or clumsy dancer
He has always had two left feet hence he never went to any dance party with his friends.
Think on one's feet/Quick on one's feet: to think clearly and effectively at the time of crisis, when there is no prior preparation
The pilot was able to think on his feet and landed the plane on the river.
*Etymology: the ability to stand in front of an audience and answer their questions on the spot
Put one's best foot forward: to try to act as the best version of oneself especially when trying to impress others
The job seeker put his best foot forward in the recruitment interview.
Drag one's feet-to do something slowly because one doesn't want to do it
Take one's time: to proceed in a leisurely fashion
Go at a snail's pace: to work at a very slow speed
Itchy feet: having a wanderlust (an urge to travel)
Sit on one's haunches: to crouch down
*Etymology: haunch means the buttock and thigh considered together
The boot is on the other foot: when a situation of holding an advantage has reversed
Earlier, England was dominated by Australia in cricket, but now the boot is on the other foot.

∎

Show somebody a clean pair of heels: to run away
The thief showed the police a clean pair of heels and got away.
Hot on someone's heels: to be in close pursuit
To tread someone's heels: to follow someone closely
To tread on someone's toes: to offend someone

Dip one's toes/get one's toes wet: to gently try out something

He has been dipping his toes into the world of Bitcoins.

Toe the line: to obey the rules; to conform

The employees were expected to toe the line and dress as per the company policy.

Bring to heel: to make someone submit to one's control

Sit at the feet of someone: to worship someone

Fall head over heels in love: to fall deeply in love with someone

Dig in one's heels: to refuse to change one's opinion despite a lot of strenuous persuasion

∎

See the back of somebody: to be glad to get rid of someone

Scratch someone's back: to do someone a favour in return of a favour

To have someone's back: to be willing to defend someone

Backroom talks/Back alley talks: secret negotiations

Back of the envelope calculation: a rough calculation

∎

Ballpark figure: a rough estimate

*Etymology: this refers to a baseball field which is an enclosed space meaning a reasonable range and out of the ballpark means beyond the reasonable range

Knock it out of the park: to do an excellent job

*Etymology: this refers to hitting a home run in baseball where the ball is hit so hard that it lands outside the stadium

Step up to the plate: to take responsibility

*Etymology: this refers to baseball, where a batter stands next to home plate (batting crease in baseball) to face the incoming pitch (ball throw)

Out in left field: weird; strange

His theories are usually out in left field as he ignores the evidence.

*Etymology: in baseball, some ballparks the left field was larger than right and thus more balls were lost there

Bench player: the reserve player on a team

*Etymology: the reserve players of a team sit in an area that is usually equipped with benches

∎

Gut-wrenching: extremely unpleasant

The documentary was a gut-wrenching portrayal of child trafficking.

*Etymology: gut means stomach

Punch to the gut: a severe blow to one's body or spirit

∎

Hard nut to crack: a problem which is difficult to solve

Selling super spicy chilli powder in the European market is a hard nut to crack.

Have a job at it: a tough task

He had a job at it while cleaning the gutters.

∎

Blue blooded: member of the royal family

*Etymology: Spanish phrase 'sangre azul', which means blue blood and refers to royalty, as their royalty used to be fairer compared to others and hence their veins would appear more blue than the veins of the dark skin common people

Born in the purple: born into the aristocracy

*Etymology: in some earlier civilizations, purple coloured dye was made from very expensive raw materials, which only the royalty could afford

Born with a silver spoon: born into a wealthy family

Hit a purple patch: coming into luck or success

The tennis player hit a purple patch and won three back to back tournaments.

Esquire of the body: an officer in charge of dressing the king

His nibs: someone acting like royalty

The upper crust: the upper class of society; the elites

The awards ceremony was his chance to mingle with the upper crust of the movie world.

Get off one's high horse: a request to someone to stop behaving in a haughty manner

*Etymology: in medieval times, leaders would show their supremacy by appearing in public mounted on large and expensive horses

∎

Lay down one's office: to resign from a post

He laid down his office after reaching the age of 70.

Through someone's kind/good office: by someone's help who used the influence and power of their official post

Under the aegis of: with the support or protection or sponsorship

The free English classes ran under the aegis of the government.

*Etymology: aegis means support or backing and it comes from Greek *'aigis'* meaning the shield used by the God Zeus
*Pronounced as ee-jis

■

Operative word: the most important and relevant word of a sentence
The operative word in the sentence 'he was a great musician' is 'was' because he died last week.
Overplay one's hand: to try to get more advantages from a situation than one is likely to get
He overplayed his hand when he asked for a promotion and a paid vacation at the same time.
Double down: to increase one's commitment to a particular course of action, especially when such a course of action is risky
*Etymology: in the card game blackjack, one doubles their bet after seeing one's initial cards but with the requirement that an additional card be drawn

■

On the nod: to be accepted without discussion
The proposals were accepted on the nod.
On the ball: to be alert
Despite less sleep the driver was completely on the ball.
*Etymology: as if looking carefully at the ball in a sports game
On the button: right on time
On the double: very fast
On the anvil: being discussed and planned but not read yet
The details of the proposed salary hike are still on the anvil.
*Etymology: an anvil is a heavy block made of iron with a flat top, on which heated pieces of metal are kept and then beaten into a desired shape with the help of a hammer

■

To play ball: to cooperate
To play hardball: to act aggressively and ruthlessly in getting what one wants
The leader of the winning party played hardball with the allies.
*Etymology: in baseball, using the hard ball as opposed to the softer one

■

To be on the side of the angels: to be on the correct side of an issue when there are two sides and one is good and one is bad
In the Civil War, the humanitarian aid agencies were on the only one on the side of the angels.
A ministering angel: a person who helps people
*Etymology: in the Bible, to 'minister' means to serve hence a ministering angel is a kind-hearted person who provides help and comfort
Fools rush in where angels fear to tread: foolish people often try to attempt tasks that wise people avoid because of the danger involved
The scales fall from one's eyes: to suddenly realise the truth
The scales fell from his eyes when he saw the forged signature and realized that he had been duped.
*Etymology: In a story from the Bible, there was a person called Saul, who had been a persecutor of the Christians. He was later blinded due to some growth on his eyes, which looked like the scales of a fish. While Saul travelled to Damascus (the capital of modern day Syria) to arrest some Christians there, God sent a man to fix his eyes and the scales fell and because of this Saul 'saw the truth of God' and converted to Christianity. This is also called a **'Road to Damascus'** conversion as in a moment where a person converts from an enemy to an advocate.
Preach the gospel to the choir/convert: to try to convince someone about something when this person is already convinced about this thing
Recite chapter and verse: to give complete and full detail
Jack knew the policy well and could recite it chapter and verse.
All hell breaks loose: an idiom used to suggest that suddenly chaos and pandemonium erupted
All hell broke loose when shots were fired.
When hell freezes over/Cold day in hell: an expression denoting that something will never happen
He said that he would do his boss's dirty work only when hell freezes over.
Come hell or high water: whatever difficulties may arise
The manager exclaimed that the task must be finished on time, come hell or high water.
Fire and brimstone: this refers to God's anger in the Bible
*Etymology: brimstone is the awful smell of sulphur

dioxide given off by lightning strikes, and lightning strikes are considered as God's punishment in the Bible

The quick and the dead: the living and the dead, referred to collectively

The president paid respect as a nation for the quick and the dead who fought in the war.

*Etymology: as per the Bible, the living are considered to be 'quickened' into life by the breath of God and hence referred to as the 'quick'

■

The devil can cite scripture for his purpose: even good things and ideas can be manipulated to serve an evil purpose

Devil's Advocate: someone who argues against his own beliefs to show that the opposite side is actually wrong

*Etymology: in the Roman Catholic Church, the 'advocatus diaboli' (Latin for devil's advocate) was an officer appointed to argue against the canonization (sainthood) of a candidate in order to find out if there were any material flaws in the candidate

Devil's luck: if something good happens to a person then something bad is coming next

Jack has the Devil's luck as he won a million dollars but his wife left him the next day.

Devil's children have the devil's luck: evil people often seem to have good luck

Go to the devil: go to hell

Give the devil his due: reluctantly give someone due credit

The devil lies in the detail: the problems lie hidden away in the details of something when overall things look simple and straightforward

■

The penny dropped: an idiom used to signify that a person finally understood something

Turn up like a bad penny: to arrive when unwanted

Packed like sardines: crowded very close together

*Etymology: a sardine is a small sized edible fish and they are packed tightly together in a metal can for distribution for consumption

Put a quarter into a pint pot: to try to cram something big into a smaller container

He tried to put a quarter into a pint pot by packing his wardrobe in one suitcase.

*Etymology: a pint is 0.568 liters and a quart is 1.136 liters

■

Turn of phrase: the ability to express oneself well

Lois Lane had a nice turn of phrase which helped her a lot in her journalism

Turn a corner: to pass a critical point in a process and then improve

The patient turned the corner and is now beginning to improve.

*Etymology: like how a train turns a corner and that is the toughest part of the journey

Turn turtle: to turn upside down in water

■

Return to the fold: to come back to a group after an absence

After teaching at the university for many years, John finally returned to the company's fold as its chairman.

Revert to type: to return to the normal state

Regress to the mean: this denotes that extreme outcomes are usually followed by moderate ones

■

Filthy lucre: money obtained dishonestly

Coin money: to make money by cheating

Rich as Croesus: to be very rich

*Etymology: Croesus was a Persian king.

Embarrassment of riches: an overabundance of something

Well-heeled: to be very rich

*Etymology: earlier, good quality shoes with thick heels were very expensive

Quid's in: to be making a profit

*Etymology: a quid is informal British for one pound sterling

Face value: the superficial value of something

Don't take his word on face value.

*Etymology: In the share market, the face value is the value printed on the share certificate but the real value of the share is the market value and that can be much higher depending on the stock market.

Put one's money where one's mouth is: to follow through on something which one talks about a lot, especially by spending money on it

The selector always praised the batsman but never actually selected him and thus never put his money where his mouth was.

To pay a fancy price: to pay exorbitantly

Cost an arm and a leg: to be very expensive

Nickel-and-dime: to harass someone by charging over small things

The café closed because it would nickel-and-dime the customers like charging for extra sugar sachets.

*Etymology: a nickel is a coin worth five cents, a dime is a coin worth 10 cents and a cent is one per cent of a dollar

Midas touch: the ability to turn any business into an extremely profitable one

*Etymology: this refers to King Midas, who had the power to turn anything into solid gold by just touching it

■

Silver bullet: a solution to all problems; a panacea

There is no silver bullet that will solve the problem of global warming and instead many different steps are needed to be done together.

Silver lining: a sign of hope in an otherwise gloomy situation

*Etymology: This idiom comes from the proverb 'every cloud has a silver lining', which means that there is always a positive side to every difficult situation.

Cross someone's palm with silver: to bribe someone

*Etymology: This refers to the practice of placing silver coins across a gypsy fortune-teller's hand so that she tells one's fortune.

Thirty pieces of silver: the reward a person receives for betraying someone

The traitor received his 30 pieces of silver from the foreign country for giving up his country's defence secrets.

*Etymology: According to the Bible, 30 pieces of silver was the reward that Judas Iscariot received for betraying Jesus.

■

Until the cows come home: for a very long time

We could talk about this problem until the cows come home, but it wouldn't solve anything.

*Etymology: Cows are slow moving creatures and make their way home, after grazing, at their own unhurried pace.

Many moons ago: a long time ago

He has the faintest recollection of the event as it all happened many moons ago.

Once in blue moon: very rarely

He drank alcohol only once in blue moon.

The year dot: since a very long time—as if from the year zero, which is said to be the first year in our recorded history

Children have been fascinated by ghost stories since the year dot.

In a month of Sundays: something which is not likely to happen

*Etymology: as if something is as likely to happen as a month full of just Sundays and no working days

Put something in mothballs: to put something into storage

■

Below the mast: this refers to a common seamen rather than officer

*Etymology: the common sailor, who is a part of the crew of a ship, lives in the forecastle (which are the living quarters located at the front part of a ship), and the naval officers live in the aftercastle (which are the living quarters on the back part of the ship).

Go to sea: to become a sailor

Nail one's colours to the mast: to publicly state one's opinion

Run something up the flagpole: to tell people one's opinion to get feedback from them

Take the wind out of someone's sails: to cause someone to lose energy or become dispirited

Ride at anchor: to be stationary by anchoring at a place

Even keel: well-balanced

The new manager succeeded in putting the business back on an even keel.

*Etymology: this is a nautical term signifying that the construction of a ship is well balanced and stable

The world is one's oyster: one can do whatever one wants

Boil the ocean: to try to do something that is very difficult or impossible, especially right in the starting of a project when one wants quick wins and gain momentum

The entrepreneur was advised to first just make a prototype and not to try to boil the ocean by looking for the perfect version.

Drain the swamp: to get rid of corruption in politics

*Etymology: this originally meant to get rid of the malaria-carrying mosquitoes by draining the swamp of all its water by using a reverse pump

■

Go to Davy Jones's locker: to be drowned at sea
*Etymology: Davy Jones's locker is considered the grave at the bottom of the sea for all those who have died at sea. Davy Jones is considered as the sailors' devil.
Keep up with the Joneses: to try to match the lifestyle of one's neighbours
Keep up with the Joneses can take a huge toll on one's finances.
Before one can say Jack Robinson: quickly or suddenly
He said that he would reach her house before she could say Jack Robinson.
*Etymology: As per the Grose's *Classical Dictionary* (1785), the original Jack Robinson was a gentleman who met his neighbours for such a brief moment that there was hardly any time to announce him before he was gone.

■

Dry as dust: very boring
Bite the dust: to lose
Kick up a dust storm: to create unnecessary drama
Make the dust fly: to work in a very vigorous manner

■

Tie and anvil around it and throw it in the sea: to forever get rid of something
The matter is on the anvil: when a matter is being discussed and not yet finalized
Put on the backburner: to relegate to a lower priority
Back of one's mind: to have something in the mind but not act on it
Turn something over in one's mind: to think about something.
Lose one's bearing: to lose one's orientation in his/her surroundings
He felt like he lost his bearings ever since he was fired from his job.

■

Have one's heart in the mouth: to be really scared
Jaw fell to the floor/One's jaw drops: to be shocked
His jaw dropped when he found out the rent of the new apartment.
Jump out of one's skin: to be very shocked or startled
He jumped out of his skin when his boss suddenly called him to deliver the presentation.
Quake in one's boots: to be very worried

■

Curry a favour: to try to gain favour by doing flattery
Scrape up acquaintance with someone: to ingratiate with someone
Pay court to someone: to attempt to gain someone's favour through flattery; to woo someone
The lobbyist paid court to all the influential members of the legislature.
Put on a pedestal: to put someone in a very high position as if more important than others
Pride of the place: the top position
Shanghai has taken over the pride of the place title from London as the world's top business centre.

■

Wax lyrical/Wax eloquent/Wax poetic: to talk in a highly enthusiastic way; *Etymology: In old English, 'wax' meant to grow. Hence in this expression, wax doesn't have anything to do with candle wax but instead means 'to grow' or to become lyrical about something exciting.
To take one's hat off to someone: to publicly praise someone
Doff one's hat/Tip one's hat: to raise one's hat in acknowledgement of another person or to show respect
*Etymology: doff means to remove an item of clothing
Pat on the back: to praise someone

■

Home Bird: someone who likes to always stay at home
Shrinking violet: a shy or retiring person
*Etymology: relates to the presumed shyness of the violet, since it grows in secluded spots, as if wanting to hide
Wallflower: a shy person especially a girl
Come out of one's shell: to discard one's shyness and become more sociable
Go into one's shell: to go into a quiet and withdrawn state and not interact with people
Silent majority: any group of people who are not outspoken and who are considered to constitute a majority

■

Yellow streak: a tendency toward cowardice
Yellow belly: a coward

*Etymology: This is an American expression referring to Mexicans who were then fighting with the Americans. The yellow could be a racist allusion to skin colour.

To show white feathers: to act in a cowardly manner
*Etymology: from the belief that a gamecock with a white feather in its tail is a poor fighter in a cockfight

To raise the white flag: to surrender
*Etymology: in the Roman empire, armies would show the white flag when they wanted to surrender as the colour white was used to signify that a person did not want to fight

Turn tail: to run away from a fight

■

In the red: this means that one is in debt or operating at a loss; also means that the person's liabilities are greater than one's assets

In the black: this means that one is debt free or operating at a profit; this means that one is solvent, that is one's assets are greater than one's liabilities
*Etymology: this refers to the old system of bookkeeping where in the accounts ledger, the left hand side entries for debt or loss were made in red ink and right side entries for assets or profits were made in black ink

In the pink: in top physical condition
*Etymology: pink refers to body tissue that is full of blood, hence signifying that this person is lively and healthy

In a brown study: to be depressed
Lack of friends can lead a man into a brown study.
*Etymology: in old times, brown referred to gloomy, and study meant thought

■

Red-eye flight: a flight which departs at night and arrives the next morning and because of this timing the passenger gets very little sleep and often ends up with red eyes due to the fatigue

Red letter day: a special day
*Etymology: this comes from the practice of marking the dates of special Church events on the calendars in red ink

Scarlet day: a special day especially in academia
*Etymology: Scarlet is a bright red colour. Furthermore, in UK universities, on special days, doctors of the university may wear their scarlet gowns instead of their black gowns.

Black day: a day when something tragic or disastrous happened

Green room: it is a room in a theatre or studio where performers wait or relax when they are not performing on stage
*Etymology: such rooms were historically painted green in colour

Green light: to give permission to go ahead
Netflix decided to not green light the third season for Daredevil.

White paper: an official report by the government, giving information about an issue

Blue book: an official book of the government

Brownie point: an imaginary point awarded to someone who tries to please or get praise or gain approval
He tried to win some brownie points with his mother-in-law by offering to clean the dishes.

■

In apple pie order: a very organized and neat and tidy state
The secretary kept all the office records in apple-pie order.

Upset the apple cart: to mess or interfere with a plan
He upset the applecart by postponing the important office sales meeting to next month.

Put the cart before the horse: to do something in reverse order

Apple of discord: the bone of contention; the issue under dispute

Forbidden fruit: something, especially sexual, that is even more appealing because it is not allowed
*Etymology: this refers to the apple from the forbidden tree in the Garden of Eden

Apple of one's eye: a cherished and beloved person

Rotten/bad apple: an immoral person in a group who has a bad influence on others

Apple doesn't fall far from the tree: a child usually has similar characteristics as that of the parents

Fruit of the poisonous tree: this is a legal principle in the US which states that evidence that is obtained illegally is inadmissible
*Etymology: if the tree is tainted then so must its fruit be also tainted and hence not reliable

■

Keen as mustard: to be very eager

183

Carrot and stick: a system in which one is rewarded for good work and punished for mistakes or undesirable actions.

Carrot on a stick: the policy of offering a reward but not delivering it

*Etymology: when a carrot is placed on a stick in front of a donkey to make it move and the donkey then moves towards it

Drinking the Kool-Aid: to show unquestioning belief and loyalty

*Etymology: the 1978 cult mass-suicide in Jonestown, Guyana, where the cult leader Jim Jones made his followers commit suicide by drinking grape-flavoured Kool-Aid (kind of a sugary drink) laced with potassium cyanide

Scrape the bottom of the barrel: to use the worst quality things because nothing else is available

Since the markets were closed, he had to scrape the bottom of the barrel and eat yesterday's stale food.

*Etymology: in the early US, food was stored in barrels and when the supplies ran low one had to scrape the bottom of the barrel to get hold of anything left over

Lock, stock, and barrel: including everything; the entirety

We lost everything in the fire: lock, stock and barrel.

Hook, line and sinker: completely and absolutely

He told the teacher a silly excuse for being late and the teacher fell for it, hook, line and sinker.

*Etymology: hook, line and sinker is a classic and a popular combination of tackle (fishing equipment) used by anglers to catch fish

Everything but the kitchen sink: just about everything one can think of

When he went to college, he packed everything in his room to take to the hostel but the kitchen sink.

■

Fortunes of war: the vagaries of war

Soldier of fortune: a mercenary (a soldier who doesn't fight for his or her country but fights for anyone who pays him or her the right monetary fee)

Reversal of fortune: to come across hard times after good

Fortune favours the brave: a winner is the one who doesn't shy away from taking risks

■

Fire and sword: the killings of war

Add fuel to the fire: to make a tough situation worse

Out of the frying pan into the fire: to go from a bad situation to an even worse situation

Get on like a house on fire: to instantly become friends

At the party, he introduced two of his friends who went to the same university as each other and they got on like a house on fire!

Hanging fire: the delay in taking action or progressing

Due to bad management, there were many projects hanging fire.

*Etymology: in the seventeenth century gun called flintlock musket, the firing powder was ignited but sometimes failed to explode that resulted in 'hanging fire'

■

Cut both ways: to affect both sides

Censorship cuts both ways as it can stop hate speech but also prevents dissemination of knowledge.

*Etymology: in a double-edged sword, both sides of the blades are sharp and can cut

Take up the cudgels: to argue strongly in support of someone or something

The union took up the cudgels for the members who were unduly fired.

*Etymology: a cudgel is a short heavy stick, used as a weapon

Tilting at windmills: to fight battles with imaginary enemies

*Etymology: the fictional character Don Quixote (*pronounced as Don Kee-hotay) attacked windmills thinking that they were giants and 'tilt' means to joust, where two knights on a horse try to hit each other with a lance (a spear)

To keep one's powder dry: to be ready to take action

*Etymology: this refers to the idea that gunpowder will not explode if it is wet

A shot across the bow: a warning shot

The company fired a shot across the bow by sending a legal notice to the journalist to stop his investigation.

*Pronunciation: bow is pronounced just like one pronounces how

*Etymology: a bow is the front part of a ship and firing a shot across the bow is a naval tactic of drawing an imaginary line in front the opponent's ship with the cannon shot thus signalling to stop or face an attack

■

Paint oneself into a corner: to get oneself into a difficult situation from which it is very tough to get out of
He painted himself into a corner by cheating on his wife with multiple mistresses.
Not have a leg to stand on: to be in a situation where one cannot prove a claim or statement
He had no leg to stand on as the alibi was disproven.
To skate on thin ice: to engage in very risky activity
He was skating on thin ice when he decided to invest his entire savings the stock market
*Etymology: during the winters in colder countries, the surface of rivers and lakes freeze and then people skate on them but if the ice layer is thin then it can break and the skaters can fall in the water
The tip of the iceberg: a small part of a large and complex problem: Routine floods are only the top of the iceberg when it comes to the perils of global warming;
*Etymology: this idiom refers to the fact that 90 per cent of an iceberg is submerged below the water and is not visible
Slippery slope: a course of action that will likely lead to a very bad situation or disaster
He went on a slippery slope the day he started to lie on government forms to avail subsidies.
Walk a tightrope: to handle a difficult situation where one has to take many decisions that are opposing in nature and balance many interests which are pulling in different directions
*Etymology: just like a Trapeze artist who walks the tightrope in a circus
Side-stepping a few landmines: to avoid problems even before they arise
Fly by the seat of one's pants: to use one's own judgment and intuition rather than a concrete predetermined plan
They started the company by the seat of their pants and without any market testing.
*Etymology: in aviation, some pilots would fly the plane only by their instinct and without using a flight plan or navigational instruments
Ground beneath the feet shrinking: this is an idiom that signifies that there is less scope and opportunity to defend oneself from the incoming trouble
The ground beneath the politician's feet was shrinking as the investigative team was getting closer and closer to unearthing the scam.
Clock is ticking: this is an idiom that signifies that the time required to accomplish a task is running out quickly
The sands are running out: to have very little time left to do something

The manager reminded his team that the sands of time are running out and that they must finish the project soon.
*Etymology: in an hourglass, the sand trickles from top to the bottom through an opening in the middle
Hear the branch creaking: to see one's support or base being taken away
*Etymology: this refers to a monkey who is sitting on a branch of a tree and then hears the branch creaking and then the monkey falls down to the ground
Drum beats are getting closer: this is an idiom that signifies that a major problem is approaching
*Etymology: drum beats refers to the beat of the marching band of an incoming enemy battalion
Noose began to tighten: to make a difficult situation worse
*Etymology: hangman's noose around the neck of a person who is about to be hanged
Caught in a cleft stick: to be in tough situation
Because of new restrictive government regulations, the company was caught in a cleft stick.
*Etymology: cleft sticks are those which are split at one end and were used to capture snakes by pinning them to the ground
Death by a thousand cuts: this means that a lot of small bad things are happening which are not fatal by their individual self, but taken together will cause massive damage
*Etymology: this refers to a form of torture and execution in Imperial China

■

Come to a pretty pass: this is an idiom that signifies that the situation has become tricky
Flashpoint: a point when a serious problem starts: the flashpoint in their relationship came early
Hot potato: a controversial topic: the abortion issue is a political hot potato in the US.

■

The thin end of the wedge: the start of a harmful development
The abrupt layoffs were just the thin end of the wedge and soon the company closed.
*Etymology: a wedge is a piece of wood having one thin and one thick end and the thin end is driven between a large objection to pull it apart
Have a thin time: to experience a difficult period

Get the rough end of the stick: to be treated unfairly

Get the short end of the stick: to come off worst in a bargain

Get the wrong end of the stick: to incorrectly understand an issue

Wide off the mark: to be very inaccurate: the predictions of the financial experts were wide off the mark

■

Spare somebody's blushes: to do something to prevent someone feeling embarrassed

Ronaldo saved the team's blushes by scoring a goal in the last minute of the match.

Spare someone's feelings: to not make the other person upset: He spared her feelings by lying about her awful new haircut

Spare a thought for someone: to think about someone who is in a bad situation

We must spare a thought for the poor farmers.

■

Move like a thief in the night: to move secretly to avoid detection

Thick as thieves: a really close friendship

Honour among thieves: thieves do not steal from each other

■

Red herring: a red herring is a smoked herring fish, whose flesh has turned red

*Etymology: British fugitives in the 1800s would rub a red herring to throw their scent off and divert the police dogs. Later, the word started to be used by investment bankers in the 1920s to warn against misleading prospectuses by calling them 'red herrings'.

Loaded dice: to gain an advantage by using dishonest means

Everyone knew that the dice were loaded and that the judges had been bribed.

*Etymology: this refers to a dice where weight has been added to one side so as to increase the chances that the dice will land on the opposite number

Stack the deck: to win by cheating

He stacked the decks against everyone by bribing the official.

*Etymology: stacking the deck means to cheat by arranging the cards to be dealt out to one's advantage

■

Witch-hunt: a campaign aimed at exposing and punishing those who hold an unorthodox view or are considered a threat to society

The President said that the investigative agencies were on a witch hunt.

Wild goose chase: a futile and foolish search for something which either doesn't exist or is unobtainable

The kids went on a wild goose chase looking for the toy, which was discontinued by the manufacturer years ago.

*Etymology: a goose is a type of a flying duck and a wild goose chase was a type of horse race in the sixteenth century, where all the riders would follow a particular lead rider, like all the wild geese follow a single goose

■

A man of straw: a weak and unreliable man

A man's word was his bond: a reliable man who honours his word

■

For keeps: forever

The car turned out to be junk but since he signed the contract, he was stuck with it for keeps.

Time hangs heavy on someone's hands: an idiom that signifies that time seems to move slowly when one has nothing to do

Watch the clock: to keep looking to see what the time is because one is eager to stop working

A watched pot never boils: an idiom that signifies that something we eagerly wait for to complete usually takes forever to be done

Be caught in a time warp: to not move ahead with the modern times and remain outdated

The town was caught in a time warp as it would celebrate child marriages.

*Etymology: a time warp is an imaginary situation in which the past becomes the present

To keep up with the times: to change one's ideas and beliefs to keep up with the modern values

To play a waiting game: to delay taking action in order to see how the situation develops and then see what the best course of action is

The army could not afford to play a waiting game as their supplies were running out.

To play for time: to use delaying tactics in order to gain time and thus avoid taking a decision or committing to action

The governor played for time by appointing a committee to advise him.

To run out the clock: a strategy used in sports like football or basketball, in which the leading team at the end of the game tries to protect its lead by maintaining the possession of the ball so as to deprive the other team of any scoring opportunity before the match clock runs out

■

Wet behind one's ears: an inexperienced person
*Etymology: just after birth, baby farm animals (who are covered in amniotic fluid) are licked dry by their mothers and the area behind the ears is the last to be licked dry

Wet blanket: a spoil sport

Whet ones appetite: to stimulate one's appetite; whet means to stimulate

■

Give someone a wide berth: to give someone space or keep distance from them

Keep at arm's length: to keep someone or something at a slight distance but not appear to be ignoring

Al Gore says politicians keep the environmental issues at arm's length.

Wouldn't touch with a barge-pole/ten feet pole: to avoid something at all costs
*Etymology: barge-poles are the long wooden poles used to push barges (boats) along

Rub shoulders (or elbows): to interact or mingle with people

He got a chance to rub elbows with the big shots in town at the charity dinner.

Silent treatment: the act of completely ignoring a person by resorting to silence, done with the aim of expressing anger at that person

Give the cold shoulder: to ignore someone

To leave out in the cold: to abandon someone

The students were left out in the cold when their college suddenly shut down.

To leave somebody in the lurch: to abandon someone in an embarrassing or difficult situation

The manager left the entire team in the lurch after he suddenly quit right before the delivery deadline.

Drop someone or something like a hot potato: to disassociate oneself

When they learned of their partner's criminal conviction, they dropped him like a hot potato.

Backhanded compliment: a compliment that actually is an insult

He gave his sister a backhanded compliment by telling her that her new haircut really slimmed her face.

Shorthanded: to be understaffed

Glad-hand: to greet someone very warmly, just like a politician

Strong-arm tactic: the use of force or threats to make someone do something

The local mob goons used strong-arm tactics.

■

To be badly off: to be in bad shape

None the worse: not damaged or hurt despite something bad happening

He seems to be none the worse, despite his car accident.

Make a virtue of a necessity: to make best of something not good

When his car got stolen, he made a virtue out of necessity and rode his bike to work and thus ended up getting in shape.

■

For what it's worth: this is said when one is giving someone information or advice but unsure if the information or advice will be of any help

He told his sister that for what it's worth, she took the right decision by quitting her job at the toxic company.

For all one's worth: to the full extent of one's powers or ability

The athlete may have lost out on the first position but he ran for all he was worth.

Worth the weight in gold: extremely useful or valuable

Experienced singers are worth their weight in gold because they bring a lot to the choir.

■

Wringing one's hands: to worry about something but not do anything about it

He just wringed his hands in fear rather than immediately calling the police.

Wring someone's neck: to get very angry at someone

The wrong side of the tracks: the poor area of a city or town
*Etymology: this idiom is based on the idea that poor areas are often divided from the rest of the town by railroad tracks
Back the wrong horse: to support the losing party

■

Wrap somebody up in cotton wool: to protect someone too much and thus not allowing them to be independent enough
Dyed in the wool: someone having extreme and strong opinions and not willing to change
He is a dyed-in-the-wool traditionalist in the kitchen and doesn't allow any modern gadgets.

■

Babe in arms: a very young baby that is carried by mother
Tied to one's mother's/wife's apron strings: to be controlled or dominated by one's mother or wife
To cut the apron strings: to become independent from someone's control or domination
Hide behind someone's skirt: to try to take shield behind some authority figure and avoid the consequences of one's actions
*Etymology: this refers to how children hide behind their mother's skirt when they get in trouble
To treat something or someone with kids gloves: to deal with something or someone very gently
*Etymology: based on the literal meaning of kid gloves (gloves which are made of a very soft and smooth construction)

■

Armchair theory: a theory based on just sitting in a room and without doing actual field research; a defective theory
Article of faith: something deeply believed which may or may not be backed up by science
Creationism (a doctrine which states that man was created by God and that evolutionary theory is false) is an article of faith for some people despite the scientific evidence to the contrary.

■

Fall between two stools: neither here nor there; to fall between two categories
The book falls between two stools as it is neither basic enough for beginners nor advanced enough for experts.
Be on the horns of a dilemma: to be in a dilemma
Sit on the fence: to not take a stand on an issue
Come down on one side of the fence: to take a stand
Have the courage of one's convictions: to do what one believes is right despite mounting criticism and pressure

■

In a flat spin: a confused state
*Etymology: an aircraft spin in which the plane's longitudinal axis is nearly horizontal rather than vertical
In a tailspin: an emotional collapse or generally a severe decline
The economy was in a tailspin after the markets crashed.

■

Tail between one's legs: feeling embarrassment and shame after a defeat
*Etymology: like a dog literally putting its tail between its legs
Add insult to injury: to make an already bad situation even worse, especially in a humiliating way
To add insult to injury, his wife left him the same day his office got raided by the police.
Meet one's Waterloo: to suffer a resounding defeat
His underprepared team met their Waterloo in the finals when they lost to the defending champions.
*Etymology: Napoleon Bonaparte suffered at the Battle of Waterloo in Waterloo, Belgium, in 1815, which ended his career.

■

Shoot one's bolt: to use up all of one's resources too quickly
He lost the marathon because he shot his bolt too early in the race.
*Etymology: in archery a bolt is a crossbow's arrow and the archer who used up all his bolts too early was a fool as he did not leave any for later
*Synonym: shoot one's wad (*etymology: in gambling a 'wad' refers to a roll of banknotes and hence this idiom means to use up all of one's resources too quickly)

Shoot the works: to use up all of one's funds for something

They shot the works on their only daughter's wedding.

Shoot a line: to exaggerate

He shot a line whenever he described his foreign trips.

*Etymology: shoot an extra line of words to describe something

■

Break the bank: to use up all of one's money

The famous football club Real Madrid broke the bank to get Ronaldo to play for them.

Go the whole hog: to do something completely thoroughly and to the fullest extent They went into the restaurant only wanting to order soup but instead they went whole hog and ended up having a full meal.

*Etymology: a hog is a pig and some customers 'go the whole hog' and buy the whole pig

Pull out all the stops: to do something with one's full effort and utilize all of one's resources

The political party pulled out all the stops for its President's retirement party.

*Etymology: a pipe organ is a piano-like musical instrument used in a church, produces sound by driving pressurized air through pipes and the stops are the knobs which control how loud the sound is and the organ plays loudest when all the stops are out

Playing for keeps: to put in one's full effort to win and not holding back anything

The captain warned the opposing team that he and his team were fully ready and playing for keeps.

*Etymology: from the game of marbles, where the winner actually keeps all the marbles won

Go to town: to do something very enthusiastically or extravagantly

The carpenter had only planned to fix some of the old furniture but then he went to town and wound up fixing all of the furniture instead.

To come out with all guns blazing: to put in all efforts and energy into trying to achieve the target

To fire on all cylinders: to work at full capacity

*Etymology: this refers to the working of an internal combustion engine where the controlled combustion of the fuel in the cylinders is what provides the power

Go for the jugular: to attack someone very aggressively and severely in order to inflict maximum damage

The prosecutor in the case wanted to make an example of the accused and went for the jugular.

*Etymology: jugular is a neck vein that transports blood between the head and the heart

Take no prisoners attitude: to be fierce and merciless in the pursuit of one's goal

*Etymology: this expression refers to the practice of killing enemy soldiers in a war rather than keeping them as prisoners

■

Get to first base: to succeed in the initial phase of something

He was delighted that he had gotten to first base in the job application process as he was called for the next round of interview.

*Etymology: this refers to the first base of baseball, which is the first step toward scoring a run

Get blood out of stone: to get something out of a very difficult and uncooperative person

Collecting the rent from his dishonest tenant was like getting blood out of a stone.

Catch a tartar: to deal with someone who is very tough to deal with

The guards caught a tartar as the new prisoner refused to obey instructions.

*Etymology: tartar is a sticky chemical and also tartar is a sticky chemical. A Tartar was a soldier in Genghis Khan's army. Tartar is also used to refer to a difficult and stubborn person.

Catch lightning in a bottle: to try to do something that's impossible

■

Draw a bead on something: to take aim at something; to focus on something

In his speech, the president has drew a bead on the fiscal deficit impeachment.

*Etymology: earlier, guns in America used to have a small knob called a 'bead' which helped the shooter take aim at the target

Be broad in the beam: to have wide hips and large buttocks

*Etymology: the nautical term 'beam' which refers to a ship's breadth at its widest point

To know how many beans make five: to have worldly knowledge; to be sensible and responsible

Jack did not go to a fancy university but he still knows how many beans make five.

■

Made no bones about it: to clearly say what is on one's mind

He made no bones about his dissatisfaction with the service at the hotel.

To the bone: thoroughly

They got chilled to the bone because of the cold winds that day.

Close to the bone: to let something get under the skin; personal and offensive

She was irritated by the close to the bone comment on her weight.

Feel it in the bones: to have an intuition

She felt it in her bones that something terrible was going to happen.

Skeleton in the cupboard: an embarrassing or shameful secret; undisclosed facts about someone which would damage one's reputation if revealed

His campaign was worried about the skeletons in his cupboard, which could be exposed by the rival team during the campaign.

■

Don't cross my path: don't come in my way

Not give a tinker's dam/curse: to not care at all about someone or something

He did not give a tinker's dam about what his classmates thought of him.

*Etymology: a tinker was a small utensils repairman and a tinker's dam was a very cheap doughy material used to repair; tinkers were also known to swear a lot and hence their cursing had no value.

■

Fool's paradise: a situation where a person is happy but unaware or deliberately ignoring potential trouble

Not to suffer fools gladly: to not tolerate irritating people

Jack is a very patient person and overall a nice guy but he doesn't suffer fools gladly.

Reel under: to suffer under the weight of something

He reeled under the responsibilities of the new job and considered quitting.

■

Wax and wane: to alternatingly increase (wax) and decrease (wane) in size, number, strength or intensity

His fortune waxed and waned over the years depending on the stock market.

*Etymology: the verbs 'wax' and 'wane' were used to describe the phases of the moon; when the moon waxes we see more of it and when it wanes we see less of it

Ebb and flow: to decrease and then increase, as with tides

The CEO had a tough time adjusting to the natural ebb and flow of business.

*Etymology: this refers to the regular movement of the oceanic tides, where ebb means to move away from the land and flow means to move back towards land

On the ebb: to be on the decline

■

Long and the short of it: the main point

Alpha and omega: the entire story

*Etymology: in the Greek alphabet line, alpha is the first alphabet and omega is the last alphabet

Pros and cons: the positives and negatives of something

He weighed the pros and cons of investing in the stock market.

■

Stink to high heaven: to stink a lot

Raise a stink: to make a strong public complaint

To cry hoarse: to vehemently object against something

*Etymology: to shout so much that one's throat becomes sore and one begins to speak in a rough and hoarse voice instead of the normal voice

In full cry: to criticize vocally

The opposition was in full cry over the arrests of the peaceful protestors; also this idiom means to do something energetically

*Etymology: this idiom refers to the sound made by hounds (hunting dogs) when they are chasing their target

A slanging match: a quarrel in which both sides use abusive language

What started as a civil and polite peace talk ended up being a slanging match between the two parties.

■

Tone-deaf: a person who doesn't listen or doesn't want to understand others opinion

The president was tone-deaf to the concerns of the farmers.

*Etymology: a person who is unable to differentiate between the different tones of a musical composition

Radio silence: a period where one hears nothing from a usually a very communicative person

*Etymology: in the military, radio silence means to deliberately not transmit anything on the radio fearing enemy interception

■

Smoke and mirrors: distraction techniques

*Etymology: this idiom refers to the practice of conjurers who use actual smoke and mirrors in their stage performances to deceive the audience and perform magical illusions

No smoke without fire: there is no rumour without any basis to it

Go up in smoke: to end in disaster

■

The calm before the storm/Lull before the storm: a period of calm and inactivity before chaos ensues

The temporary ceasefire between the two warring groups was just the calm before the storm.

Eye of the storm: the area of calm in the centre of a tornado or hurricane; the temporary peaceful time amidst trouble and strife

The weather agencies warned to not venture out as this was only the eye of the storm.

Be in the eye of the storm: to be in the middle of a chaotic situation

The holidaying tourists were unfortunately caught in the eye of the storm when civil war suddenly broke out in the country.

In the eye of the wind: in a direction moving against the wind

We were having trouble navigating as the ship was sailing in the eye of the wind.

■

Eyes are bigger than their stomach: an idiom used to signify that a person has taken more food than they can eat

To have hollow legs: to have a great capacity or need for food or drink

Eat like a horse: to eat large amounts of food

■

Stir up a hornet's nest: to cause trouble

Let the sleeping dogs lie: to not create drama and just let things be

Flutter the dovecotes: to cause a commotion

The loud and boorish mannerisms of the tourists fluttered the dovecotes of the orthodox old town.

*Etymology: a dovecote is the cage for domestic pigeons

To set the cat among the pigeons: to create unnecessary trouble

Open up a can of worms: to create a complicated situation

The investigation into the source of funding opened up a can of worms.

Wake the dead: to make a lot of noise

Rock the boat: to cause a disturbance

Pour oil on troubled waters: to attempt to calm a problematic situation

*Etymology: in earlier times, oil was deliberately poured onto the sea surface to calm choppy waters as the oil had a calming effect on the waves

■

Sangfroid: a very composed person in face of trouble

*Etymology: sangfroid is French for strong blood

Cool as a cucumber: to be very calm in a stressful situation

Ronaldo is always cool as a cucumber no matter how much pressure.

A sting in the tail: a disappointing end to something that began positively

The love story had a sting in its tail because of the tragic ending where both the lovers die in a plane crash.

*Etymology: this idiom refers to a scorpion, which looks small but it has a poisonous sting in its tail

From the sublime to the ridiculous: to go from great to bad

■

Fly in the ointment: an irritation that spoils the fun

Fly on the wall: an unnoticed observer of situation, who closely observes the situation but doesn't interfere or participate at all

He wanted to be a fly on the wall in his friend's house when she would tell her father that she had wrecked the family car.

*Etymology: this is a documentary film-making

191

technique whereby events are recorded realistically as they are happening

■

Gild the lily: to unnecessarily decorate
She decided against any alterations to the beautiful dress as otherwise it would just gilding the lily.
*Etymology: to 'gild' means to cover with a thin layer of gold and a lily is a very beautiful flower in its original form and doesn't need any decoration
Gild the truth: to sugar coat; to make hard facts more digestible
Glad rags: special occasion clothes
Gird up one's loins: to get ready for a tough task
Both sides are presently girding their loins for the tough battle that lies ahead.
*Etymology: the tucking up of the traditional long and loose robes into a girdle (a belt) so they would not hamper physical activity

■

Put someone out to grass/pasture: to retire someone
The ruthless board of directors put the founding CEO of the company out to grass CEO.
*Etymology: farm animals are sent to graze in the fields all day when they are old and no longer useful for other farm related work
Not let the grass grow under one's feet: to not waste time
Rolling stone gathers no moss: a person who is always involved in some activity or the other doesn't stagnate

■

Half and half: in equal proportions
The homemade grease required a half-and-half mixture of motor oil and turpentine.
Don't know the half of it: this idiom is said when one knows that a situation is bad but unaware of the actual severity
To have half the mind to: to be on the verge of doing something
He had half the mind to report his colleague's rude behaviour to the company CEO.

■

To be above the board: to be completely legitimate and lawful
To sweep the board: to win all the prizes in a competition
To get on board: to agree with a course of action
Go back to the drawing board: to start planning again as the first idea failed
*Etymology: a drawing board is a large wooden board on which paper is spread for designers to work on

■

To run point: to lead a group
*Etymology: the 'point guard' in basketball is the player that runs the team's offense
Moot point: the issue under debate
The matter is now moot: this idiom is used to indicate that a matter is now only academic and has lost all its practical significance

■

Leave someone high and dry: to leave someone helpless and without any support in a tough situation
The sudden departure of several key executives left the company high and dry.
*Etymology: sometimes ships were left stranded on a beach due to a low tide and could only be helped when the tide picked up again and re-floated the ship
Leave someone holding the bag/To leave someone holding the baby: to leave someone appearing to be guilty
The bank robbers ran away and the innocent and clueless taxi driver was left holding the bag.
Throw the baby out with the bath water: to discard something valuable along with something undesirable
By scrapping the entire project rather than fixing the specific issue, they threw the baby out with the bathwater.

■

The smoking gun: an indisputable evidence of guilt
*Etymology: this refers to the best evidence in a murder case which is the recently shot gun; and because it was recently shot, there is still smoke still coming out of it.
Stick to one's guns: to keep one's position even though one is under severe criticism and disagreement
The president stuck to his guns and decided to go ahead with the tax hike despite massive public protest.
Stare down the barrel of a gun: to face imminent danger

Jump the gun: to act hastily; to start something before it was appropriate

His boss was angry because he jumped the gun and went ahead without getting the final approval.

*Etymology: this refers to how a runner in a foot race starts running even before the starting gun has been fired by the official

Under the gun: to be under pressure

The entire sales department was under the gun because of the new aggressive new sales targets.

Under the radar: to be under surveillance or scrutiny

In the crosshairs: to be targeted

The politician was in the crosshairs of media because of his recent racist remarks

*Etymology: crosshairs is a fine thread on the lens of a target scope of a gun used to mark out a target

Have a target on someone's back: to be identified as the chief rival or primary contender

He had a target on his back since the day he reached the top of the goal scorers' chart.

■

Move up in the world: to gain social status; to climb the social ladder

He moved up in the world when he joined the elite New York law firm.

Man of the world: a person who has a lot of experience in the ways of the high class and sophisticated society

Man of letters: a scholarly man

Confucius was a man of letters.

Man about town: a male socialite

■

Extract mileage: to get a lot of use from something

The president extracted a lot of political mileage from the reform plan.

*Etymology: an referring to the number of miles a car can travel before it is time to refuel

Toot one's own horn: to show off one's own achievements

To reinvent the wheel: to waste time trying to develop something that is already in existence

There was no need to reinvent the wheel and find a new cure when there were already very effective drugs in the market.

Wheels within wheels: this idiom is used to refer to a very complex situation in which there are many secret or indirect forces at play

In making political deals there are always wheels within wheels and no one can be certain of anything.

*Etymology: Bible: 'And their appearance and their work was as if it were a wheel in the middle of a wheel.' (Ezekiel 1:16)

■

Be in a minority of one: to be the only person who has the particular view

Too clever by half: to try to be over smart

The lone voice in the wilderness: someone who expresses an opinion that is not popular

For many decades she was the lone voice in the wilderness, writing for the need for immediate agrarian reforms.

■

Spin a yarn: to tell a long and far-fetched story usually as an excuse

She came home very late after midnight and then spun him a yarn about the bus breaking down.

*Etymology: earlier womenfolk used to spin yarn on the spinning wheels and would tell stories to pass the time

Grist to the mill: a useful resource

All the free publicity due to the sex scandal was grist to the popstar's mill.

*Etymology: grist is the corn that is brought to a mill to be ground into flour

■

Cut a sorry figure: to make a poor impression

He cut a sorry figure at the job interview because he wore jeans and T-shirt rather than a formal suit.

More's the pity: an old expression that is said to express regret and disappointment

The host exclaimed 'more's the pity' when he found out that his caterer had cancelled at the last minute.

■

To take the occasion: to take on an opportunity that presents itself

He took to the occasion and networked with everyone at the conference.

To take ill at something: to get offended at something

■

To be under a cloud: to be under suspicion
Everyone in the office was under the cloud after it was revealed that someone had stolen money from the company safe.

Fair-weather friend: a friend but only in the good times
It is the hard truth but a fair-weather friend is of no help in an emergency.

Wear one's heart on one's sleeve: to display one's feelings openly
His father was a very reserved person and never wore his heart on his sleeve.
*Etymology: Knights in the Middle Ages would traditionally wear colours or symbols on their arms to signify the ladies for whom they were jousting

Ace up one's sleeve: a secret advantage or plan to help achieve one's goal
The prosecution lawyer had an ace up his sleeve in the form of the murder weapon with the accused's fingerprint.
*Etymology: reference to cheating in a poker game by hiding a favourable card up one's sleeve

Have two strings to one's bow: to have backups
She has two strings to her bow because if her career in politics fails she can always go back to her legal practice.
*Etymology: archers who went into battle used to carry two or more bowstrings if in case one snapped

Take one's belt in a notch/Tighten one's belt: to cut on one's expenditure to prepare for lean times
Since their father got fired, the family decided to take their belts in a notch till the time he found a new job.

Wash/Air dirty linen in public: to air private problems in public for all to see
The daughter-in-law thought that she gained sympathy by washing the family's dirty linen in public.

Get one's knickers in a twist: to become extremely upset about something very unimportant
He sarcastically told his father to not get his knickers in a twist after his sister banged up the family car.

■

Throw one's hat into the ring: to become a participant in a contest, especially an election
The movie star was slow to throw his hat in the ring in the presidential race but is catching up quick.
*Etymology: in boxing, throwing a hat in the ring used to indicate a challenge to fight

At the drop of a hat: with very little provocation
She is so emotional that she cries at the drop of a hat when watching any family movie. Also, at the drop of a hat means freely and immediately.
He could not just leave the office at the drop of a hat because he needed his manager's permission first.

■

No holds barred: without any restrictions or limits
The election campaign was no holds barred with the candidates going after each other's families.
*Etymology: a hold is a kind of a wrestling move and this idiom refers to a wrestling match in which all holds (no matter how dangerous) are legal

To have someone on the mat: to put someone in a tough situation and near defeat
*Etymology: this idiom is from the world of wrestling, where a wrestler scores a point by pinning the other on the mat

Move the goalposts: to change the target unfairly, usually in order to make it more difficult for someone to achieve something or change the target to make one's progress seem substantial when it is not
The graphic designers had a tough time working as the client kept moving the goalposts every day.

Par for the course: when something happens which is very much on the expected lines
*Etymology: this idiom comes from the world of golf where a 'par' is considered a standard score after playing a round of golf

Follow suit: to act the same as another person's actions
*Etymology: this idiom comes from the world of card games like bridge when one has to play a card of the suit of the leading card

Come a cropper: to fail
*Etymology: crop means swelling in Norse and cropper means to fall off a horse and get a swelling and thus come up a cropper means to fail at something

■

Play to the galleries: to behave or act in such a way to gain maximum audience approval
Politicians are always more interested in playing to the gallery than doing what is correct.
*Etymology: how some musicians play to gain audience applause satisfaction and not for technical perfection

Punch above one's weight: to perform at a level generally considered beyond one's abilities
Everyone thought that Mahatma Gandhi was punching

above his weight when he took on the might British Empire.

*Etymology: in boxing every boxer has a weight category to fight in and sometimes they take a risk and fight in a higher weight category for glory

Last twelve rounds: last the entire fight or battle without defeat

No one thought that the novice small time politician would last the twelve rounds against the savvy old Governor in the debate last night.

*Etymology: in boxing, usually a fight consists of 12 rounds and it is a sign of strength if someone lasts the entire 12 rounds without getting knocked out

Prepare for twelve rounds: to come prepared for a long fight

Because of the extensive and long mock interviews at his college, he came prepared for 12 rounds at the company's job interview.

On the ropes: to be in trouble or near collapse

The company has been on the ropes ever since the massive failure.

*Etymology: in boxing when one is getting hit hard, they get pushed to the ropes surrounding the ring

Down for the count: to be unconscious and about to be defeated

The management concluded that the company was down for the count because of its huge debt obligations.

*Etymology: in boxing, when a boxer knocks the other down to the mat (the floor of the boxing ring) and the referee counts till 10 and if the person doesn't get up then he or she loses

First-round knock-out: to defeat someone right in the start of the battle

To throw in the towel/sponge: to give up

The company decided to throw in the towel and file for bankruptcy because it did turn a profit for five years.

*Etymology: a boxer's coach duty is to towel dry the boxer between rounds and when the coach sees that the boxer would get heavily injured in a round then he or she would throw the towel in the ring to signal quitting

Pull no punches: to not hold back in one's criticism

The media decided to not pull their punches during the press conference with the president over the crumbling economy.

*Etymology: in boxing, if someone pulls a punch then it means that this person is holding back so as to not hit with full force

Gloves are off: an idiom that is used to denote that people have started to fighting in an overly aggressive fashion

The gloves were off when the couple started throwing plates at the each other in the kitchen.

*Etymology: boxers wear gloves in a fight as bare fists can cause serious injuries

Below the belt: unfair and cruel

It was below the belt for the journalist to ask the president about his marital troubles rather than questioning the president on his actual job performance.

*Etymology: in boxing, it is illegal to hit an opponent near the groin area, which is located just below one's belt

■

To stand in good stead: to be qualified

The recruitment committee held him in good stead for hiring as the technical manager.

Suit down to the ground: perfectly suiting

The bride's beautiful wedding dress suited to the ground.

Saving grace: a redeeming feature

The only saving grace of the traffic jam for hours was that the couple got to spend time with each other.

Rough around the edges: someone who is not very sophisticated; having a few imperfections

The workers at the factory were rough around the edges but they were all very hard working.

■

Stuck in a rut: to be stuck in a boring old pattern

He did not like his job as he thought that he was stuck in a rut.

Vice-like grip: a very tight and firm grip

The dictator had a vice-like grip over every aspect of the country.

*Etymology: a vice (also known as a clamp) is a mechanical tool for holding things in place

Keep something at bay: to hold off a trouble

He kept the creditors at bay by promising the repayment with his first salary.

Nip in the bud: to halt something at an early stage

The chef made all the workers wear gloves to nip any hygiene issues in the bud.

*Etymology: this refers to the destruction of a flower bud before it blooms

■

To eat humble pie: to admit mistake

The complete eat humble pie in the board meeting when his expensive marketing plan failed to get even a single new customer.

*Etymology: humble, here, comes from a mid-nineteenth century word 'umbles' which meant offal (inferior meat like internal organs: liver, guts, etc)

Rich ate the good parts and the servants would eat offal.

To receive one's just deserts: to get the punishment one deserves

The CEO got his just deserts when he was sent prison for defrauding his investors.

*Etymology: the word 'deserts' in this idiom means 'things deserved' in old thirteenth century English

This idiom has nothing to do with 'desserts' which are the last and sweet course of the meal, like a cake or pudding.

That's the way the cookie crumbles: the situation is so and we must accept it even if it is something that we do not like

There's many a slip twixt cup and lip: it means that many bad things might happen before something is finally concluded so be on guard and not get complacent

The proof of the pudding is in the eating: this means that something can be judged only after trying it first.

Too many cooks spoil the broth: if too many people are involved in a task then it will not be done well because of mismanagement and confusion

Sell like hot cakes: to sell quickly and in large quantities

Have one's cake and eat it too: one can't have two good things at the same time if one of those things come at the expense of the other

We can't have our cake and eat it too by saying that that we want better hospitals but refuse to pay more tax.

*Etymology: to 'have' one's cake means to 'retain' one's cake, as in if one eats their cake then the cake is necessarily gone

■

To walk the talk: to act according to the ideals one espouses

The proclaimed vegan never really walked the talk and regularly ate meat.

To talk a big game: to speak very confidently about one's abilities but not necessarily back it up with results

He talks a big game but when it comes to an actual tough situation he just runs away.

To pay lip service: to agree with something but not back it up with actions

The politicians merely paid lip service to the farmers but did nothing when they came to power.

*Etymology: Bible mentions that many followers would honour Jesus only with one's lips but their actions revealed a different story

■

Pound the pavement: to walk or run

The marathon participants pounded the pavement for several hours every day.

Scratch the surface: to barely begin

We are only scratching the surface of what AI (artificial intelligence) can accomplish.

Get the ball rolling: to cause something to start

The students got the ball rolling for next year's exam by joining a test series.

■

Climb on the bandwagon: to join something or get involved with a cause that has recently become popular

Ever since universal free health care has become popular, many politicians have started to climb on the bandwagon.

Circle the wagons: to unite in order to collectively defend against a threat

The NGOs decided to circle the wagons to defend against the powerful tobacco lobby.

*Etymology: in old America, people would make a circle with their band wagons and stay inside that circle for protection from enemy fire

Hitch one's bandwagon: to attempt to benefit from someone else's success by closely associating with them

The fashion label hitched its wagon with the rising football star to achieve brand promotion.

■

Cutting edge: very advanced or innovative

The company produced cutting-edge mobile phones.

Wafer-thin: very thin

He won his election by a wafer-thin majority.

Razor-edged: very sharp; extremely incisive

The politician was the receiving end of some razor-edged criticism from the press.

■

Plumb the depths: to get to the bottom of something
The detectives plumbed the depths of the case to find out who was the killer.
*Etymology: a plumb line is used by masons and carpenters to see if the wall or structure they are building is perfectly perpendicular to the floor
Out of one's depth: to be in a situation which is beyond one's capabilities
He was out of his depth in the new job position because he was unqualified.
In over one's head: to be in a difficult situation which one cannot handle the problem and nor get out of this difficult situation
He was in over his head with his girlfriend as she wanted to marry him but he was not ready.
*Etymology: this refers to being in water that has risen above one's head

■

To brook no dissent: to not heed any opposition and have one's own way
The president brooked no dissent and just did whatever he wanted.
To ride roughshod over: to treat someone with contempt
The dictatorial president rode roughshod over all other democratic institutions.

■

Have a chip on one's shoulder: to always carry a grudge because of the feeling of being treated unfairly
He's got a chip on his shoulder about not getting into any top college.
*Etymology: 'chip' here refers to a piece of wood and not potato chips; earlier, when a person was looking to fight, they would place a 'chip' on their shoulders and dare others to knock it off
Chip off the old block: a person who resembles their parent in appearance or behaviour
Mike is a real chip off the old block since he looks just like his father.
*Etymology: 'chip' here refers to a small piece of wood that has come from a large piece of wood (block)
When the chips are down: a difficult situation: His friends helped when his chips were down
*Etymology: 'chips' here refers to the plastic tokens used in gambling
When all the bets are placed, the chips are said to be laid

down on the table and this represents a critical moment as the winner of this hand will take all and everyone else would have lost all their money.

■

A square meal: a wholesome, nutritious and substantial meal
The government runs a scheme which provides square meals for children.
A square peg in a round hole: a misfit, a person who doesn't fit in a particular situation like a job or a position
Everyone branded him as a square peg in a round hole because of his rebellious nature.
Back to square one: to go back to the beginning
The negotiations broke down over a trivial issue and both the parties ended up back to square one.
*Etymology: this refers to the board game snakes and ladders where a player can end up at the beginning square after an unlucky throw of the dice

■

Be no oil painting: to not be very attractive
Lend colour to something: to make something more interesting
The master of ceremonies lent colour to an otherwise dry panel discussion.
To scale up: to make something larger, especially a design or model
He scaled up the startup from two employees to one hundred in one month.
Cross the t's and dot the i's: to pay a great deal of attention to the details
Jane took a long time in filling up the college forms because she insisted on dotting the i's and crossing the t's.
*Etymology: this refers to cursive writing, where adding the dot to the letter i and the crossbar to the letter t is done after one has written the full word
To go off on a tangent: to digress from the point of discussion and start talking about something unrelated
The speaker on heart disease went off on a tangent and gave a full lecture on the importance of being on time.

■

Learning curve: a graph that depicts the rate of learning, especially a curve of skill level plotted against the time
A steep learning curve means huge knowledge gains in quick time.

Lean on: to derive support from someone or to pressurize them

He leaned on his friends for emotional support after he broke up with his girlfriend.

In it for the long haul: to be involved in a matter for the long term with the determination to see it through one way or the other

The president said that he was in it for the long haul and that he wouldn't leave easily.

■

No sooner said than done: immediately

The pizza was delivered to the office no sooner said than done.

Crack of dawn: very early morning, right at sunrise

They left for the long road trip at the crack of dawn.

■

Argue the toss: to refuse to accept a decision and argue about it

The football player was detested by the referees because he would always argue the toss, even for the minor decisions.

All agog: surprised and amazed

The audience was all agog as the speaker told about his harrowing experience in North Korea.

Boon in disguise: a blessing in disguise

It was a boon disguise that he lost his job because then he got time to start his own business.

By dint of: by means of

He rose up in the world by dint of his hard work.

Not an earthly chance: no possible chance for an event to occur

There was no earthly chance that he would pass the exam because he had not studied the course material at all.

Not put it past somebody to do something: to find it possible that a person could engage in shockingly bad behaviour because of their past actions

The cyber expert said that the government could spy on its citizens and that he wouldn't put it past them because of the authoritative nature.

For all intents and purposes: in every practical sense

For all intents and purposes, the true CEO of the company was not the CEO, but the vice president, since the CEO never really came to office.

Prodigal son returns: this is a phrase used to denote that a wasteful child has returned after having left his family in order to do something which the family disapproves and this son has now returned home after having learnt his lesson and feeling sorry for what he did

Under protest from family members, the father welcomes his son home.

*Etymology: it's a reference to the biblical story in which a son asks for his inheritance in advance then squandered it all and is forced to return home.

In tow: following or going along under someone's control

She usually goes shopping with her three children in tow.

*Etymology: based on the literal meaning of a vehicle or ship in tow (being pulled with a rope or chain)

Turn king's/queen's/state's evidence: to give evidence for the State in response to an offer from the prosecution for reduced sentence

The mob hitman turned in State's evidence and testified against the mob boss.

Hazard a guess: to make a guess

The student decided to not leave any question unanswered as there was no penalty for hazarding a guess.

*Etymology: originally hazard was a game played with dice and is derived from the Arabic word *az-zahr*, meaning 'the dice'

■

www.ingramcontent.com/pod-product-compliance
Lightning Source LLC
Chambersburg PA
CBHW080543220326
41599CB00032B/6351